I0649290

Caribbean Reasonings

The George Lamming Reader
The Aesthetics of Decolonisation

Other Titles in the Caribbean Reasonings Series

After Man, Towards the Human: Critical Essays on Sylvia Wynter

Culture, Politics, Race and Diaspora: The Thought of Stuart Hall

George Padmore: Pan-African Revolutionary

The Thought of New World: The Quest for Decolonisation

Caribbean Reasonings
Series Editors
Anthony Bogues
Rupert Lewis
Brian Meeks

Caribbean Reasonings

The George Lamming Reader:
The Aesthetics of Decolonisation

edited by
Anthony Bogues

IAN RANDLE PUBLISHERS
Kingston • Miami

First published in Jamaica, 2011 by
Ian Randle Publishers
11 Cunningham Avenue
Box 686
Kingston 6
www.ianrandlepublishers.com

Introduction and Editorial material
© 2011 Centre for Caribbean Thought, University of the West Indies

All rights reserved. While copyright in the selection and editorial material is vested in the Centre for Caribbean Thought, University of the West Indies, copyright in individual chapters belongs to their respective authors and no part of this publication may be reproduced, stored in a retrieval system or transmitted in any form or by any means electronic, photocopying, recording or otherwise, without the prior express permission of the author and publisher.

National Library of Jamaica Cataloguing in Publication Data

Caribbean reasonings: the George Lamming reader: the aesthetics of
    Decolonisation / edited by Anthony Bogues

    p. ; cm – (Caribbean reasonings)

Bibliography : p. - Includes index
ISBN 978-976-637-515-7 (pbk)

1. Lamming, George, 1927- – Criticism and interpretation   2. Lamming, George, 1927 – Political and social views   3.   Caribbean Area – Intellectual life – 20th century 4. Caribbean Area – In literature   5. West Indian literature (English) – History and criticism   I. Bogues, Anthony   II. Series

823.914   - dc 22

Cover Image: An artist's impression of the Atlantis Hotel, Bathsheba, St Joseph, Barbados, W.I. reprinted from a Mark Waterman mural located in the hotel's dining room prior to its refurbishment in 2009.

Cover and Book Design by Ian Randle Publishers
Printed and Bound in the United States of America

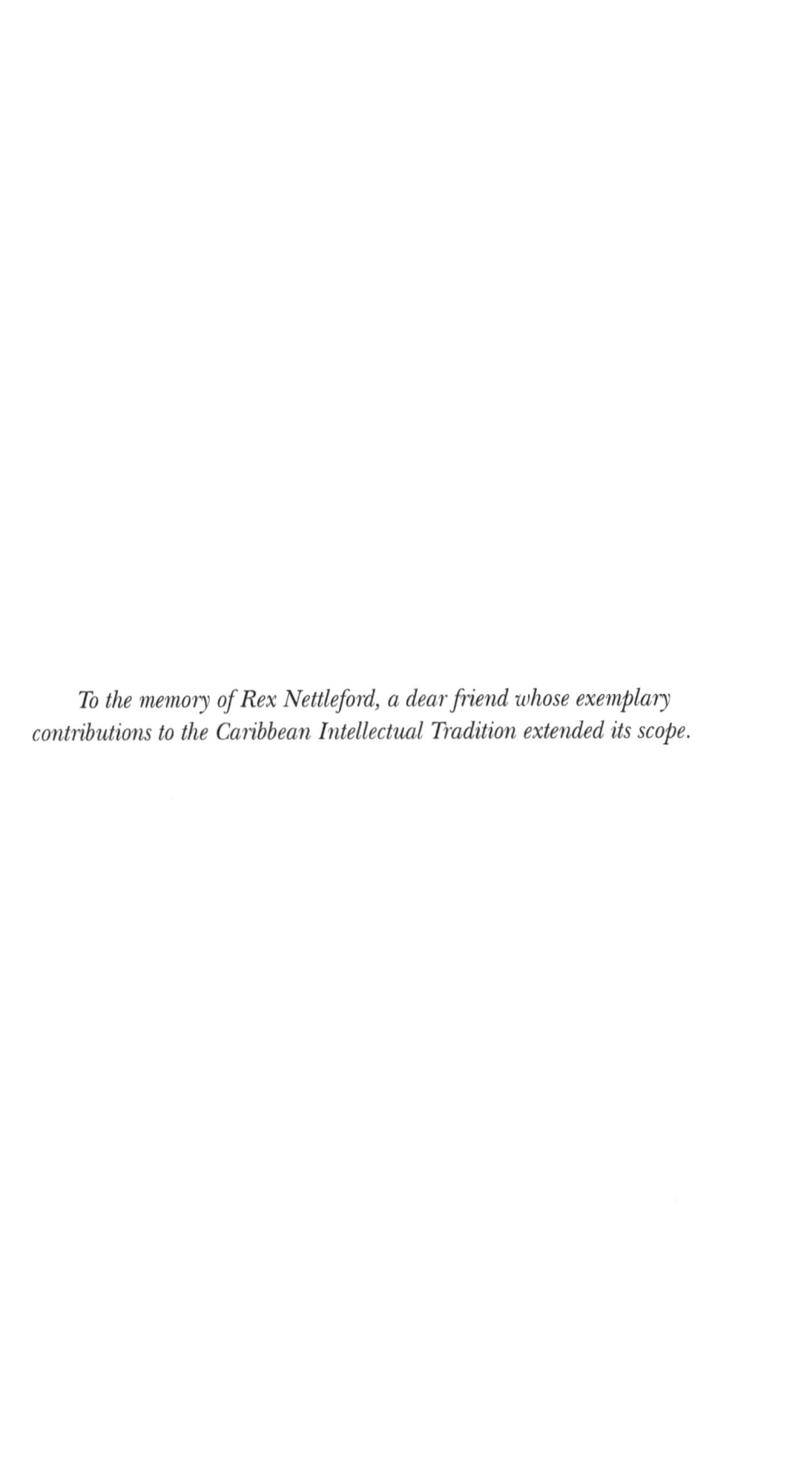

To the memory of Rex Nettleford, a dear friend whose exemplary contributions to the Caribbean Intellectual Tradition extended its scope.

George Lamming with Eusi Kwayana in Guyana in 1987

Table of Contents

SECTION 2: LAMMING IN CONVERSATION

SECTION 3: REFLECTIVE NOTES: THE PAST AND THE PRESENT

SECTION 4: CRITICAL REFLECTIONS ON THE POLITICS, ART AND AESTHETICS OF GEORGE LAMMING

SECTION 5: EXTRACT OF NOVEL IN PROGRESS

SECTION 6: BIOGRAPHIES

George Lamming is a seminal Caribbean intellectual and thinker. He is part of the post-Second World War wave of Caribbean writers who migrated to London to become a writer. He is the author of six novels, *In the Castle of My Skin,* (1953); *The Emigrants,* (1954); *Of Age and Innocence* (1958); *Season of Adventure* (1960); *Water with Berries* (1971); *Natives of My Person* (1972); three books of critical essays *Pleasures of Exile* (1960); *Coming, Coming Home, Conversations II* (1995); *Sovereignty of the Imagination;* and *Conversations III* (2009). Lamming is the editor of *Cannon Shot and Glass Beads; Modern Black Writing* (1974); and has edited and co-edited what are now critical documents of Caribbean intellectual history including, *Enterprise of the Indies* (1999); and Barbados and Guyana independence issues of the *New World Quarterly.* His awards and honours include, Guggenheim, the Somerset Maugham Award and an honorary doctorate from the University of the West Indies. He has been a distinguished visiting professor at many universities most recently as a professor of Africana Studies and Literary Arts at Brown University. He continues to live in Barbados where is the consulting editor for the journal *BIM.*

Anthony Bogues is Harmon Family Professor of Africana Studies, Brown University, an honorary professor at the Center for African Studies, University of Cape Town and associate director of the Center for Caribbean Thought, University of the West Indies, Mona. His latest book is, *Empire of Liberty: Power, Desire and Freedom* (2010).

Foreword

Freeing the Imagination: Lamming's Aesthetics of Decolonisation

Ngũgĩ wa Thiong'o[1]

Introduction

It was Whitehead who once said that Western philosophy was a series of footnotes to Plato. By this he did not mean that there was no originality in later Western philosophy but rather that many of the themes that came to dominate that tradition were anticipated in Plato's work. There is a way in which the same can be said of the literature of decolonisation in relation to Lamming's work, in particular his text, *In the Castle of My Skin* which in many ways anticipated many of the themes in Fanon's *Wretched of the Earth*; Albert Memmi's *The Colonizer and the Colonized* and numerous other contemporary anti-colonial texts. Lamming's work that followed, *Of Age and Innocence; Pleasures of Exile* and *Season of Adventure* were to elaborate on themes already touched in that seminal text of the aesthetics of decolonisation written by one just past his early twenties.

Even the date of its publication, 1953, marks a great moment in the praxis of decolonisation. It is a moment pregnant with the tension between what had been a century of European Imperial ascendancy in the globe with French and British Empires at the helm, and what was about to be, the redrawing of the power map of the world by the forces of decolonisation. The redrawing had already started with India's independence in 1947; the Chinese Revolution in 1948; the defeat of the French in Vietnam at Dien Bien Phu in 1954; the start of the Mau Mau armed challenge of the British colonial state in Kenya in 1952; and a similar armed challenge against the French in Algeria. There was also Ghana's Independence in 1957; the Cuban revolution in 1959; the rise of Civil Rights Movement in America marked by the now famous act of Rosa Parks refusing to give her seat to a white person in

Alabama; not to mention the workers movements in Asia, Africa and the Caribbean often marked by general strikes and mass uprisings. In short Lamming emerges at the high noon of anti-imperialism, the forcible entry of the masses into history. His work is simultaneously a product, a reflection and a celebration of a people making history.

The narrative structure of *In the Castle of My Skin* reflects that centrality of people in history. The community of ordinary men and women and children is the principle actor. Multiple voices are given equal space in the narrative. Their awakening from just a people in themselves with lives governed by a mythic consciousness and local allegiance to a people for themselves governed by a vision that goes well beyond the boundaries of the village, the Caribbean shores to the outer arena of black and social struggles world wide is the central drama of the narrative.

Trumper's remarkable journey to America and back illustrates this. You will recall that Trumper is one of the group of youth with whom boy G, one of the narrative voices, grows up. We are told that after going to America, in the midst of the Civil Rights Movements, he comes back with an outlook that confuses the others while it also fascinates them. In America, among other things, Trumper has gone through experiences that make him understand the baritone voice of Paul Robeson singing *Let My People Go*. The concept of the people, my people, becomes the centre piece of Trumper's new vision.[2] But who are my people, the other youth ask, for clearly Trumper is talking of a reality that embraces more than the village, more than Caribbean nationalism, more than race even. *My People*. In the tone with which Trumper repeats the vision, it is suggestive of Garvey's racial pride, Du Bois's social consciousness in *Souls of Black Folk*, and of the earlier Toussaint L'Ouverture, whose entry into history through mobilisation of the slaves as *My People* is dramatised and celebrated in C.L.R. James's *Black Jacobins*, a text which Lamming himself discusses in *The Pleasures of Exile*, as Caliban Orders History.[3] He describes the book as a West Indian classic, and recommends it as bible reading.[4] That concept of my people underlies James's analysis of both the rise and the fall of Toussaint L'Ouverture. After initial hesitation to join the revolt of the masses, Toussaint, the liberator is seen as connecting with people; while Toussaint, the fallen, has become so, through disconnecting with the people, a judgement that James renders on the hero of his narrative and which Lamming endorses in his summary of the classic.

Sovereignty

What is this encapsulated in the phrase *My People* and which even Trumper is not quite able to give words? I want to suggest that it is the concept of the subject becoming the sovereign, the sovereignty of the people. The notion of the sovereign, the one who, whether embodied in a person or a state, 'renders habitual obedience to no one' as opposed to the subject who 'renders habitual obedience' to the sovereign,[5] is important in theories of the state and legal thought. Thus the notion of sovereignty residing with the people is not unique or original to Lamming. It is in fact central to European theories of the state and state power.

In Hobbes's *Leviathan*, the people, to escape the state of nature marked by 'warre of everyone against everyone' which of course makes their life 'solitary, poore, nasty, brutish, and short,' surrender their sovereignty to the state and its ruler. Although Locke of the *Two Treatises of Government*, takes the opposite view, that the state of nature is not governed by *constant warfare and strife*, still he shares the view that people surrender their rights of self-rule to the state. Though the sovereign power remains with the people who have the right to recall or reclaim their rights by dispensing with the government officials and even dismantling pre-existing orders, and unlike the Hobbesian ruler from whom the surrendered sovereignty can never be recalled, they both share the common starting point of people first surrendering their agency to the safekeeping of the sovereign, resident in the state or a central political power.

Rousseau differs with the two because for him sovereignty which began with the people, remains there: it cannot be represented, for the same reason that it cannot be alienated: an active citizenry was the central pillar a well-functioning political system where the affairs of the political authority and the citizens are closely intertwined.

Rousseau's concept of the sovereignty of the people comes closest to Lamming's. But while Rousseau's people are undifferentiated, Trumper's *My People* hints of the working people in the Gramscian tradition or that assumed by Walter Rodney, in his histories of *How*

Europe Underdeveloped Africa and *A History of Guyanese Working People*, the preface to the latter, written by Lamming.

In Lamming sovereignty lies with the subject freed from his subjection to an oppressing other, free to regain his own subjectivity as an agent of his being. For to be subject to another, an oppressing other, be he a foreigner or a national, is to have one's capacity for imagining a different future limited. In a colonial context, this sovereignty is not yet realised, it is an ideal for which to struggle.

It is this concept of the people which underlies the totality of Lamming's sensibility from *In the Castle of My Skin* to *Natives of My Person*. It is the possibility of *My People* being organised, taking back their sovereignty, which terrifies the colonial state and the nascent middle class of the colonial stage of Imperialism, and for whom, the real enemy is my people. 'My people don't like to see their people get on. The language of the civil servant. The myth had eaten into their consciousness like moths through the pages of ageing documents.' (p6) Nothing dramatises this terror better than the overseer of *In the Castle of My Skin* who sees this people as jealous and about to destroy his privileged position as recipient of the remnants from the colonial master's table. The overseer mutates into the entire slimy group whose historical mission and destiny is that of replacing the colonial settler. Trumper comes back with the greatest contempt for this group which he sees as being in league with the Creightons of the colonial world. In short settler/colonial state may depart through the front door but it leaves behind its representatives in the newly independent estate, what Lamming used to call the caretaker government in both the sense of acting on behalf of imperial interests and also its short-lived/temporary character. Thus in *In the Castle of My Skin*, Lamming anticipated the betrayal of Independence, a theme he takes up in *Season of Adventure*, in a narrative that dramatises neocolonialism long before it had been part of common political parlance.

The Slimies of the colonial world have taken over power and what they reproduce is a mimicry of the mother country.

This slimy class is tied with cultural umbilical cords to the culture of the mother country through education as mutilation of memory or else as production of amnesia about a people's history. It is, once again, in *In the Castle of My Skin* where mutilation and amnesia are dramatised. One of the most memorable scenes is where the school kids are discussing slavery as something which belongs to a myth of a distant past. Slavery has nothing to do with them, it happened to others. The school reproduces the notion of Barbados as Little England, a replica of Big England. This is more real for it is played over and over again in the colonial narrative in books and on the blackboard. In *Season of Adventure*, the narrator stops the narrative to describe his relationship to Powell about to face murder. It is the school that differentiates their two fates; one accessed the school; the other did not, but, according to the narrator, he still bears responsibility for his brother's fate. He accepts responsibility but how many of the middle class inheritors of Independence accept the responsibility of mass poverty and degradation?

In the colonial and even the post-independence school, language plays a crucial role in producing and reproducing cultural dependency on the mother country for language is the rubber stamp that certifies that the neocolonial mind as truly made in Europe. In all his works, both creative and critical, Lamming comes back to the issue of education, culture and language. The two icons of this system are English and Shakespeare. They are also the greatest exports of the Empire. Note that in themselves there is nothing wrong but it is how they are used. The colonised has never, can never produce Shakespeare. And Caliban has no language. He can only be taught/given language.

Caliban

Prospero keeps on reminding Caliban of his debt to Prospero's language and culture. You did not know yourself until I gave you language. I created you but, of course, in my image. We encounter this phenomenon in Defoe's Robinson Crusoe where Crusoe is teaching Friday language. Your name is Friday. My name is Master. Language here is being used to reproduce a master and slave consciousness to reinforce the material reality of the same. If Friday or his earlier manifestation in Caliban were to accept that language as used by the master, then he would enter a permanent state of auto-enslavement, surrendering his own sovereignty forever.

That is why Lamming's work as a whole is a continuous argument with Shakespeare and English. He must deconstruct the two icons to reveal the way they have been used as an enslaving aesthetic in order to construct the foundation of a liberating aesthetic reflecting a sovereign people whose capacity to imagine a new world, whole, unfragmented, is set free. This would be a people who have overcome a state of alienation imposed on others.

For colonialism, as it emerges in Lamming's work, is indeed a system of alienation. It turns a people's land, labour, power, values, psyche even, into an enemy, a threat in the case of the overseer. Colonialism is a totality of alienation and when this is later nationalised into a norm in the postcolonial state it becomes the most dangerous threat to our imagination of a different sovereignty.

Lamming's project is an interrogation of the colonial process seen as integral to a capitalist modernity now mutating as globalisation with a global slime in power subjecting the globe to its narrow view of what it is to be human. This interrogation is a necessary step in the decolonisation of the economy, the politics, the culture and the psyche of the formerly colonised and now still dominated.

Central to the concept of the people, is labour, as a moulder which nurtures. The highest representative of labour is the artist, for labour itself is seen as having the power to transform. The artist, seen as belonging to the category that Lamming often describes as cultural workers, draws from the imagination as his primary means of production. Imagination is the supreme sovereign for it is not bound by time and space and authority. No authority can enforce a command: Don't imagine. Don't dream. In that sense even within an oppressive system the artist can still exercise the sovereignty of his imagination to dream of new worlds. The artist and the worker are allies in the quest for freedom.

A constant image in his work is the Ceremony of Souls. The invocation of the ceremony is like an artistic process that connects and heals. Lamming's own literary project is truly a huge artistic strife for the recovery of memory and the resurrection of the mutilated. The totality of his work is itself then a ceremony of resurrection, the recovery of our right to imagine, and it belongs to Caribbean, African, Asian and European peoples, indeed to all the social forces seeking unity to create a world reflective of human need not greed. His work is a site of the aesthetic of resistance and human liberation. He has built an artistic house for *My People*.

Notes

1. Address at the conference on 'The Sovereignty of the Imagination; The Writings and Thought of George Lamming', University of the West Indies Mona campus, Kingston, Jamaica, June 5–7, 2003.
2. As a 21 year old, Lamming, who by then had left Barbados for Trinidad did attend a concert given by Paul Robeson on his only visit to Trinidad, at the Carib Theater, about 1948. 'That was an extraordinary moment! It was one those holy moments,' Lamming describes the experience in an interview with David Scott, *Small Axe, a Caribbean Journal of Criticism*, September 2002.
3. *Pleasures of Exile*, London, 1960, p. 118.
4. Ibid., p. 119.
5. H.L.A. Hart, *The Concept of Law*, Oxford 1961.

Acknowledgements

Working on this reader has marked a critical moment in my intellectual life. The volume was edited alongside my preparations of another manuscript on Caribbean thought and the radical imagination. As I wrote the latter, it became clear to me that in probing questions of the radical imagination I had taken up issues which had been raised in the many intense conversations with two individuals that I have had over a five year period: George Lamming and Sylvia Wynter, both seminal figures within the 20th century Caribbean intellectual tradition and a larger radical anti-colonial intellectual tradition. I point this out because the reader should be aware that this volume forms part of a larger project on Caribbean intellectual history which I am engaged with. In this project, I am attempting to examine both the conditions for and the history of Caribbean thought as radical practices of the imagination and as one way to think about the categories which shape and continue to influence our contemporary world. The project is part of a larger enterprise of writing and thinking about radical anti-colonial thought as well as the radical black intellectual tradition. But it is also part of a project to understand some contours of the world we currently inhabit. The radical anti-colonial intellectual and political tradition and the black radical intellectual tradition engender habits of thinking and posed questions which are in danger of erasure in our contemporary world governed by the dictates of neoliberalism.

Within the Caribbean we face not only neoliberalism as an economic and ideological system which celebrates and integrates the ethic of an unbridled market as part of constructing a self; it is clear as well that we are in a new intellectual and political dispensation as the nationalist and regionalist dreams have crashed and many forms of legitimacy and importantly understanding of self and society have taken on frameworks and forms which are deeply shaped by neoliberalism. To think about the Caribbean post-colony is to understand issues of death, of political parties which are bankrupt, of a globalisation process in which the region has been inserted primarily within a international division of labour as a zone for tourism; it is to understand that since the collapse of the nationalist and federal projects, the implosion of the Grenadian Revolution and the reformist attempts in the 1970s in Jamaican society, that Caribbean societies have been in perpetual crisis. In such a context one does not wish to return to the past to find answers nor to indulge in forms of nostalgia; rather one returns to a past to ask questions about the present. So to write and think about the radical anti-colonial intellectual tradition and the Caribbean intellectual tradition is to think about the questions posed in these traditions. Now, it is not that the questions posed by the struggles against colonial and racial power by the writers and thinkers within these traditions are all alive and the sole ones which face us. No. We live in a different world, one not governed by the colonial power although it is clear that racial power has yet to be overcome and of course within our current post-colonial Caribbean new questions have been posed. So what this project seeks to do is by working through the questions and habits of thinking within the Caribbean intellectual tradition, the radical anti-colonial tradition and the black radical tradition, one seeks to suggest new questions that emerge from an examination of these traditions within the historical, intellectual, cultural and political spaces that constitutes the Caribbean. Let us take for example the question of violence. How does one begin to grapple with violence as a form of power in the Caribbean post-colony without historising it? Thus one element of this project is a certain historisation of the present in order to understand the present in all its complexities. Additionally the questions posed by the radical anti-colonial intellectual and political traditions may be helpful for an understanding of power today and the possibilities of freedom. Editing this volume has made it clearer to me that frames of our thinking are in need of change and perhaps thinking through radical anti-colonial thought might be an important part of generating this change.

The idea for this volume in its present form emerged sometime after the Centre for Caribbean Thought and the Department of Literatures in English at the University of the West Indies, Mona hosted a 'Caribbean Reasonings' conference on the thought of George Lamming. In assembling the volume I have had the unstinting support of Lamming. Over the past few years we have had numerous conversations about Caribbean politics, literature, culture and life. In all of these I have encountered leading figures of the 20th century Caribbean intellectual tradition in ways which I had not known. Lamming knew most, if not all of the major figures in some way and he openly shared with me the experiences of his contact with them. Working with Lamming has been historically educative as he opened letters, old newspapers, searched for original drafts of essays and answered my numerous queries. As well, he was extraordinarily generous with his time. In a real sense the volume was a collaborative enterprise and could not have been done without his input. So thank you George.

As I searched for Lamming's essays, articles and speeches many individuals and libraries were extremely cooperative. Bill Schwarz directed me to the Institute of Race Relations in London as a source for newspapers where the staff there was very helpful and I thank them very much. In Barbados the staff at the Errol Barrow Centre for the Creative Imagination at the Cave Hill campus of the University of the West Indies (UWI) located the DVD required. I want to thank them for this. On my various visits to Barbados two individuals not only welcomed me but facilitated this work in many ways; Esther Phillips whose remarkable poetry I now often return to and Valance whose knowledge of Bathsheba in the parish of St Joseph was unparalleled giving me insights into contemporary Barbados life. Many thanks to Sara Pfaff who transcribed some of the tapes of Lamming's talks and to Sachelle Ford who complied the bulk of the annotated biographies. Their work was funded by a Brown University Departmental Humanities grant. My frequent travels to Barbados for research, interviewing of Lamming on different occasions and the final compilation of the volume was sponsored by my Harmon Family Professorship. I wish therefore to thank Brown University for their support of this work. This volume would not have been possible without the efforts of Ms Dawn Jackson who until recently worked at the Africana Studies Department. From the beginning of the work on this reader she has been central to its production. Indeed over the last two years, she has worked with me in the preparation of three book manuscripts and I want to thank her deeply for this work.

Acknowledgments are in order to Andaiye who gave permission for me to use some of the essays from the volume *Conversations*. My thanks also go to two of my colleagues at the Centre for Caribbean Thought, Brian Meeks and Rupert Lewis for their support. Deepest appreciation is due to Christine Randle my publisher who without hesitation supported this volume and the entire *Caribbean Reasonings* series. Nuff respect Christine.

Finally a note about the cover of this book. The cover is Mark Waterman's rendition of a mural which adorned a wall at the 'old' Atlantis Hotel. The 'old' Atlantis Hotel was built in the 1880s as a resort hotel at the end of railway line in Bathseba, in the parish of St Joseph. Perching on cliffs washed by the waves of the Atlantic ocean, the 'old' Atlantis was for years the home of George Lamming. For many years its cuisine called ABC (All Bajan Cuisine) was hailed as the best on the island. There is, however, another history to the Atlantis which marks it has an historic site in 20th century Caribbean intellectual and cultural life. Many editorial meetings of the New World Group where held there and the late Lloyd Best and James Millette held many meetings at this site. Leading Caribbean figures stayed there for some time, including Rex Nettleford, M.G. Smith, Andaiye and George Beckford. C.L.R. James stayed for a few months. Then there were the literary and artistic personalities from the Caribbean and US, Paula Marshall, Nina Simone and Sonia Sanchez, all making the Atlantis Hotel an exceptional space. The format and conceptualisation for this reader happened there in my many conversations with Lamming which occurred between 2006–2008.

Anthony Bogues
Bridgetown, Barbados & Providence, RI
January 2010 & May 2010

Introduction

The Aesthetic Quest for an Insurgent Caribbean Intellectual Practice: George Lamming and Caribbean Thought

Anthony Bogues

I do not think that there has been anything in human history quite like the meeting of Africa, Asia, and Europe in this American archipelago we call the Caribbean and that[it] is the most urgent task and the greatest intellectual challenge: how to control the burden of this history and incorporate it into our collective sense of the future.
George Lamming

I shall have failed to communicate my meaning if I leave the impression that I am constructing theories...I believe that what a person thinks is very much determined by the way that persons sees.
George Lamming

Introduction

To write about George Lamming is to immediately confront the entire scaffolding of 20th century Caribbean intellectual, cultural, political and literary life. Perhaps no other figure spans the gamut of all these elements of 20th century Caribbean life in the way that he does. In embodying all these elements Lamming works in the first instance during the period of late colonialism in the Caribbean and from a radical anti-colonial stance. In the present moment he operates from an anti-imperialist position in which labour and the 'people from below' are not only the makers of Caribbean history but its humane future. As a writer and critic Lamming developed a style, a form, a particular voice of critical intervention which both anchors us to history while beckoning us to a future we have yet to construct.

To see Lamming primarily as a novelist is to narrowly reduce his intellectual labour. He himself makes the point that he is both a 'writer and a critic of the cultural history of the region.' But what does it mean to be a writer and critic with a focus on issues of culture and the history/ histories of a place? Within 20th century Caribbean letters, there have been many arguments about the different genres and character of Caribbean literature. In particular Wilson Harris has argued that the 'novel of the West Indies, the novel written by West Indians of the West Indies...belongs-in the main-to the conventional mould'.[1] By this Harris means that the Caribbean novel, and here he is speaking primarily of post-war Caribbean writing in what some have called its nationalist phase, belongs to different genres of realism. However, my point here is not about different genres of the Caribbean novel but rather it is to suggest that there is a lacuna in 20th century and contemporary Caribbean letters. It is one where there is an absence of robust debate about the function of the writer and the relationship of writing to the practices of the critic.

Writing as Raymond Williams tells us has specific properties. One of these properties is the way in which it becomes a fixed discourse and then the ground through which a text is created. With regard to literature, Paul Ricoeur has noted that once the text becomes literature (and here he is speaking about Western literature) it destroys the world. But importantly he further notes, 'Nevertheless, there is no discourse so fictional that it does not connect up with reality. But such discourse refers to another level more fundamental than that attained by the descriptive, constative ... discourse which we call ordinary language.'[2] Writing does create a form of language and in doing so it names. As a writer and critic Lamming has been preoccupied with language and as C.L.R. James once noted, 'I have talked with George Lamming on this question of language and he has very definite views on it.' This preoccupation of language I would argue is the central way through which Lamming shapes his interventions either as a novelist or critical public intellectual. So for example, in his novel, *Season of Adventure*, we read the following passages. It is the opening conversation between Crim and Powell and takes place after a bit of drinking of a local gin and both men are on their way to the *tonelle* and the ceremony of the souls.

> 'Who say I's a man'? And Crim's voice meant what he had asked.
> 'Is you self say so'
> 'When'?

'The very day you born.'
'But I couldn't make a note with words that day,'Crim argued.
'Is words make a note with you,' said Powell. 'like how you beat your drum till it shape a tune , words beat your brain till it language your tongue.'[3]

For Lamming, although speech and language are central to the human enterprise, it is only when language engages in critical questioning do we become aware of self and ultimately are able to conduct the inventory of ourselves. Continuing the same conversation between Crim and Powell, the latter says, 'But talk aint nothin'till it ask' said Powell. 'Man is a question that the beast ask himself.'[4] Lamming's intellectual labour as critic and writer has been to ask these questions: Who and What are the Caribbean people? What has been their history and what are the possible futures? It is asking these questions at every turn and then making an attempt to find a language which both names and communicates these answers that has been his lifelong preoccupation. For Lamming to think about language is not just to think about communication but it is to develop categories, names if you wish, in which the Caribbean understands itself and its history. It is a preoccupation which moves across literature and politics. Let us again return to *Season of Adventure* but this time to its conclusion.

Language and Writing

After *In the Castle of My Skin* and the book of essays, *Pleasures of Exile*, and the novel *Emigrants*, all of Lamming's novels, *Of Age and Innocence; Season of Adventure; Water with Berries; Natives of My Person* occur on the island of San Cristobal. Sandra Paquet notes that, 'Lamming peoples the island of San Cristobal with characters who are representative of the various forces at work in the society as colonial rule gives way to a popular independence movement.'[5] I suggest that the imaginary island of San Cristobal emerges in Lamming's writing at the moment when he begins to think about how Caribbean anti-colonial nationalism had secured a formal political independence that shattered the possibilities of West Indian federation and established nation states. In this formal constitutional decolonisation process the middle classes became the new political elite without any rupture from the forms of political rule established by British colonial power. Lamming is deeply concerned about this formal decolonisation process and his novels from *In the Castle of My Skin* to *Natives of My Person* tracks the history of the region from colonialism to a configuration of the post-colonial in which the legacies of colonial power and today, imperial power hold sway. So as the first republic (a state formed in the early aftermath of San Cristobal's political independence) collapses, we read in *Season of Adventure:*

> But the main problem was language. It was language which caused the First Republic to fall. And the Second would suffer the same fate; the Second and the Third, unless they tried to find a language which was no less immediate than the language of the drum.[6]

Many critics have noted that Shakespeare's play *The Tempest* figures a great deal in Lamming's writings and as is typical of many anti-colonial thinkers, the characters of Caliban and Prospero litter his essays. Although Caliban learned Prospero's language and in turn uses it to curse him, the future of Caliban and the language he deployed in Lamming's eyes was not a closed one and he notes 'however independent it was, [it] would always be in some way inextricably tied up with that pioneering aspect of Prospero. Caliban at some stage would have to find a way of breaking that contract, which got sealed by language in order to reconstruct some alternative reality for himself.'[7]

Lamming's preoccupation with the creation of a language is an effort to construct a decolonisation process in which the ordinary Caribbean person experiences him/herself *inside* the politics and culture of society. We already know, and Lamming acknowledges, that the ordinary Caribbean person has created a language and therefore categories which describe their experiences and life. Stuart Hall observes about Lamming's writing that in his 'hand, the rhythms and idioms of West Indian speech are brought to a condition of sensitivity where language is capable of expressing the deepest reaches of West Indian personality.'[8] So to whom is Lamming addressing his preoccupation about language and why his he so preoccupied with this issue? I would suggest that what drives Lamming's preoccupation is his concern that the Caribbean intellectual both in the colonial and post-colonial periods is distant and disconnected from the ways of life and general life of the ordinary

Caribbean person. It is one reason for his extraordinary author's note in *Season of Adventure*. In part the note reads:

> Powell has never appeared since that night he tried to finish his work on Fola. But his life has provided the literature of San Cristobal with two important themes. By historians and analysts, he is presented as a man who saw freedom as an absolute, and pure...Until the age of ten Powell and I had lived together, equal in affection of two mothers...and then the division came. I got a public scholarship which started my migration into another world, a world whose roots were the same, but whose style of living was entirely different from what my childhood knew. It has earned me a privilege which now shut Powell and the whole tonelle right out of my future...Instinctively I attached myself to that new privilege....[9]

Thus one feature of Lamming's criticism about Caribbean life is the role and function of the 'native' intellectual. It is why in his eulogy for Walter Rodney, he says: 'But he had a rare gift of intellect to which he felt a special duty. It was a tool a reservoir of power which could only justify itself ...[when] put into service, and on behalf of social need.'

The Vocation of Writing

In his own practices as a critic and writer Lamming has attempted to carve out a space in which his own special talents operate 'on behalf of social need' in the Caribbean as he sees it. Thus for him to be a writer demands engagement with Caribbean society and a special duty of responsibility. Such a responsibility means calling to order, speaking against the grain while writing against the conventional styles which marked the   Caribbean novel of the 'nationalist period.' In doing these things Lamming does not attempt to reconstruct the world of the 'people from below' similar to ways in which other novels of the period did, in particular, Roger Mais in *Brother Man* or Sylvia Wynter's *Hills of Hebron*. Nor would he seek to distill elements of Caribbean history like, Vic Reid's *New Day*. Rather for Lamming his novels were the *site of ideas*. In Lamming's novels there is no process of character fulfilment since there is a collective character: the village in *In The Castle of My Skin* or the island of San Cristobal and its rejection of colonialism in *Of Age and Innocence*. In this regard for Lamming instead of individual characters whose interior lives we follow, there is what he calls, 'characters of place.' It is the complexities of the colonial and then post-colonial situation which he wants to unravel for the reader. Thus for him what becomes critical is a form in which this can occur. Since Lamming is preoccupied with investing his prose with ideas and searches for a form where this can happen, oftentimes the prose of the novel reads like dialogue in a dramatic play.

Lamming himself in many interviews notes his deployment of the dramatic form in his novels and sometimes the multi-genre forms of his writing. The use of the dramatic form is not an unsurprising feature of Lamming's work and in part can be explained by the genre of drama itself which bends itself to a dialogue of statements. Raymond Williams observes that, 'drama is a special kind of use of quite general process of presentation, representation, signification... it is now so often associated with what are called myth and ritual... drama is a precise separation of certain common modes for new and specific ends.'[10] So there is a way in which the dramatic form facilitates experimentation. For Lamming this is important since he desires to develop a new language which will explain the Caribbean from within. Thus even though Lamming has argued that the Caribbean writer added a new 'dimension to writing about the West Indian community,' and that the novel was the genre and medium for this addition there is I suggest an element in Lamming's work which pushes the form and style of the novel. The ground for this kind of push can be located in a certain aesthetic that takes literature in its oppositional form as a counter-language which maintains an intimate relationship with life. The aesthetic practiced here is one which Sylvia Wynter calls a 'deciphering aesthetic' one which seeks in her words to 'decipher *what*...texts do,' in addition to what they may mean.[11] In such an aesthetic what becomes important are practices and ways of life and form is then shaped by these practices as seen by the writer. From this framework literature reveals the substrata of history/histories and the politics of a society. This is of central importance for Caribbean thought since as Lamming reminds us in an interview published in this volume, there are two things which give oxygen to Caribbean thought: history and politics. So what is the relationship between this kind of aesthetic and what can be called politics?

Politics, Writing and Criticism

Lamming has been called a 'political novelist,' a term which he eschews. However reading Lamming one cannot escape the *political density* of his novels. So the question which is posed is both a general and specific one: what does one mean by a politics of literature with an aesthetic which embraces politics? Or to put it in the words of Jacques Ranciere, is there a 'specific link between politics as a definite way of doing and literature as a definite practice of writing?'[12] Note here that the issue I have signalled circles a relationship between practices. We are not here probing conceptual forms or models but grappling with how different sets of human practices relate and illuminate each other. Thinking about politics is a practice of framing, of trying to make sense of forms of associative life that humans engage in. Political thinking in great part is about how we shape a common world which we make, inhabit and then act upon. In enacting this world we erase things; some things have no visibility, are given no presence nor have speech within the order that is enacted. Ranciere makes a point worth recalling here, that politics as a practice is about 'ways of being, ways of doing and ways of speaking.'[13]

For the Caribbean inhabiting a historical moment in which the colonial gave way to a juridical post-colony but continued to haunt our horizons, then our 'ways of being' were rooted often times in the traces of this colonial power. Many of our institutions born during the colonial period now in the post-colonial one often develop strange twists to them which unfailingly exacerbate that which was the signature marker of colonial power: might and its companion, violence. So how do we frame these colonial traces which haunt us?

With very few exceptions the framing of politics in the Caribbean has been about resource allocation, the capturing of state power and the electoral fights to capture this state. In this context there has emerged a figure who Lamming calls, 'The Honorable Member.' Politics in the Caribbean and the parties which practise this form of so-called politics have become over time the bane of Caribbean society without any conception of what constitutes humane forms of associative life, so much so that it is accurate to say that 'politics' has had debilitating effects upon Caribbean society. How to decipher this debilitating effect has been a feature of Lamming's novels and his many essays and public statements. In executing his literary art and performing his role as a public critic, literature in Lamming's hands becomes a form of practice which presents an alternative framing of our common world. This makes literature for Lamming a practice of criticism.

In working through this form of literature as an art of criticism, Lamming understands the vocation of the intellectual as a representative figure who takes witnessing and testimony as serious critical engagements. It is why I would suggest in eulogising C.L.R. James he describes him as having the 'zeal and urgency of an ancient evangelist.' This evangelism Lamming tells us had nothing to do with religion nor with any special display of knowledge rather it had to do with the ways in which James's thinking was an 'act of pure and complete participation.' For Lamming writing as a vocation means to be a critical witness of Caribbean history. It means that many of his novels are historically framed.[14] Let us take for example *Natives of My Person*. Lamming notes that the novel is 'a way of going forward by making a complete return to the beginning.'[15] This makes Lamming's criticism profoundly routed through an examination of history. And because he also wishes to develop a new language through which alternatives can be imagined his practices of criticism cannot be described as just speaking truth to power.

Lamming's work has a complex relationship to history. It is true that in his most historically detailed novel, *Natives of My Person*, he constructs a fictional history of European colonial and racial power. As well in the novel one of Lamming's preoccupation is how the act of colonisation creates individuals who are themselves morally bankrupt once they embrace the colonial project. In the novel Lamming also identifies women as a radical force for the future.[16] It is interesting to note I think that, this latter theme which appears most forcefully in the novel as the last chapter and the novel's third segment, simply titled, *The Women* is written in dramatic dialogic form primarily between wives and the 'Lady of the House', confirming I think, that for Lamming, dramatic prose and form gives him the widest scope for his expression. However if one returns to the question of history we would see that for Lamming history is not a time past but rather is one in which the dead and living co-mingle. Hence for him the Haitian Ceremony of Souls becomes the site in which both living and dead, present and past can speak to each other. This is what he writes in the introduction to his current manuscript, 'Columbus: A View From the Other Side':

The story should be set within what is described in my novels as the Ceremony of the Souls. This is a moment in Haitian mythology when the Dead return to discuss and dispute with the Living all those issues which were left unresolved when Death separated them...examples of this dialogue between the Living and Dead would be: the intellectual and moral conviction which determined the conduct of the Spanish...and those who came after, as well as the consequences of that dramatic intervention for the native populations whom they encountered. And the story is narrated from the point of view of the violated hosts: Arawaks, Caribs, Tainos, etc.

Thus for Lamming history is a burden from which we must be released. Therefore writing is an aesthetic quest for a decolonisation in which the burden of history has been transformed and where the dialogue between the living and the dead can now occur within a context where previously unresolved matters can be dealt with. For Lamming the Ceremony of the Souls is about a drama of possible redemption, the drama of return and a drama of cleansing for a commitment towards the future.[17] So while there is a general understanding in much of current historiography that the present poses the questions of history, for Lamming when we confront history we do so with an eye towards the future. In the end, if politics and literature are both critical practices which frame, for Lamming it is history which provides the passages that link them. This element of Lamming's thought is a common one in radical anti-colonial thought particularly of course in the work of Aimé Césaire.[18]

Given his long life Lamming has been a witness to the various ways that the current Caribbean condition has been shaped by neoliberalism and globalisation. Of note is his observation that tourism is now a primary economic activity in many of the islands and so he has mused that 'the source of our humiliation has now become our living.'[19]

With the collapse of the nationalist and federal projects Lamming began to outline a possible way in which the decolonisation process could continue. For him what is currently critical for Caribbean sovereignty and indeed for more humane forms of living in the region is, 'the sovereignty of the imagination.'[20] Developing the idea in an interview with David Scott, Lamming states:

> ...but a limited sovereignty acknowledged in the public domain does not necessarily demand a limited sovereignty in the power of the self to perceive why you have to limit that sovereignty. In other words there is a sovereignty which remains intact in spite of the limitations which you must concede...in the public domain... And I am in a way arguing that there remains an area for *choice*, for independent free choice, about the meanings you place on events[21] (emphasis in the original)

It is interesting here because Lamming has moved or perhaps has returned to his preoccupation about language, but now language is not linked to politics but instead it becomes primarily about interpretation and naming within limited spaces. Such interpretations and exercises in naming are for Lamming marks of a cultural sovereignty. This continues a theme in Lamming's thinking since for him both colonial and imperial powers operated through hegemonies. About the former he has observed that there was a certain 'terror of the mind'. We of course find this 'terror' most eloquently teased out in *The Castle of My Skin* in the following passage:

> That's what the woman meant – the Queen did free some of us in a kind of way. We started to think about the Empire more than we thought of the Garden, and then nothing mattered but the Empire. Well they have put the two of them together now – Empire and Garden. We are to speak of them the same way – they belong to the same person; they both belong to God. The Garden is God's own garden and the Empire is God's own empire.[22]

Reflecting on the contemporary Caribbean and the unresolved dilemmas of decolonisation, Lamming calls for a cultural sovereignty as, 'the free definition and articulation of the collective self, whatever the rigor of external constraints.' I would argue that Lamming has become so driven by this concern that public speaking and therefore public statements of critical intervention have over the years become the major modality for him to think aloud about Caribbean society. What began in the late 1950s when he was asked by the Barbados Workers Union to give a public address about the state of the 'Black Man in the world' has become his signature as a public critic and intellectual.

Speaking as a Vocation

Lamming has developed an oral style of critical intervention which he calls a 'language of statements.'[23] In describing these statements, he notes that the 'speeches are addressed to the mind' in order for the 'mind to feel'. While the novels are written with the 'specific intention of making the feeling think.' There are a set of juxtapositions here which should give us pause. Literature, Lamming is arguing, is about feeling and his writing is about 'educating' that feeling which is why I suggested earlier on that his novels are sites of ideas. However in a profound sense both Lamming's writing and speaking are the two sides of the same purpose, the practice of criticism. The difference between the two is audience. For example listening to a Lamming speech say to the Barbados Workers Union or to a group of progressive political people is to enter a kind of dialogue in which politics, history and questions of culture all meld into a statement about who we are and what we can become. There is always a historical sense to the speeches, an analysis of the moment and an appeal or call to future possibilities. One of the most astute political figures in contemporary Caribbean society Andaiye, makes this telling observation about Lamming's eulogy to Walter Rodney.

She writes: '...for the first time in my experience, a eulogy in a Guyanese church provoked a standing ovation. Afterwards, I asked some of the youth what had happened. They said that the ovation was not for George, it was for Walter. George had brought Walter into the Church...'[24]

Bringing things back to us, always engaging in acts of critical retrieval while beckoning towards a future we must learn and a present we must understand, those are the themes that shape Lamming's statements and therefore his function as a critic.

A Tentative Conclusion

One does not need to write an introduction for this volume to guide the reader nor to follow the conventional academic fashion of summarising articles. The bulk of this volume is composed of Lamming's writing. The reader will determine for himself or herself what these pieces and critical essays mean. I have made an attempt to structure the volume in such a way that Lamming speaks and that there is an internal textual conversation between his 'language of statements' and the critical essays composed by the different contributors. So I want to conclude not with this volume and its structure but rather with a few statements about Lamming himself.

I first met Lamming in the 1980s when he spoke at a seminar organised by what was then the PNP left in Jamaica. We were at that time deeply engaged with a political education programme aimed at nothing less than building a radical mass democratic party that could transform Jamaican society from one of gross inequities with its deeply held class and colour privileges structured within an economy dominated by imperial power. The implosion of the Grenadian Revolution had occurred and in many ways we felt isolated. In thinking about the figures whom we should invite, Lamming's name was agreed upon because we felt that over the many years he had become the voice that represented both our past and possible future. I mention this invitation because there is another kind of intellectual labour that Lamming engages with as a critic and public intellectual. He has never joined a political organisation and his failed attempt to join the Communist Party in England in the 1950s might have left him with the feeling that his work was not within any party structure but more as a public figure unfettered by any specific party position; a public figure whose voice could only be unvarnished not just because he spoke truth to power but because his work embodied the history of that truth. Thus he is always in a position to remind us; to be our critical memory which does both forward and backward glances simultaneously. This is what Lamming's work as coordinator of the Regional Committee for Cultural Sovereignty in the late 1980s was all about.

There is a picture in this volume which gave me reason to pause when it was shown to me. It is of Lamming and Eusi Kwayana sitting beside each other speaking. Lamming had gone to Guyana heeding the call of some members of the Working Peoples Alliance to persuade Eusi to end his hunger strike. The photograph shows two extraordinary figures of Caribbean life, both individuals of action and thought. One had spent his life in Caribbean politics making tremendous and courageous attempts to construct a politics in which humane forms of associative life was possible within the region. The other had been a voice which kept alive the deepest impulses of the ordinary person, those who made 1937/1938 such years of significance in 20th century Caribbean history. Because it is the mass uprisings of 1937/1938 which opens up for Lamming an intellectual trajectory. It is these events which gives him his gaze. It is what he considers to be the deepest significances of these events which makes him think about the possibilities of a Caribbean future founded in freedom. I want to end with Powell, the figure that causes Lamming to write the remarkable author's note in *Season of Adventure*. Lamming writes:

> The politics of freedom has always haunted Powell's imagination. Day after day he would punish his friends with argument in the Forest Reserve...Independence aint nothin'till it free.' ...Free is how you move from the start, an' when it look different you got to move, just move, an' when you movin' say that is a natural freedom that make you move. You can't move to freedom, Crim. Cause freedom is what you is, an where you start, an where you always got to stand.[25]

It has been Lamming's position to stand for freedom and to do so he has developed within the Caribbean intellectual tradition an insurgent intellectual practice that has created a fusion between literature and politics which will stand as marker in 20th century Caribbean life and letters. His writing and voice as a critic can be aptly described in the similar way that the Cuban artist Wifredo Lam described his own paintings. He says that his art was an 'act of decolonisation'. Lamming's insurgent intellectual practice was about writing and speaking while enacting an aesthetic of decolonisation for Caribbean life and letters.

Notes

1.   Wilson Harris, *Tradition, The Writer and Society: Critical Essays*. (London: New Beacon Publications, 1967) p. 29.
2.   Paul Ricoeur, *From Text To Action*, (Evanston: Northwestern University Press, 1991) p. 85.
3.   George Lamming, *Season of Adventure*, (Ann Arbor: The University of Michigan Press, 2002) p. 15.
4.   Ibid.
5.   Sandra Pouchet Paquet, *The Novels of George Lamming* (Kingston: Hienemann, 1982) p. 49.
6.   *Season of Adventure*, p. 363.
7.   Cited in *The Novels of George Lamming*. p. 7.
8.   Cited in *The Novels of George Lamming*, p. 6.
9.   *Season of Adventure*. p. 331.

10. Raymond Williams, *Writing in Society* (London: Verso, 1983) p. 15.
11. For a fuller discussion of this concept see, Sylvia Wynter, 'Rethinking Aesthetics: Notes Towards a Deciphering Practice.' in Mbye Cham, *Ex-Iles: Essays on Caribbean Cinema* (Trenton: Africa World Press, 1992) pp. 237–79.
12. Jacques Ranciere, *Dissensus On Politics and Aesthetics* (London: Continuum International Publishing Group, 2010) p. 152.
13. Ibid.
14. See for a further discussion of the relationship between history and Caribbean literature, Nana Wilson-Tagoe, *Historical Thought and Literary Representation in West Indian Literature* (Kingston: The Press, University of West Indies, 1998).
15. See Interview with George Kent in this volume where Lamming develops this point.
16. For a discussion about the role of gender in Lamming's work, see Curdella Forbes, *From Nation to Diaspora, Samuel Selvon, George Lamming and the Cultural Performance of Gender* (Kingston: The Press, University of the West Indies, 2005).
17. See Lamming's talk, 'The West Indian People: A View From 1965.'
18. For a discussion of this see Anthony Bogues, *And What About the Human?: The Politics and Literatures of Radical Anti-Colonial Thought* (forthcoming).
19. Conversation with George Lamming, January 2010. Bridgetown, Barbados.
20. The phrase is David Scott's see his introduction to the interview of Lamming in *Small Axe*, (No. 12, September, 2002) pp. 72–75.
21. Ibid., p. 123.
22. George Lamming, (Introduction by Richard Wright) *In the Castle of My Skin* (New York: McGraw-Hill Book Company, 1954) p. 67.
23. While Lamming has argued that this style of speaking was the result of the many public statements which he makes, he also notes in an interview that the process begins with his writing of *The Pleasures of Exile,* suggesting to me that he is making a general distinction between forms of writing and criticism not only between orality and writing.
24. Richard Drayton & Andaiye (eds.) *Conversations* (London: Karia Press, 1992) p. 8.
25. *Season of Adventure*, p. 18.

SECTION 1

Language, Politics and Literature (1953–1990)

1 | *The Negro Writer and His World**

I was invited, originally, to speak on the subject of the Negro novel in English, but I have chosen, with your permission, to consider a situation that is at once wider and more manageable: the Negro writer and his world.

We shall find in the challenge of the word "Negro" a strange and conflicting set of factors. It would be very difficult to establish, from the premise of literature, the close connection between the matter and method of three such writers as Mr Richard Wright in *Native Son* and *Black Boy*, Mr Amos Tutuola in the *Palm Wine Drinkard*, and the late Jamaican novelist Roger Mais in *Brother Man*. America, Nigeria, and the British Caribbean have met here under the embracing function of an activity called writing; but the manifestations of that activity in the work of these three are at once delightful and perplexing. The only thing which holds them together, apart from the belief they are men, is the fact they are black.

My second reason for extending the first title has to do with my impression that you are concerned with matters which go far and fast beyond the strictness and delicacy of creative literature. It is not without reasons, other than dedication to your particular disciplines, that you should want to establish the validity of the African contribution to human civilisation. There is on the whole a psychology here at work which prompts us to remind others of things we know already, or at worst, to prove something that the Other tends to dismiss or deny. Our speculations lean so heavily on the attention of the Other, that it is difficult to think at all without being constantly mindful of the

---

*   This address was delivered at the First International Congress of Black Writers and Artists in Paris on September 21 1956. Three versions of the text have been previously published: *Presence Africaine* 1~56, No.8, 9, 10: 318–325; and *Caribbean Quarterly*, 1958, 5: (2). And in conversations: *George Lamming, Essays, Addresses and interviews 1953-1990*. (Karia Press: London, 1992).

sympathy and attitude of the Other. The Other being, of course, the equally wide category of men we must, for the purposes of such a conference, regard as Non-Negro.

I shall consider the term Negro, first of all, as a word which represents at one shot a fact and a fallacy, although I am not at all sure that the fallacy I have in mind is not itself a fact, or the fact I shall try to define is not, after all, a fallacy. Our speculations and actions are so often reactions to the Other's impact in our world. They lean heavily on the very fact that the Other exists. It is this aspect of the word Negro which I want you to consider as fallacy.

If we are going to be honest with ourselves, it is necessary too to consider, and to express with some indignation, some of the ways a Negro may use to cash in on this fallacy, and in our concern with the afflictions and the possible prosperity of one group of men, we must take care not to construct props for a man who may not differ in any way from his enemy in the quality of their bad faith. Rumour has it, and rumour may be right, that many a Negro is doing extremely well in the skin trade; cashing in, that is, on the extraordinary and perverse privilege of being a quite fascinating black in a world of well-meaning and unthinking whites.

This aspect of the word leads straight to the Other, which I am suggesting represents a *fact* of the man's existence as a Negro. This is not now the case of the Other defining the Negro, but rather of the Negro becoming conscious of his own presence as a result of the regard of the Other.

The Negro writer is a writer who through a process of social and historical accidents, encounters himself, so to speak, in a category of men called Negro. He carries this definition like a limb. It travels with him as a necessary guide for the Other's regard. It has settled upon him with an almost natural finality until he has become it. He is a reluctant part of the conspiracy which identifies him with that condition which the Other has created for them both. He does not emerge as an existence which must be confronted as an unknown dimension; for he is not simply *there*. He is there in a certain way. The eye which catches and cages him has seen him as a man *in spite of* ... As a result he encounters himself in a state of surprise and embarrassment. He is a little ashamed, not in the crude sense of not wanting to be this or that, but in the more resonant sense of shame, the shame that touches every consciousness that feels it has been *seen*.

The Negro is a man whom the Other regards as a Negro; and the dichotomy, the split, as it were, which may exist at the very centre of this consciousness, shall have been created by that old, and it would seem eternal conflict between the naming of a thing and a knowledge of it. For it is one of the mischievous powers of language, and particularly that aspect of language which relates to names that it enables us to rob things of their power to embarrass us. Language in this respect is intentional, and the intention seems clearly part of the human will to power. A name is an infinite source of control.

We attribute to any class of objects (stones, leaves, birds, insects) these names, and we have immediately found a way of avoiding the mystery which clothed these objects in their original state of silence and anonymity.

A good example turns up in *Hard Times*. Dickens calls that chapter, *Murdering the Innocents*, and although it is a savage comment on the crudeness of educational method of the time, it suggests much more. Let us for a brief moment watch Dickens situate his character, Sissy Jupe.

> "Girl number twenty," said Mr Gradgrind, squarely pointing with his square forefinger, "I ain't know that girl. Who is that girl?"

> "Sissy Jupe, sir," explained number twenty, blushing, standing up and curtsying.

> "Sissy is not a name," said Mr Gradgrind. "Don't call yourself Sissy. Call yourself Cecilia."

> It's father as calls me Sissy, sir," returned the young girl, in a trembling voice, and with another curtsy ..

> "Then he has no business to do it," said Mr Gradgrind. "Tell him he mustn't. Cecilia Jupe. Let me see. What is your father?"

> "He belongs to the horse-riding if you please, Sir," says Sissy. Mr G. frowned and waved off the objectionable calling with his hand.

> "We don't want to know anything about that here. You mustn't tell us about that here. Your father breaks horses, don't he?

> "If you please, sir, when they can get any to break, they do break horses in the ring, sir."

"You mustn't tell us about the ring here. Very well, then. Describe your father as a horse-breaker. He doctors sick horses, I dare say?"

"Oh, yes, sir."

"Very well, then. He is a veterinary surgeon, a farrier and a horse breaker. Give me your definition of a horse."

(Sissy Jupe thrown into the greatest alarm by this demand).

"Girl number twenty unable to define a horse!" said Mr Gradgrind for the general behalf of all the little pitchers. "Girl number twenty possessed of no facts, in reference to one of the commonest of animals! Some boy's definition of a horse. Bitzer, yours."

Of course Sissy knows all about horses, but it is, in the particular context, an irrelevant knowledge. It is a knowledge which suggests participation, and where there is real participation there tends to be an absence of determinants, definitions, directions. But let us hear from Bitzer who is an alternative to Sissy.

"Bitzer ," said Thomas Gradgrind. "Your definition of a horse."

"Quadruped, Graminivorous. Forty teeth, namely twenty-four grinders, four eye-teeth, and twelve incisive. Sheds coat in the spring, in marshy countries, sheds hoofs too. Hoofs hard, but requiring to be shod with iron. Age known by marks in mouth. Thus (and much more) said Bitzer.

"Now girl number twenty," said Mr Gradgrind, "You know what a horse is."

This is a sad knowledge but it is appropriate; for having found our references we can all, with the exception of Sissy Jupe, move forward. Following such an example, we can see a contradictory intention at the very heart of words. They may equip us through their power of symbolisation for an investigation into what is not known to us and they may also be an unconscious mechanism for our fear of the unknown.

In my book, *The Emigrants*, the African Azi (who, I suppose is, in Bitzer's terms of knowledge, a real Negro) has had a brilliant career as a mathematician at Cambridge. He experiences certain dislocation of facts, in historical sense, and meanings. He is stricken by a lack of references, and as a result is forced to consider the whole problem of significance. Here is an extract from a letter he wrote to his tutor:

... I think I begin to understand two things. One is the accidental nature of social relations. This is what I think they call History. All the roles which different classes play in any collectivity might just have been reversed. Privilege is simply a relation which defines one group in terms of another, and if you examine the matter, you'll see, Andrews, that the dominated might very well have been the dominant. If you like you can explain the relations in terms of their historical *development*, but beneath the history, there's no *reason* we can detect for these things being what they are.

The other is the insignificance of events. The same errors are committed, the same consequences crush us. But nothing really *happens*. We adjust to some abstraction as easily as we adjust to some concrete occurrence. It does not matter what is involved, massacre or mystery. If we need things to occur before we can change, it seems that what happens is wasted on us, or nothing ever really *happens*. Azi again.

So I arrived at a point, a stand-still. First of all I must leave Cambridge for a while. And I realised that I was just drifting, a bit of flotsam, if you like, but conscious of itself in that drift. I didn't know what to choose. If I acted on instinct, I couldn't call that choice because choice ultimately implies a relation of transcendence. An ultimate value by which I choose, and I had no experience of such a value. There was, only habit. Honesty, telling the truth rather than a lie the instinct to survive, this opposition to death, all these constituted habit, or rather habit dictated these, and I couldn't admit that ,such was the true foundation of my action, my choice. For a *man* there is something profoundly humiliating about such an admission. But I felt there was freedom, that I was even free to do away with this humiliation. Freedom! I don't mean, Andrews, some exemption from a social force – nothing that shows my relation to another in a group – I mean something alogical, something that seems always outside the reach of any demands a particular situation might make of you, freedom as an experience of the self in a state of unconditional awareness. I do not attain to this freedom. It is an attribute of *me*...

7

And there is always contained in such a statement of feeling a confession of one clear desire. It is the desire for totality, a desire to deal effectively with that gap, that distance which separates one man from another, and also in the case of an acute reflective self-consciousness, separates a man from himself. In the isolated case of the Negro it is the desire, not merely to rebel against the consequences of a certain social classification, but also a fundamental need to redefine himself for the comprehension of the Other, and in the hope that the stage shall have been set for some kind of meaningful communication.

The Negro writer joins hands, therefore, not so much with a Negro audience, as with every other writer whose work is a form of self-enquiry a clarification of his relations with other men, and a report of his own very highly subjective conception of the possible meaning of man's life.

To speak of his situation is to speak of a general need to find a centre as well as a circumference which embraces some reality whose meaning satisfies his intellect and may prove pleasing to his senses. But a man's life assumes meaning first in relation with other men, and his experience which is what the writer is trying always to share with the reader, is made up not only of the things which happen to him, in his encounter with others, but also of the different meanings and values which he chooses to place on what has happened. What happens to him depends to a great extent on the particular world he happens to be living in, and the way he chooses to deal with his own experience is determined by the kind of person he considers himself to be. In other words, he is continually being shaped by the particular world which accommodates him, or refuses to do so; and at the same time he is shaping, through his own desires, needs and idiosyncrasies, a world of his own. And since a writer's work is meant for public consideration and, through the wonderful devices of printing, translation and distribution, is continually extending to places and people, with whom he may have no direct experience, another world is being created about him.

What, then, we may ask, is really meant by the term 'world' in the particular context of these remarks? There are, I would suggest, three kinds of worlds to which the writer bears in some way a responsibility, worlds which are distinct, and yet very deeply related. There is first of all the world of the private and hidden self, a world which turns quietly, sometimes turbulently, within one man, and which might be only known by others after that man has spoken. Each who becomes aware of himself as a separate existence shares this solitude, each man has had, an experience, momentary or prolonged, of the meaning of being alone. I do not mean loneliness or any similar illness of certain self-important natures. I am speaking of the experience proceeding from the depths of one's being, of *existing*.

It is a moment marked by silence. It is a moment when a man's utterance cannot catch and convey the shape and shade of his thought and his feeling. Language, it would seem, has actually surrendered just when his need is greatest. It is then he requires this weapon of words to enter that hidden area of his consciousness, and bring back with it, so to speak, the kind of picture which another's eye cannot conceive. In ordinary circumstances this effort is never carried through. A verdict of guilty may be directed against others who have been betrayed not by their guilt, but by that appalling and impotent failure to communicate their innocence. And when there is no condemnation the matter is easily forgotten. The ordinary person is, time and again, seized by an experience a meaning perhaps, and quickly abandons the attempt to grasp it completely, because the exercise, from the start, seems too much of burden; and after all, he will say it does not really matter. Or even if the desire to struggle is real, the urgencies of living make it very difficult to sustain his interest: because there is something to be done, something which requires his immediate attention if life is to be liveable. Day-to-day living keeps intruding on that private and solitary world of concerns. It may take the form of the bad-tempered husband who makes trouble when he cannot find something more dramatic to occupy his energy. Or the rent is overdue. All these things make for a great nuisance. They are what the Danish philosopher Soren Kierkegaard, calls, 'the immediate neighbourhood', one's family, sometimes one's enemies, and always one's friends.

But for the writer this private world is his one priceless possession. It is precisely from this point that everything else will proceed. And in these circumstances it cannot be sacrificed to his immediate neighbourhood (even when that neighbourhood means a group defined by an artificial misfortune which includes him). Nothing can take its place. It is his initial capital. He may gain by it, or lose by it, but without it he cannot function. Why he should be possessed in this way is a matter we do not wholly understand. We must accept it as a fact of his experience. But it is this possession which is responsible for his relation to words. He has failed until he has caught some part of that world and given it form in language. Words are his anchor and his spear; he has got to keep them in preparation and in order, and when they begin to wear under their work, he must find new ones, or new combinations of the old ones, for the work must go on. A writer does not only use language. He helps to make language. To any decent man who is anxious to feed his children and comfort his wife and be amiable to his neighbours, this personal rage with words must seem a kind of lunacy and that judgement will not be far wrong; for the writer is, in fact, a kind of lunatic whose insanity is only kept in control by his occasional triumph of expression. *In the Castle of My Skin* opens with a passage which may help to throw some light on the mechanics of this private world as well as the process through which certain currents of emotion move to touch and assimilate the world of social relations. The passage reads:

> Rain, rain, rain ... my mother put her head through the window to let the neighbour know that I was nine, and they flattered me with the consolation that my birthday had brought showers of blessing. The morning laden with cloud soon passed into noon, and the noon neutral and silent into the sodden grimness of an evening that waded through water. That evening I kept an eye on the crevices of our wasted roof where the colour of the shingles had turned to mourning black, and waited for the weather to rehearse my wishes. But the evening settled on the slush of the roads that dissolved in parts into pools of clay, and I wept for the watery waste of my ninth important day. Yet I was wrong, my mother protested it was irreverent to disapprove the will of the Lord or reject the consolation that my birthday had brought showers of blessing.
>
> It was my ninth celebration of the gift of life, my ninth celebration of the consistent lack of an occasion for celebration. From a window where the spray had given the sill a little wet life I watched the water ride through the lanes and alleys that multiplied behind the barracks that neighboured our house. The white stalks of the lily lay flat under the hammering rain, then coaxed their roots from the earth and drifted across the upturned clay, into the canals and on to the deep black river where by agreement the floods converged. The water rose higher and higher until the fern and flowers on our verandah were flooded. It came through the creases of the door, and

expanded across the uncarpeted borders of the floor. My mother brought sacks that absorbed it quickly, but overhead the crevices of the roof were weeping rain, and surfacing the carpet and the epergne of flowers and fern were liquid, glittering curves which the mourning black of the shingles had bequeathed. No one seemed to notice how the noon had passed to evening, the evening to night; nor to worry that the weather had played me false. Nothing mattered but the showers of blessing and the eternal will of the water's source. And I might have accepted the consolation if' it weren't that the floods had chosen to follow me in the celebration of all my years, evoking the image of those legendary waters which had once arisen to set a curse on the course of man.

As if in serious imitation of the waters that raced outside, our lives – meaning our fears and their corresponding ideals – seemed to escape down an imaginary drain that was our future. Our capacity for feeling had grown as large as the flood, but the prayers of a simple village seemed as precariously adequate as the houses hoisted on water. Of course, it was difficult to see what was happening outside, but there were paddling splashes of boys' feet and the choke of an engine stuck in the mud.

This world is private. It contains the range of his ambitions, his deceits, his perplexity, his pride, his shame, his guilt, his honour, his need. All these qualities are there, hidden in the castle of his skin.

But that private world of the writer is modified, even made possible, by the world in which he moves among other men. Much as he might think it otherwise, it is through the presence of others that his own presence is given meaning.

What then is the relation of a writer to a society in which for reasons which have nothing to do with his work, he is regarded as different? When the differences carry consequences of injustice, his relation is not different from that of any other who shares a similar misfortune. Any identical suffering holds him together in defence or attack with those who are part of his misfortune, and since this misfortune of difference enters his private world, one expects his work as a writer to be, in part a witness to that misfortune. Not because there is a moral law which demands he address himself to his social world, but rather because there is a fundamental need to present his private world in all its facets, and one of its vivid experiences will of necessity be the impact which that social world, with all its reservations and distinctions, has made on his consciousness. This is the sense in which it is true to say that a writer has a real and primary responsibility to himself.

From the point of view of imaginative literature, this social classification which manifests itself most violently through race, is a peculiar torment and a peculiar challenge for the writer who suffers its disadvantage. About the situation in America, I would say briefly, that the torment has been real, and so overwhelmingly challenging that the meaning of the challenge has not always been clearly seen, in all its largeness, by all Negro writers of distinction. And the reason is simple. If you are continually and ruthlessly bombarded by floods, you can easily forget how precious a gentle shower of rain can be. And the floods, which may spring from rain, soon lose that identification with rain in their common source of water. It seems after a while that there is no real connection between water and water, the gentle shower and the opposing flood; for the abundance of the one has severed it from its real link with the other.

Similarly, if through the character and the fate of his country, a writer's senses have been consistently assaulted by the vast pressure of a single issue, it is not difficult for him to lose sight, for a time, of the connection between the disaster which threatens to reduce him and the wider context and condition of which his disaster is but the clearest example. The Negro in the United States symbolises an essential condition of Man, not merely in his urgent need to correct a social injustice through powers of law, but also in his need to embark upon a definition of himself as man in the world of men.

For the third of his worlds, the world to which he is condemned by the fact of his spirit is the world of human beings. He shares in their community. What he cannot escape is the essential need to find meaning for his destiny, and every utterance he makes in this direction is an utterance made on behalf of all men. And his responsibility to that other world, his third world, will be judged not only by the authenticity and power with which his own private world is presented, but also by the honesty with which he interprets the world of his social relations, his country, that is, for those who have no direct experience of it, but are moved by the power of his speech, his judgement and his good faith.

2 | *The Education of Feeling*[*]

When I left the island of Barbados as a youth, that is, when I was much younger than I am now, I went to Trinidad where I lived and worked for some years. This was very important in my later formation. I have a deep gratitude for Trinidad. I think my life would have been very different if I had gone straight from Barbados to England: it was Trinidad that redirected my head. I went as a teacher, which was a very funny thing. You see in Barbados they had tried to expel me from this school where I was. But then they wanted somebody to teach in a boarding school in Trinidad and the school recommended me as a teacher. Very interesting that! I really went from rebel to custodian or warder.

But in Trinidad I had this friend. This was around 1947, '48, '49. Cliff was his name. It was through Cliff that I first saw names like Stalin. They had books there, which they read – this isn't exact – the books we didn't read them. Because the books were in Russian. It was a very interesting thing. Fervour can take peculiar forms sometimes.

He would say; "Come, come, come, you see that?" "Yes. The name is Stalin. What's that?" "It doesn't matter. It don't matter."

As long as it was Russian you were doing justice. But we had important, critical discussions about the society because of those

* In November 1982, under the umbrella of a conference on Culture and Sovereignty, writers, artists, scholars and intellectual workers of all descriptions met on the island of Grenada. Lamming had been a pivotal figure in the organisation of the conference and went on to edit the papers delivered there for the Regional Committee for the Cultural Sovereignty of the Caribbean. After the conference, Lamming together with Ngũgĩ Wa Thiong'o, the Kenyan author, journeyed to Carriacou in the Grenadines. While there he delivered an informal address to an audience composed of Grenadian teachers, members of the New Jewel Movement, and many working people from Carriacou itself. The original text has not survived; this is a transcribed and edited version of an audio recording made on that occasion. It was originally published in the volume, *Conversations* (1992) under the title, 'A Visit to Carriacou'.

names-Stalin, Lenin, and so on. And needless to say, as men of that age, we were fun loving, we were meat eating, we were rum drinking men. And Sunday was a very special kind of day – that was the one day when you were likely to eat in the house where you had slept. A very special day. We were close, very close. And then we parted.

I went to London.[1] Cliff followed about a year or so later although I didn't know he was there. Until one day I was going down one of those streets and saw him, and we greeted each other warmly as before. He had done a very odd thing. He got married. What I mean is that he was not a man given to that type of arrangement. Not the man I had left in Trinidad. But anyway he was married, and his wife was a woman whom I had known when she was in high school.

He asked me to lunch the first Sunday after I met him. So I went and I really wanted to be happy there. It was Sunday and I went through that ritual I had picked up in London. I got up at 11 o'clock. I went to the park. I took no breakfast – I was making myself hungry for this thing. So I went and I noticed that – you know when you can tell changes in a man by the rhythms of the body – how he moves – different walking – slightly different feeling. Strange thing. But I had not seen him for two years, and it is a fatal mistake to assume that you can pick up from where you left off. Anyway we had a drink, and it looked like things were normal. Then it was time for lunch and they brought out some little plates with what looked like dry grass on it. Very peculiar. But I was well brought up – our house was poor but very rigid in courtesies. So I ate this little dish that looked like dry grass. And then they brought out another course in little bowls, that looked like boiled grass and the pattern of the meal moved in that way.

So at the end of the thing he got up: "I didn't tell you that we have gone through a food reform. We are now vegetarian."

Now I didn't mind this change. (That is what I am coming to: processes of change and transformation). What I objected to was that I had not been warned, you know, I would have made arrangements. I'd have taken along my own pork chops. I didn't mind this vegetarian business, but I thought it unfair that a man should impose his conversion on me without my going through the same process. It didn't seem right.

Cliff and I are great friends today. But I mention that Sunday for two reasons. First of all, it is about food. Food is the first stage. Food is the first plan of human life. Men and women have to eat in order to survive. Man is of nature but he is also situated in nature and discovers that survival is not possible unless he engages with nature in some alliance that will allow him food. And that engagement when it elaborates itself over a series of processes is what you call work. One of the profoundest insights, perhaps from my reading the most profound and revolutionary insight of Marx pertains to that: not the identification of classes – lots of people knew about that before he started. It is that critical and unbreakable connection which he makes between man's engagement with nature for the purpose of survival, and in the elaborated stages, his engagement for the purpose of turning nature into the path of his own history. That is the profound revolution in Marx's thought. That relationship to nature called 'work' which is demanded by the need for food is at the centre of history. What interested me after a while was not that Cliff was a vegetarian. What interested me was how he came to that. And that is always the important question for me, whenever a man tells me he has become something, a Jehovah's Witness or anything. I have spent a lot of my life in association with Marxists of a variety of colours. But I have never in my life met a Marxist baby. Never. Never. Nor have I ever met a Christian baby. When a man tells me he is a Marxist, that is of great interest, but there is a matter that fascinates me more. I want to know how he got there. I want to know what was the particular journey that took him from wherever he was to that point of perception and conviction and redemption which he calls Marxist. It is that journey when he reveals it to me that allows me to see his connection with what he is calling himself.

And I want to give an example now from my own life of these processes of change and transformation. There is a very remarkable ceremony held in Haiti in which every seven years relations of the dead meet. The cosmology is simple; it is based on the fact that in life we have quarrels. Men and women have quarrels about various things. Sometimes one of them dies before the quarrels wear out. The Haitian Gods demand that the quarrels be resolved. The dead cannot be released into eternity unless there is a resolution. And the living are very uncomfortable about what will happen to them until the quarrel is solved. What fascinated me about this ceremony was the extraordinary dependence of the dead on the living. The dead whose destiny is eternity cannot be unlocked from water until they have this dialogue with the living. The symbolic function of the ceremony for me, as an artist within the Caribbean situation, is the necessity of reconciling the past with each moment of conscious living. That the dead need to speak with the living. And in the way we work I discovered this was about my own life. For the Haitian suggestion about change and transformation troubled me. It troubled me personally.

I was born in what was not an ordinary village. I was born in what was called a 'bad' village. It was bad in the sense that there were some extraordinary men there who were not afraid of anyone. You see, if there was a fight in my village it took a long time for the police to come because there was always a big argument in the station as to who should go. It was that kind of village. A very, very serious village. Although I felt perfectly safe in the village – they had a certain ambivalence to me. My mother was investing heavily, heavily, in something called education. The village was the source of a lot of my problems in school, because one of the first difficulties I had in school was in open class giving my address. That is a serious thing because I did not want anybody to know that I came from that village. That is not a joke. Not a joke. I said, 'on Alkins Road near Belmont', hoping the emphasis would be on Belmont. Because after Belmont the white people started. Belmont was still the black district. But those were painful moments of having to put down that kind of detail. And I was in a situation in which I lived in two worlds. This high school was intended for people to go into the Civil Service, the professional classes and so on. But I was alright there: I was a good cricketer, I redeemed myself in that way, my football was very good. But, and this is the one that hit the vein, if I left that school at ten after three in the afternoon, and that laboratory of democracy was still going on, and we were walking down the main streets into town and without warning I saw my mother coming towards me – that was very serious – should I acknowledge her or not? And in those situations she just caught my eye and I caught hers and as we come nearer to each other we are both thinking about the same thing because I am not too sure that I want to be identified there. And in a curious kind of way she does not mind if I don't because of who I am with now – Dr Somebody's son. So when I hear people discussing class, I did not discover that in Marx. I lived it, from the age of ten. I lived with class. Then much later, I had to try and understand what had happened to me. But I did not discover how class society deforms human relations from Marx. I lived it. And so I have developed an extraordinary nose. I can smell middle class people everywhere.

I am much older now but obviously this experience is still penetrating, moving through me all the time. It is in *Season of Adventure*, which I wrote after my visit to Haiti. It is the first book of mine in which the central character is a woman, a young girl – a 'break away.' It is a very prophetic book. It is a strange book in terms of structure and some people have been confused by it. It goes on as what seems a normal novel and then at a certain point I intervene. I, Lamming, intervene to say, "Look – there are some things that the fiction has not yet said that I want to say personally." It is a very peculiar thing to do in fiction. It was not peculiar for me. It took some critics fifteen years to say: "That intervention is working." But this was it:

> Until the age of ten Powell and I had lived together, equal in the affection of two mothers. Powell had my dreams; and I had lived his passions. Identical in years, and stage by stage, Powell and I were taught in the same primary school.

> And then the division came. I got a public scholarship which started my migration into another world, a world whose roots were the same, but whose style of living was entirely different from what my childhood knew. It had earned me a privilege which now shut Powell and the whole tonelle right out of my future. I had lived as near to Powell as my skin to the hand it darkens. And yet! Yet I forgot the tonelle as men forget a war, and attached myself to this new world which was so recent and so slight beside the weight of what had gone before. Instinctively I attached myself to that new privilege; and in spite of all my effort, I am not free of its embrace even to this day.

> I believe deep in my bones that the mad impulse which drove Powell to his criminal defeat was largely my doing. I will not have this explained away by talk about environment; nor can I allow my own moral infirmity to be transferred to a foreign conscience, labelled imperialist. I shall go beyond my grave in the knowledge that I am responsible for what happened to my brother.

> Powell still resides somewhere in my heart, with a dubious love, some strange, nameless shadow of regret; and yet with the deepest,

deepest nostalgia. For I have never felt myself to be an honest part of anything since the world of his childhood deserted me.

Powell is being hunted down because he is a political assassin. *Season of Adventure* is a political novel, there is a revolt that is initiated by the drums. They try to ban the drums and the drums took to the streets and the whole population took to the streets and the government says that the President is murdered by Powell. He has not been found in the book, and I suspect he is still around.

This brings me to the question of liberation. I said it is a word which suggests process. It is a process of trying to free self and society from various forms of imprisonment. The imprisonment of social injustice, the imprisonment of intellectual backwardness, the imprisonment of disfigured spirits. We liberate ourselves from a condition that is undesirable or intolerable but there is an implication in this word that we have to liberate ourselves into some other kind of being. You fight a struggle in order to construct something of the future. And there is, sometimes, in the moment of struggle, no way to predict what new problems and challenges that freedom will confront you with. Many forms of imprisonment. I was very troubled and shaken up in St George's when Pearl Springer[2] was reading that poem about the man. The man who wanted to bury his head in his kind of gravity when confronted with a woman. This man, this poet, this intellectual could not cope with what he saw as a challenge, which should have been no challenge at all, of sharing life with a gifted woman. Nine and one half West Indian men out of ten cannot cope with that. And it poses a peculiar isolation and pain for a new woman. Where in hell do I find a man that by my criteria is a man? And nine and a half out of ten men who have to deal with that dismiss it with language [which is what I am coming to now]: "She is weird. She is very weird." And then that does not become just a word. That becomes a total state. Wherever she goes they point to the weird one. Nobody even knows her name now. The weird one. And it may surprise you to know that there is a very close connection between language and liberation. One of the major failures of the intellectual left for me in this region is the failure to think about the problem of language in their attempt to communicate ideas with a people who are victims of a scarcity of knowledge and do not share those modes of perception.

Now language is made of words, but it is made of more than words. I want to give you an example. If I say: "That chair is comfortable," the word 'chair' does service as normal language and signals a convenience. It does not do more than that. But if I say: "That man is behaving like a chair," the word 'chair' in that context applies completely new meanings. That is a man who has been letting everybody sit on him – that has all kinds of resonances. If a poet writes: "The sky is blue" that 'blue' is a dead word. All that 'blue' does is to indicate the inherent qualities of a colour called blue. But if you come up with a line that says: "The sky turned the stones blue," something very peculiar is happening with words. What that blue is doing is opening up the senses to the penetrative power of the sky, now as 'blue,' and to the predicament of stone in the context of such a sky. Same word, but the range and resonances are very different. And I would ask you who use words like 'consciousness' and 'revolution,' 'individual consciousness,' 'social consciousness,' 'political consciousness,' to consider that these are words whose meaning must be sharpened unless you would rather they become just like the blue. And the biggest insult to revolutionary struggle is for the revolution to become just like the blue. This is the critical importance of language.

In recent years I have been invited to all kinds of places to speak, particularly for the trade union movement, journalists, all kinds of places to give speeches and yet nobody asked me to speak on literature. It is a very peculiar thing. I am a novelist. I have not in recent times had an invitation from any Caribbean institution to address the question of literature. I understand that and I go. That is quite clear. But when I make a political speech to journalists or when I make a political speech to the Barbados Workers Union or the Trinidad Oilfield Workers Trade Union, I write a speech. And one of the things about being a novelist is that I give it structure. It is very structured. But it does not work like the language of the novel. It is a very different kind of language. The speeches are addressed to the mind. With the intention of making the collective mind of the crowd feel – if you can get them – to make the mind feel. That is really what I am trying to do. The speeches are given in what we would call a language of statements. But statements given and structured in such a way that makes the mind feel. The novels, on the other hand, are directed to an area of feeling and with the specific intention of making the feeling think. And therefore the novels are more subtle, the novels are more complex. A character in the novel does not only do this or say that. We try to show what precisely is his relation to what he is doing or what he is saying. That is not the technique of the speech. The novel does not only depict aspects of social reality. It explores it. It ploughs it up. There are writers who take an easy short cut and go around photographing the absurdities that appear on the social landscape: but they have no plough.[3]

They do not ask where that strain of absurdity comes from, nor do they plough it up.

The serious revolutionary writer must always try to make that which is only seen and felt as possible into a moment of living reality. And one of the important functions of the arts and cultural activity has to do with an aspect of education which is on no curriculum at all. *I am speaking of the education of feeling*. And I think this may be our most dangerous omission, not just for the schools but for the revolution: not to educate feeling, not to educate in loving, as distinct from 'being in love'. To educate in love is really the function of the creative imagination. The work of art, be it theatre, music, novel, or poem is not seen primarily by the artist as a call to revolution, or a call to anything else nor as a celebration of victory. Artistic expression can do those things and in particular situations may regard or must regard this function as its priority. But the central and seminal value of the creative imagination is that it functions as a civilising and a humanising force in a process of struggle! It offers an experience through which feeling is educated. Through which feeling is deepened. Through which feeling can increase its capacity to accommodate a great variety of knowledge. How many of you have gone into a theatre when they are rehearsing? What is going on there is that the man is being educated into making the body speak a language of absolute precision about the feeling it is about to communicate. "That is it. Do it again. The head is in the wrong place. The arm is wrong," and so on. That is not histrionics. It is about making the body speak feeling.

The same is true for the poet and novelist and it is with some of my own work that I am going to finish. In my first book, *In the Castle of My Skin*, there are some boys who spend all day on the beach talking about everything in a metaphorical and incoherent way – love, life, marriage, the house, the village and so on. But as they are going back to the village they discover that they are doing a very wasteful thing.

They are discussing serious matters and they are not educated people. That is what they discover. And this is the collective monologue which is going through their minds on the way back. This is one passage:

It was hours since we had left home. We had talked and talked and talked. We had talked a lot of nonsense, perhaps. But anyone would forgive us. With the sea simmering, and the sand and the wind in the trees, we received so many strange feelings. And in the village in the cellar, at the school, in this corner or that corner of the house, something was always happening. We didn't notice it then, but when something bigger appeared like the sea and the sand,... we had to say something was like something else, and whatever we said didn't convey all that we felt. We wouldn't dare tell anybody what we had talked about. People who were sure of what they were saying and who had the right words to use could do that. They could talk to others. And even if they didn't feel what they were saying, it didn't matter. They had the right words. Language was a kind of passport. You could go where you like if you had a clean record. You could say what you like if you know how to say it. It didn't matter whether you felt everything you said. You had language, good big words to make up for what you didn't feel. And if you were really educated, and you could command the language like a captain on a ship, if you could make the language do what you wanted it to do, say what you wanted it to say, then you didn't have to feel at all. You could do away with feeling. That's why everybody wanted to be educated. You didn't have to feel. You learnt this and you learnt that, and you knew a Jack for a Jack and Ace for an Ace. You were alright. Nothing would ever go pop, pop, pop in your head. You had language to safeguard you. And if you were beginning to feel too strongly, you could kill the feeling, you could get it out of the way by fetching the words that couldn't understand what the feeling was all about. It was like a knife. If you wanted to slaughter the pig, you got your knife. The knife hadn't a clue what was going on in the pig's head, but when you wielded it, the job was done. It was so with language. When the feelings came up like so many little pigs that grunted and irritated with their grunts, you could slaughter them. You could slaughter your feelings as you slaughtered a pig. Language was all you needed. It was like a knife. It knifed your feelings clean and proper, and put an end to any pop, pop, pop in your head. Perhaps we would do better if we were educated. For the time being we weren't going to say a word to anybody. Not a word.

The education of feeling must be at the heart of any struggle for liberation.

Notes

1. See George Lamming, "Birthday Poem for Clifford Sealey," *Bim*, 1951, 4 (14): 132–33.
2. Pearl Springer is a poet from Trinidad and Tobago. The Poet Laureate of Port of Spain, her poetry focuses on social issues and the African heritage of the Caribbean.
3. Perhaps a reference is being made here to V.S. Naipaul, the Trinidadian author. See Lamming's comments in his *Pleasures of Exile*, Allison & Busby, London, 1984 (1960), pp. 224–25.

3 | In the Castle of My Skin: *Thirty Years After**

_____

The reading of fiction involves a certain conspiracy of feeling between the writer and his reader. They have both agreed to accord every act of the imagination the status of an absolute truth. And the world of fiction must work towards this end. It may be helpful, therefore, to alert readers to the kind of device which this writer has employed in the creation of that world, and especially since his methods denote a break from conventional practice. *In the Castle of My Skin* introduces us to a world of poor and simple villagers: and the village functions both as place and symbol of an entire way of life.

> The village was a marvel of small, heaped houses raised jauntily on groundsels of limestone, and arranged in rows on either side of the multiplying marl roads. Sometimes the roads disintegrated, the limestone slid back and the houses advanced across their boundaries to meet those on the opposite side in an embrace of board and shingle and cactus fence [...] There were days when the village was quiet: the shoemaker plied lazily at his trade and the washerwomen bent over the tubs droned away their complacency. At other times there were scenes of terror, and once there was a scene of murder [...] But the season of flood could change everything. The floods could level the stature and even conceal the identity of the village. With the turn of my ninth year it had happened again. From the window I looked at the uniform wreckage of a village at night in water...I went away from the window over the dripping sacks and into a corner which the weather had forgotten. And what did I remember? My father who had only fathered the idea of me had left me the sole liability of my mother who really fathered me [...]

_____

*   This is an essay written by Lamming in 1983 as an introduction to the first Schocken Books edition of his classic 1953 novel. George Lamming, *In the Castle of My Skin*, Schocken Books, New York, 1983 pp. ix-xx.

This world is not really the creation of individual wills. There is no privacy since the secret of each household can never escape communal scrutiny. I know your business and you know mine. The mother of the novel is given no name. She is simply G's mother, a woman of little or no importance in her neighbourhoods until the tropical season rains a calamity on every household; and she emerges, without warning, as a voice of nature itself.

> Then she broke into a soft, repetitive tone which rose with every fresh surge of feeling until it became a scattering peal of solicititude that soared across the night and into the neighbour's house. And the answer came back louder, better organised and more communicative so that another neighbour responded and yet another until the voices seemed to be gathered up by a single effort and the whole village shook with song on its foundation of water.

I cite that passage in order to introduce readers to a characteristic of this type of fiction which has caused some difficulty for the conventional critic of the novel. And what I say now of *In the Castle of My Skin* is also true of other Caribbean writers. The book is crowded with names and people, and although each character is accorded a most vivid presence and force of personality, we are rarely concerned with the prolonged exploration of an individual consciousness. It is the collective human substance of the Village, you might say, which is the central character. When we see the Village as collective character, we perceive another dimension to the individual wretchedness of daily living. It is the dimension of energy, force, a quickening capacity for survival. The Village sings; the Village dances; and since the word is their only rescue, all the resources of a vital oral folk tradition are summoned to bear witness to the essential humanity which rebukes the wretchedness of their predicament.

In this method of narration, where community, and not person, is the central character, things are never so tidy as critics would like. There is often no discernible plot, no coherent line of events with a clear causal connection. Nor is there a central individual consciousness on which attention is focused, and through which we can be guided reliably by a logical succession of events. Instead, there are several centres of attention which work simultaneously and acquire their coherence from the collective character of the Village.

The novel has had a peculiar function in the Caribbean. The writer's preoccupation has been mainly with the poor; and fiction has served as a way of restoring these lives – this world of men and women from down below – to a proper order of attention: to make their reality the supreme concern of the total society. But along with this desire, there was also the writer's recognition that this world, in spite of its long history of deprivation, represented the womb from which he himself had sprung, and the richest collective reservoir of experience on which the creative imagination could draw.

This world of men and women from down below is not simply poor. This world is black, and it has a long history at once vital and complex. It is vital because it constitutes the base of labour on which the entire Caribbean society has rested; and it is complex because Plantation Slave Society (the point at which the modern Caribbean began) conspired to smash its ancestral African culture, and to bring about a total alienation of man, the source of labour, from man, the human person.

The result was a fractured consciousness, a deep split in its sensibility which now raises difficult problems of language and values; the whole issue of cultural allegiance between the imposed norms of White Power, represented by a small numerical minority, and the fragmented memory of the African masses: between White instruction and Black imagination. The totalitarian demands of White supremacy, in a British colony, the psychological injury inflicted by the sacred rule that all forms of social status would be determined by the degrees of skin complexion; the ambiguities among Blacks themselves about the credibility of their own spiritual history.

All this would have to be incorporated into any imaginative record of the total society. Could the outlines of a national consciousness be charted and affirmed out of all this disparateness? And if that consciousness could be affirmed, what were its true ancestral roots, its most authentic cultural base?

The numerical superiority of the black mass could forge a political authority of their own making, and provide an alternative direction for the society. This was certainly possible. But this possibility was also the measure of its temporary failures.

I was among those writers who took flight from the failure. In the desolate, frozen heart of London, at the age of 23, I tried to reconstruct the world of my childhood and early adolescence. It was also the world of a whole Caribbean reality.

Migration was not a word I would have used to describe what I was doing when I sailed with other West Indians to England in 1950. We simply thought that we were going to an England which had been planted in our childhood consciousness as a heritage and a place of welcome. It is the measure of our innocence that neither the claim of heritage nor the expectation of welcome would have been seriously doubted. England was not for us a country with classes and conflicts of interest like the islands we had left. It was the name of a responsibility whose origin may have coincided with the beginning of time.

Today I shudder to think how a country, so foreign to our own instincts, could have achieved the miracle of being called Mother. It had made us pupils to its language and its institutions; baptised us in the same religion; schooled boys in the same game of cricket with its elaborate and meticulous etiquette of rivalry. Empire was not a very dirty word, and seemed to bear little relation to those forms of domination we now call imperialist.

The English themselves were not aware of the role they had played in the formation of these black strangers. The ruling class were serenely confident that any role of theirs must have been an act of supreme generosity. Like Prospero, they had given us language and a way of naming our own reality. The English working class were not aware they had played any role at all and deeply resented our arrival. It had come about without any warning. No one had consulted them. Occasionally I was asked: "Do you belong to us or to the French?" I had been dissolved in the common view of worker and aristocrat. English workers could also see themselves as architects of Empire.

Much of the substance of *In the Castle of My Skin* is an evocation of this tragic innocence. Nor was there, at the time of writing, any conscious effort, on my part, to emphasise the dimension of cruelty which had seduced, or driven by the force of need, an otherwise honourable black people into such lasting bonds of illusion. It was not a physical cruelty. Indeed, the colonial experience of my generation was almost wholly without violence. No torture, no concentration camp, no mysterious disappearance of hostile natives, no army encamped with orders to kill. The Caribbean endured a different kind of subjugation. It was a terror of the mind, a daily exercise in self-mutilation. Black versus black in a battle for self-improvement.

> Each represented for the other an image of the enemy. And the enemy was My People. My people are low-down nigger people. My people don't like to see their people get on. The language of the overseer. The language of the civil servant [...] Not taking chances with you people, my people. They always let you down. Make others say we're not responsible, we've no sense of duty. Like children under the threat of hellfire they accepted instinctively that the others, meaning the white, were superior, yet there was always the fear of realising that it might be true. This world of the others' imagined perfection hung like a dead weight over their energy. If the low-down nigger people weren't what they are, the others couldn't say anything about us. Suspicion, distrust, hostility. These operated in every decision. You never can tell with my people. It was the language of the overseer, the language of the Government servant, and later the language of lawyers and doctors who had returned stamped like any envelope with what they called the culture of the Mother Country.

This was the breeding ground for every uncertainty of self. In the riot scene of the novel, a group of men armed with knives, and ready with stones, have ambushed the white landlord on his way home. There is a clear intention to kill him, but the act of political revenge is delayed by argument about its timing.

Should we strike now or a little later? Their deliberations go on and on, and betray a latent ambivalence which is finally resolved by the arrival of their labour leader who pleads with them to withdraw. The landlord escapes, unharmed.

When I read this scene some 20 years after its publication, I was surprised by the mildness of its resolution. From the distant and more critical vantage point of London, the past now seemed more brutal. I wondered why I had allowed the landlord to go free. Was it the need to make the story conform to the most accurate portrayal of events as I had known them? No white man had been killed by rioters in Barbados in 1937. But I had taken greater liberty with other facts and done so in the interest of a more essential truth. Now I had begun to think that the most authentic response to the long history of shame and humiliation which had produced the riots demanded that the white landlord should have been killed.

The novelist does not only explore what has happened. At a deeper level of intention than literal accuracy, he seeks to construct a world that might have been; to show the possible as a felt and living reality. So for a long time I remained haunted by the feeling that the white landlord should have been killed, even if it were presented as the symbolic end of a social order that deserved to be destroyed.

The novel was completed within two years of my arrival in London. I still shared in that previous innocence which had socialised us into seeing our relations to empire as a commonwealth of mutual interests. The truth is there was never any such reciprocity of interest, and the various constitutional settlements which would gradually lead to the recent status of independence had a decisive influence in preserving much of the social legacy of the colonial period. Today the region is witnessing with alarm what is, in fact, an upheaval too long delayed. But the tactical withdrawal which the British now so proudly call decolonisation simply made way for a new colonial orchestration. The Caribbean returns to its old role of an imperial frontier, now perceived as essential to the security interests of the United States.

It is interesting for me to reflect on the role which America was to play in shaping essential features of the novel. If England dominated our minds as the original idea of ultimate human achievement, the United States existed for us as a dream, a kingdom of material possibilities accessible to all.

I had never visited the United States before writing *In the Castle of My Skin*; but America had often touched our lives with gifts that seemed spectacular at the time, and reminded us that this dream of unique luxury beyond our shores was true. This image of America has not changed. Almost everyone had some distant relation there who had done well. I had never heard of anyone being a failure in the United States.

And Christmas was evidence of this when postal orders arrived with money and gifts of exotic clothes.

But the United States had also provided the character, Trumper, with a political experience which the subtle force of British imperialism had never allowed to flourish in the islands. After his sojourn in the United States as a migrant labourer, Trumper returned home with a new ideology, and the startling discovery that his black presence had a very special meaning in the world. He had learnt the cultural and political significance of race.

Europe had trained black men to wear those white masks which Frantz Fanon wrote so bitterly about, and which the racist culture of the United States would tear asunder. America was really the extreme example of Europe, stripped naked of all pretense about having a civilising mission in the dark corners of the earth: a vast energetic extension of that demonic Europe which the novelist Joseph Conrad had so maliciously identified as a 'Heart of Darkness' in Africa. Conrad writes:

> They were conquerors, and for that you want only brute force – nothing to boast of, when you have it, since your strength is just an accident arising from the weakness of others. They grabbed what they could get for the sake of what was to be got. It was just robbery with violence, aggravated murder on a great scale, and men going at it blind – as is very proper for those who tackle a darkness. The conquest of the earth, which mostly mean the taking it away from those who have a different complexion or slightly flatter noses than ourselves, is not a pretty thing when you look into it too much.

Conrad, a child of Europe, understood the cultural racism of his own ancestry. Africa, a human continent to its own people, existed in Conrad's consciousness as a proper symbol of the demonic force which had driven his own white race to raid and vandalise every corner of the globe.

And so, in the United States, the black man was forced to recognise himself as a different kind of creature. Trumper *In the Castle of My Skin* embraced this new status, and on his return home offered it to the astonished villagers as the only foundation for a free human dignity among black people.

> You'll hear 'bout the Englishman, an' the Frenchman, and the American which mean man of America. An' each is call that 'cause he born in that particular place. But you'll become a Negro like me an' all the rest in the States an' all over the world, 'cause it ain't have nothin' to do with where you born. 'Tis what you is, a different kind o' creature. An' when you see what I tellin' you an' you become a Negro, act as you should, an' don't ask Hist'ry why

you is what you then see yourself to be, cause Hist'ry ain't got no answers. You ain't a thing till you know it.

This stark and bitter message of Trumper, pan-African in character, is supported in argument by the recorded music of black people, *Let My People Go*. The voice of Paul Robeson becomes his weapon.

It is difficult to write soberly about the persistent influence of race in the formation of human thought. It holds a unique place in the consciousness of black people wherever they may be; and this is unlikely to change until Africa becomes a black continent whose sovereignty is the product of her own institutions and is protected by an economic and military strength that can defy any intruder. The cordiality which exists between African countries and their former French imperialist masters, and the harassment of Angola by apartheid South Africa are an odd and cruel sequel to the various declarations of African independence. It is as though nothing had changed except the flags and the expanding scale of western robbery.

There is a sense in which the Afro-American has acquired a critical awareness of this racial drama. He sees through the language of negotiation and diplomacy imposed upon African and West Indian leaders, and is often appalled by the terms of our accommodation to white privilege. But he doesn't often see with the same clarity how the process of colonisation may have divided black majorities into conflicting social strata, pruning away from the main body of the trunk of our human tree those elitist branches that are trained like termites to work corrosively on its roots. The overwhelming torment of race has made it difficult for Afro-Americans to perceive how central is the conflict of class in the ultimate liberation of black countries. On the other hand a false preoccupation with social status seduces the black West Indian into wishing the racial component away.

Africa broods over the faces, the canefields, the broken huts and sugar fortunes of *In the Castle of My Skin*. But it is not recognised until the land is asleep, and the ocean threatens the island with the memories of that fatal crossing. An ancestral voice breaks through the dream of the village elder, Pa:

And strange was the time that change my neighbour and me, the tribes with gods and the one tribe without. The silver of exchange sail cross the sea and my people scatter like clouds in the sky when the waters come. There was a similar buying and selling 'mongst tribe and tribe, but this was the biggest of the bargains for tribes. Each sell his own [...] A man walked out in the market square and one buyer watch his tooth and another his toe and the parts that was private for the coming of a creature in the intimate night. The silver sail from hand to hand and the purchase was shipped like a box of good fruit. The sale was the best of Africa's produce, and me and my neighbour made the same same bargain. I make my peace with the Middle Passage to settle on that side of the sea the white man call a world that was west of another world [...] We were for a price that has no value; we were a value beyond any price [...] I see the purchase of tribes on the silver sailing vessels, some to Jamaica, Antigua, Grenada, some to Barbados and the island of oil and the mountain tops. And then as 'tis now, though the season change, some was trying to live and some trying to die, and some was too tired to worry about either. The families fall to pieces, and many a brother never see his sister nor father the son.

The ancestral spirit, speaking through the voice of an old man on the eve of his death, provides the kind of history which the village could not have learnt from its official school. A different myth was planted there, interrupting and, in the view of some students, actually eliminating beyond recall the continuities of feeling and perception which linked Africa to her transplanted sons and daughters in the New World. It is this area of twilight which has attracted and teased the imagination of many Caribbean poets and novelists; and in more recent times has offered a promise of redemption for the cultural nationalist and the political activist.

In 1950 I could not have foreseen the drama that would launch Africa like a hurricane across the ocean and into the hearts of islands and cities of the black Americas. Many who were once afraid of Africa had now become afraid for Africa. The murder of Lumumba reminded us of an old conspiracy within our ranks. "There was a similar buying and selling 'mongst tribe and tribe". But these contradictions were not wholly negative. When the Kenyan novelist, Ngũgĩ Wa Thiong'o, told me that *In the Castle of My Skin* was the signal which alerted him to what he had to do as a Kikuyu and a pan-Africanist writer, I too was assured that the continuities which united Africa and the Black Americas were at work.

This theme had been the main thrust of Edward Brathwaite's work as a poet and historian. But it is a difficult terrain. The demands of labour introduced a more complex world than either Europe or Africa could have bargained for.

> Now there's been new combinations of those that come after made quite a different collection [...] Now not only black nor white, but all colours that give credit to the skin in these islands of the west.

Neither China nor India had then left any mark on Barbados. We had lived as a black majority under the fearful domination of a minority of white sugar planters and merchants. There was evidence of considerable miscegenation, but there was always a rigid code of separate development. Blacks divided among lines of complexion, and all were kept severely at a social distance from the white world. The island has never really overcome this barrier; and a concordat of silence descends on any crisis which appears to have its origins in race and colour.

Africa existed in Barbados and throughout the Caribbean, and refuses to be buried by the institutions which sought to render it impotent and void of any spiritual force. School, church, the language and ritual of English courts of law, the mysteries of parliament: all these had to be learnt in the interests of black survival and social advancement.

But Africa has remained a source of embarrassment here, although the actual nature of the embarrassment may have changed. Once we were truly nervous at any suggestion that we were part of a world that had not graduated to the status of human. We held this truth on the authority of the institutions which mediated our daily lives. We lived the purest racism without acknowledging that any such calamity had really touched our lives.

Today the embarrassment is more likely to be felt if there is a charge that we seek to deny Africa any part in our spiritual formation. The other response is a rhapsodic and uncritical embrace of Africa as a mother once stolen and now miraculously restored to our embrace. It was perhaps this fear the ancestral spirit tentatively warned against.

So if you hear some young fool fretting about back to Africa, keep far from the invalid and don't force a passage to where you won't yet belong.

Sometimes the twilight startles with signs of recognition: an old woman who places bits of food under a tree and for no one in particular; the spontaneous libation of the rum shop drinker; the hallucinatory form of worship that may suddenly strike a simple believer who cannot explain what world she had been transported to. And always, there, a reluctant faith in the supernatural force that heals, or intervenes in moments of domestic crisis. The politician is frequently in search of an obeah man. Africa invades us like an invisible force we dare not acknowledge, fearing the journey may take us beyond the boundaries of our approved instruction. And all this subliminal life goes on in spite of the determined resistance of the official institutions. The white myths, firmly planted by conquest and enslavement, have been internalised, and continue to work like litmus on the black rock whose history we have not yet summoned to our rescue. Sometimes the twilight darkens and threatens to obliterate all memory in the tidal wave of capitalist consumerism. America spreads itself like a plague everywhere, capturing the simplest appetites with the fastest foods and nameless fripperies the advertising industry instructs us are essential needs. It is this obstacle the world of the ancestral spirit may not survive. A new class of black housewife now flies from these islands to Los Angeles for some novel brand of underwear. This barbarism has become the style of a new ruling group: a new breed of professional nationalist who may be heard in international councils arguing the case for a new economic order. They are the adolescent offspring of that slave culture which has persisted through school and college, university and people's parliament.

In his introduction to the first American edition of *In the Castle of My Skin*, Richard Wright made this observation:

Notwithstanding the fact that Lamming's story, as such, is his own, it is, at the same time, a symbolic repetition of the story of millions of simple folk who, sprawled over half the world's surface and involving more than half of the human race, are today being catapulted out of their peaceful, indigenously earthy lives and into the turbulence and anxiety of the twentieth century.

Turbulence is at work everywhere, but anxiety does not adequately describe what has been happening with that half of mankind since Richard Wright wrote his introduction. The catapulted ones have become the subjects of their own history, engaged in a global war to liberate their villages, rural and urban, from the old encirclement of poverty, ignorance and fear.

This is the most fundamental battle of our time, and I am joyfully lucky to have been made, by my work, a soldier in their ranks.

4 | *On West Indian Writing**

In order to protect my flanks I thought that I would state a formal introduction to let you know the kind of terrain on which I would operate, and beyond which, perhaps, I would not be seduced to travel.

I realise that I speak to you, assuming that you are Puerto Ricans, against a somewhat difficult background of mutual ignorance. For example, I do not have, as indeed I should have, a working knowledge of the contemporary creative writers of Puerto Rico. This is very lamentable; and many of you, I believe, are only vaguely familiar with the very abundant literary activity of the English-speaking Caribbean during the last 30 or 40 years. And it seems to me at once very sad, and a little humiliating – if there are degrees of humiliation about this that there are people, and a considerable number of people, in Europe and in North America who are considerably more informed about us in the Caribbean than we are about each other.

Now, in the past this was also true about islands in the English-speaking Caribbean. Jamaica, you've heard, was once very ignorant of Barbados; and Trinidad, for example, was very ignorant of the others. But this is no longer so; at any rate, it is not so to the same degree that it was some years ago.

Today in those islands we share a much deeper knowledge of each other than we could have boasted of some 20 years ago. I believe that a major factor contributing to that knowledge has been the creation and survival of the University of the West Indies, particularly the individuals working in that University whose commitment has always been to the realisation of a regional Caribbean community.

Professor Figueroa, as Head of the Department of Education, UWI, has been one of the central and most moving spirits in such a commitment; and so has Dr Gordon Lewis at the University of Puerto

* First published in *Review Inter Americana*, 1975, 5 (2), pp. 149–62. It is a transcribed and edited version of a talk given at the Inter American University in Puerto Rico on November 24, 1974.

Rico, who through his consistent and scholarly attention to the affairs of the region has made an immense contribution to our sense and to our understanding of a Pan Caribbean reality. I'd like, therefore, to regard a simple visit like this as in its way a contribution, however small, to the work and to the concern of men like Dr Lewis and Professor Figueroa. I realise that there may be others, but I simply ask your indulgence to mention those I am most vividly aware of.

I would like to give you two anecdotes – we are very good at anecdotes in the South and Eastern Caribbean – that illustrate one of the manifestations of this ignorance which sometimes doesn't make for very healthy relationships. Some years ago I was talking to a young lady from Barbados who was explaining to me what happened when she wrote her father to tell him that she was going to marry a Jamaican. He wrote back: "Well, I would neither say Yea nor Nay; but all I would say is that the only one of them I ever met, I met when he was here – in prison." And then there was also the following account, which I'm not inventing. A friend of mine, a Guyanese who is now a professor in Ithaca, upstate New York, wrote – not his father this time but his mother – that he was going to marry a French girl who was white, and that he wanted her to know she was white, but she was nice. Black people also use that 'but.' I don't know whether white people are aware of it "She was white but she was nice." And the mother wrote back to tell him "I don't care what colour woman you marry, provided she is not Trinidadian."

These stories may seem amusing, but they are, as they say, manifestations of some things that go a little deeper than the popular surface would suggest. Now, I come of course from a unique island. There is no island in the Caribbean quite like my island, like Barbados. We are, in Barbados, what you could call the colonisers. We are to be found everywhere in the Caribbean, and when we arrived in the Caribbean we often arrived in the role of organisers of other peoples' lives. We are either the policemen or the schoolmasters or the overseers on plantations. Since we often have to make our living outside of Barbados, in Trinidad or Jamaica or St Lucia, we colonise the local population by marriage, so that today all the most important grandchildren, not to speak of the great-grandchildren, really belong to us. I have not yet been able to locate this fact in Puerto Rico, but I am absolutely sure that there must be an important Barbadian ingredient in the Puerto Rican bloodstream. If it is not so, then there may be something very seriously lacking in the Puerto Rican ethnic consciousness. This is not my personal view; but it is simply a reminder of what Barbados will expect me to tell you. And since I have to return to Barbados in a matter of days, it seems to me only sensible to perform this simple task of letting you know what my island country would expect you to be told.

I believe that *In the Castle of My Skin,* my first work, is perhaps the work with which those people who get interested in the literature of the English Caribbean are most familiar; I thought it wise to begin by saying something about that. This is a book which has created some difficulty, I believe, for conventional critics and for teachers. First of all, it is very difficult to say precisely what it's about. It's about many things. It is, in a curiously paradoxical way, the book of all my books which has continued to hold the greatest fascination for readers both inside and outside the Caribbean. I have not myself found that very helpful. And I think one of the reasons is that one could perhaps define it essentially as an account of childhood and adolescence; and since everybody, or nearly everybody, has had a childhood and an adolescence, there is some connecting link between their experience and that of the book. It is an account of childhood and adolescence in a particular place, which is that particular island of Barbados. And what happens, it seems to me, is that because it is about the universal theme of childhood and experience, it tends to move up and around. It's what happens, for example, if you throw a pebble in water. You see one circle, and then a wider circle. And so it begins from the point of a simple household, the relations of a father and son and mother. And then the world, the world of the house, moves out into the world of the village, and then the world of the village moves out into the world of the town, and the world of the town to the world of the island; and the world of the island to the relations of the island to other islands; and then those relations move further and further out into all the historical resonances of plantation societies, of the middle passage, of colonialism, and so on.

The passage that I'm going to read you – I think it best to introduce you to the material not by reading the whole of it, but bits and pieces – I propose to read in order to suggest to you what were the particular influences at work on the writers in this kind of society. It seems to me that there were perhaps three; there were probably more, but one can be sure of three. I am not putting them in their order of importance. There is, first of all, the kind of influence which is uncritically received through the particular system of education, through the particular texts that you are given to read. Everybody starts with teachers who tell you what to read, and when you are what is called a student you do not know how to tell teachers, "I don't want to read that." You read what she tells you to read. And these are spiritual foods that are consciously and unconsciously received. The act of reading is, metaphorically speaking, an act of eating. And just as food has an influence on the physical metabolism, what one reads has some influence on the consciousness. It has some influence on the way the ear receives rhythms, it has some influence on the way the senses take one into certain experiences. And so I belong to a generation which, when it had any formal education at all, was moulded by all the traditional figures of English literature. They started with Chaucer, in a very fragmentary kind of way. They would then make a great leap to Shakespeare and the seventeenth century. Then they were very heavy on what were called the Romantics – Wordsworth, Shelley and Keats, then they moved about in prose with people like Jane Austen. They could not, unfortunately, avoid Dickens; and then there were bits and pieces of the twentieth century; there were people like Thomas Hardy, Joseph Conrad. And then, as we started to get fashionably modern, we had to go through the intolerable experiences, which we didn't see then but I see now, of people like Aldous Huxley.

What is very interesting is that when I was a boy in school – and this is true of my generation throughout the area, although historically and geographically we were an essential part of the Americas – there was no influence of America on this reading. It was a long time after I left school – that sort of school we went to until 18 – that I discovered that there was such a thing as the American writer! Up until the age of 18 I did not encounter Melville, and had barely heard of *Huckleberry Finn* as a boys' book.

In other words, the system of education, the people who organised it and who applied it, did not accept that there was something called American literature, or if there were something called American literature, it was exclusively for something called American consumption. It did not acquire the status of promotion within our kind of school. This was not only so when I was a boy. I always remember one of my most vivid experiences on returning to the Caribbean in 1955 or '56 or thereabouts, and going to the University of the West Indies and having a talk with a man who was then chairman of the English Department, and asking whether Faulkner was done in the course of English studies, and he said, "What is there of Faulkner to do?" This was in 1955, the chairman of the Department of English Studies in the University of the West Indies. So that was one of the influences on the writers on whose work I shall reflect, the influence of received readings.

This was not wholly a negative thing because among that received reading were works, indeed, which one should never miss. One should never, if one wants to go back in time, never miss Shakespeare. And in terms of my own preferences, as far as modern literature is concerned, I would never have wanted to miss Conrad, whom I regard as perhaps the greatest genius who ever touched the language in the twentieth century with the possible exception of D.H. Lawrence.

The second influence (the second and third are tied together) was the influence of the Bible. This was true both for people who had an extended formal education and for people who did not. The King James Bible is a continuing echo in the language of the masses of the Caribbean population in places like Jamaica and Barbados. And, along with that, the third and very seminal influence is what we would call the influence of popular speech. We live, in the West Indies, in a situation in which there is more than one kind of English. There is a kind of English which is used, say, in official situations, in the civil service context, in the context of parliament, in the context of school and so on. This is when you have to get on with authority. You use then a standard or formal English. But there was always, in any given territory, another kind of English, the English of popular speech, the language which the mass of the population use, at market, on the streets, whenever you are going to abuse somebody, or when you are going to laugh at somebody there's another kind of language there. It is not the language of negotiation, but what one might call the language of action.

So these are the three, it seems to me, of several influences. But there would have to be a lot of explanation of the degrees of their weight that would have affected these writers: the influence of received readings, the influence of the Bible as a pervasive force in literacy in that area, and the inescapable influence of popular speech – which is the way that language is being used even while you are not paying attention to what is being said. And those of you who are interested in the language problem – it does not particularly interest me except when I am making it; I'm not particularly interested in analysing its derivatives and so on – would find that if there is one source of great interest in the Caribbean novel, it is the source of language, the different levels on which the language operates, not only between different writers, but quite often in the same book. There are sometimes three and four different levels of language at work in the same book.

Now, I want to give you some examples of this language where there is the mixture of all three influences: the influence of received readings, the influence of the pervasive force of the Bible, and the influence of what we call speech in action – that is, the language that ordinary people are using. I shall read a passage from *In the Castle of My Skin*. There may be better passages to illustrate this but it is the one which does it easiest for me. And it is a section of the book which describes an old man, an old man who is called 'Pa' and who with 'Ma' functions as a kind of chorus in the novel. This is the passage on the eve of his death: and he is asleep and he is talking in his sleep. But it isn't really Pa who is talking; it is really the ancestral voice talking through Pa – a man of African descent, an old man, an archetypal grandparent of the village. He is heard by the old woman talking in his sleep but not really talking. It is his voice which is conveying a message from the dead, the ancestral dead, to the living. This is the passage:

> And strange was the time that change my neighbour and me, the tribes with gods and the one tribe without. The silver of exchange sail 'cross the sea and my people scatter like clouds in the sky when the waters come. There was similar buying and selling 'mongst tribe and tribe, but this was the biggest of the bargains for tribes. Each sell his own. A man walked out in the market square and one buyer watch his tooth and another his toe and the parts that was private for the coming of a creature in the intimate night. The silver sail from hand to hand and the purchase was shipped like a box of good fruit. The sale was the best of Africa's produce, and me and my neighbour made the same bargain. I make my peace with the Middle Passage to settle on that side of the sea the white man call

a world that was west of another world. The tribes with gods and the one tribe without we all went the way of the white man's money. We were for a price that had no value; we were a value beyond any price. For the buyer and the seller 'twas no difference 'twixt these two, price and value, value and price, since silver is solution for every ready-made sorrow. And so 'tis today in the islands left and right of this your little island and for the village too that's not very important. Silver is more than what pass from hand to hand. 'Tis also a way of what you call getting on. If the islands be sick 'tis for no other reason than the ancient silver. Your motto now is price or power which mean the same thing. Sinner and saint are alike in this matter. I see the purchase of tribes on the silver sailing vessels, some to Jamaica, Antigua, Grenada, some to Barbados and the island of oil and the mountain tops. And then as 'tis now, though the season change, some was trying to live and some trying to die, and some were too tired to worry about either. The families fall to pieces and many a brother never see his sister nor father the son. Now there's been new combinations and those that come after make quite a different collection. So if you hear some young fool fretting about back to Africa, keep far from the invalid and don't force a passage to where you won't yet belong. These words not for you but those that come after.

From part of you that's neither flesh nor bone in a sleep before your last and longest, I come to say what I say. Tomorrow you won't remember the visit made by your father's forebears, for what you call a dream the morning after has quite a different meaning from what your silence made safe the night before. Now not only black nor white, but all the colours that give credit to the skin in these islands of the west. Let sackcloth be the flag they fly whatever the limits of the freedom they talk. The beginning had the best intentions. A sailor called Christopher followed his mistake and those who come later have added theirs.

Now he's dead, and as some say of the dead, safe and sound in the legacy of the grave. 'Tis a childish saying, for they be yet present with the living. The only certainty these islands inherit was that sailor's mistake, and it's gone on and on from father to son amongst the rich and the poor: in Slime and Creighton, landlord and politician, those who play at ruling and those at being ruled, and those who are neither one nor the other: the mob that is always good but will never understand the face of the devil nor the equal smile of the deep blue sea. The fate of islands I do not know, but man must live like a god or a dog, or be a stone that is neither dead nor alive, a pool no wind will ever wrinkle. For there's always two worlds to one man if you're a man, two darknesses to one light, one light, one light....

This is an aspect of the language product that I was speaking about, operating in one particular island, the island of Barbados. And now I want to give you an example of a different but closely parallel language product – from another island, exactly 1,000 miles away, the island of Jamaica. And the writer whom I choose for this is a very distinguished novelist, a man by the name of Mr V.S. Reid, who was born in 1913 and whose novel *New Day*, the one I shall use, was first published in 1949. This is in many ways a very fine novel and remarkable work of fiction.

It was the first time in the history of Caribbean fiction that a novelist would try to render the entire work of fiction in a form of the vernacular. Now what has often happened in these novels, as I have said, language is operating on three or four different levels. Now it is recognisably standard, now it moves from standard in the sense of English standard to something that might be called West Indian standard. Then it moves in to various forms of vernacular, all in the same book. Usually the formal standard takes care of the narrative, the vernacular takes care of the dialogue. But in *New Day* what Reid does – an extremely bold thing for a writer to do – he renders narrative and dialogue in the vernacular, in a very highly stylised vernacular. And what he also does that I think was perhaps the first attempt of this kind, he used this novel as an epic rendering of the history of the evolution of the nationalist spirit in Jamaica.

Very briefly, what happens in this novel when it opens is that we meet an old man, John Campbell, who is about 80 in the year 1944, a very important year for Jamaica. It was the year in which self-government was to begin, that is, the Jamaicans were going to be responsible for all of their internal affairs. And John Campbell was a boy of about seven or so in 1865. The year 1865 is the date of a very famous rebellion, known as the Morant Bay Rebellion on Jamaica. On that occasion there was a suspension of representative government to return to what is called Crown Colony government, where the island is directly ruled from London. The year 1944 is the "New Day".

On the eve of this "New Day", on the eve of self-government, this old man begins to recall the history of his island from the Morant Bay rebellion to the New Day of 1944. I shall read just three very, very short passages to give you an idea of how, first of all, the language is being used to summon the dead. This is an example of the biblical rhythm being married, more closely than it is, I think, in *In the Castle of My Skin*, to the local speech.

> Then, now! Pa John and Ma Tamah, and mother o'sorrow – are you hearing? And my brethren, Emmanuel, David, Samuel, Ezekiel, Ruth, Naomi, are you hearing?
>
> Are you a-hear, George William Gordon? And Paul Bogle, Abram M'Laren, and the good Doctor Creary?
>
> And you too, bloody Governor Eyre and your crow Provost-Marshal Ramsey, are you hearing wherever you are? Tell me, Bro. Zaccy O'Gilvie, are you a-listen of me tonight?
>
> Then, now! All o' you Dead Hundreds who looked at the sun without blink in your eyes, you Dead Hundreds who fell to British redcoats' bullets and the sword o' the wild Maroons, the wild men o' the mountains, tell me, you Dead Hundreds o' Morant Bay, are you hearing that tomorrow is the day? And that sorrow and restlessness are here with my joy, for I am standing here alone?
>
> Aie – me, John Campbell, youngest o' Pa John Campbell.

What he is doing in this is: he is resurrecting all of these names, family names, names of all the public figures, the governor, the officials, all of those people who were present on the morning of 1865 when the court house in Morant Bay was destroyed. And then he uses this language to do something similar now, not with the resurrection of the dead, but with the restoration of nature in the consciousness of those who were beheaded here. He is reminding us that the rebellion is not only the bloodshed and bullets and so on but there were other factors, creative and positive factors, the factors provided by nature. To continue:

> Eh, but now I am restless tonight. Through the half-opened window near where I sit, night wind come down the Blue Mountains to

me. Many scents come down on the wind, and I know them all. I know all the scents o' the shrubs up on the mountains. There are cerosee, mint, mountain jasmine, ma raqui, there are peahba and sweet cedars. I know that the bitter cerosee will drive away fever, that ma raqui will heal any wounds – even wounds from musket balls.

This recall of nature is a reminder that it is during this moment of rebellion, during this moment of physical destruction that the inhabitants of nature learn the curative power of nature – cerosee, mint, and so on. These are not just dead immobile furniture in nature; these plants are active and curative forces. So we see two or three different things happening here in a novel of this scale and imagination. We see this peculiar marriage of different levels of language, which is not just an exercise in language. It is an exercise in language which, as I say, brings back all the historical resonances, all the historical associations which have in common the weight and continuity of plantation slave economy.

It is noticeable and, I think, it will have to be explained some time that when you look at the prose written then by two of the leading Caribbean novelists from Trinidad, men of the same generation, there is going to be some difference in the prose, some difference in the texture of the language. The first is Mr Selvon. Mr Selvon, who was born in 1923 and in a sense is one of the pioneer people of this period, has the distinction of using that vernacular speech with a greater authority than almost any other Caribbean novelist. And sometimes only Mr Selvon can really do justice to reading what he writes. Here you find not the same luxuriance of metaphor and image that you find in the other pieces. It's spare now, and it's a racy kind of rhythm. I'll just give you a small bit of him, this from a book called *Lonely Londoners*. Now we have in a sense moved out of the archipelago to the metropolis. This is a book about the predicament of West Indians who have immigrated to London, and what Selvon is doing in this section is reminding us of the magic of the exotic, of how people go from one place where there are things they grew up with, which they are familiar with, and so on; and then they go to another place which by its exoticism has a way of astonishing you, stupefying you. I witness this: I live in London. Every summer you have great hordes of Americans who come as tourists and they queue up in rain outside the Tower of London to see the kind of sword which one king used to remove the head of the ex-king with and so on, and they will queue up there for hours in rain to get in there and see these pieces of rusty iron. This is an example of the exotic, the stupefying. Or if on Sunday morning you go to an East London market, they are buying very strange things, some little bottle marked 1863. This was a beer bottle of 1863, and they will pay $15 to $20 for this idiotic thing. This is an example of the exotic, the stupefying, a beer bottle for $15 or $20 with this label 1863. The English are very funny people and I've always suspected that those labels are in fact made the night before for those bottles. But once you see "1863," people who have got a colonial past are always stupefied by dates, particularly if it is 100 years old. They lose all sense of judgement.

And what Selvon is doing is showing how the exotic works on a man from the Caribbean. As happens in many calypsos, these fellows have very odd names, they take on the names of royalty and of medieval titles, and so on. This fellow is Galahad and the other fellow is Moses. This is how it would go. This is Galahad who is going to meet a girl. Galahad is a very peculiar kind of black man. In winter, when it is freezing, Galahad walks about in summer clothing. For some peculiar reason he gets hot in cold weather. And in summer, when it is hot, he goes about in a winter coat because he gets cold in summer. He gets hot in cold weather and he gets cold in hot weather. It is not explained why Galahad should be biologically so strange but that is, as Mr Selvon says, that is how Galahad is, and he is going to meet this girl:

> When that first London summer hit Galahad he begins to feel so cold that he had to get an overcoat. Moses laughs like hell. "You getaway from the weather, eh?" he say. "You warm in the winter and cold in the summer, eh? Well is my turn to put on my light suit and cruise about."

It is really a very delightful thing. I really do not want to do damage to it. He does it in a magnificent kind of way. But the point I'm getting at there is that texture and pace of language has not changed. It is swift, it is spare, and I think this may have something to do with how the varieties of English have worked in Trinidad as distinct from Barbados and Jamaica.

The passage I want to read next, which also represents an important novelist from Trinidad, is a passage from Mr V.S. Naipaul. I didn't think that I would have to explain it, but I've forgotten to say that in the cases of Naipaul and Selvon we are dealing here not with Caribbean men of African descent, we are dealing here with Caribbean men of Indian descent, what is called East Indian, Indians of Asia.

Mr Naipaul, who is in some ways influenced by Mr Selvon, is an example also of that spareness but is an example also of a certain formality. The structure is very formal, very sophisticated but never that racy vernacular overtone, and never, in Mr Naipaul, that luxuriance of metaphor or image that you will find in a Mr Reid. Listen to this. It's the prologue to *A House for Mr Biswas*, a very remarkable book – I think it is Mr Naipaul's most outstanding work of fiction – in which tracing a Hindu family over three generations gives us a picture of what that particular house, that Indian house, felt like, looked like, moved like, that self-contained Indian house against the background of the wider Trinidad house. He does some very interesting kinds of novelistic tricks: for example, he opens with a prologue which tells us how the book comes to an end. Then he has this most interesting thing, we have this very, you might say, ridiculous situation, in which when we first meet Mr Biswas in chapter one, he's a baby. Its a very odd thing for a baby to be a mister, so Mr Biswas sneezes as a baby sneezes. He plays some very interesting comic turns and tricks. It is done very well, because the prologue takes care of it. In the prologue we learn of what happened to Mr Biswas, and it is very spare.

> Ten weeks before he died, Mr Mohun Biswas, a journalist of Sikkim Street, St James, Port of Spain, was sacked. He had been ill for some time. In less than a year he had spent more than nine weeks at the Colonial Hospital and convalesced at home for even longer. When the doctor advised him to take a complete rest the Trinidad Sentinel had no choice. It gave Mr Biswas three months' notice and continued, up to the time of his death, to supply him every morning with a free copy of the paper.

There is no fanfare, no dramatics; very spare, very lean but very charged. And then, the end of Mr Biswas, who after a lifetime of 46 years or so of trying very desperately to own his own house, has just managed to survive living in a house which he has bought but which has not yet been paid for:

How terrible it would have been, at this time, to be without it: to have died among the Tulsis, amid the squalor of that large, disintegrating and indifferent family; to have left Sharna and the children among them, in one room; worse to have lived without even attempting to lay claim to one's portion of the earth; to have lived and died as one had been born, unnecessary and unaccommodated.

Two examples, I think, of a certain movement of language, although there is considerable difference between Mr Selvon's movement toward the vernacular, his manipulations of it, and Mr Naipaul's particular manipulation of a spare, almost classical usage of the language.

I think I'm going to hurry through, and just read one or two poets in whom this can also be demonstrated, this pervasive force of the Bible the way this imagery is always summoned, sometimes unconsciously, sometimes highly consciously, by the poet. The first example I shall look at is a poem (we move to another island now) by the poet, the very distinguished poet, Mr Derek Walcott. Mr Walcott is a very interesting figure, in some ways a unique figure, one of the very few major Caribbean writers to have spent all of his working life as a writer in the Caribbean. He has not lived and worked outside of the Caribbean. Also, very interestingly, a poet who is also responsible for a theatre, the Trinidad Theatre Workshop; I think this is the fifteenth year that it has not only been in existence but also has been very active.

This is one of Mr Walcott's early poems. He started very early; he was only about 17 or 18 when he brought out a little volume. I always make jokes with Mr Walcott now and again about that little volume, because it sold out; it was a bestseller. There were only 150 copies and it sold right out in no time at all. I think he is the first West Indian who has had a first edition sold right out. And in that volume was this remarkable poem, derivative in many ways, about a concrete situation, the situation of the destruction, almost the total destruction by fire, of Castries. Castries is the capital town of the island of Saint Lucia.

Now there is an interesting thing, a little confusing thing about St Lucia as far as the language is concerned. There is not only the formal English and a vernacular, but when you move into the vernacular in St Lucia, you do not move into an English vernacular but you move into a French Creole. It's a very peculiar language situation. The official language is English. The language of negotiation is English.

The language of action is French Creole, not English Creole. This is the kind of linguistic situation which produced Mr Derek Walcott, who speaks French Creole perfectly. It has started to come up more recently in his plays, but there is not much evidence of that in the early poems. He was, I suppose, rescued by the diligence of the Methodists, and this was the kind of results he got – very strong influences of the Welsh Valley in this poem:

> After that hot gospeller had levelled all but the churched sky,
> I wrote the tale by tallow of a city's death by fire;
> Under a candle's eye, that smoked in tears, I
> Wanted to tell, in more than wax, of faiths that were snapped like wire.
> All day I walked abroad among the rubbled tales.
> Shocked at each wall that stood on the street like a liar;
> Loud was the bird-rocked sky, and all the clouds were bales
> Torn open by looting, and white, in spite of the fire.
> By the smoking sea, where Christ walked, I asked why
> Should a man wax
> tears, when his wooden world fails?
> In town, leaves were paper, but the hills were a flock of faiths;
> To a boy who walked all day, each leaf was a green breath
> Rebuilding a love I thought was dead as nails,
> Blessing the death and the baptism by fire.

This literature did not just produce itself, just as the men did not produce themselves. In all of these territories, you would have found, particularly in the '40s, very active individuals and groups of people whose names are not now as well known as these, but who were really responsible for creating the ambience, for creating the atmosphere that first gave validity to the activity of writing. These were the men who were responsible for creating the literary journals. I think that you will find in the literature of all countries, certainly in the modern literature of all countries, this peculiar, this unavoidable, this invaluable role of the literary journals in the formation of taste, in the formation of critical judgement, and ultimately in what is called the encouragement of the creative artist. And what is very striking about these journals is that they appeared in three different territories – Barbados, Jamaica, and the mainland territory of Guyana – quite separately, with no collaboration between the territories, each journal springing up quite separately but obviously part of the same historical continuity, part of the same kinds of experience. In 1942, in Barbados, the magazine *Bim* was started by Mr Frank Collymore, perhaps the most famous of all the editors, not only famous for the magazine, but also famous as a schoolmaster, certainly responsible for my education, for my introduction to literature as an activity which I now perform.

In Jamaica you have the figure of Mrs Edna Manley, responsible for the journal *Focus* in 1943. And in Guyana, a little later in 1944–5, you have the figure of Mr A.J. Seymour, responsible for the magazine *Kyk-Over-Al*. Now, what is important about these journals is that the writers I have mentioned here and all the writers whom we do not have time to mention tonight literally came out of these journals. Their first experience of being in print, their first feeling that writing was something that was all right for me to do, their first sense of receiving some kind of attention, however small, for what they did, was in these journals. These journals were the cradles, and their editors served as the midwives, as it were, of these particular writers.

Every essential novelist, every important poet produced in the Caribbean over the last 30 years started the writing career in one or other of these particular journals – in some cases, as they got to know each other, in all three of them. Then, at that period, as a matter of historical interest, another factor which was important in the development of this literature was the role of the B.B.C., which worked in collaboration with these journals.

What happened was that sometime in the 1940s, from about 1942 or 1943 and until as late as 1959, the B.B.C. Overseas Service carried a regular literary programme which was beamed overseas, particularly to the Caribbean area, and which was devoted to the work of writers from the West Indies. Quite often much of the work used by the B.B.C. had come from that particular cradle of the journals, and sometimes the work originally broadcast from B.B.C. was later used in the journals. The importance of the B.B.C. was that for the first time in the writing life of these people – they were very young at the time – for the first time they had this very novel experience of getting money for writing. This was a very peculiar thing at the time, writing was not an activity that you were paid for. You know, if someone printed something you had written, they did you a favor. That goes on in some ways with radio. Somebody comes and asks you to do a broadcast and is working on the peculiar assumption that he is helping you, not that he is asking you to help him. So the B.B.C. functioned in this very important way, that writing then became not only a seriously spiritual activity but a serious activity, that is, it was paid for.

One of the problems which I shall leave open with you, that I have been trying to do, is to concentrate on certain aspects of this predicament which may have parallels. As I say, unfortunately I do not have a working knowledge of the contemporary creative writing situation in Puerto Rico. I hope if there is an opportunity for these remarks to be discussed by Puerto Rican writers, that maybe the thrust of that discussion might simply be the parallels in our experience.

5 | *Politics and Culture**

Your Excellencies, Ladies and Gentlemen, Comrades and Friends. As most of you know I have never been a Minister of Government. Nor have I ever held public and distinguished office in any of the institutions of this region; and I own no wealth which would qualify me to be a donor of aid to the needy. It is reasonable to assume, therefore, that the University's decision to confer this honour must be related to the facts of my working life as a West Indian writer and their genuine recognition of this work as a possible contribution towards the cultural and political future of our people. I would like to express my appreciation of their judgement, and to do so on behalf of all of my colleagues, dead and alive, who have engaged in the art and labour of creating a literature on behalf of the peoples of all languages in the Caribbean. I think in this moment especially of Roger Mais of Jamaica, Edgar Mittelholzer of Guyana and E. M. Roach of Trinidad and Tobago. My debt and eternal gratitude to Frank Collymore of Barbados are already on permanent record.

Men make their own history but we can only make that portion of it which our concrete circumstances allow. We do not choose the time or place of our birth, nor the parents who make this possible; but the process of our thought, the hidden nature of our needs, the character and quality of our imagination may be decisively influenced by these origins. Our struggle towards freedom is experienced always within the external constraints of nature and the invisible limitations of our own consciousness.

I was born in a small village where the women were mothers and servants. The men worked by chance – casual labourers, house painters,

---

* In 1980, the University of the West Indies gave Lamming an honorary Doctor of Letters. At the Graduation ceremony of that year, Lamming delivered an address at the Cave Hill Campus of the U.W.I. to the assembled graduates, faculty, staff, and other guests. This address, printed above in its entirety, was previously published in Kathleen Drayton and George Lamming, *The Most Important People in Barbados*, pp. 1–7.

shoemakers, sharpeners of knives, and messengers for a great variety of occasions. And since the island was small and could be viewed as one large cane farm, we lived within the shadow of the plantation and at the rigorous mercy of the merchant. Our relation to bread, our relation to God, our relation to the courts of law were influenced daily by these demons. We were the children of an old and enduring servant class.

Small size offers here, in its most extreme form, a social order which prevailed elsewhere in these islands. If culture is the means whereby people feed themselves and the ways in which they experience their existence, then poverty and the calculated impoverishment of the mind were essential ingredients of our culture.

For we had inherited a region which was not designed for social living. It was intended exclusively for production. Men and women and children were common hands summoned or ordered to create wealth, a source of fortune for hostile strangers. They were a reservoir of cheap labour, the material base on which kingdoms of luxury or convenience would be constructed elsewhere.

A dominant class, exclusively white, laid the foundations of a cultural force that would influence all our lives. It was the ideology of racism; a morality whose guiding principle was the excessive privilege of the skin. To be black was to be a commodity identified with the cheapest of labour. White was the symbol and source of all authority. The priest and the planter, school and church, legislation and the law, all gave the weight of their authority to this social and economic arrangement; and they did so in the name of decency, honour, and Christian democracy. And I want to emphasise that in spite of the modifications which we observe in contemporary West Indian society, we have never, never been truly liberated from the persistent legacy of this system.

This system of economic and cultural imperialism remains in profound conflict with the struggle of labour for an alternative society, a national dwelling-place which would be the material reward and the spiritual symbol of that labour; how to transform production into creative forms of social living that derive from the free and informed choice of those whose labour makes our survival possible. But the power of the system prevails.

You do not have to be a Marxist to recognise these truths, although, in my view, Marxist analysis provides us with the most penetrating insight into the formation of this system and the purpose which it serves. It is clear to me that no institution of learning, be it University or Labour College, in the modern world, especially in that vast area we name underdeveloped, and by which we mean exploited, can do its duty with honour and not come to terms with the fundamentals of Marxist thought. Just as you do not have to be a Christian to recognise the importance of coming to terms with the history and the radical significance of that great religion – only one, I remind you, among others. For oil, you will have noticed, has restored the authority and respect of Islam, even among bankers.

What are you new graduates really doing here this evening? What will be your business when you leave? Where shall you stand in relation to that system which will offer you a marketplace for the highest bidder for your skills? These questions have their origin in my novel, *Season of Adventure*, in which I offered the prediction that the new independence arrangements would, inevitably, fail; and in which I examined the predicament of a political assassin, Powell, whom I called my brother. This is what I wrote:

> Until the age of ten, Powell and I had lived together equal in the affection of two mothers. Powell had my dreams; and I had lived his passion. Identical in years, and stage by stage, Powell and I were taught in the same Primary School.

> And then the division came. I got a public scholarship which started my migration into another world, a world whose roots were the same, but whose style of living was entirely different from what my childhood knew. It had earned me a privilege which now shut Powell and the whole village right out of my future. I had lived as near to Powell as my skin to the hand it darkens. And yet! Yet, I forgot the village as men forget a war, and attached myself to this new world which was so recent and so slight beside the weight of what had gone before. Instinctively I attached myself to that new privilege; and in spite of all my effort, I am not free of its embrace even to this day.

> I believe deep in my bones that the mad impulse which drove Powell to his criminal defeat was largely my doing. I will not have – this explained away by talk about environment; nor can I allow my own moral infirmity to be transferred to a foreign conscience

called imperialist. I shall go beyond my grave in the knowledge that I am responsible for what happened to my brother.

Powell resides somewhere in my heart, with a dubious love, some strange nameless shadow of regret, and yet with the deepest, deepest, nostalgia. For I have never felt myself to be an honest part of anything since the world of his childhood deserted me.

And here we encounter one of the sharpest contradictions of our inheritance. You are a minority; and you are a minority because education is scarce; and was intended to be a scarcity so that it might serve as an instrument of continuing social stratification, an index of privilege and status, a deformed habit of material self-improvement. This has created acute problems for all forms of leadership. The political leader is the educated one. He leads from above. It has also complicated the role of the intellectuals in their relation to the mass of the population. These are men and women who live and work in an orbit of privilege, and share in those material interests which bind them to the dominant ruling group. Their relation to the mass of the population is a dubious relation; it is a fragile relation; and in some circumstances it is an utterly fraudulent relation. This scarcity of education amidst the mass of our people has given this minority an easy access to comfort; it confers a superficial and sometimes tyrannical authority. It breeds a dangerous self-importance.

The power of the old white planters derived from what they owned. The power of the new black planters derives from what they know. To explode the mystique of the educated one while retaining a genuine respect for the creative power of learning: that is the task of organised labour.

Our recent exercise in sovereignty may yet degenerate into an electoral pantomime, a four- or five-year party go-round, orchestrated by foreign interests, unless organised labour throughout the West Indies can eliminate this obstacle of disparity in practical learning between a technical and bureaucratic elite and a labouring mass whose main argument is confined to questions of wages and conditions of service.

Whom does your labour serve? And towards what vision of mankind?

The symptoms of this minority class extravagance have already received attention from the most distinguished of your writers across more than one generation, and have been recorded with bitter regret

by so humane a poet and person as Derek Walcott of St Lucia. The time
is night; the ritual is the party assembled in one of the new temples
built to the glory of the Prophet, Hilton.

> In our upside-down hotel, in that air-conditioned roomful of venal
> vengeful party-hacks
> lunch-drunk, scotch-drunk, cigar and brandy-stoned,
> arguing, insulting till incoherence cracks ...
> ... Guilt, Sweated
> out in glut, while outside, a black wind
> circles the room with jasmine, like a whore's
> perfume or second secretary's lotion. Fear those laws
> which ex-slaves praise with passion. Pissed, dead
> drunk, I soar to hellish light. In the lobby,
> cigars with eyes like agents drilling me.

Throughout the literature of the Caribbean, this theme of spiritual
dispossession and self-mutilation remains central to the thought
and perception of your writers; and it's no wonder that the gradual
infiltration of their books into the education of our youth is made a
cause of grave concern.

But it is the function of the writer to return a society to itself; and
in this respect, your writers have been the major historians of the
feeling of your people. To separate them by open or hidden forms
of censorship from a generation which needs to be provided with a
firm sense of historical continuity would be to inflict upon us a second
stage of isolation.

We started out as men, some of us younger than you graduates, who
had to conduct the most bitter struggle simply to retain a minimum of
confidence in ourselves, and in our feeling that we could, with a little
luck and a fair chance, do what our instincts and our gifts demanded.
Ridicule and a habitual neglect were the social barriers which always
threatened us with destruction. And in desperation we started on that
fateful journey which had always been the saving doom of our people.
We took flight; hence the phrase and paradox which would become a
continuing source of argument, my own *Pleasures of Exile*.

But it is often forgotten that we did not leave as men, certificated
and equipped to bargain in the intellectual marketplaces of Europe.
Like other forms of migrant labour, we were journeying, hopeful and

powerless, towards an expectation. This exile was, then, a historical necessity, and the logical consequence of that social and economic order I have asked you to consider and reject.

But such are the contradictions of this imperial arrangement, that this same power which had organised the castration of our creative energies, would be responsible for returning our names where they belonged. The enemy had rescued us from total anonymity. That is the pleasure and paradox of that exile. And our modest achievement has been that, in spite of this separation from the sources we needed for our survival, we were able to produce a body of work which would, in time, become the base from which other men would carve their own careers as teachers and critics in this University and similar places throughout the world.

Which brings us back where we began: to the charmed circles of the educated ones, and the obstacles of disparity in practical learning between that minority and the starved mass of our populations. One stage towards a solution would be to use the communications media in the service of your literature and on behalf of those whose lives have made it possible.

But the media, as it functions today, is the major agency of that cultural imperialism we would escape; a major obstacle in our progress towards the liberation of this region.

These reflections are not spontaneous. They have a certain origin; they have grown out of a particular soil. They have been fertilised, so to speak, by a certain reservoir of experience; and they travel with me like a passport everywhere.

Half a century is long and not so long. For it was the triumph of the Cuban revolutionary response that alerted many of us to the fact that a new chapter had begun in the politics and cultural life of the Caribbean people. And Cuba is an integral part of our historical reality. In 1960 the economic and cultural boycott of that country was total. In 1979 all the island parishes of the Caribbean met in Havana to participate in the Third Caribbean Festival of Arts. Caribbean literature in English had discovered through Cuban publications in Spanish a new intellectual and blood connection with the reading classes of the Spanish speaking Americas. The Jamaica National Dance Company had become a regular and prestigious feature in Cuban cultural life. Half a century is really not so long!

And we have now a criterion of achievement in the miraculous birth and flowering of the Cuban revolution; the most profound and creative political event in this region in my lifetime, and in the lifetime of all of you here this evening. It was fought by the Cuban people; but it was not won for the Cuban people alone.

Such a battle against the exploitation of your region is also your battle. The victory is one you can honourably share. And it must always be rewarded by a pan-Caribbean embrace; and defended, whenever necessary, by a pan-Caribbean resolution. Yet Cuba must not be applauded for the wrong reasons, or taken as the final prescription for change. Out of the concrete circumstance of our reality each must forge the appropriate method towards the model which transforms.

So that when the question is asked again 'What were you really doing here in this Cave without a Hill, and what was your business when you left?' Your answer may be taken from Martin Carter of Guyana, the truest, the purest, and the most authentic poetic voice of my generation:

> And so
> if you see me
> looking at your hands
> listening when you speak
> marching in your ranks
> you must know
> I do not sleep to dream,
> but dream to change the world.

6 | *Tribute to a Tragic Jamaican**

You were silly like us: your gift survived it all;
The parish of rich women, physical decay,
Yourself, mad Ireland hurt you into poetry.
Now Ireland has her madness and her weather still…

In Memory of *W.B. Yeats.*
W. H. Auden.

And like Yeats, whose death was the occasion for the preceding lines, the late Roger Mais had created and entered a personal mythology. I do not join these names to make a comparison of their particular gifts; for such comparison, like all argument, is irrelevant and wasteful. I do it to suggest that every poet, regardless of his size, is a worthy participant in the unfinished architecture of language.

Roger Mais was a poet; and poetry, we are reminded by the example of its effect, is more than an arrangement of words in a formal pattern, more than an imaginative report on private experience. It is a way of living.

But his life became a role, as his name to the innocent has turned into a tale and a label for laughter. He understood this laughter, and he lived with it and through it, until its power of annihilation turned his passion into a sense of persecution, and he felt his energy being

---

* This piece was published originally in *Bim*, 1957, 6 (24), pp. 242–44. Its subject, Roger Mais, was born in Jamaica in 1905, where he died in 1955. Author of *The Hills were Joyful Together, Brother Man* and *Black Lightning*, Mais was also a stalwart of the nationalist movement of Jamaica. He was jailed by the colonial government in 1944 on a charge of sedition for writing a pamphlet entitled *Now we Know*, which castigated the hypocrisy of those who talked of democracy but clung on to colonial empires.

pushed gradually towards aggression. And so he used extravagance as a protective attitude.

It started, I believe, as a gesture, a mask of naughtiness, a preparation, as it were, for some calculated impertinence. But his audience was tough. Their strength, a strength which the creative spirit seldom survives, was their capacity to assume the other; and to assume is already to annihilate.

One's meaning is sorted before one's utterances have been made. One's feelings are measured with a frightening efficiency, checked, and locked forever after in that capacious kennel called the Stereotype. One's total desire, in all its manifestations, is dissected, analysed and judged finally by the bright and unfeeling imbeciles who claim to know the history of its formation. 'The trouble with so and so is...'

This was the sentence of rebuke which enlarged his gesture to an assault and made of an attitude a fixed reaction. He became predictable. He was condemned to death without receiving the customary pleasures of the morning before. His life turned into a series of minor and sometimes imagined crises, a gradual and barely tolerable adjustment to his personal suffering; for he was a Romantic (that is a man with the perennial hunger for an alternative) in a society which had had no deeply felt experience of individual exile.

Prose was a way of assembling the strangers and like children who knife their names into monuments that are a reward for their journey, he wanted and needed to leave, humbly, his signature on the heart of a people he loved, and, I believe, understood with terrible clarity.

It is not my intention to attempt any evaluation of his books, and particularly since his relation to language and the concerns which that language served were so different from mine. I want simply to pay tribute to his memory, and to register, in all humility, my homage to the eternal power of his spirit. For it is this spirit, that huge generosity of feeling which everyone who knew him shared, that made his presence always an occasion.

And it is not inappropriate, I hope, at a time when Beauty Queens are as abundant as the blue-bright air, to honour a dead man who was, in many ways, a very beautiful person. The Jamaican Tri-centenary celebrations would not be wholly complete without some voice celebrating its pleasure on his behalf.

Also, my reason for remembering him at this time is more personal than my participation in this or any other Tri-centenary. He was almost 25 years my senior, but he belonged to my generation and a generation of young men who during and after the last war, emerged, with astonishing suddenness, to offer a body of work which, whatever its ultimate stature, has significant meaning for their society.

West Indian writing, in the most organic sense of literary expression, begins with people like Roger Mais. And he is, I am reminded, the first to die. His work, like his death, preceded mine; and his fortunes in the same activity also have been different.

This difference of age, which made for a greater opportunity in my case, helped me to understand the kind of change which has taken place in these islands. It is essentially a change of awareness. The search for a manageable and genuine identity, which is the West Indian's greatest concern, was already an issue when I was a boy.

He had to start from scratch; and as an individual he came of age before his society had quite caught up with the adolescent illusion of its safety and its peace. He was bound to be out of step; for it is only quite recently that West Indians, as a collective body, have tried to understand the kind of world they live in.

His political excitement was, I believe, a small part of the rebel's nature. It was a reaction to a status which he felt was damaging to the human personality. But it was really the Jamaican middle class which hurt him. They made his wound, and later by a dumb and obscene lack of sympathy, proceeded to widen it.

There was nothing to do but work; and he worked while many much younger than himself were complaining that the time was not ripe. Enslaved by a vegetable lethargy, they became natural heirs to the evenings' boredom. They talked about the books they had in mind, and the places it seemed wise to visit. 'If only...only if...'

He kept working, for it was the only way his existence could be justified. But his profession was not an impressive one, for one needs an axe to get it into some people's heads that there is a genuine connection between writing and working. Later one is shocked by the impertinence, the nasty audacity contained in the question: 'When are you going to give me a copy of your book?' One can understand why a certain French writer never enters his publisher's office without his knife.

But Mais's endurance was astonishing, and his devotion and conviction are part of the splendour of his example.

I met him for the first time in London. Isolated from his own generation by its natural unawareness and from his country by a certain logical inadequacy of interests, he decided to migrate. He became a refugee. But London, which he wanted to choose as a base, was as wrong as the particular season in which he was born. For he had reached an age when he needed respect, attention and intelligent sympathy.

He found a world where privacy is real like a human eye, and enthusiasm is always suspect. Enthusiastic friendship, indiscriminate sharing, was the kind of food his appetite craved; but in London, solitude, like an overcoat, is the common refuge. And his impatience, which was natural, prevented him from encountering, by chance perhaps, those isolated pockets where there is real warmth.

London became for him an association of stale porridge, wet blankets, inactive gas rings and silent neighbours. It was always Sunday afternoon with the four o'clock night waiting leisurely, absurdly, outside the window.

Meanwhile he worked with a fury which, now one recalls the time, must have been a secret warning that there wasn't really much time left for work. But he devoured time with his fingers. Hour after hour for days and weeks a demon battled with his brain. And then he made, as though it were a reward, a trip to Paris.

I had seen him shortly before he left, and he was much the same, except for a slightly increased irritability. He was still cheerful, the short man with the earnest, messianic gaze. His clothes still hung about him in a pleasing disorder.

He was still consuming his measure of fuel which I, too, can hardly function without; still a formidable walker at night, with no sense of direction, and eyesight that was sometimes very unwilling, and still talking interminably, amusingly, and sometimes, in retrospect, angrily.

It was then I learnt how a charge of sedition had enabled him to become, as he put it, a guest of Her Majesty's Government in Jamaica. It was his favourite story which he told with great expansiveness and elaborate care; and I have often wondered whether there were any Jamaicans who rose to the occasion and gave him the appropriate homecoming party.

Three months later I met him in Paris. He loved Paris, but it was too late to love anything. Roger looked 50 years older.

Already he was dying.

When he returned to Jamaica, it was simply to be buried. But it was at this time that his will reached the height of its fury. He thought the doctors were making a fuss about nothing; at least that was what he kept saying. He wanted to work, work, work, and I saw, during a visit to his house in Jamaica, the torture of a certain kind of impotence. He couldn't lift a hand while his brain was bursting with intentions, and his fingers spilt words that would never reach paper.

The typewriter was a kind of wooden leg for which he could not honestly have any more use. That was the last time I saw him.

I remember him as a man who was blessed with passion and energy, silly like many of us, more loveable than most of us. His integrity was unquestionable, his devotion to his work the most accurate rebuke to those whose function is simply to carp, complain and wait for the possibility of better times.

Jamaica may have her weather and her madness still, and have them forever; but the hills were certainly joyful to receive so honoured a guest.

7 | *Builders of Our Caribbean House**

The first leader of a Caribbean government who brought my attention to the necessity of gathering in this scattered family of artists where they belong was the late Dr Eric Williams.

After the victory of the People's National Movement in 1956, his invitation to the novelists, Samuel Selvon and V.S. Naipaul, to return and move within the region at their pleasure was a stage towards that ambition.

It was the transmission of this idea, taking root by chance in Guyana, that started the pattern of reunions which has brought us here.

Williams was also the man who a decade earlier had first brought my attention to the names of two of our honoured guests – Nicolás Guillén of Cuba and Aimé Césaire of Martinique.

It was his wish that people of my generation then would ignore the imperial barriers of language, and enter the world which was being made by Guillén and Césaire.

He was, essentially, a Caribbean person, and through his work, both as historian and man of public affairs, he became a great pioneer in helping to lay the cultural foundations of this regional house.

But a political life, especially a long political life, carries within it the burden of great contradictions, since critical moments will often show action to be in conflict with intention and idea.

And, whatever controversies may surround the career of Eric Williams, I think it consistent with our purpose here, that we should, on this occasion, remember him with reverence and with gratitude.

---

*   The fourth celebration of the Caribbean Festival of Creative Arts (CARIFESTA) was held in Barbados in July 1981. Six artists were specially honoured on that occasion: Beryl McBurnie, dancer and theatre organiser of Trinidad and Tobago; Edna Manley, sculptor of Jamaica; Nicolás Guillén, poet of Cuba; Aimé Césaire, poet of Martinique; Mighty Sparrow, calypsonian of Grenada and Trinidad and Tobago; and Frank Collymore, writer and artist of Barbados. Lamming delivered this Opening Address on July 19, 1981.

That influence is at work in the selection of these six West Indians for special honour. It is the recognition of a family of islands including the mainland island of Guyana, peopled by the same blood, and shaped by the same historical experience.

Many of you will have good reason to know that Barbados, your host, has secreted itself in the bloodstream of every Caribbean territory. Wherever you go within this region, the signature of that sperm is there.

Federation may have failed to create common institutions, but the ceremony of marriage has certainly succeeded in reinforcing that first tradition of kinship by blood. To speak of the Caribbean family, therefore, is to speak of a collective and personal experience of the deepest intimacy. And this has been a dominant characteristic of the work of those we honour: their recognition of common predicament, of common need, and of common destiny.

It is not by whim or fancy that Mrs Edna Manley, Jamaican in her experience, should welcome the Trinidad poet, Wayne Brown, to be her official biographer.

From the great Sparrow in Trinidad, through the sparkling voice of Aimé Césaire in Martinique, to the earliest pre-occupation of Nicolás Guillén in Cuba, each has sought to make permanent a vision of this regional house where no member of the family would conceive of calling another 'expatriate' or 'alien'.

Common decency tells us that it would be an act of the greatest perversity to train a Barbados-born child to think of its Vincentian or Jamaican mother as an expatriate in the island where she resides as mother and person who contributes to the continuity of this family. Such language promotes a mischievous disruption, and threatens all of us in the most sacred areas of our domestic experience.

And so, we warmly congratulate the Barbados Government for using its authority and its power to confirm, by this particular choice, the possibility of that vision, of a common family, which has influenced almost every creative, cultural worker in this region.

It is not only an excellent choice. It is also a very courageous one. When we consider the details of the work and lives of our honoured guests, we recognise that, in their different ways each has been an agent of creative upheaval for ruling groups at different times.

I do not think it necessary to emphasise that the prevailing values of a society (the codes you respect and obey) are, to a large extent, the wishes of the dominant ruling group. And the most urgent need of all rulers is to achieve and maintain an order of stability.

But these honoured guests have all been led, by the nature of their work, to explore aspects of our reality which brought them into conflict with established and official ways of seeing.

While the soldier may applaud stability with his gun, the creative, cultural worker forces us to question the content of that stability, to rethink, even to redefine the terms of our meaning.

The grave is, after all, a very stable place, perhaps the most stable of places. But it would be a strange intelligence which chose the cemetery as a model kingdom of development.

The late Frank Collymore who had the greatest genius for being loved, will always remain the most memorable father of the family of Caribbean writers.

The magazine *Bim* became a regional home for all. But he was by occupation a schoolmaster whose reputation for kindliness and humane concern will never be surpassed in this island.

It was his business to train boys into the habit of being stable, yet he always performed this function with a certain gentle mockery. It was his humour which concealed from us how deep was his creative suspicion:

> And I think of these youngsters, large or small, earnest or wayward, or frankly indifferent, but all, however, quite sure, that the ablative absolute and the Acts (by Marshall) are proven paths to a status that's secure.

Then there's prayers every morning and double-entry bookkeeping; one foot in Heaven, and one on the things that really matter, plenty of time afterwards to fornicate, guzzle and chatter.

> See how nicely his tie sits underneath his collar, you can always tell an educated man if you know just where to look. See, he takes his hat off when the band is playing the national anthem. That man's no bloody fool: he owns three houses and a drugstore in Port-Market. He has learned to use both edges of the golden rule. Yes, he won't have to use a hoe, or lie out in the open wondering what things are or why they go.

The privilege of school, and a gift for private accumulation, would later transform three houses and a drugstore into a miraculous haven of condominiums and boutiques, and all the expensive mysteries of un-real estate. But there remains the same virus of that stable man who perceives himself to be in a stable place.

It was once a condition of stability in this region to ignore the existence, and deny the human worth of the enormous majority of men and women whose labour made that order possible. The mark of their exclusion was the black skin.

'On that day,' cried Frantz Fanon, 'completely dislocated, unable to be abroad with the other, the white man, who unmercifully imprisoned me, I took myself far from my own presence, far indeed, and made myself an object. What else could it be for me but an amputation?'

I know there are those among you, who tremble at the sound of that blunt and simple word, 'black;' and who, apologising for your own victimisation, nervously anticipate a message of race. But when we say black, it has no biological meaning, nor is it used in the service of racial applause. When I say black, it is the name of a profound and unique historical experience, borne by a particular group of men and women whose presence in the world was destined to transform the eyes and ears of the world, and whose ultimate liberation will be the decisive contribution to the liberation of mankind.

It is, precisely, in this connection, that we must perceive the meaning of those we honour today. For each of them has waged a war on that amputation Fanon speaks of: each has battled consistently to heal and restore the rhythm and beauty of that battered black body, which Europe argued, and continues to argue, is ugly, graceless and without history.

For Europe and their successors, the United States, have been trapped in the deceiving habit of seeing themselves, not as a portion of mankind, but as the custodians of all human destiny.

But we know, as Marx observed more than a century ago: 'Labour cannot emancipate itself in the white skin, where in the black, it is branded'.

And the significance of the Rastafari Movement in its native Jamaica is that they confront us, in the most dramatic way, with a question which remains central to the politics of our culture. Where do you stand in relation to blackness?

It is curious that in so cautious a land as Barbados, the answer was being offered by the native poet, Mr H. A. Vaughn, in a rebuke to the black classroom of this island:

Turn sideways now and let them see
What loveliness escapes the schools,
Then turn again and smile and be
The perfect answer to those fools
Who always prate of Greece and Rome,
The face that launched a thousand ships
And suchlike things, but keep tight lips
For burnished beauty nearer home
Turn in the sun, my love, my love
What palm-like grace, what poise, I swear
I prize these dusky limbs above
My life. What laughing eyes, what gleaming hair.

Each of our guests came to their work on behalf of a family whose history is an example of a people, throttled by the embrace of imperial guardians (be they English, French, American), whose generosity demands our total acceptance of their will, and their interests.

It was this condition of self-denial that Mrs Manley encountered in the Jamaica of the late '30s and '40s when her participation in the political lives of the ordinary and the poor alerted her to the astonishing beauty of their physical presence. And she set out, as sculptor and painter, on a remarkable labour of love and duty to return that black face to its own eyes, and to train those eyes to see again what they should never have forgotten. It is the measure of her stature that an authentic history of Jamaica could not be written without focusing on the role she has played in the development of a national culture there.

The same role fits exactly the career of Beryl McBurnie of Trinidad and Tobago. The language of sculpture and the language of dance are different aspects of the same function. They are tools, devices of the imagination, which, encountering a moment in reality, sets out to discover the meaning, the essence of that moment, by creating an order out of what had appeared too ordinary for serious attention.

The imagination teaches us to see.

Beryl McBurnie, as dancer and teacher of the dance, created a wholly new vocabulary for the people of Trinidad and Tobago. She made the body laugh; she made the body sing; she made the body weep. This range of mood and emotion could be heard through different accents: the Amerindian, the African, the Indian, and a creolising synthesis of all these. But she is also a builder of institutions. The 'Little Carib' theatre, born from the most fragile dream, would later grow into a resource centre for many a corner in the Caribbean. The first independence celebrations of Guyana could not have been the same, if the 'Queen of the Little Carib' was not there.

I do not believe it is possible to find anywhere outside this region an example of creative, cultural work, where the imagination of individual artists is so completely dominated by the lives of people from down below. Whether it be literature, music, dance, or the visual arts, each form has derived its power from an involvement with the realities of the poor.

It would ordinarily be a presumption to draw the Mighty Sparrow to your attention, for he, as a total creation of the Caribbean people, is also, perhaps, the most complete of all Caribbean artists.

His art embraces all forms. He sings, he dances, he employs, in the telling of a story, all the narrative devices of a novelist. His act is visual. His themes, for all the laughter they provoke, are a source of great disturbance. Sociologists will never be able to formulate what his critical intelligence and quick perception so easily communicates.

> Outcast
> The slave
> Congo man
> Dan is the Man in the Van
> Monica Doudou
> Rose
> Why, why, did you leave me?
> Why did you deceive me?
> Rose, you looking for blows.

The enslavement of our educational system, the chaos in our sexual relations, the political leader in the role of the 'bad john'. He offers us back our several humiliations. But there is behind the extravagant vigour of this musical genius a persistent legacy of rage. For Sparrow was descended from a dangerous decade, before the steel bands got elevated to the status of national orchestra, and the streets of Carnival were ruled by warriors.

The sound was 'Desperadoes', 'Renegades', 'Red Army', 'Hell Yard', 'Conquistadors'. These are clearly not the names of patron saints in communion with a holy spirit. They are declarations of war on behalf of a turbulent folk who reminded all agents of power that space was not for sale. This tradition of resistance is at the heart of Sparrow's art. And it is an inescapable Caribbean phenomenon whenever the artist goes seriously to work.

There has recently been universal mourning for the loss of Bob Marley.

Get up, stand up;
Stand up for your rights.

But to accept Marley is to accept the moral necessity of entering into battle against all those forces that would halt or extinguish the possibility of men and women becoming truly human.

It is to aid, by all means possible, that process of struggle against the racism of white power, the epidemic of class discrimination, nurtured in these neo-colonial cells, by a new breed of aspiring blacks, the assault on individual dignity by the personal abuse of official power.

Get up, stand up;
Stand up for your rights.

Behind those drums of steel, the agitation of Marley, and the joyful mockery of Sparrow, there was, across the water, an ancestor of the same faith whom we recognise and honour as a resident of this regional house: Comrade Nicolás Guillén.

Recording his witness to the Spanish Civil War of the '30s he could say:

So here we have this Cuban from Camaguey;
this West Indian from Cuba:
this American from the West Indies,
proclaiming to his brothers from Spain:
I who love freedom so simply. .
As one loves a child, or the sun or the tree

planted in front one's house
I shout to you with the voice of a free man
that I shall match my step with yours,
Simply and happily,
Pure, serene and strong,
With my curly hair and brown body.

He created the greatest scandal among the ruling classes in Cuba when, in 1934, his book, *Motivos de Son*, drawing upon the African orgins of a popular dance, the Son, affirmed that there was no Cuba without Africa, that the fundamental blood of the Cuban flowed from that black continent. There was no need, you might say, that a man of his complexion should offer himself up as target for such national villification.

We have special reason to embrace him. At the age of 17 his father was murdered by the 'democratic' government of the day. And for more than half a century Comrade Guillén has combined the gifts of a great poet with the heart of a man of conscience.

As he enters the eighth decade of his turbulent life, he is often heard rejoicing that the Cuban revolution was the greatest Caribbean poem written in his time.

What does that poem say?
When I look at and touch myself,
I, John-only-yesterday-with nothing,
and John-with-everything today,
With everything today,
I glance around, I look and see
and touch myself and wonder
how it could have happened.

I have, let's see
I have the pleasure of walking my country,
the owner of all there is in it,
Examining at very close range what
I could not and did not have before.
I can say cane
I can say mountain,
I can say city,
I can say army,

Army say,
Now mine forever and yours, Ours,
And the vast splendour of
The sunbeam, the star, the flower,

I have, let's see:
That I have learned to read,
To count,
I have that I have learnt to write,
And to think
And to laugh.
I have that now I have
A place to work
And earn
What I have to eat, I have, let's see
I have what was coming to me!

This example of dream has never had a more urgent voice in contemporary literature than that of Aimé Césaire of Martinique. He is the product of a particular French intellectual tradition which knows ideology not as an epidemic to be controlled or exterminated, but as an example of theory and practice which all men, in different ways, bring to the conduct of their daily lives.

Of the humblest origins, where the house of his childhood could hardly boast a roof, his gifts have taken him into the academies of the world, through the ranks of the working people, and back to the original Africa which lent its heart to Martinique.

He was the teacher of Frantz Fanon: that Fanon who so abrasively warned:

Leave this, Europe/America where they
Are never done talking of man
Yet murder men everywhere they find them,
At the corner of their own streets,
In all corners of the globe.

Carifesta is not about spectacle, it is a celebration of work accomplished and work that is still in progress: and it is sometimes the work of men and women of whom it might be said:

We who tried to lay the
foundations of friendliness,
could not ourselves be friendly.

If you plant a breadfruit tree, it is unreasonable to expect that it will bear pineapples. The tree is known by its fruit. In a similar way it might be said that a nation is made known to itself by the creative cultural work which grows out of the soil of that society.

Yet there is an important difference between the tree of man and the trees of nature. The history of a tree is fixed since it can only obey the laws of its own nature. But men do not only enter the world. They transform the world by their work. They alter the chemistry of their own soil, and they change in their perceptions and their needs with every radical change they bring about in the material conditions of their existence.

If some of our children find us strange, it is, perhaps, because they live, as a fact of experience, what we had only dreamt of as a vague possibility.

Just as many of us take for granted a measure of freedom which other men, at other times, beaten and enslaved, could only dream of as a distinct and achievable reward of struggle.

The dream is not an idle exercise. It is the very foundation of a future reality. And that is why it often carries the cost of an untimely death.

Let the voice of Césaire seal that dream:

> For now we know in truth
> that man's work is by no means complete
> that we have not nothing to contribute to the world
> that parasites we are not
> that no more need we squat at the gate
> but that man's work has only just begun
> and that he has to release his energies and conquer
> and that no single race has a monopoly of beauty,
> intelligence and creativity and that there is room
> for all to conquer.
> And now we know that our land too
> is within the orbit of the sun
> which shines on the little plot we have willed
> for ourselves;

that without constraint we are free to move heaven, earth
and the stars.

Distinguished, honoured guests: mine is a single voice through
which an entire region now thanks you for the gift of your life and
your work to this unique family. And in asking the Governor General
to confirm these honours, I am deeply conscious that your presence
here confers a permanent honour on this island, perhaps the greatest
and most humane visiting honour it has ever known.

8 | *Portrait of a Prime Minister**

Parents have no idea what damage their love may inflict on children. Similarly, we do not know where an influence begins; nor can we trace with any certainty that subtle process whereby it works an effect on the choices we make. My own political curiosity didn't start with the man's interest in philosophy which dominated my reading after the 1950s.

But it may have had something to do with the boy who loitered among the crowds in Queen's Park, learning the acid and embattled language of men who aspired to be our leaders. And I had watched the riots at close quarters. Or even at an earlier date, when I feared and distrusted those white priests who led us in prayer at the apartheid church of St Cyprian's. Belleville is still a difficult memory for me.

A reflection on the source of influence is appropriate to any serious observation of Errol Barrow, the new Prime Minister of Barbados.

He has been here before, from 1961 to 1976. Even in Opposition, he sometimes gave the impression that he had lent the other office to his successor. A man of slow voice and very gentle manners, he surprises and often shocks Barbados by the things he says.

Once he apologised to an immense crowd in Independence Square for an unfortunate appointment he had made to the public service. On a similar occasion, he has lamented the fact that he helped to draft the Constitution which gives special liberties of speech to members of the House, explaining that he didn't anticipate the Chamber would so quickly accommodate such a great variety of vagabonds.

I have heard him warn the poor to avoid taking their disputes into the law courts. He appears to have doubts about the honour of his own profession, and he has said so.

---

*   On May 28, 1986, Errol W. Barrow, who had led Barbados into independence in 1966, won a resounding victory at the polls which brought him and the Democratic Labour Party into power after ten years in Opposition. In June of that year, Lamming wrote this tribute to Barrow which was published in the *Nation* newspaper. Less than a year later Barrow was dead.

And yet, in person, he is the least offensive of men; easy, accessible, almost ordinary in his style of discourse. Be it fish market or supermarket, back alley or modern highway, the humble chattel home or posh ministerial office, he moves through these different orbits with a total lack of pomp or ceremony.

It is difficult to think of a public figure in Barbados who commands such a wide and genuine affection from his people. But there is a complex personality behind this veneration, and one example is provided by his relations with the Press.

> If the media do not make you, they cannot break you. Consequently, even well-meaning and honest journalists find it difficult to secure interviews or responses from me as they will all confirm; chiefly because in public life, I am a private person. If my name never appears in the Press even if I won a prize of great value, I would remain completely unconcerned.

This is a very revealing admission, and it says more than Mr Barrow may have intended. In the first place, I do not think it is true that the Press selects its targets with such care. The Press can destroy a career which they played no part in making; and may, indeed, do so for precisely that reason. But the passage is drawing our attention to an important aspect of Barrow as 'a private person'.

A public figure who can remain completely unconcerned about neglect or critical dismissal is making a declaration of astonishing self-assurance; a quality which might otherwise be perceived as arrogance.

And Barrow does have a degree of social confidence which is rare in most Barbadians, who always need to check out each other's origin before relationship can be approved.

It is as though he had escaped the pervasive inferiority complex which cripples the mind and imagination of most black men and women of the middle class.

Barrow has a powerful sense of his social and ancestral connection; and at the heart of this security is the O'Neal clan, and especially the heroic figure of his uncle, Dr Duncan O'Neal.

O'Neal, who was born in 1879, graduated from Edinburgh University as a medical doctor and returned to Barbados in 1924. For the next 12 years his life became an example of sacrifice and dedication which has never been surpassed in the political history of Barbados. He declared himself a socialist, identified with the cause of longshoremen and field labourers and every sector of wretched black life in the island. He launched the Democratic League, created the Working Men's Association, and fought to teach a voteless black populace the importance of organisation.

Almost alone, he confronted the merciless citadels of white power, demanding the abolition of child labour, free medical and dental care of old people and children, a universal pension scheme, and the disestablishment of the Church on the grounds that no man should be asked to pay for another man's religion.

Barrow was the nephew, in a sense the son, of a man who came to be known as the father of democracy and who had earned that honour. He absorbed this influence as a boy and must have come to see O'Neal as the rock on which he would one day build his own spiritual house.

Barrow has this innate conviction that he has come from great stock. It is not at all surprising that may years later, in a public appeal to Caribbean Heads of Government, he should say:

> I place special emphasis on defending the dignity and self-respect of our people, since it must never be thought that poverty is a good enough excuse for abandoning these virtues.

His preparation for public life has another and quite different source of influence. The journey to Britain is critical in understanding the mental climate of his generation. Barrow didn't arrive as a student. Like any other loyal colonial of his time, he went to serve in a war. Crisis is a good opportunity for learning the anatomy of a society. The rigidity of the British class system would have been temporarily dislocated, narrowing the social distance between men and women of different origins. But the English are branded on the tongue, and accent immediately betrays every citizen's social formation. Barrow would have met English people of all classes, now forced into various forms of social intercourse which would have been impossible in more normal times.

A product of Empire, he caught a glimpse of those who had made the rules by which his own childhood had been indoctrinated. The next stage was inevitable. He would become the colonial in revolt. If he did not wish to be a revolutionary, it is also true he did not degenerate into that status we call conservative. For the colonial has nothing to conserve unless he consciously settles for a life of voluntary enslavement.

By the end of the war, Barrow would be a student with a difference. He was ripe for the influence of the London School of Economics, dominated at the time by the socialist theoretician, Professor Harold Laski. It was an influence which bore strange fruit across more than one continent. It was here, too, that the triumvirate of friendship, later known as the Barrow–Burnham–Manley axis, found its earliest soil. Years later, they would have settled many a discord by recalling the political intimacy of the London days.

It was a period of great change. The British people had repudiated their war hero, Sir Winston Churchill, in as decisive a manner as the people of Barbados have dealt with the party of the late Tom Adams.

The anti-colonial struggle was irreversible. London was the city and the intellectual training camp of many men who would become the dominant influence on the liberation struggles of their countries until independence was conceded: Jomo Kenyatta, Kwame Nkrumah, and his political advisor, the great Pan-Africanist, George Padmore. This was the political environment which Errol Barrow knew personally and whose influence he has never been quite able to escape. The radical tone of many of his recent statements is not new. It has a root and a line of continuity from Duncan O'Neal, to Nkrumah and Padmore and the honourable and courageous visit he made with his old friend, Michael Manley, to the Debt Conference in Havana. This could only have provoked controversy from commentators whose general backwardness included a specific ignorance of Barrow's political ancestry.

It is important to remind a younger generation in all territories that his political career is an inseparable part of the history of the regional integration movement; from his first meeting with Sir Alexander Bustamante, Dr Eric Williams and Dr Cheddi Jagan in 1963, to the formal launching of the Caribbean Community at Chaguaramas in Trinidad in 1970.

Until 1975, he had played a central role in helping to convene no less than 13 Heads of Government meetings which bore fruit in a variety of Caribbean institutions: the Caribbean Free Trade Area, the Caribbean Development Bank, the Caribbean Meteorological Institute, the University of the West Indies Campus at Cave Hill, the Law Faculty, the Common Market and the Caribbean Community.

His credentials as a regional patriot are very impressive; and it is to be expected that his presence in Georgetown next week will carry the weight and authority of this personal record in the conduct of Caribbean affairs.

He would be less than human if he was not conscious of this singular distinction; for no other present Head of State would have had a comparable history of regional involvement.

Barrow has always avoided ideological debate; and in this respect he is very different from Burnham or Manley. He has that pragmatic liberal conviction that ideology should never be a precondition for arriving at agreement in specific areas which affect the human development of the Caribbean people.

His comment on the early meeting with Bustamante and Jagan is very instructive:

> Indeed, an examination of the diversity of political methodology between Sir Alexander Bustamante, Dr Williams, Dr Jagan, and your humble servant, will disclose that ideological pluralism and a high level of political tolerance informed our discussions from the outset.

His recent pronouncements on foreign policy confirm that he is essentially a regional nationalist with an old ambition to promote and defend the political sovereignty of the Caribbean people.

He is, therefore, suspicious of the motives which lay behind the Regional Security System, fearing that it is no more than a 'justification for dependency on the United States of America; and from their side of the coin, an excuse for them to make interventions in the Caribbean when certain policies of Government do not coincide with what they consider their best interests.

Barrow is not afraid of that anti-Christian virus which goes in the name of anti-communism; a shabby despicable campaign to rape the minds of all ill-informed people. In this respect, he represents a new force of moral resistance in the struggle for cultural sovereignty.

But there are certain areas of his thinking which cause friends and students a certain apprehension. It came as a shock that a man of his sophistication should hint that state-owned Caribbean Broadcasting Corporation (CBC) might be abandoned to the commercial whims of a private sector which has no record of involvement in the cultural development of this country. It would be an unforgiveable blunder for him to proceed in that direction.

He has also provoked unhappy controversy by the charitable view he takes of the Guyana regime; and it is to be hoped that he will speak of this matter with greater candour than he has done in recent months. Personal friendship cannot be a substitute for political integrity.

On the other hand, he has wasted no time alerting us to the exploitative strategies of the governor of Puerto Rico:

> The Puerto Ricans as a people have never displayed any interest in the Caribbean people...Now they have an economic problem, here is their governor rushing and saying, "We have something which will be very good for you."

It is timely that he should draw our attention to the colonial degradation of Puerto Rico. But if he is right about Puerto Rico, he has got to be wrong about Singapore as an alternative model for Barbados. Frank Walcott would not be safe in the care of Prime Minister Lee Kuan Yew who feels no pain in locking up trade union leaders. And prison is not a place we should ask Mr Walcott to contemplate.

Barrow is not a stranger to us; but there is something quite novel about his return to power. He has aroused great expectations among honourable patriots within the region as well as the Caribbean external frontiers in Europe and North America.

It is generally admitted that he has no great interest in personal power. He is not hungry for material wealth. And the vulgarities of social status have never attracted him.

These are the ambitions which normally motivate the region's political men, and apply with equal force to the appetites of many political women. He is singularly free from such distractions.

What then can be his ambition except to have a rendezvous with history? In a way, he had stated this in his open letter to the Heads of Government in 1982:

> We have survived a long history of servitude and colonial exploitation, and there is no other road for us to take now, but a journey towards a larger freedom for all our people. Caribbean solidarity and regional integration can never be achieved as a by-product of United States foreign policy.

There is a distinct possibility that the next five years of his working life might be recorded as the most creative and memorable of his entire political career.

9 | *On the Murder of Rodney*[*]

Citizens of Guyana, and the islands of the Caribbean, Comrades and friends from beyond the region, I speak to you as one who has loved this country, as one who ever since his first visit 25 years ago had always applauded the Guyanese as perhaps the kindest and most hospitable people in this Caribbean region. As one, who in the year of your independence amidst some controversy was even given the assurance by the then and present Prime Minister that he had earned the right to speak freely in this land on matters of common concern to this region. There have been great changes in fortune and method in your country, including the ungracious curtailment of my stay among you to a brief 48 hours, and yet I experience no change in the quality of my affections for this place.

Sometimes it may take a death and a special kind of dying to quicken the truth that is not urgently alive in our own consciousness. Today, we meet in a dangerous land, and at the most dangerous of times. The danger may be that supreme authority, the supervising conscience of the nation, has ceased to be answerable to any moral law, has ceased to recognise or respect any minimum requirement of ordinary human decency. Walter Rodney's death, like the manner of his dying, has quickened this truth and provoked within and beyond Guyana a rage

---

[*]   Walter Rodney was blown up in his car on June 13 1980 in Georgetown, Guyana. In the space of just 38 years, Rodney had earned for himself worldwide distinction for his intellectual contribution as a historian of Africa, as a teacher in Jamaica, Tanzania and West Germany, and as a political activist and leader of great courage and skill. He was author of *History of the Upper Guinea Coast*, *Groundings with My Brothers*, *How Europe Underdeveloped Africa*, and the posthumously published prize-winning, *History of the Guyanese Working People*. At the time of his murder, Rodney was at the centre of a broad-based tide of opposition to the Guyanese government of Forbes Burnham, as a leader of the Working People's Alliance of Guyana which he helped to found. Lamming delivered this address at the funeral of Rodney. The government of Guyana refused to release his corpse for the ceremony.

and grief which official authority could never have anticipated. To turn murder into a mockery of the dead is the ultimate blasphemy against all forms of living. But this is not new, although history may record that at this time Guyana has made its own contribution to a long, long, tradition of nightmare and terror which has always been at the heart of the history of these Americas.

For democracy has never, never, been an organic part of our experience, from conquest through slavery and colonisation to the present arrangements we endure. The need for democracy is often a conscious and courageous effort to exorcise those twin demons of the tyrant which have pursued us from the past.

What did Rodney represent that was so special? And what is it about his loss to us that has caused such sorrow? His closest colleagues will have their answers. I speak as a man of the Caribbean who knew him through conversations over the years, through correspondence and through his work as a historian, a teacher and an intellectual worker among those who had been deprived of his advantages.

He was, first of all, a serious man; and that, in our territories, does not always make for comfort. He was not 'smart.' He was not 'bright.' He did not seek to score points for the sake of argument. But he had a rare gift of intellect to which he felt a special duty. It was a tool, a reservoir of power which could only justify itself if it were put into service, and on behalf of social need. He was an intellectual in the sense that all men and women are intellectuals. For to be alive is to have a concept, a view of life, to be engaged in or be condemned to making choices about your actions.

But Rodney impressed us by a constant struggle to live his view; to bring to his work, as a historian and teacher and political comrade, a certain integrity of commitment. It is as though he wanted to live each day as though it were his last.

This gift of seriousness, this struggle for personal decency, and this courage, left their impression on all who came within his influence from Africa to the Americas, to Europe and back to the heartland of Guyana which he loved.

I came in this morning from Barbados which is known to be a country of excessive stability, and I am really struck by the deep respect and affection which he has generated among the most conservative elements in that country. And I was hearing a story this morning on the plane as we came in of a simple woman hearing Rodney on the radio, and her only comment was 'He must be a Christian.'

To his wife, Pat, and their children, to his mother and immediate family, I take this liberty of saying that all his comrades embrace you. We thank you for the contribution you made in the shaping and creation of so fine a human being. And we walk with you now and into the future.

A few weeks ago I received a letter from Walter telling me of the completion of the first part of his *History of the Guyanese Working People*. It ends with this sentence:

> There is still much work to be done here, but I expect that we will meet at the rendezvous of victory.

I think we shall meet; since the struggle for humanity in this region will always be identified with his name; and any just victory will have been influenced by the powerful contribution of his intellect and the gentleness of his caring. And so I close with the poem which Martin Carter gave me this morning:[1]

For Walter Rodney

Assassins of conversation
They bury the voice
they assassinate, in the beloved
grave of the voice, never to be silent.

I sit in the sky's wild noise
of the feet of some who
not only, but also, kill
the origin of rain, the ankle
of the whore, as fastidious
as the great fight, the wife
of water. Risker, risk,
I intend to turn a sky
of tears, for you.

Note

1. Martin Carter of Guyana is a poet who Lamming has elsewhere described as, 'the purest, clearest, and most authentic poetic voice of my generation.' Carter was a major figure in the anti-colonial struggle in then British

Guiana, and was a minister in the People's Progressive Party government of 1953, which was the first to be elected under universal adult suffrage. When British troops suspended constitutional democracy in that same year, the colonial government jailed Carter among others. While in prison he wrote his *Poems of Resistance*. He is the author of several books of poetry, including two major collections: *Poems of Succession* and *Poems of Affinity*.

10 | *The Imperial Encirclement**

There are two words which frequently appear as a kind of symbolic representation for two conflicting movements of thought and action in our region. These words are Freedom and Liberation.

A mode of thought, called the Left, is engaged in a struggle of liberation from the imprisoning freedom of the Right; and the Right desperately seeks to protect this freedom from the menace of liberation from the Left. Let me share my involvement in this dilemma.

I was born and grew up in one island of a region whose history offers the most fundamental contradiction. Caribbean society, historically, was never conceived as the coming together of people with any design for social living. That is not how it came about. It is a society into which men and women were brought for one purpose and one purpose only labour, to be transformed from persons into instruments of production.

They were brought here to meet the requirements of production whose fruits would be appropriated and then redistributed by other men who were often absent from the actual landscape and who could in fact be regarded by the producers as hostile strangers. So if we conceive of human labour as the basis on which men will freely create their design for social living, the history of our region continued to be the history of extreme contradictions: the contradictions between men perceived only as instruments of production, and labour experienced as the basis for social living.

We have endured a series of social settlements: Crown colony rule, various exercises in constitutional reform, one more elected seat here, and another two there; the rehearsal of ministerial rule for the arrangement of self-government; and the latest settlement which we

---

* Address given at the Annual Dinner of the Jamaica Press Association in Kingston, Jamaica on December 12, 1981. The introductory remarks, which have been cut, acknowledged Mr Theodore Sealey, a former editor of the Gleaner newspaper in Jamaica. The text has been slightly edited.

now know as Independence. In every instance the stages of this journey were initiated, the frontiers of social justice extended by a struggle of liberation by men and women from down below.

The old imperialism of Europe, appropriating the destiny of the region through a strategy of fragmentation by language (French West Indies, British West Indies, Dutch West Indies, Spanish West Indies and so on) has given way to a new and more challenging menace of imperial encirclement.

One of the most formidable difficulties in discovering the history of the Americas and of recreating the meaning of the Americas has to do with the disproportionate power of one area of the Americas. It is the formidable power of the United States which obscures and distorts the reality of the Americas.

I do not think it would be an exaggeration to say that the most formidable obstacle to the progress of that discovery is the power of the United States, and the perception which derives from that power. This has been simply and brutally put by the Mexican novelist Carlos Fuentes: 'When Americans hear the word Mexico, all they see is an oil well.'

The vision which derives from an individual sensibility is tied up with the fact of nature. We are of nature. We experience something we call our human nature, and by which I think we vaguely mean our human impulses, our human instincts, our individual senses. But these are not fixed, these do not have a given permanent history. The character of this human nature, it seems to me, is dependent on, and very influenced by, the kind of relation we have to nature as the physical world, as external reality. And how we encounter nature, the physical world, individually, has to do with how the individual mode of perception has been shaped by men at work in organised societies. For humanity through the process of *work* makes nature a part of its history. That is, our experience of nature is really a social experience, which determines then our experience of ourselves.

If our immediate neighbourhood is the neighbourhood of our personal relationships, of how to be with our neighbours, it seems to me that any education which equips us for how to be with each other has got to be political education. It has got to be an education, which, first of all, lets us know, helps us to understand, what is the context of power, the character of that social reality within which those individual personal relationships take place, because those personal relationships cannot be regarded as having an autonomy. Those individual personal relationships have got to be in some way a reflection of another reality which is social.

And so the history and character of that social reality, the mechanisms whereby these are organised and directed, must be learnt if we are going to have a more comprehensive preparation for knowing what it is we are trying to do when we set out to be with each other in what we call a human way.

It is this particular view of the relation of the individual sensibility to the social collective, this view of the correspondence between individual liberation and our particular relation to the physical world of nature and work which causes many of us the greatest concern about the dominant role of the United States in defining the reality of the Americas.

I will read you something which crystallises the worry and concern which I have been communicating. It is a small extract from a statement by a Chairman of a giant corporation, called Allied Stores, responsible for clothing people not only in the United States but outside it.

And I want to alert you that it is not said by way of entertainment. It is a directive to executives about the nature of what they are doing, and the ways which they have to do what they are doing, if the enterprise can be justified.

It reads thus:

> Basic utility cannot be the foundation of a prosperous apparel industry. We must accelerate obsolescence. It is our job to make women unhappy with what they have...We must make them so unhappy that their husbands can find no happiness or peace in their excessive savings.

I want to suggest to you that this represents the clearest articulation not just of a Chairman of a garment industry. It is the essence of a total philosophy and I believe that this philosophy, articulated here, is essentially the philosophy that underpins the faith and practice of corporate capitalism, whether it is garments or foods or whatever. Utility is not their purpose. That purpose is the creation of false needs in order to justify a demand for an expanding consumerist society. That is what we are dealing with.

When groups of men in a given society have been able to command the peaks of power which enable them, through the control of all institutions, to organise an entire society in their own interest and in the image of that philosophy, there is no way that you can begin to think of a vision of personal relationships, a vision of how you are going to be with your neighbour outside of the context of the power of that collective minority.

And the question for us is how do we relate to that, because it is the overwhelming and dominant authority of that philosophy which determines our relation to nature and to work, and which many of our regional leaders uncritically embrace as their last desperate hope of anaesthetising the consciousness of our people.

In other words, it is not possible in the circumstances of this philosophy for strategies of development to proceed without the continuing violation of the human person in the process of work. And therefore a system that is in this profound and lucrative conflict with nature and human labour, is a system that may be engaged in a conspiracy against the liberation of the poor.

It is that power, through the development of science and technology and the remarkable flexibility of its capitalist system, which now reaches everywhere. The United States does not only offer itself (and this is the curious paradox) as the leader of the free world, with which the Chairman of Allied Stores would agree, but it offers itself to its surrounding neighbourhood, by which I mean the world that comes within that system, as the model of freedom.

Barbados is a very small island. It is not more than 20-odd miles from top to bottom; beyond that there is the sea. It has a most remarkable network of roads. In its 20 miles length and 14 to 15 miles of width it has something like 600 to 700 miles of road.

They weren't there when I was a boy. You would have thought that this was the perfect infrastructure for the most up to date transport system. The result of this material improvement has produced a public transport system that threatens every Minister of Transport with an early death, because the local population is enraged morning, noon and night about the bus service. Yet on the other hand, in this small island where you would have thought there were no serious problems of mobility, the ratio is one car to every 10 to 11 people. In other words, we have a situation which must be construed by the political leadership as development, and stability, and the aspiring model of freedom is to buy. It is part of the concept of the Chairman of Allied Stores.

What makes it truly sad, and takes us into the area of real tragedy, is that nobody in Barbados makes motor cars or motor car parts. In other words, leaders of societies characterised by the deprivation of very large sections of the population, trapped into the notion of being a model of this freedom, have engaged the energies and the ambitions of their population in raising their living standards to those of a very well off industrial working class in the United States and Britain and Japan.

But as I say, no motor car is made in Barbados and similar territories.

It is really one of the problems we have with the paradox of the word freedom. Any politician would have been thought completely out of his mind, who says in an election campaign: 'Look, I am going to make it perfectly clear that we will have to deal with the car problem. I want two-thirds of the private vehicles off the road'.

It would be the end of his political career. In these circumstances, sanity is suicide.

Today we live a global inequality which drives men and women from the soil that gave them birth, the immediate landscape that shaped their childhood, across oceans, since any dream that they may have of rescuing life, in dignity, from poverty, that dream is elsewhere, it is not in the landscape where they were born.

So we are in this history of migration. The United States is the most extreme example, but the United States is not alone. The economies, which they call strong, of Germany and France, have been built by over 10 million migrant labourers over the past two decades, drawn from every poor sector of the world: Southern Italy, North Africa, Turkey, Portugal. Men and women leaving their families and drifting into these streets they do not know to rescue their dignity from a permanent deprivation.

Because of our proximity to the United States, and because we almost imagine ourselves to be in the valley of the moon, it is extremely difficult to get the local population of the Caribbean to think critically of the United States.

If you go to Jamaica or Barbados there is not a single family who has not got some relation in the United States. And this person, in a relative sense, is doing well. Jean who has not worked for two years has gone up, she has been there for a year, got a night job or a day job, she is at school, she thinks she may be able to come home for holiday next Christmas. There has been a transformation in Jean's expectations. It would be crazy for anyone to tell Jean's aunt that Jean is living in a sinister place.

This deceptive magic of the dream of milk and honey, to the ones who have not yet visited Canaan, makes for a tremendous resistance to any sane perception of the world in which we live. I say the situation is extreme because what this particular arrangement or system has so far succeeded in doing is to provide to a large extent a level of material comfort sufficiently different from preceding deprivation to make its human victims also its uncritical defenders.

What road has brought us to this fantasy?

As a result of our historical indoctrination, we have developed and absorbed a view that education is the best and safest means of escape from labour. That is, to grow up through education is to grow away from the very foundations that made social living possible.

And so in those arrangements which are usually political arrangements, you find that for us in the region education has always been made a scarcity. It is a scarcity and its market value is high. So you have always had in the Caribbean a broad mass of the population whose destiny was to be what the society understood as instruments of production; and a small minority siphoned off into higher levels of certification.

By virtue of its uniqueness, that is as a minority, by virtue of its training and its skill, which in certain areas were superior to those of the masses of the population, it assumed as a right the status of leadership. It would have seen itself as the head of the society, unaware that a head cannot move without its belly, for it is the belly which feeds the head in that particular society. And it is the ancient neglect of the belly that has made for the continuing impoverishment of our head. That head has certain skills, but it is an impoverished head because it has had no reciprocal relationship with the belly of its society.

And it is only by alerting that belly to that fact that it is the decisive force in the liberation of the society that you will in fact liberate that head from the imprisoning relation that it has to the belly.

The problem that we have is that this belly of the society, by which I mean the great work force, has historically been conditioned to see the agenda of its concern as always exclusively the question of wages, and survival through wages.

I take the view that an articulate and educated labour force should be a decisive factor in the cultural programming of a nation. The present arrangement whereby what you call the culture of a society is the monopoly and concern of that head, is to turn the world upside-down. Questions of education and culture; the whole question of national policy should be at the centre of the agenda of any labour movement.

But the labour movement is kept effectively immobilised because it has been trapped into the notion that what are called industrial questions are exclusively its business, and it is only when it is liberated from that agenda that you will have a quickened and deeper democratisation of the total society, which cannot be brought about simply by a minority leadership, of whatever political persuasion, however well meaning its individuals may be.

This minority which has been elevated by the struggles of working people into a new political and technical bourgeoisie poses a critical problem for us. They are nearly all the children, certainly the grandchildren of poor people. A great social investment in education by their poor parents and guardians, as well as the various social settlements of the imperial power, has brought them to dominant positions of power and authority. But they are a fragile class in the process of formation. If we trace their immediate ancestry (not to go any further) we shall not find there, either by blood or adoption, any great landowner, or merchant banker; no industrial capitalist or great ship builder: they are unique as a dominant ruling group, without any historical social experience of ownership or control of the means of production in their own country. It makes for a great fragility in their negotiations with an external power, and illuminates one of the most vulnerable areas in the national defence of the region.

For their recent elevation from poverty has made them desperate to consolidate their new material interests, and reproduce themselves by rapid personal and private accumulation. This exercise in self-production through rapid accumulation of money and the conspicuous display of social power, is bringing them into conflict with the base from which they sprang.

This ambiguity, this ambivalence which they now experience in relation to their own base of working people, makes for a corresponding ambivalence in their negotiations with the external power on whom they may have to lean for their protection as a new ruling group. This explains, in a way, their uncritical commitment to that liberal, electoral democracy which they inherited from the former imperial power.

I have asked this question before, and I will repeat it:

> Why do you think western capitalist imperialism should be so concerned about the electoral democracy which their economic vassals practise in the developing world? How is it that these alien strangers who have always been indifferent to the hunger of our children should suddenly be so eager to rescue us from a lack of democracy, to save us for freedom?

Is it not that they understand very well the arena of politics in which the new class organise their careers, and find in that national cockfight we call elections, the easiest and safest entry into our domestic affairs?

I put it as a speculation, and no more, that these imperialist salesmen of electoral democracy recognise that the contending political parties, in their fierce pursuit of office, create an artificial division within the ranks of working people, and make the power of labour that much easier to control.

Power at any time, and by whatever means it realises itself, always seeks to create the means of its own defence. It knows itself to be futile if it cannot defend itself. And so we must expect that the internationalising of Capital will seek the means of internationalising its defence. And culture, as a weapon of ideological penetration is one of its most formidable assets. The Argentine professor Garcia Canclini recorded his personal and intellectual experience of this phenomenon:

> Not only do the United States provide the Latin American armies and police with weapons, but they also elaborate patterns of counter-rebellion and communication techniques from every area of social life: from trade unions to schools, from churches to the means of mass communication. The totality of social relationships and of the system of ideological representation is programmed internationally.

When the contradictions between this system and a native resistance sharpen, the internationalising of defence will assume a greater rigour in the internationalising of repression.

Canclini out of his experience again observes:

> Chilean political prisoners are interrogated by Brazilian policemen.
> Brazilian journalists are detained in Uruguay, assassinated in
> Argentina; Argentinian officers train Bolivian and Central
> American soldiers; all this under the coordination and advice of
> intelligence personnel of the United States.

As part of the logic of this encirclement, it is likely that men and
women who had once thought themselves secure may experience what
are for them very novel forms of punishment: the articulate may be
driven to silence by various forms of censorship, highly certificated
elements of the middle class may be forced by a hostile regime into
unemployment, or become new recruits for prison. I say novel, since
they have too often retained class expectations that never saw prison
as a place built for them, and always regarded unemployment as
exclusively the burden of the poor.

In the general circumstances I have outlined, I see the function
of an authentic press, and all engaged in communication, to be the
vanguard in helping to create a cultural resistance to the increasing
penetration of this new imperialism. A press which is truly rooted in
the collective consciousness of its masses will discover there is a great
cultural capital that has never been released by the institutions which
mediate their lives. The press, in its various forms, would be the crucial
link which forges that organic connection between the now isolated
head and the troubled belly of our society. Its immediate task would
be to conduct a relentless battle for democratising all the conventional
structures of Party and Trade Union to which our people have often
innocently given their loyalty, as to a church; and in the process of
this linkage, we may discover within the ranks of our working people
an intellectual tradition whose wealth of experience and perception
we have rarely drawn upon.

To return to Canclini:

> If we think that culture is not a question of refinement and
> erudition, but the totality of processes that contribute to the
> understanding, the reproducing or the transformation of the social
> system, through the symbolic representation or re-elabouration
> of material systems, a cultural policy, then, cannot be seen as an

added complement nor as a luxury task to be taken up after the economic and political changes have taken place.

Men and women technically have the means of collaborating with nature in the liberation of man and woman, and yet the paradox of those means is that today, nature is endangered by man. This is to some extent the climate of my preoccupation. In my concrete corner of the world as an organic part of the writing of books, my work is for me really a record of the ways of seeing and recording the collective experience of those to whom I am joined by history. That is, I do believe that labour, which is the basis of all culture, must also be the motive force in the humanising of working people.

11 | *C.L.R. James, Evangelist**

In saying farewell to Nello, I thought I should speak in a very personal way. This is very much in keeping with his own style of expression, since he had, in a way I had not encountered before or since, a certain tone and clarity of delivery which made any historical event or the most abstract idea, come alive as though these were a part of his personal experience.

If he made reference to the French Revolution of 1789, you got the impression that he was actually there; he saw what happened, and had a special claim to the truth about that explosion. He would pronounce the name Robespierre with the same ease and familiarity that he would say 'Sparrow'.

He spoke of the tragedy of Shakespeare's Lear as though the king was a turbulent, old man he had met way back in Tunapuna. And always he spoke about such matters with the zeal and urgency of an ancient evangelist.

And this is, indeed, the correct word to define his role and function in our lives. C.L.R. James was an evangelist. But it took me some time to recognise the real nature of this kind of performance. It had nothing to do with display of knowledge, or parading the wide range of reference which supported such discourse.

This eloquence was of a different order. He literally believed what he was saying. There was no distance between head and tongue; and each judgement established a direct and organic connection between what was said and how he felt.

To think was to engage in an act of pure and complete participation: hence the immediacy and the spontaneity of view as well as the zeal and urgency of the evangelical style. These were characteristics of what

---

*   Eulogy delivered by Lamming at the funeral of C.L.R. James in Tunapuna, Trinidad and Tobago. James died at the age of 88 on May 31, 1989, in London, England.

might be called his intellectual personality. This certainty of purpose was a source of immense strength. It was also the cause of more than one grievous error. This view of mine is the result, over years, of very close and frequent contact. We met for the first time by chance on the Charing Cross Road in London in 1954. He had recognised me from a photograph on the jacket of a book of mine which he had read. He introduced himself.

We spent the next hour in a coffee shop. To my innocent eye, he had the air of a vagrant, lean and frail, and I was alarmed to discover that he could not raise, with both hands, this simple cup of coffee to his mouth.

I was wholly ignorant of the extraordinary life he had lived in the United States; that it was less than a year since his detention on Ellis Island. And I had no grasp at all of the real implications of his deportation back to an England which he had not seen for 15 years.

I call attention to these omens of adversity in order to emphasise a very different point. Four years later, on the eve of his departure for Trinidad in 1958, I had to marvel at the stamina, the perversely triumphant spirit of a man whom I had earlier thought to be on his way out.

And I am convinced that this miracle of perseverance could not have been of his own making. You had to know the apartment at Parliament Hill to realise the immense wealth of love and care with which wife Selma and son Sam had, as it were, cradled him. This was not exclusively a domestic service, overwhelming as that was; it was a reservoir of human relationship which kept alive the continuity of his work and his certainty of purpose. As James would say, 'I have no doubt about that'.

They created a human neighbourhood which, through the reciprocity of their interests, and the space of their hospitality had earned the right to summon whoever arrived from whatever community of resistance.

Let me quote from a letter written to Martin Glaberman on March 25, 1957:

> Yesterday the Rev. Martin Luther King and his wife had lunch with us and stayed here from 12:30 until nearly 5 p.m. With us was George Lamming, the writer from Barbados, who is shortly on his way to Ghana. There was also Dr David Pitt who is likely to be the first West Indian to run for Parliament in England. After two hours

of general conversation, Luther King and his wife began to speak about the events in Montgomery, Alabama.

The year before, the visitor was the new Premier of Trinidad and Tobago, Dr Eric Williams, who had come to discuss with us preparations for the festival of Arts in Trinidad. It was to be the PNM's first cultural gift to the nation; and, indeed, it was the first time I had ever heard from a head of government in the English-speaking Caribbean the concept of what is now known as Carifesta. Williams took copious notes including whether the writers would be seated alphabetically or according to the order of their importance. Wherever these notes may be, I regret to say we never heard anymore further about these plans.

And Trinidad has never hosted a Carifesta.[1] I do not think it was due to neglect; but Dr Williams had no confidence in the ability of his colleagues to fulfil tasks which he had conceived as his own. But the exchange was lively, instructive, and for me an unusual opportunity to observe men of power at close range. Over all the years I had known C.L.R., and with every change of abode, this was the environment which he created: a simple space where men and women of every race, and across a great variety of political cultures, met to explore the burdens of this planet, I mean that literally.

Change has been so swift that we may easily forget that London, in the 1950s, was still an important political capital. And it was the safest place to hide. Or so it seemed. It was through this association with James, in the context of his home, that I became aware of the global character of modern rebellion. Not in newspapers, not from textbooks, but in ordinary social intercourse with his regiment of renegades who arrived: one from India, another from Ceylon, a fallen activist from Malta, ambitious lawyers from every corner of the African continent; and always the West Indian with an eye firmly fixed on his territory's throne.

I did not know that the world was so full of complaint. And I was reassured that if I was wrong, it was, at least, the right kind of error.

This is for me C.L.R.'s supreme contribution to our time, not just the books, the pamphlets and the public lectures, but these passionate exchanges in small groups, about the nature of a national crisis, and the principle and method which should inform strategy. There is no way you can document these vital moments in the consciousness of those individuals, or their true meaning for the territories to which they would return.

James was and will remain, like all great teachers, a permanent and invisible asset. You can identify the printed page, but you cannot identify, with any such precision, the subtle transmission of thought from one generation to another.

He may not be unique in this respect, but it is a correct national and regional response that we should take great pride in the fact that it was this soil which gave him to the world of his time. What is the essence of James's thought? I shall indicate it by two quotations which related specifically to the Caribbean, but which lose none of their validity when they are applied to other political cultures.

In his essay on *The Birth of a Nation* he wrote:

> For one thing is certain, any new and genuine economic development of the Caribbean has to begin first of all with the involvement of the mass of population. Those responsible for plans and production are not even aware that this is missing. For them, the business of workers and peasants is not to concern themselves about industry, bringing to bear their accumulated experience, their practical knowledge, and their creative handling of the materials that they use every hour of the day. And that is why the West Indian economists are barren in productivity and insular exchange.

The second quotation is a philosophical reinforcement of this observation:

> The citizen is alive when he feels that he himself in his own national community is overcoming difficulties. He has a sense of moving forward through the struggle of antagonisms or contradictions and difficulties within the society, not by fighting against external forces.

James's intellect rested on one solitary pillar of faith. He believed in the creative power of the working masses of the population. And in all his enquiry into human achievement, he looks for the evidence that will prove this to be true. But this judgement did not come about by chance or divine intervention. The boy, James, had lived this experience from that window of his parents' house which separated him from the lawless good-for-nothing lout, Matthew Bondman, a man whose art and craft of batsmanship was James's first and lasting experience of the hero as a man from down below.

Childhood is the most pervasive influence in the decisions of the adult. This symbol of the vagabond, Matthew Bondman, batsman extraordinary, is at the heart of all James's formulations about society and its potential for self-transformation. Through all his seminal books, from *The Life of Captain Cipriani*, the novel *Minty Alley* to the astonishing and unorthodox brilliance of *Black Jacobins* and *Beyond A Boundary*, this theme will be affirmed: to engage the collective energies of the world down below is the first and only certain path towards the liberation of person and community.

But there is an obstacle at once external and within. The shadow of a new plantation class slides across this vision in the form of a professional salariat of politician and technocrat and numerous functionaries of an expanding bureaucracy.

This class is almost brand new. They have arrived very recently, children of the poor, without ancestry in wealth, unfamiliar with the chairs they sit in, always dressed for work as though they were going to a wedding, and in a desperate hurry to correct a previous history of personal deprivation.

Politics is, in a literal sense of the word, a serious business of protecting bread and private banks of butter. They are a nervous class, apprehensive, vulnerable, fragile. And they recognise the potential dynamic in this process between their role and the wider terrain of ordinary folk.

They recognise, too, that this enclave of experts can be mobilised into a force of intellectual mercenaries, mediating on behalf of the existing state power, and they are often successful with this strategy.

They are not wicked men; and it may be argued that they are not wholly without honour. But they are like those men the Nigerian novelist, Chinua Achebe, talks about in his novel, *A Man of The People:*

> A man who has just come in from the rain and dried his body and put on dry clothes is more reluctant to get out again than another who has been indoors all the time.

> The trouble with our new nation...was that none of us had been indoors long enough...We had all been in the rain together until yesterday. Then a handful of us – the smart and the lucky and hardly

ever the best – had scrambled for the shelter our former rulers left, and had taken it over and barricaded themselves in. And from within they sought to persuade the rest through numerous loud-speakers...that all argument should cease and the whole people speak with one voice.

I went to see James in July, along with our mutual friend, the American historian, Professor Vincent Harding. Nello looked very neat, almost formal in the courtesy of his greeting. There was an attractive serenity about him.

He asked after Jesse Jackson and his prospects in the American presidential campaign. Harding gave, stage by stage, an account of Jackson's rise to prominence. And then C.L.R. said, with that old, characteristic circle of the hand: 'I have been following this rise, but tell me, does he know where he is going to land?' It was a very Jamesian question; and it led me back to his philosophical position on what you might call a meaningful life. The passage is from *Beyond A Boundary*:

> Time would pass, old empires would fall and new ones take their place, the relations of classes had to change before I discovered that it is not the quality of goods and utility which matters, but movement; not where you are or what you have; but where you have come from, where you are going, and the rate at which you are getting there.

July, 1988, and the question about Jesse Jackson was the last and among the most vivid memories I have of him: shrewd, alert, mischievous in his humour, and always concerned. Until the eve of his death, he was a victim of the saddest kind of neglect a country can inflict on one of its national treasures. If we forgive, it is perhaps because a certain social and intellectual backwardness did not allow the political directorate to recognise that such a treasure existed. But he has laid, for us in this region, the foundations of a native intellectual tradition, and set the highest standards of political morality.

To have known you, Nello, and shared so much of your life is a blessing I do not want to measure.

Note

1.   Trinidad did host Carifest in 2006.

12 | *The Honourable Member**

I want to offer you the social portrait of a man you have often seen, and whom many of you may have some reason to admire. He was born some 40-odd years ago in an urban village with a local primary school. Later he attended two secondary schools before going on a Government scholarship to a university abroad. He qualified as a lawyer, felt a passing interest in the study of economics, but was persuaded by his godfather, a senior public figure, to return to Barbados where his chances of a political career looked very promising. He had a moderate success at the bar, before he successfully contested an election. He has served as a Minister of Government and represented his country in various international negotiations. Today he owns three houses and a chicken farm. There is also substantial rumour of investments in an auxiliary transport service locally known as the mini-bus, and shares in various tourist resorts. His known assets are estimated to be in the region of a figure, not under three quarters of a million dollars.

He occupies a large four-bedroom house in the rural suburbs with an ample view of six parishes, and a horizon of sky that disappears into the deep-water harbour. His tastes have been influenced by foreign travel. The furniture is modern Scandinavian. There is a conspicuous assortment of Moroccan rugs, exquisitely patterned in crimson and gold. These were acquired as a gift after a brief romance in southern Spain. The walls, on all sides, are disfigured by juvenile souvenirs of illuminated nights in New York, eating out along the Bay in San Francisco, racially mixed couples at play around a kidney-shaped swimming pool in Miami. There are no books anywhere. An electric trolley moves itself around with drinks. The family has two cars: one

---

*   This address, made to the 40th Annual Conference of the Barbados Workers Union on August 29, 1981, a detailed treatment of the Caribbean middle class, particularly – but not only – those of the class who function as 'Honourable Members'. Parts of this description recur, explicitly or by echo, in other speeches by Lamming.

Italian, the other Japanese. But his cultural preference in magazine reading and film is irreversibly American.

He is careful in his choice of clothes. Abroad he was known to wear pink carnations in his button hole, but promptly dropped this style of decoration on his return, since flowers on a man encourage Barbadians to question his sexual tendencies. He lunches frequently in hotel restaurants on the south coast; dines about twice a week on the west coast. On Sundays he may take small parties for a buffet feast at the Atlantis hotel. Much of this eating has to do with political business.

He has two children: a girl who went to St Winifred's from a junior school called St Gabriel's and a son who, after problems at home, was placed in a minor public school in the South of England. Neither has ever seen the inside of a government elementary school. Neither has any recollection of ever travelling by bus in Barbados.

I refrain from offering you a physical description of the Honourable Member, since he is of a type who bitterly resent any reference to the skin in analysing social relationships in this island. It is a sufficient guide to add that his wife is a lady, distinguished by her hair, which we have been trained to call, 'good.' They have both retained certain travel documents which allow them indefinite residence elsewhere.

Many of his contemporaries had a privilege of schooling similar to his. They may have been less enterprising, but they have all made notable contributions in education and at the upper levels of the Civil Service. Some have been chairmen of corporations; junior functionaries in development banks of one kind or another. A few are in general medical practice. No one of his acquaintance went into business.

Let us identify him as the Honourable Member, a man who sees his achievements as the base for an expanding personal prosperity in the years ahead. If we are to understand the true history of this man, and his relations to his public duties, we cannot concentrate only on the period of those 40-odd years you have seen him around. Nor can we view him exclusively in the context of his personal life without any reference to his social formation. Such a limited perspective can only lead to fruitless and self-degrading gossip. So let us try to see that process of social evolution which has brought him to this criterion of success which he and a whole class of men like himself now embrace as the most desirable reward of their efforts in this life: social power and material wealth.

His great grandfather was born in the parish of St George in 1877, a year after the Confederation Riots. He was put out to labour as an estate hand at the age of nine. Twelve years later, an ox-cart crippled him for life. He had already had a son of four. But it would have been useless in those days to argue a case for compensation. He lingered until the age of 40, elaborating on the stories he had heard in his childhood about the great insurrection which had engaged a turbulent underclass of workers against elements of the merchant/planter class of the day. Plantation families fled their homes to seek refuge on the ships at anchor in Carlisle Bay. In St George alone, at Salters plantation, labourers had stolen or captured 12 acres of potatoes. Their adversaries said it was the work of communistic agitators. That charge, as you will see, has been the official explanation of any disruptive social action for more than a century. It is amazing that, to this day, men can still successfully make it their major appeal in what is thought to be an honest election.

The Honourable Member would be in this category.

His grandfather who was born in 1894 continued to pass on his own father's recollections of the Confederation Riots. He could never understand why Governor Hennessy should have included in his famous six points the outrageous proposal that 'the mental asylum in Barbados should open its doors to receive lunatics from other islands'. It made him adopt a conservative and unwelcoming restraint towards all foreigners who looked a little like himself. But he is very important for our understanding of his grandson, the Honourable Member, since his own work career introduces us to a remarkable category of men whose struggle for an independent form of employment influenced a development which led towards the achievement of the Honourable Member. This grandfather had distinguished himself as a cooper. He made and repaired every kind of wooden cask and tub you could imagine, and by this achievement of a technical skill, also made himself and the artisan class he represents indispensable to the technical function of the plantation. They were stubborn men, this artisan class of coopers, carpenters, masons and blacksmiths. They were men who had cultivated an immense pride in the excellent quality of the things they made. They had a simple and genuine dignity.

The Honourable Member would hardly remember him. But it was this grandfather who preached the absolute necessity of education.

He perceived the school as the only possible means of rescuing his offspring from the humiliations his ancestors had endured. The book, the lesson, pen and ink: these were his images of redemption. And that's why his son, the Honourable Member's father, born in 1914, was destined to be a teacher. The elementary school became their chapel, Harrison College their cathedral, and an English university, the Kingdom of Heaven.

And behind this immense effort was an even greater sacrifice of courage and will: the women who fathered many a household, nursed man and child without a wage and have remained to this day the last surviving example of legalised slave-labour.

Those indolent critics who treat the past as though it were an amputated limb to be buried and forgotten and who complain about my insistence on restoring it do not pay serious, critical attention to the society they describe. For a large proportion of those who rule our lives today from the executive, the judiciary, and all corners of the bureaucracy are the products of that tutelage I have described, and profoundly shaped by that social experience which has made the Honourable Member who he is. And I do not have to argue with you this morning that our rulers are not only very much alive, but may be with us for some time to come. And this is the point I want this social portrait to emphasise.

If we follow, in greater detail, that honourable line of ancestry from the estate hand in the 1880s to the professional great grandson in 1981, we shall not find a single dominant landlord, a powerful merchant banker, certainly no industrial capitalist or great shipowner. But it is precisely these categories of men and their representatives whom the Honourable Member and his class have to deal with in very complex negotiations on our behalf in the political and industrial centres of the world: from Tokyo to Toronto, London, Brussels, and New York. Our Honourable Member and his class, bright, ambitious and often patriotic men, assume these challenging tasks without any historical social experience of ownership and control of the means of production in their own country: just functionaries who take care of other people's business. It makes for a certain fragility at the heart of all their protestations against unfair terms of trade, or the subtle and not so subtle bullying by capitalist powers to make us shape a foreign policy that may not be in the interests of our people. It is a grave predicament for the Honourable Member and his class; and it is made all the more dangerous when this class, putting its own self-interests above and beyond social incentives, is so eager to separate itself, by lifestyle and the hunger for status, from the working-class base from which it derived. It is important for you, on the fortieth anniversary of this great Union of yours, to recognise very clearly that such a division in the social fabric makes you, the working class, the main bastion in the people's national defence. Not the army, nor the police, nor any arm of the state power, but you whose productive labour is the foundation of the country's survival and the major factor which will always determine what are our objective needs and how these should relate to genuine social demand. There is little or nothing mercenaries can do before a united working class that is absolutely clear about what it has to defend. But if we were to follow the lifestyle of the Honourable Member, a style which now threatens to be the dominant value for all ranks of the people; we shall stumble into a way of living where we consume what we do not produce, and produce what we scarcely consume.

Barbados will cease to be a distinct and recognisable society. All it would aspire to be is an efficient service station. Then, one mercenary could be enough.

It is clear, therefore, that the responsibilities of the Trade Union movement are essentially, and inescapably, political. There are dangers you must attend to, the most serious of which is the strategy to distract your attention from the politics of your life as an organised body of labour, and a distinct class in the country's production relations: to pin you down to concerns and preoccupations which do not go beyond disputes about wages and conditions of work; to limit your capacity to intervene as a dominant force in the creation of national policy.

Karl Marx is very prophetic on this point. In a speech to a delegation of German trade unionists in 1869, he said:

> Trade Unions are the schools of socialism. It is in Trade Unions that workers educate themselves and become socialists, because under their very eyes and every day the struggle with capital is taking place. Any political party, whatever its nature and without exception, can only hold the enthusiasm of the masses for a short time, momentarily; unions, on the other hand, lay hold on the masses in a more enduring way.

They alone are capable of representing a true working class party, and opposing a bulwark to the power of capital.

The fundamental basis of democracy should be the workers' control of their place of work, where every choice of programme and personnel from management to the floor, remains decisively within workers' power. That would be the most authentic arena of elections. Those who are afraid of such a development are afraid of genuine democracy.

The trade union, as a school of socialism, has a duty to encourage responsible debate about the relevance, and the function, of certain inherited models of government which evolved out of a social history that is not our own. It is not true that this particular electoral system is the only guarantee of a people's freedom, or that it is, indeed, such a guarantee from fear.

Since the independence of Barbados in 1965, both political parties have come to power. I think it is true to say that neither the Democratic Labour Party, nor the Barbados Labour Party, can be accused of repressive rule. Neither party in power has any history of political harassment of the people. Neither party has produced a leader who remotely resembles Gairy or Burnham. It would be impossible to defend a Barbadian who, any time after 1965, would claim abroad that he was a political refugee. On that score the record of both parties is excellent.

But I have observed the hardening of a social attitude which may confront the society with one of its greatest dangers: I refer to the increasing party tribalism which smothers all critical judgement about social and political issues, and makes the ordinary decent citizen afraid of being overheard.

It is as though members of the political parties see themselves as loyal warriors of two rival primitive tribes, each regarding the other's existence as a threat to his own; and where the tribe that comes to power takes possession of the total political estate, free at last to reward prizes to the most diligent of its own henchmen; and to punish, by careful exclusion, those whose tribal allegiance lies elsewhere. This party tribalism has nothing to do with politics, but leads to an exercise in petty victimisation which imposes silence on those who might otherwise contribute to shaping the critical intelligence of the nation.

It would be unjust to identify such practice exclusively with the present Administration; for I have listened, in the past, to volumes of similar complaint during the reign of the other party. In any case, it is idle at this stage to engage in distributing blame. The fact of the matter is that such an atmosphere exists; and members of this great national institution, the Barbados Workers' Union, who straddle both parties, have a political duty to deal with this example of dysfunction. I put it that way because I do not believe that such practice derives from the particular viciousness or vindictiveness of any particular Minister of Government at any time. The average professional politician is no less virtuous than the average citizen in other occupations: the businessman or the academic who conducts a faculty politics of a particularly sinister kind. But there is, I think, an important connection between the practice of punishment and reward, and a system which confers such an undemocratic range of patronage on those who hold office. This dysfunction becomes particularly acute in the tribal politics of small islands.

Sir Arthur Lewis in *The Agony of the Eight*, speaking of small islands and Government says:

> Everybody depends on the Government for something, however small, so most are reluctant to offend it. The civil servants live in fear; the police avoid unpleasantness; the Trade Unions are tied to the party; the newspapers depend on Government advertisements.

A one party mentality advocating a two party arrangements, is a recipe for disaster. I have followed political movements in Jamaica very closely since the 1950s and observed during my visits over the years how this party tribalism grew; became institutionalised; and ultimately nurtured the political violence that was to afflict that country.

There is another danger you have lived with, and which has been eroding the consciousness of our people, almost without notice. It is what Professor Gordon Lewis, of the University of Puerto Rico, has referred to as 'recolonisation by religion'. Capitalist promotion of liberal democracy in developing countries goes hand in hand with the commercial sponsorship of Jesus Christ; and it has nothing to do with Jesus, who was not a man for the marketplace.

I take the view that among the most undesirable bandits probing Caribbean society are the vagrant religious evangelists. They have been able to buy their way into the approval of those who manage our radio stations. They wake us at dawn, and pursue us throughout the day, with these militant appeals to withdraw our attention from the most urgent issues that affect our lives. It is a form of collective hypnosis by radio; and no one seems to question their motives. They have an assignment to put the minds of our people to sleep, and to mobilise that psychic energy which has no outlet into other and more honourable forms of organisational activity.

The success of the People's Cathedral reflects a critical failure of the Trade Union Movement in educating the consciousness of our people out of such joyful stupor.

These are not anti-religious sentiments; for I have a deep respect for the religious sensibility in its search to give life a creative meaning. But what you ought to place at the centre of national debate is this unforgivable, commercial blasphemy against our people's capacity to believe; for it weakens their resistance to all other forms of external penetration.

My predecessor in this role drew attention to the tasks of education which confront the Union. The Labour college should be a national institution familiar as the political parties throughout the land, as the main centre of a popular intellectual culture, attracting men and women of all races and social backgrounds, and of every level of learning.

The Trade Union Movement has the financial capacity and the human resources to give birth to a popular theatre, assigning its own actors, directors, and writers to translate the day-to-day problems of the working class into a form of entertainment and instruction with which every member of the working class can immediately identify. It may perhaps win back the victims of the People's Cathedral to an arena of genuinely spiritual communion.

I don't know what are the creative consequences of Carifesta. But whatever critics of its organisation may justly say, as a cultural event, it was a most remarkable success. There was the demonstration of the Jamaicans that their country has now provided us with a formidable school of drama, the admirable professionalism of the Cubans who came and left without doing us any harm, and were even admired and embraced by those who saw them, and the vibrancy of the Surinamese at all times. This was a moment of cultural resistance in which the

Barbados Workers Union might have played a central role. It must prepare itself for such a role.

The political sovereignty of a people is impossible unless it rests upon an authentic cultural base created by its working people.

13 | *Nationalism and Nation**

This is, I think, my second visit to Dominica; I came here very many years ago. But this morning was the first time I had ever seen the island from the air, and coming from Martinique one watches this landscape which looks so utterly undomesticated, a landscape that seems almost to be asleep waiting for some hand to arouse it. And I kept wondering in that plane what secrets were buried in those hills that would be the evolution of a future for you.

Men and women, from the beginning of history, have had to enter into some alliance with nature. They have had to observe nature to see what it is that nature produces or what it is they can make nature produce in order to secure their physical existence. This process of man trying to bend nature to his will, of man forcing nature to meet his own needs is what we call work. There is no way in which man can turn nature into his own history except through his work or through his labour.

It is therefore absolutely impossible to understand a society or the culture of a society without reference to the history of labour. That is, labour is the foundation of all culture. And that is what I meant when I was saying in an article in *Contact* that we have to understand that the farmer and the fisherman are cultural workers; and that all questions relating to the processes of social transformation are essentially cultural questions.

I want to show you by a short illustration from *In the Castle of my Skin* how the movement of culture from the tending of plants and animals to the cultivation of the mind takes place as we live in society. The passage I'm going to use is intended to show how the way people come to think is determined by the way they feed themselves. This is one passage:

---

* Extracts from a talk given in Dominica in 1982, transcribed from a tape on which there was unfortunately no information about its precise date, audience or sponsorship. The extracts have been edited. The newspaper *Contact* was a major regional newspaper in the 1980s sponsored by the Caribbean Council of Churches and edited by journalist Ricky Singh.

An estate where fields of sugar cane had once crept like an open secret across the land had been converted into a village that absorbed some three thousand people. An English landowner, Mr Creighton, had died, and the estate fell to his son through whom it passed to another son who in his turn died, surrendering it to yet another. Generations had lived and died in this remote corner of a small British colony, the oldest and least adulterated of British colonies…

This is a glimpse of plantation society with sugar the base of the island's physical existence. And what we go on to do in that passage is to show how, through a division of labour, tensions develop between people whose livelihoods are made on that sugar estate. There is this tension between the overseer, who is a black man, and the rest of the village. The overseer, in order to maintain his authority, is always very austere and very aggressive; and he sees in the ordinary folk on the plantation a potential enemy to this authority of his.

My people are low-down nigger people. My people don't like to see their people get on. The language of the overseer. The language of the civil servant. The myth had eaten through their consciousness like moths through the pages of ageing documents. Not taking chances with you people, my people. They always let you down. Make others say we're not responsible, we've no sense of duty. That's what the low-down nigger people do to us, their people. Then the others say we've no sense of duty. Like children under the threat of hell fire they accepted instinctively that the others, meaning the white, were superior, yet there was always the fear of realising that it might be true. This world of the others' imagined perfection hung like a dead weight over their energy. If the low-down nigger people weren't what they are, the others couldn't say anything about us. Suspicion, distrust, hostility. These operated in every decision. You never can tell with my people. It was the language of the overseer, the language of the Government servant, and later the language of the lawyers and doctors who had returned stamped like an envelope with what they called the culture of the Mother Country.

The plantation, the base of the material existence, is going to produce a particular mode of thought; and the theory around that is that those who control the material production of life will also control the mental production of life. If I own and control the productive forces of a society I will dictate what is the mode of perception in that society; I will dictate how that society defines itself. And because plantation society was racist and needed to be racist in order to survive, racism permeated the thought and the consciousness of all who lived in plantation society. That is the particular lesson of that passage: in all society, those who control material production will also control mental production.

There are a variety of ways in which, in human history, nations have come about. But there are perhaps two components that are necessary for nation. One has to do with specified territory, a more or less homogeneous people living in a specified territory; and the other has to do with this people having a consciousness of itself as nation. Let me read you two passages that establish this.

The novel *Of Age and Innocence* is a study of colonialism in its last stages, that is, when they are coming to the social settlement of internal self-government. And this is part of a speech that a man, a writer attached to a political movement, makes: in a way, it is his definition of nationalism, the ingredient that will make nation.

> Nationalism is not only frenzy and struggle with all its necessary demand for the destruction of those forces which condemn you to the status we call colonial. The national spirit is deeper and more enduring than that. It is original and necessary as the root to the body of a tree. It is the source of discovery and creation. It is the private feeling you experience of possessing and being possessed by the whole landscape of the place where you were born, the freedom which helps you to recognise the rhythm of the winds, the silence and aroma of the night, rocks, water, pebble and branch, animal and bird noise, the temper of the sea and the mornings arousing nature everywhere to the silent and sacred communion between you and the roots you have made on this island. It is the bond between each man and that corner of the earth which his birth and his work have baptised with the name, home.

In other words, he is rooting this nationalism first of all in what he calls a possession, not a material possession, but a spiritual possession of the landscape in which you live. A landscape in which you know the rhythm of the wind. A landscape in which you know the smell of the sea. A landscape in which you know the texture of the stone and rock.

These are not objects outside of you: they are a part of your consciousness. This is one of the foundations of nationalism and of nation.

The question that is being put by that passage is: in what part of the Caribbean do West Indian people feel that about the landscape when so much of the landscape is owned by hostile strangers?

The second passage comes from *Season of Adventure*. It is now after Independence and what we see in the book is an independent country collapsing. The First Republic is going to fall. The idea is that these social settlements called independence cannot last. The book is also a celebration of the steel band. These guys, drummers, are going to a ceremony and they are discussing Independence. They are discussing this freedom that the Republic of San Cristobal has just won. Their names are half nicknames, half real names: you know how we do this in the Caribbean. Crim and Powell. Powell is the really dangerous one. Powell is the one who assassinated the President. And Powell has not yet been found. And they are arguing, in a way, about freedom. Gort is the greatest drummer and the most believing of them.

And Powell says:

> "A man must got somethin' that he can't let go,' said Powell, 'like how Gort hold that drum."

> The drum dipped its sound; then surfaced through the air, calling like a human voice from the tonelle. The women's voice grew suddenly loud, exulting in the chorus which started to summon their dead. Crim pondered the gradual retreat of the tenor drum.

> "I was thinkin', he said, 'how the Independence would change all that wipin' out, change everythin' that confuse."

> Powell's pride had been aroused. His voice came loud and fretful.

> "Change my arse," he shouted, "is Independence what it is? One day in July you say you want to be that there thing, an' one day in a next July the law say all right, from now you's what you askin' for. What change that can change? Might as well call your dog a cat an' hope to hear him mew. Is only words an' names what don' signify nothin'."

113

The politics of freedom had always haunted Powell's imagination. Day after day he would punish his friends with argument in the Forest Reserve. He would relate the news as though it were domestic rumour he alone had heard.

"Independence aint nothin' till it free," he said. "An' it don' have two freedoms any place. Is how I see it, Crim, clear an' straight like you beat you drum."

Crim was more docile. He could never understand why Powell should suspect any gift he had been offered. Powell's pride was like the woman's shame whenever he had to receive.

"I say it was a real freedom happen when the tourist army went away," Crim said. "It look a real freedom they give San Cristobal."

"It don't have that kind o' givin'", said Powell, trying to restrain his anger. "Is wrong to say that, 'cause free is free an' it don't have no givin'. Free is how you is from the start an' when it look different you got to move, just move, an' when you movin' say that is a natural freedom make you move. You can't move to freedom, Crim, 'cause freedom is what you is, an' where you start, an' where you always got to stand."

This nationalism that these two characters are speaking about; this sense of nation which is both political and cultural, I am suggesting to you that it does not exist in this region. Whatever colour the flags, whatever rhyme the music to the anthem, what these men are talking about does not exist in this region. Let us see if we can arrive at the reason why, so far, it does not exist.

Historically, the move to nationalism has often come in developed places from what is called the bourgeoisie, who have very real interests to defend against alien powers. The equivalent to this in the Caribbean would be called the middle class, which does not exist: what we have in the Caribbean is a class in formation. And I want to say that because of the particular social formation of this class, it is an extremely vulnerable class. It is the most vulnerable point of the nation in our experience. It seems to me that if you wanted to ensure the defence of the national integrity you may have to turn to another group of people and that would be organised labour. The problem for us here is that these tendencies we identify in what is called the middle class emerge in the leadership of organised labour. And that is what the rank and file of the working people have got to keep their eyes on: the compromise, the ambivalence of leadership throughout the trade unions of this region.

I want to deal now with what I call the imperial environment. Our political leaders have to do a lot of business with the United States. Within 48 hours of winning an election they are on a plane and in Washington. But most unfortunately for us, it seems they have little knowledge of the history of the relations of the United States to the rest of the Americas, even, say, from a cut-off point of the beginning of the century. And what I want to offer you now quite seriously is a self-portrait of the United States' image and presence in the Americas from about 1898 to the 1980s. I say self-portrait because I am going to let Americans speak for themselves. And I want to begin with a most remarkable document, written in November 1935 by a Marine Commander by the name of General Smedley Butler. This is what he says:

> I spent thirty-three years and four months in active service as a member of our country's most agile military force, the Marine Corps. I served in all commission ranks, from a second lieutenant to a major general and during that period, I spent most of my time being a high class muscle man for big business, for Wall Street and for bankers. In short, I was a racketeer for capitalism. Thus I helped to make Mexico, and especially Tampeco, safe for American oil interests in 1914. I helped make Haiti and Cuba a decent place for the National City Bank to collect revenues in. I helped to purify Nicaragua for the International Banking Houses of Brown & Bros. from 1909 to 1912. I brought light to the Dominican Republic for American sugar interests in 1916. I helped make Honduras right for American fruit companies in 1923. In China in 1927, I helped see to it that Standard Oil went its way unmolested. During those years I had, as the boys in the back room would say, "a swell racket." I was rewarded with honors, medals, promotions. Looking back on it, I feel I might have given Al Capone a few hints – the best he could do was to operate his racket in three city districts, we marines operated on three continents.

Eric Williams has identified that between 1898 and 1960 the United States was involved in no less than thirty-two invasions or comparable violations of the territories of its neighbours. The second self-portrait is more complicated than Butler's. This is a memorandum set in 1953 by the late Nelson Rockefeller to President Eisenhower. He is reporting to Eisenhower on two things, the importance of aid and the meaning of natural resources to the United States. I am quoting him:

> We should not ignore the vital fact that virtually all our natural rubber, manganese, chromium and tin, as well as substantial proportions of our zinc, copper and oil and a third or more of the lead and aluminum we need comes from abroad. And furthermore, that it is chiefly drawn from the under-developed areas of Africa and Asia which are in the orbit of one or more of the military arrangements we have set up.

You have been led to believe that throughout the world, the United States has a great preoccupation with communism. But it is not communism that worries the American power structure: what concerns the American power structure is keeping within the orbit of its control this manganese, this chromium, this copper, this zinc, this oil, because it is upon these natural resources and only upon these natural resources that the industrial empires of the United States can exist and flourish in the future.

Anti-communism is not part of an American belief so much as it is part of an American device: any time there is an attempt among people to look after their interests, which may be in conflict with the interests of the United States, they will get people to identify you as a communist. You may be a Catholic priest; you may be a member of the Salvation Army: if it appears that you are in any way promoting your interests and those interests come into some conflict with those of the United States, your immediate environment is asked to identify you as communist. And they have got our political leaders to buy it and even to use it in their elections.

In the same memorandum to Eisenhower, Rockefeller moves on to add:

> The most significant example in practice of what I mean has been the Iranian experiment with which, as you will remember, I was

directly concerned. By the use of economic aid we are now well established in the economy of that country. The strengthening of our economic position in Iran has enabled us to acquire control over her entire foreign policy and in particular to make her join the Baghdad Pact. Sir, at the present time, the Shah would not dare even to make a single change in his Cabinet without consulting our Ambassador.

Have you heard that? The function of aid is to control the domestic and national policy of a foreign country: 'At the present time the Shah would not dare even to make a change in his Cabinet without consulting our Ambassador'. And when, 25 years or so later we read of extraordinary explosions in Iran, people are asking what is wrong with these people, are they crazy? Who is this Ayatollah?

You must reflect on the accumulated rage. The accumulated hurt. The accumulated humiliation that those people would have felt living under the arrangement described here by Rockefeller. They weren't crazy; they were just acting out of a history of rage and humiliation that had been imposed on them.

Now I come to something that is very near you here. If there are any members of the Peace Corps present, try to understand that this is not an attack on you. I am trying to show the pattern of thinking that has been the United States' relation to this hemisphere. I am going to read you a long extract from a memorandum issued by the United States Department to Peace Corps volunteers:

A war of ideas is being waged in the world. In the present stage of the world it is of imperative importance that the developing countries be kept within the framework of the West. It is essential to reinforce the struggle against the ideas of neutralism and national egoism.

That is, the nationalism we were speaking about. It goes on:

A volunteer is a frontline soldier in the fight against communism and despotism for freedom. Teach the American way of life and show the people of less developed areas how to think rationally and act effectively. Use all means and opportunities for strengthening the positions of those political personalities and groups which support the ideas of the West. Direct their effort in the field of political and social development to counteract the spread of communism. Foster and inculcate the ideas and methods of private enterprise and personal initiative and demonstrate their obvious superiority. This is the only way the developing countries can expect the establishment of effective cooperation with the West. In countries where the leaders adhere to the principles of nationalism or socialism volunteers should cautiously but steadfastly oppose the dissemination and acceptance of their theories.

Mark the words well: 'In countries where the leaders adhere to the principles of nationalism or socialism, oppose them.'

There is no reason we should be surprised by that. A state power which has imperial interests has got to defend those interests; and in order to defend these interests it has to collect battalions of intellectual mercenaries to help it defend those interests.

When President Reagan was about to be inaugurated he had a report made for him on what should be the strategies of the United States in dealing with the Americas. It is called the Santa Fe report. It covers all areas, but the area I want to bring briefly to your attention is the area of education and some advice given to President Reagan which, incidentally, has been executed. The opening phrase reminds one of the Peace Corps statement. 'The war is for the minds of mankind': that is how it opens.

> The war is for the minds of mankind. Ideo-politics will prevail... Education is the medium by which cultures retain, pass on and even pioneer their past. Thus, whoever controls the education system determines the past – or how it is viewed – as well as the future. Tomorrow is in the hands and the heads of those who are being taught today. [The United States] should export ideas and images which will encourage individual liberty, political responsibility and respect for private property. A campaign to capture the Ibero-American elite through the media of radio, television, books, articles, pamphlets, grants, fellowships and prizes must be initiated.

And this is the insult, what he is saying is:

> We know them. They like scholarships to the United States. They like fellowships. They like the things they write published. We will

facilitate that. And since we know that that is how they see their career mobility there should be no problem.

In other words, the Caribbean intellectual is up for sale. That is 1980. And the last portrait is from this year.

Very remarkable, this piece. In April this year, the CARICOM Foreign Ministers met in Belize and during this meeting there was a document under consideration which dealt with the conditions which the United States was laying down for investment aid under the Caribbean Basin Initiative. The document said that to be defined as a qualifying country for investment purposes, a country had to enter into a bilateral executive arrangement with the United States for the exchange of information, including information that would otherwise be subject to non-disclosure under local law. The United States is saying that one of the conditions of its Caribbean Basin Initiative is that in the interest of the United States, you will have to suspend your own law to meet a request of the United States; and that what you call your sovereignty is a status which the United States may or may not recognise as the United States sees fit.

It is a repeat of the Shah all over again. All countries have information which it is illegal for anybody, including the Prime Minister of the country, to disclose; the United States' condition for receiving CBI money is that your law of non-disclosure will have to be suspended.

Now, with the exception of *Caribbean Contact*, the only decent newspaper in the entire region, not a single national newspaper saw fit to expose and attack this insult. This press which now offers itself as a great crusader of people's sovereignty; this press: the *Daily Gleaner*, the *Advocate*, the *Nation*, the *Express* – none of them, crusaders of people's sovereignty, saw fit to deal with this insult to the Caribbean people. And it was left only to the Leader of the Opposition in Barbados, Mr Errol Barrow, in a statement on the eve of the Heads of Government Conference in Ocho Rios; Mr Barrow using the weight of his stature as a regional statesman to come out and identify this condition as an insult to the dignity and self-respect of the Caribbean people.

From 1898 and the confession of the Marine Commander to the 1980s and the conditions of the Caribbean Basin Initiative, we see in the history of the United States's relations to the rest of the Americas a consistent pattern of motive and intention for which the only word is imperialism. And we have to ask ourselves, given the mistakes they have made over and over again in this region, why do they maintain this consistency of error? Why? I think a large part of the reason has to do with the racism of the United States. Racism is an organic part of the culture of white America. They started their democratic history with the wanton destruction of a great Indian people; and they continued that history with the slave crucifixion of a great African people. This is their intellectual ancestry; and they have never been able to perceive any portion of the non-white world as qualifying for equal status with white men.

In the light of that intellectual ancestry of racism it isn't even that men like Reagan are particularly wicked; it is that in that area of perception they are utterly crippled. They are products of a particular disease which they are not at this stage in any position to heal. In these circumstances, it would be a great mistake if the Prime Minister of Dominica or the Prime Minister of Barbados or Antigua or St Lucia or wherever imagined that when one of the men in the White House looks across at them from that table he does not see, first and foremost, a nigger. Some may be good niggers and some may be bad niggers: in their view, Maurice Bishop is a bad, bad, bad nigger. He is a very bad nigger, compared to others who are reasonably decent niggers. They make a mistake if they don't see that. It is against that kind of background – that background of the Marine Commander, that background of the Rockefeller memorandum, that background of the Santa Fe report, that background of the insulting condition for being eligible for the investment; it is against that background that all Caribbean people will have to decide where they stand when imperialism and the newspaper mercenaries of imperialism make attacks against Grenada. When the chips are down and you have to choose between an honourable brother of this regional family and a hostile stranger, I stand with that brother. That's where I stand.

14 | *Labour and the Humanising of the Landscape**

On the evening of June 23, 1980, Walter Rodney was buried, at the age of 38. It was a people's funeral. Earlier in the day, thousands of Guyanese had walked over a distance of 12 miles behind the murdered body of this young historian. He was not the first victim of political murder in Guyana, but the radical nature of his commitment as a teacher and activist, the startling promise that his life symbolised, made of his death something of a novel tragedy.

Directives had gone out to government employees that they should avoid this occasion; yet no one could recall, in the entire history of the country, so large and faithful a gathering assembled to reflect on the horror that has been inflicted on the nation. For Guyana has become a land of horrors. Democracy was no longer on trial here. The question was whether it would survive this official crucifixion.

The Caribbean has been deprived of a great creative mind; but Walter Rodney had achieved at an early age, the special distinction of being a permanent part of a unique tradition of intellectual leadership among Africans and people of African descent in the Americas. He belongs to the same order of importance as Marcus Garvey and W.E.B. Dubois, George Padmore and C.L.R. James. Products of various doctrines of imperialism, they had initiated through their work, as writers and orators of distinction, a profound reversal of values. It is not possible to have a comprehensive view of all the ramifications of Africa's encounter with Europe without reference to these men.

Walter Rodney consolidated and extended that work. His scholarship was sure, but it was also a committed and partisan scholarship. He believed that history was a way of ordering knowledge which could become an active part of the consciousness of an uncertified mass of ordinary people and which could be used by all as an instrument of

---

*   Foreword to Walter Rodney, *A History of the Guyanese Working People: 1881.1905*, Johns Hopkins University Press, Baltimore, MD., 1981.

social change. He taught from that assumption. He wrote out of that conviction. And it seemed to have been the informing influence on his relations with the organised working people of Guyana.

Rodney begins this enquiry some two centuries after the introduction of slave labour and about 50 years after the formal emancipation. It is an indication of his sense of priorities, his critical realism as a historian, that he should deliberately focus our interest on the peculiar character of the landscape. It is not just a casual reminder that this coastal strip of Guyana was hazardous terrain. It is the emphatic and persuasive way he situates men and women in nature. He can be at once elaborate and precise in defining the categories of capital and labour; but first he plunges us into the sodden realities of mud and faeces, the menace of flood either from the sea or from overwhelming torrents of rain.

Unlike many a Caribbean island, Guyana did not offer itself easily for human settlement. There was no instant welcome. Every triumph of cultivation was subdued by the constant fear that overnight the ocean would advance and swallow up the achievement. The morning would awaken men to the smell of animal corpses. For days there would follow the spectacle of a rotting goat or sheep or cow, a decomposition of carcasses stuck or afloat across the hidden landscape. Workers quenched their thirst from the same mud water. Fever struck; gastroenteritis prevailed. They waded through a catalogue of pestilence. Transport was impossible. Work had to stop. It was a daily battle for survival. Sometimes they recovered just in time to lament the arrival of fierce and prolonged drought. One tries hard to imagine the fate of children and it may not be surprising that there is little mention of them here. Meanwhile, the planter fretted over the disintegration of roads, the inconvenience of sick workers. The harshness of their rule reflected the panic and impatience they felt at the loss of capital.

Dutch agricultural engineering had devised a way of reclaiming the land, and African labour found in the concept of the polder a means of digging and draining while setting up a structure of dams that would offer some defence against the sea and other threats of flood. It was a stupendous effort by labour to make the land suitable for cultivation of sugar cane, and the maintenance of the polder would be a continuing anxiety. Reflecting the scale of labour involved in the original construction of waterways, the Venn Commission of 1948 estimated that each square mile of cane cultivation involved the provision of 49 miles of drainage canals and ditches, and 16 miles of higher level waterways used for transportation and irrigation. The commissioners noted that the construction of these waterways must have entailed the moving of at least one hundred million tons of soil.

The point Rodney wants to be remembered is the means whereby such labour was undertaken.

This meant that slaves moved 100 million tons of heavy water-logged clay with shovel in hand, while enduring conditions of perpetual mud and water...Working people continued making a tremendous contribution to the *humanisation* of the Guyanese coastal landscape.

It is the operative word, humanisation, that confirms his real intention. Such an emphasis leads to an overwhelming conclusion. The history of humanising this landscape is primarily the history of those hands. Retelling this history was the task Rodney had set for himself over two volumes, the first of which must now be the last. It was the task of excavating and reaffirming that particular history.

Caribbean scholars have, on the whole, concentrated on the intricate arguments and provisions made by those who ruled the land, those whose concept of social responsibility was confined to their exercise of power and to the protection of their interests as a dominant ruling group. This is an important contribution, but Rodney was engaged in illuminating our understanding from a different perspective. Working people of African and Indian ancestry in Guyana have had a history of active struggle, which it has been our habit to omit or underestimate in political discourse about the past.

If they often met with failure against the combined power of planters and the imperial parliament that sponsored their oppression, it remains true that every struggle planted a seed of creative disruption and aided the process that released new social forces in the continuing drama between capital and labour. Moreover, it is in the course of that struggle that we can discover the origins and growth of the middle and professional classes. And it is their failure to grasp the meaning and possibilities of this connection that still makes them so vulnerable to continuing external influence.

But it is also in that dramatic encounter with nature that Rodney offers us a view of certain tendencies that help to define the mind of the ruling group. Neither planters nor parliament could legislate the contingencies of nature; rich and poor alike were condemned to live in a state of emergency. The politics of survival were argued in the language of dams, dikes, canals, drainage, and irrigation. Flood and drought were alternating names for the same demon, which could visit dispossession and even total disaster on the unfortunate. But a common defence against natural disaster was often undermined by rival capitalist interests.

When Rodney begins this enquiry, in 1881, the legislature was the exclusive forum of the white planter class. Justice in the swamps was ordained by the rule of skin. This abnormality would further complicate what started as a history of contradictions. Work makes possible a process of production, and the planters perceived this to be true. But work is also the essential base on which people struggle to create a design for social living. Planters could not perceive this to be true without contradicting their original reason for being there. The workers' achievement of humanising the landscape and creating a design for social living had to be interpreted and dealt with as a threat to the foundations of the planter enterprise. Planters were therefore unanimous in their recognition of labour as a potential enemy. But such agreement could not always survive the conflict within their own ranks. And so in Guyana in the last decades of the nineteenth century, this social defect of the planter class would be brutally exposed by the challenge of nature.

It was certainly in everyone's interest to provide a common defence against the sea; flood water did not discriminate among its victims. When the dams burst, and the dikes gave way, and the canals were drowned, the subsequent damage could be seen as a collective disaster. But there was no binding concept of community to meet a challenge of such scale. The villagers, enduring at their subsistence level, were without any resources of wealth. They didn't qualify for credit, and loans for the purpose of sea defence would only be granted if there were an absolute certainty these would be recovered. Any obligation of a collective character had, therefore, to be met by the planter class, the only body of men whose personal fortunes and political authority could guarantee some measure of protection against the possibility of destruction. But even when individual fortunes were at stake, many of them worried over the apparent conflict of development costs and returns on capital. It seemed unsound business to tie up capital in costs of protecting their property over a period that might prove such protection to be unprofitable.

In spite of the impartial fury of the elements, many would calculate their first priority according to the advantage of the individual estate. They were profoundly resistant to any experiment in social collaboration. It is as though the principle of material self-interest feels itself betrayed by such forms of human partnership.

If this point is emphasised, it is simply to invite the imagination to grasp how utterly naked and defenceless poor villagers were in this sordid conflict of planter self-interests. Engineers might argue until the sky came down, yet many a planter found it difficult to grasp why the impoverished village could not possibly be asked to meet the cost of their own defence against the sea.

But it was, perhaps, inconceivable that a sense of communal responsibility could develop in this planter type, since Guyana was perceived as just one corner in a wider imperial playground for private speculation. The international character of the capitalist experiment encouraged the imaginative and energetic to shift scene whenever fortunes waned and disenchantment set in. So Quintin Hogg, a wealthy planter with large holdings in Guyana and the Caribbean, could tell the West India Royal Commission of 1897:

> I myself have just gone in for a block of land in the Malaya peninsula for putting in coffee, exactly the coffee I should put in Demerara. I pay for my labour there 4 pence or 5 pence per day. Why should I go and put coffee in Demerara? My machinery will not serve me, and I should have to pay double and treble for my labour to what I have to pay in the East.

Sugar or coffee, it made no difference what the crop was. Malaya workers or Guyana workers, it made no difference which hands made possible the process of production that would satisfy Hogg's expanding self-interest.

There is abundant evidence that this imperial approach to the Caribbean has not changed substantially. The region is still defined, in some areas, as a blue chip investment. A new breed of speculators arrive from Europe and North America with the assurance that labour is cheap and that the workforce can be made stable with the promise of becoming modern consumers. The earliest signs of serious revolt within the working class persuade them that it is time to depart. And they shift, Hogg-fashion, to more accommodating regions.

It is the history of this class, emerging from the ordeal of free labour, that enables us to see how external factors worked to impose very definite limitations on the initiative of the Guyanese people; how the scale and special character of the landscape, grander and more varied than the islands, encouraged the imagination to vary its response to other possibilities of survival than the dominant activity of the sugar plantation. But it was the politics of sugar that determined the frontiers of struggle.

The African workforce was hardly emancipated from slavery when they recognised that free labour had provided them with a new mode of organised resistance. Rodney records 1841 as the year in which the Guyanese workers successfully organised the first strike in the history of the working class in that country. They had initiated a pattern of resistance that would take different forms.

Later, men would organise themselves into mobile task gangs, visiting different plantations and checking out the conditions of work before committing themselves to any agreement with an employer. It was an exercise of freedom that threatened the Planters' monopoly of control over the conduct of the existing labour force. And since sugar cane was the kind of crop that had to be gotten from the field to the factory within a very short time, excessive delay could mean ruination. Planter and worker understood this urgency. Workers would, therefore, effectively time the withdrawal of their labour when it would be most needed.

It is Rodney's contention that the ex-slaves became plantation workers immediately after slavery was abolished and proceeded to think and act very much as modern proletarians would. We cannot grasp the cultural history of the Guyanese people without investigating further the mode of thought and struggle that resulted from this conscious resistance of workers to the exploitative rule of the planter class. Each struggle would alert the planters to the need for a new strategy of control, and each strategy served to introduce a new stage of conflict between the workforce and the planter class. More crucial to our understanding of this history is the nature of the conflict that would arise within the ranks of the workers themselves.

In their attempt to curb the bargaining power of free labour, the planters used their political authority to provide them with alternative supplies of labour. This was the decisive role that Indian indentured labour would play and that would make for a wholly new development in the cultural history of the region. There was no objective need for new labourers, but the planter class felt it an absolute necessity to control the threat always present in the exercise of free labour.

Indentured labour was bound labour. It was deprived of all mobility and was therefore condemned to provide that reliability of service a crop like sugar demanded. The planter class, with the full permission of the metropolitan power, had given itself the legal right to deploy this labour as it pleased. As Rodney emphasises here, with great relevance to many a contemporary situation, what the ruling class could not acquire by the normal play of the market forces had now been appropriated through legal sanctions. Indentured Indian labour was enslaved by the tyranny of the law that decided their relations to the land where they walked, and worked, and slept.

The state in a capitalist society is never an impartial agent mediating the conflicts that arise between contending classes. It is, in open or devious ways, always an instrument of the existing ruling group.

The presence of this indentured labour had a direct and immediate effect on the bargaining power of the free labour force. Time and again the planter class would, without apology or misgiving, affirm this point. Sandbach Parker observed,

> so long as an estate has a large Coolie gang, Creoles must give way in prices asked or see the work done by indentured labourers – and this is a strong reason why the number of Coolies on estates must not be reduced…

The Royal Commission of 1897 confirmed this evidence of the real motive behind this strategy of an alternative labour supply.

QUESTION: What is your opinion with regard to increasing the supply of coolies when there is in the colony at present time an excess of labour?

ANSWER: The supply of labour has no bearing on the sugar industry; the origin of immigration hinges on this point. You may have work for a black man or a coloured man, and they will not do it. In planting cane, if you leave certain agricultural work over, your crop is ruined. Therefore it is absolutely necessary that you should have bound labour that you can command. There are certain kinds of work which absolutely must be done at certain times – such as replanting in rainy weather – and for this an indentured gang is absolutely necessary.

Here we can perceive the origins of what would later be known as the racial conflict in Guyana. This has become a normal way of responding to all forms of crisis in that country. And some scholars are even disappointed when they investigate situations that do not provide them with the evidence of social disruption they had anticipated.

But Rodney rivets our attention on the nature of the labour experience that Indians shared with the Africans who had come before. There can be no question that Indian workers were now condemned to a history of humiliation almost indistinguishable from the memories of African slavery. The rigidity of the labour laws made every hint of recalcitrance an occasion for criminal conviction. Doctors and magistrates became instruments of the planters' will. Since pain was invisible, the Indian worker often had to argue his illness before doctors who were paid not to believe what they had heard. Indian women were made a new target of sexual assault by the lawless white overseers.

But there is an aspect of this persecution that demands close attention, for it refutes the rumour of docility that influenced relations between Indian and African workers. Arrests, however frequent, never persuaded the Indian workers to cease resistance. There were 31 strikes in 1886, 15 in 1887, and 42 in 1888. This is not the conduct of a docile labour force. The contradiction was too obvious to go unnoticed, and one white overseer, W. Alleyne Ireland, was persuaded to emphasise it in recording his experience of Indian labour in Guyana.

As to immigrants submitting like blind men to their employers as willingly as one would desire, the annual reports of the Immigration

Agent General show contrary evidence. Between 1874 and 1895, 65,084 indentured immigrants were convicted of breaches of the labour contract.

But there also appeared among the Indian indentured labour force highly politicised elements who could analyse and articulate the nature of the enterprise that had brought them from their homes. Bechu, a Bengali, instinctively drew comparisons with the African predicament and showed how well he understood the system that he had been forced to serve.

> My countrymen like myself, have had the misfortune to come to Demerara, the political system of which colony has very appropriately been divined and defined by Mr Trollope under a happy inspiration as "a despotism tempered by sugar." To these twin forces, the Immigration System is as sacred as the old system of slavery in former days, and for one in my humble position to have ventured to touch it with profane hands or to have dared to unveil it is considered on this side of the Atlantic to be a capital and inexpiable offence.

Peter Ruhomon, representing a later generation of Creole Indian, repeated Bechu's comparison with slavery, and went on to name the system that organised their lives.

> No trick of sophistry or twist of logic can ever avail to defend the system of semi-slavery paraded under the guise of indentured immigration, under which Indians were brought to the Colony to labour on the sugar plantations, in the interests of a powerful and privileged body of capitalists.

Nevertheless, the emotive language of race and race conflict has dominated our mode of perceiving the relations of the Guyanese working class to the politics of national liberation. Over the last three decades, as the struggle for workers' democracy has intensified, politicians of all races have found it convenient to use this mode of perception in explaining their failure to mobilise the total Guyanese workforce. The difference of cultural legacies between African and Indian workers has made little contribution to the experience of conflict, but it is clear that race was effectively adopted both by planters of the nineteenth century and contemporary leaders as an effective strategy of control in their bid for the allegiance of the Guyanese working class.

It was Walter Rodney's tireless opposition to this betrayal of a people that finally cost him his life. He sought with colleagues of his own generation to cut through this miasma of race which had been nurtured with such mischievous care and which served to obscure that fundamental unity of interests that might otherwise have advanced African and Indian labour in a decisive struggle to control their common destiny.

Admirers of Rodney's earlier work *Groundings with My Brothers* must come to realise that the great emphasis he placed on the moral necessity of Black Power – the ancestral dignity that African peoples must rediscover and keep alive was only part of a larger assignment in his intellectual life. It was no part of his intention to promote a racial sectarian attitude in our approach to the problems of human society, and especially in the concrete circumstances of Caribbean society. He takes great pains, therefore, to make us open and generous before the predicament of Indians, to make us register and internalise the fact of their suffering and the very great contribution they have made in the struggle for the creative survival of the Guyanese people. An authentic history of the Guyanese working people is equally their history.

This perception of the Indian as alien and other, a problem to be contained after the departure of the imperial power, has been a major part of the thought and feeling of the majority of Afro-Guyanese and a stubborn conviction among the black middle layers of Guyanese society. Indian power in politics and business has been regarded as an example of an Indian strategy for conquest. And this accusation persists even though, in the fashionable arithmetic of democracy, their numerical superiority might have justified such an ambition for supreme political power.

It is, of course, a dangerous fallacy to calculate human response on the basis of percentages. A specific group comprises ten per cent of the population and is therefore confined to a comparable share of responsibility and reward. We know there is no such thing as ten per cent of a person.

Every implication of this work serves as a corrective to this mode of thought. Rodney marshals an abundance of documentary evidence to demonstrate how ex-indentured Indians, like the ex-slaves who acquired land, were the beginning of new social groups, responding to new forms of economic activity. And whenever accumulation occurred, social stratification would emerge. It makes for great distortion, therefore, when we speak of Indians as a monolithic group, identifying the interests of the poor agricultural sugar worker with those of a large rice farmer.

It is one of the most instructive aspects of this book that we are allowed to see how the original force of estate labour, supplied by both groups, would acquire new levels of social function and open out into the emergence of new and distinct class formations.

The Afro-Guyanese, who had had a longer association with the culture of the dominant European group, now made a huge investment of talent in education. The school became the most accessible means of rescuing their offspring from the enslavement of estate labour. The history of the Afrro-Guyanese middle class is the history of the school. Many a black lawyer would have started his career as a primary school headmaster, a position of great status and importance to a mass of unlettered and aspiring ex-slaves.

But what began as a necessary strategy of self-emancipation would become, in our time, a major obstacle to national liberation. For the mystique of the educated one has proved to be a mystifying influence on the Guyanese and West Indian masses throughout the process of decolonisation. It has been one of the permanent features of the imperial experiment. Education was a means of escape from the realities of labour, a continuing flight from the foundations of society. To grow up was to grow away. Cultural imperialism is not an empty or evasive phrase. It is the process and effect of a tutelage that has clung to the ex-colonial like his skin.

It is the supreme distinction of Walter Rodney that he had initiated in his personal and professional life a decisive break with the tradition he had been trained to serve. And throughout this work, the reader is made to feel that his academic authority is always fused and humanised by a sense of personal involvement with the matters in hand. He lived to survive the distortions of his training and the crippling ambivalence of his class.

He worked on the assumption that men deserved to be liberated from those hostile forms of ownership that are based exclusively on the principle of material self-interest that negate the fundamental purpose of work. At the deepest levels of a man's being it cannot make sense that he should voluntarily labour for those whose style of thinking declares them to be his enemies and whose triumph in the management of human affairs remains a persistent threat to the dignity of his person. This book is further confirmation of that thesis. It was the last contribution Rodney would make during his life to our understanding of the history of labour in the transformation of his country and to our perception of the role of class in the continuing struggle for social justice.

15 | *Sovereignty, Mobilisation and Popular Consciousness**

I have been asked to speak on the subject of Sovereignty, Mobilisation and Popular Consciousness, and as I always do on such occasions, I think is it very helpful to you and reassuring for me to start with definitions. That is to let you know what I understand by the particular meaning of the words I am using. So I shall just give some brief definitions of these terms, which make up the title, then later share my reflections in such a way that they illustrate these definitions.

By sovereignty I think the literal meaning that we have in mind is really the freedom from external control or at any rate freedom from the controlling influence of an external factor. To look at it then from our side, that is in our relations to ourselves, you can say that by sovereignty we mean the collective power to exercise control and direction over the means of our material existence; and by sovereignty we also mean the freedom to define and to redefine all the processes material and otherwise which make up our social reality. Now if we accept these definitions, particularly the latter, it will be clear, as P.J. Patterson indicated, that a characteristic of our history in the Caribbean has been the continuing constraints which have been placed on this power to exercise such control as well as the constraint placed on our freedom of self-definition.

When we come to the word mobilisation, I think the first thing that strikes us is that it is a word usually connected with war. That is, mobilisation really means the act of putting into movement. That is the act of assembling say an army corps, or a fleet and putting

---

* This is an edited version of a talk given in December 1984 in Kingston, Jamaica at a regional seminar held by the People's National Party. Held in the aftermath of the implosion of the Grenadian Revolution, the seminar's theme was 'Caribbean Sovereignty: Mobilisation for Development and Self-Reliance; The Tasks of Political Education.'

these in a state of readiness for active service in war. The process of putting in movement in order to deal with what appears to be a state of disaster. I want to suggest that I do think that there is a sense in which the Caribbean is at war, not only in relation to an external force, but also in relation to the tensions which exist within the social formation in each territory. The term popular consciousness raises a certain complexity. In the first place we can use the term popular relating to the general public, that is to the whole people as distinct from a specific group or class. But there is also a sense, and I think it may be appropriate on this occasion, in which we may use the word popular to mean representing the common people as distinct from a specific class. Now when we come to consciousness, what we mean is the awareness of an external state, the awareness of what is really at stake in our situation. It means the recognition of difference, and the knowledge of difference. And I want to use this term consciousness, meaning knowledge of difference as it pertains to labour.

I think it is here, that we can see a meaning of popular and a meaning of consciousness. I think that we have been watching in the Caribbean the evolution of a new governing elite who have had no social experience of wealth. And if you go from one point of the Caribbean to the other and meet people who go by names of ministers of this and minister of that, people who occupy positions in the bureaucracy and all forms of state institutions of a certain generation, what we are dealing with are men who really are the children of poor people, not to mention the grandchildren of poor people. This new governing elite, without the social experience of wealth, have no background that ever had a claim to production. They never owned land; they never owned banks; they never owned insurance companies. This new governing elite have had to use the state as the means of accumulating wealth for this class.

And because they are aware of the fragility of the society (what someone once has called the vagaries of the democratic process), this pursuit of wealth has got to be very fast. As I put it sometimes, they do not only have to steal as much as they can, they have to steal it as fast as they can. Speed is very essential. Now if we examine such a group in relation to this predicament, it brings to us the heart of the crisis. There is a sense in which their interests coincide with the interests of the external power. That is, both have to extract as much as possible in the shortest time possible. It is therefore not an accident that we see and will continue to see an accommodation between this new governing elite and United States imperialism. Coming from different backgrounds and different heritages they meet at the road where there is a coincidence of interest. And I want to suggest that there has to be a force of resistance to this development; and the most powerful agent in that force of resistance will be the agent of organised labour.

There is a tendency, more than a tendency, it has been almost a tradition not to use certain terms like culture and intellectual in relation to labour. But there is a very important sense and I want to clarify this, in which the word intellectual may be applied to all forms of labour which could not possibly be carried out without the exercise of the mind. The fisherman and the farmer must be regarded as cultural and intellectual workers in their own right. Social practice has provided them with a considerable body of knowledge and the capacity to make discriminating judgement in their daily work. If we do not regard them as cultural and intellectual workers, it is largely because of the social stratification which is created by the division of labour and an educational system which was designed to reinforce such stratification.

I think Caribbean society, especially within the context of the English Caribbean, has been crippled by this artificial status, which separates what is called the educated from the uneducated. Experience, and my own personal experience, of our middle class confirms that literacy may sometimes be a form of self-enslavement. We have among us in this region, some men and women whose brightness blinds and sometimes makes it very difficult for them to see the peculiar darkness through which they go. We have never been short of people who were called bright, but we have been surrounded by a number of people whose brightness blinds. I want, therefore, to suggest a kind of task that has to be done in order to show labour as an agent of change, and as perhaps the essential moving force in the re-ordering of history. And I think a good way to begin is with reference to Walter Rodney in his last book *The History of the Guyanese Working People*. He goes to great pains to show us what has been the meaning of labour in the formation of that society. He says:

> In 1948, the Venn Commission estimated that each square mile
> of cane cultivation involved the provision of 49 miles of gradings

of canals and ditches and 16 miles of high level waterways used for transportation and irrigation. The construction of these waterways must have entailed the moving of at least 100 million tons of soil and what he wants us to remember is the means whereby such labour was undertaken. "This meant the slaves moved 100 million tons of heavy waterlogged clay with shovel in hand, while enduring the conditions of perpetual mud and water. Working people continued, making a tremendous contribution to the humanisation of the Guyanese costal landscape."

It is the word humanisation which tells what is Rodney's intentions. The real history of the country begins here, not with Governors, not with the British Parliament, not with the planters, but with these working hands which humanised through mud and waters, the landscape which we now know as Guyana.

Now we have had some very interesting and enlightening Caribbean scholars, who have on the whole concentrated on the various arguments and provisions made by those who rule the land, those whose concept of social responsibility was confined to their exercise of power and the protection of their interests as a governing group. But Rodney was engaged in illuminating our understanding from a different perspective: that working people of African and Indian ancestory in Guyana have a history of active struggle, which it has been our habit to omit or underestimate in political discourses about the past. They often met with defeat against the combined power of planters and the imperial power; yet it remains true that every struggle planted a seed of creative destruction, and in the process released new social forces in the continuing drama between capital and labour. Moreover, it is through that struggle that we can discover the origins and growth of the middle and professional classes. But it is their failure to grasp the meaning and possibilities of this struggle which makes them vulnerable to continuing external influence.

As was mentioned earlier, a more recent example of this humanising struggle was the period which can be called the decade of the hurricane – the period of the 1930s. Throughout this region, the enormous masses of men and women arose in a direct and spontaneous confrontation to the colonial authority. That is in St Kitts, in Barbados and Trinidad to Jamaica. The streets were transformed into popular parliaments and arenas of power. It was only, I think, the interruption caused by the Second World War from 1939 to 1945 which halted the maturing of this movement, since all domestic politics were suppressed by the colonial power. But, and this is the point I want to emphasise, because I think it has been underestimated if not omitted, that it is a point that has not really even entered, as it should have, the consciousness of labour. It was, in my view, this struggle which helped to democratise the existing social relations. The battle for trade union organisation, like the battle for adult suffrage, was won through this struggle. The racism of the governing class was eroded by this struggle. The black policeman who could never get beyond the rank of sergeant was later elevated to inspector and commissioner because of this struggle. The black priest, whose skin deprived him of a church to become Vicar or Rector, was rescued as a result of this struggle.

All areas of social living were positively affected by this struggle. All, except land, the merchant citadels, the financial institutions. But it was this struggle which helped to humanise the landscape everywhere. I think it is a supreme task of political education and research in all disciplines to plant and propagate the theme, that it is labour in all its stages of organisation which has been the most powerful democratising force in Caribbean history, and which today represents the greatest potential for Caribbean liberation. It is not only important to document this fact, but a way must be found to make such a body of knowledge easily available to working people themselves. It is the failure of the intellectual classes to root this knowledge within the ranks of working people which made the latter hostage to their own leadership, and the prey of all external forces. In other words, political education must contribute to the development of a workforce, which in its turn will produce its own intellectual agents. This emphasis will have an influence on the content and the direction of the curriculum in all institutions of learning.

The second consequence bears on the relations of West Indians of African and Indian descent in those areas where this is critical. This is the case where the concept of race and racial difference has been very effectively used during and since the colonial period. This perception, for example, of the Indian as alien and other, became a problem to be contained after the departure of the imperial power, has been a major component of the thought and feeling of the black West Indian, and a very stubborn conviction among the black middle class in Trinidad and Guyana. Indian power in politics and business has been regarded as an example of an Indian strategy to conquest and this accusation persists, even though in the fashionable arithmetic of democracy, their numerical superiority in both places might have justified such an ambition. But it makes, I think, for a very great distortion when we speak of Indians as a monolithic group, identifying the interest of poor struggling agricultural sugar workers with those of rich rice farmers or the emergent entrepreneurial cliques in Port of Spain. It is very important to establish by research the common history of exploitation endured by African and Indian in the Caribbean, and the common engagement in resistance which has been the history of both groups.

The intellectual worker in the Caribbean, therefore, or the intellectual worker outside of the Caribbean, on behalf of the Caribbean must assume, I think, an almost evangelical role on behalf of the region which should be perceived and interpreted as one unit of historical experience. Every attempt should be made to see that study and interpretation are regional in character; to establish with the greatest insistence that no single territory whatever its language or size has a meaningful destiny that is not the destiny of the entire region. Scholarship and political education should therefore be committed unapologetically to the forging of a regional consciousness in each territory to make it impossible with time for anyone of the region to be regarded as an alien by any part of the region. It was a shameful lack of this genuine regional patriotism which made the invasion of Grenada a welcome event by the majority of the Caribbean people.

Now, as you have heard my specific area of contribution has been as a writer and a critic of the cultural history of the region; and I have been very active trying to share this view, especially with people of authority in the labour movement that, and I emphasise this, a political struggle will always be a very fragile process if it is not rooted in a cultural base. This failure to recognise the organic connection between cultural activity and political struggle has been in my view, an astonishing weakness among people who claim to be of the left. In many cases, the most difficult of the philistines are among the intellectual left in this matter. Because there is a view that culture is a form of refinement, that it is a form of adornment and when you have got through with establishing the new political structure, and a new economical structure and so on, then you will call some people in to dance. But I want to suggest that it is not all a luxury for a political movement or a trade union, it is not all a luxury for such institutions to treat as a priority the organisation of a competent and dynamic popular political theatre. If there is one country that has taught me that, it is revolutionary Cuba. They do not treat culture as marginal or aberrative.

They see the cultural act as one of the major weapons in the struggle for the defence of the revolution. There is a fundamental difference between that conception and what has prevailed elsewhere. And I think that this has been so with us because one of the areas that we have rarely concentrated on in the history of education is the education of feeling. We have very rarely concentrated on the education of feeling and this I think may be a most dangerous omission from what is called a curriculum.

Creative expression, be it theatre, music, dance, literature, is not to be seen primarily as a "call to revolution" or anything else, nor a celebration of such a victory. Artistic expression can do these things; but the central and seminal value of art is that it functions as a civilising and a humanising force in a process of struggle. It offers an experience through which feeling is educated; through which feeling is deepened; through which feeling increases its capacity to accommodate greater and greater varieties of knowledge.

The major adversary which we confront is not new, although I think the form in which it now comes is more sinister. I want to read you a short extract and you may have come across it, but it will be worth hearing again. It is written by a marine commander, General Smedlay Butler, and it was written in November 1935, and it appeared in a journal called *Common Sense*. I quote:

> I spent 33 years and 4 months in active service as a member of our country's most agile military force, the marine corps. I served in all commission ranks from the 2nd Lieutenant to the major general and during that period I spent most of my time being, a high class muscle man for big business, for Wall Street and for bankers. In short I was a racketeer for capitalism. And thus, I helped to make Mexico and especially Tampico safe for Americana oil interests in 1914. I helped make Haiti and Cuba a decent place for the National City Bank boys and to collect revenues. I helped purify Nicaragua for the international banking house of Brown Brothers

in 1909 and 1912. I brought light to the Dominican Republic for American sugar industry in 1916. I helped make Honduras right for American fruit companies in 1923. During those years, I had as the boys in the backroom would say, a swell racket. I was rewarded with honours, medals, promotions. Looking back on it, I feel I might have given Al Capone a few hints. The best he could do was to operate his racket in three city districts. We marines operated that racket on three continents.

The commitment and the psychology behind this relation to the world outside the United States is precisely the commitment and psychology of the present administration of the United States to Latin America and the Caribbean to this day. But I want especially for labour people to make a second point.

Caribbean trade unions are being brought increasingly under the influence of the AFL-CIO training programmes. The intention is to Americanise these unions into the soft underbelly of the political directorate, since United States imperialism understands the relation of union to party in our political culture. In other words, the leadership of the unions in the region may be severely under the temptation or pressure to join that new governing elite in a common purpose: a coincidence of interest with United States imperialism.

The question that we have to reflect on, (we cannot answer in one go), is how do you build and how do you consolidate a force of resistance against not only the external threat of imperialism, but the internal threat of pressure from the new governing elite? One of the areas that is now perhaps the most oppressive and the most difficult is that wide area that is called communications. If you can, in our kind of society, control at source the agencies of the communication media you have won two-thirds of the battle of controlling the mind and the direction of the mind of your entire community; and nobody can stop that. It is very difficult to get Caribbean people sometimes to understand that the task of the minister in charge of communication is no less important than that of the minister in charge of foreign affairs. It is the control of that means which not only feeds with information, but feeds with selected information; not only feeds with selected information but also feeds with specific interpretation of that selected information: that control is precisely a capturing and even holding permanently in certain circumstances, the mind of an entire society. And that is why today we find even among men and women who are supposed to be intelligent such political illiteracy when the word communist is mentioned. The man who is talking cannot say what this communist is. What is a communist? Well, you know, what is communism? You know. No, I don't, I am asking you.

It is a new form of political demonology which by the means of this media, has helped to put to sleep the mind of even the most intelligent men, when they have to discuss what has been a major development in modern history and civilisation. It is not a question of whether you like or do not like, it is a question of whether you are allowed to cultivate a critical sensibility to question what is in front of you. This political demonology is now reinforced by an evangelical demonology. One of those dangerous networks exploiting what is a genuine religious sensibility of Caribbean people. There has never been any question about that – that religious sensibility in the Caribbean people. But what threatens to debase this religious sensibility is the political character, the political motivation, the political intention of this new evangelism that sweeps across the region. The demonology is so powerful that you have to be extremely careful when you are talking to ordinary, decent, sensible people from Jamaica, to Barbados. You have to be very careful to make a critique of this without appearing to be making, a critique of God. And any man who thinks that he can gain political leverage in this part of the world without paying attention to how he speaks about God is very remote from the realities of the region. Here we must choose language with the greatest of care.

I think within the next two days, we will be able in various ways to discuss the ways and means whereby you may be able to get around the established channels of communication. Are there alternative means of getting at elements of our population around the established means of communication? There is no way you can answer this in one meeting. But for the time being, where there does not exist the immediate possibility of a seizure of the communications media in most of those regions, a strategy for the working out of alternative means of communication for correcting the political illiteracy of the region must be thought of. And that is why it is not possible to think of political struggle without the central role of the cultural act.

16 | *In Defence of Cultural Sovereignty**

The original meaning of the word, culture, had to do with the tending of plants and the care of animals. In other words, this word, and the process it describes, has its roots in the practice of agriculture, and it has never lost this sense of nurturing; of feeding, of cultivating, whether it be a body or a mind that is under consideration.

The first and essential meaning of culture is, therefore, the means whereby men and women feed themselves, clothe and shelter themselves; the means whereby they achieve and reproduce their material existence. No food, no life. No food, no book, no religion, no philosophy, no politics, no performing arts. No one is exempt from the demands of the material life. So we need to understand, therefore, why the farmer and the fisherman are cultural workers, and that all questions relating to the process of social transformation are cultural questions.

Secondly, we mean by culture the variety of ways in which men and women interpret and translate, through the imagination, the meaning of that material existence in the light of their concrete experience – religion, philosophy, art, and the institutions which mediate their daily lives, all these – religion, philosophy, art – are influenced, in one way or another by the circumstances of our material existence.

A characteristic of our history in the Caribbean has been the continuing constraints, which have been placed on the power to exercise sovereignty and on our freedom of self-definition. If there is one area in which we can identify the neglect, even the abandonment of cultural sovereignty, it is in the area of food production.

---

*   Edited version of Lamming's address to the Second Conference of the Regional committee of Caribbean Cultural and Intellectual Workers held in Trinidad in January 1984. Originally published in the regional newspaper *Caribbean Contact*, March 1985.

The Caribbean is a fertile sea. We occupy lands, which accommodate a great variety of crops. It is a region, with the distinct potential for meeting the basic food needs (basic, I repeat) of the Caribbean people. Yet the Commonwealth Caribbean (the English-speaking corner) spends $700 million a year on imported food. There is a crisis in cultural sovereignty when patterns of consumption bear little relation to basic needs, and cannot be supported by the productive base of the societies. A Minister of Agriculture, in our region, whether he knows it or not, is engaged in what is essentially a cultural problem: How do you decolonise the eating habits of a people who have surrendered their very palates to foreign control? The synonym of breakfast is Kelloggs.

In these circumstances, it is (if I may use 'primeministerial' language) wicked to arouse and titillate the labour and expectations of local farmers to engage in a rivalry with imported food on the scale of US$700 million a year. But it is not only the local farmer who experiences this assault on his struggle for sovereignty; the native actor, the native dancer, writer, musician, all those who strive for an authentic definition of themselves and their society are in much the same position as the local farmer. They are condemned to a hopeless struggle against the massive insult of imported television. It is not only imported, it is the garbage of another world, unloaded on a mesmerised and uncritical populace.

Political leadership is innocent if it does not recognise that the mass-production of culture in this form is intended to ensure and reinforce the underdevelopment of our people.

Professor Rex Nettleford makes similar emphasis when he says:

Part of the suffering of developing societies like the Caribbean is that the new ruling and governing classes are sometimes the most effective and uncritical carriers of the values of the old imperial dispensation making the new order little more than the old in black or brown skin. Notions of elegance, manners, morals, and customs carry the head, heart and limbs of the metropolitan cultural ethos. Some of these are trivial and harmless enough. But a major question for the new nation is perennially how does one transform the empty power of manipulated symbols into power with substance? Is it not the capacity of a people to make definitions about themselves on their own terms and to be able to follow through to action on the basis of those actions? No development strategy is likely to succeed without resting its objective and intent on such definitions.

But listen to the Prime Minister of Dominica in an interview with CBS 60 Minutes on October 14, 1984: 'I don't go following new fads, if I can put it that way. We see eye to eye with America and England because of the traditions we've been brought up in.' Recolonisation of the Caribbean is a simple process if our political directorates represent the general cultural and intellectual backwardness of Ms Eugenia Charles.

Unfortunately, the West Indian historian is not an active and informing influence in the popular consciousness. The language of economic advisers conveys little or no meaning to the people outside their immediate circle of colleagues. Novelists function without a substantial and continuing reading class, even among the certified graduates of the region's university. This literature has hardly aroused the active interest of many who make up the political intelligentsia. The philistinism of the Left is a source of tragic political errors.

The organising agents of communications media (radio producers, television managers etc.) are vaguely aware of the region's creative writers. They may know their names, and a few episodes of scandal which shadow their personal lives. This failure of involvement coexists with the widespread and vivid enthusiasm for a great volume of imported drama which advertisers make available through the television stations of the region. The hypnotic appeal of current television shows suggests, in a definitive way, that there is a general interest in the dramatisation of human situations, 'Dallas', 'Love Boat', 'Days of Our Lives', are (it cannot be denied) drama of a kind.

What form of resistance can be organised in defence of cultural sovereignty?

Drama may be used, in my context here, as a focus of all cultural activities. It is a form of expression which allows people of very different social and educational background to share common experience about themselves. I would invite you, therefore, to examine the possibilities of popular theatre as an instrument for the distribution and dissemination of knowledge: the ways in which this particular form of popular expression can be put in the service of historians, novelists, economists, social scientists, community health workers; and how this can be done without in any way neglecting or violating the theatre's more familiar function of entertainment. The purpose of such an exercise is obvious; and it should be the basis of a national T.V. policy.

In all the areas of statistical and imaginative enquiry about Caribbean society, there remains an enormous distance between those who produce (artists, teachers, technocrats) and the general populace for whom the social product is intended. And I'm working from the assumption that this failure of participation by the general populace in the social product of the intellectual classes presents the greatest threat to our regional and cultural sovereignty. This deprivation works both ways. It impoverishes the popular consciousness; and in turn it places a very rigorous constraint on the development of the intellectual workers themselves.

It is the minimum condition for the survival of any regional institution; and the Caribbean is doomed to permanent recolonisation without institutions which are regional in character and function, and which express with the boldest insistence our own definitions of Caribbean reality. The alternative is the design of the Caribbean Basin Initiative, and that is an alternative which must be fought.

I'd like, therefore, to pose here, as I've done before on similar occasions, the following questions What kind of theatre does the average Caribbean historian envisage as expressive of his or her interests as these relate to the distribution of a knowledge and a sense of Caribbean history? What forms of collaboration could take place between economists who formulate strategies of development, and theatre directors who are preoccupied with raising the social and political consciousness of a given community? And how should such forms of collaboration proceed? What should be the role of organised labour in the production and managements of cultural activity, and in the creation of the People's Theatre?

There is no objective reason why organised labour should not be a major producer of popular theatre. They have the finance base for such an enterprise, and easy access to the human resources available: directors, writers, actors. The problem is that labour has never been sufficiently liberated to see itself in this role; as an architect of cultural policy. This is not wholly the fault of labour. It derives also from the negative attitude of the intellectual classes to labour.

It was this range of concerns which brought together the group of men and women who now make up the Regional Committee for Cultural Sovereignty. We share this fundamental conviction.

SECTION 2

Lamming in Conversation

17 | 'A Future They Must Learn': An Interview by George Kent*

KENT: You take a good deal of care in devising titles. I'd particularly appreciate your commenting on what you meant by the title of your latest book, *Natives of My Person*.

LAMMING: In 1958, during a visit to Ghana, I was spending some time with an Ashanti family, and the father showed me a postcard which presumably was a Christmas card he had made to send out to friends, business associates and so on. On this postcard were about 25 or 30 people of different ages who, to my surprise, I learned were his children. But what the postcard said was, 'These are all natives of my person'. Many years later – I think 12 years later – when I was coming to write this novel you are referring to, that phrase leaped out of my consciousness as the title that was exact for what was happening here – that everything going on in the book was in a way a native of my person, that I might in some way contain all of that experience, that anything created from that experience became, in that manuscript, *Natives of My Person*.

KENT: The book has sometimes been spoken of as a parable.

LAMMING: You might say that. It's unusual, I suppose, because in a way two sets of things are happening simultaneously – two sets of historical situations, two sets of times. Although it is true that on the surface the book appears to be about Europe and Europeans in search of conquest and colonisation, what is running through my mind all the time is that the world represented on this ship, 'Reconnaisance', is, in many levels

---

* This interview was first published in the March 1973 issue of *Black World*. At the time, Dr Kent, now deceased, was Professor of English at the University of Chicago.

of authority and power, not very different from the world of many post-colonial territories.

So, in considering the relationship of the Commandant in charge – that is, his relation to the officers, and the relations of the officers to the crew – what is also going on in my mind is my experience of the parallel relationships which take place in post-colonial territories between the leader, the cabinet and the masses. And the same kinds of authoritarianism, suspicion, disillusionment and being kept in the dark that hang over the ship, also more or less characterise the evolution of the new independent countries. In our own time, the Commandant is a type of figure found in the Caribbean and in many African countries – that is, in the nature of his relation to those he's working with.

KENT: A specific relationship to the slave trade. The Commandant represents in some sense, doesn't he, a corruption of the power quest?

LAMMING: There is in the Commandant a central paradox which, in spite of all his effort, he does not resolve. He is a man who, when the book opens, is an example of what most ordinary people would have liked to be. He is a man who has known what it is to be wealthy, who also takes pride in his achievements as a soldier, as a commander and, more than that, in the knowledge that these achievements were not really due solely to privilege of birth. They are achievements which are acknowledged and recognised by friends and foes alike.

These are no kinds of ordinary material ambition, ordinary social status, or ordinary power status that he's after. He's gone through all of that and has put that behind, but he's driven by an impulse to create a new kind of world – a world that would represent a break from the world which produced him. He wants to create a new order of relations between men. Here his creative pride is at work, for he feels that, in spite of the weight of the past, he can do it. What drives him, too, is that he is doing it anyway against the approval and the authority of the established powers of his homeland.

An endless, major obstacle for him is the question of his relation to the women in his life. A psychological difficulty confronts him there that is far more complex and far more challenging than the question of managing men or establishing a new colony.

KENT: Would you say that the woman or women in this book represent something of the density of reality, something that you cannot constrain completely by rigid patterns and therefore, who must be confronted with a greater openness? On another level, aren't they the future in the sense that the relation between man and woman, if fulfilled, represents a higher kind of evolution of men?

LAMMING: In a sense, I'd say that the intention at work there is to suggest that if the man/woman relationship is aborted, is perverted, there will be a corresponding perversion in the relation between man and what he calls his work or his conception of fulfillment. The other aspect of that is that the relation between the man and the woman will always be characterised by the prevailing concept of man/woman relationships held by the society in which the individual relationships are taking place. The corruption in the individual man/woman relationships between Steward and his wife, between Surgeon and his wife, and the difficulty between Boatswain and his woman – these are symptoms of a wider and more pervasive corruption of the society in which they lived.

KENT: So that the women at the end are saying that they are the future...

LAMMING: ...which the men must learn. The suggestion there is that men would really have to reorganise their emotions regarding women.

KENT: And if they reorganise those relations?

LAMMING: Then there would be an experience of a new liberation. I do not suggest that this will in any way automatically lead to a facile notion of harmony, but that there would be a new liberation of spirit, and the future encounters between them would be an innovation, as distinct from a continuation, of the past they have known.

KENT: Somewhere in the book, someone says – I think referring to specific women characters – that they are being related to as one would relate to a cow. In the case of the Commandant, the woman is supposed to validate all his activities, to validate the meaning and, actually, the value of his journey. I sometimes feel a sense of hysteria developing between the Commandant and his wife...

LAMMING: Yes. There are slight differences in the quality of the relationships between the different officers and their wives. In the case of the Commandant, it perhaps reaches its supreme form. The Commandant cares very deeply for his woman. He is in a way possessed by a certain aspect of her – her capacity for self-scrutiny. Now, the problem he encounters with her is one of choice, a choice which I see as an example of the nature of the society in which they are living: their moments of great distress always occur when he is about to make a new voyage. She remains. She is going to experience alone the loss, isolation and frustration of his not being there. How she endures the waiting is by living in her imagination every moment of the return. Now, he realises that this distresses her, and there is a part of him that wants somehow to console her, which he does try to do, by promising that each voyage will be the last. But every time the promise is broken, not because he was lying in the first place, but because of the nature of the work he is doing. The challenge of the adventure in that work is always presenting him with a new kind of situation which has to be mastered, making him feel that, as a man with such a career, he would be incomplete until he had mastered it. So he has to go again. She's confronting him now with this choice – that you choose what you call your work, or you choose me because I am also in an important sense your life. She tries to corner him with this by bringing home to him the nature of his work.

He is an imperialist; he conquers peoples' countries, is involved in the killing of people, in the dispossession of people. By the nature of his work, the greater his achievements, the greater his contribution to human slaughter. She is really telling him that, if you look at it in a fundamental way, you are making a choice between being a murderer – which your work demands – and being a part of me that I want you to be, which, indeed, is the very opposite in terms of human experience, as it entails being a part of the love that holds us together. Which do you choose?

KENT: Presumably, if the Commandant had been able to choose his wife in the full human range, then he would have been liberated for a broader vocation.

LAMMING: Yes. And this is, towards the end of the book, what he's really trying to do. When he goes out on that illegal expedition, his relation to what he's doing is really in reverse. He's no longer going as the man who wants to set up a colony in which his wife will be an equal partner, a real person. This new world, with these new relations, would be the world in which this feeling she has for him and the feeling he has for her would flourish. Thus, he has ultimately chosen to make her an essential part of that new world which he wants to establish.

KENT: The Steward's wife is deliberate, too, isn't she?

LAMMING: There is a slight difference with the Steward's wife. Steward is the example of a man who is not on the same scale as the Commandant, but a man who also has a driving ambition to do things on his own, without the props, the cradling, the promotion of other people. He feels this all the more strongly because his wife happens to be a woman who was in a position to help, and he now interprets her affection and gestures not as positive help, but as her strategy for colonising him, for keeping him in a particular relation to her. But the more he struggles to transcend himself, the more he really feels this tremendous prison of her affection, the prison of her concern. He is also worried by the notion that in her eyes he's not done as well as his ability and his industry had promised. This in fact is not altogether true; she was quite committed to be with him in any kind of circumstances. He feels that even where he is a success, it is a success which is largely due to her and to her birth and superior social circumstances.

KENT: Surgeon has a similar problem, doesn't he?

LAMMING: The Surgeon is caught in similar difficulty, except that he is a coarser type than Steward. Steward is a man who believes, in a curious way, in his innocence and in the purity of his intentions. Surgeon is not at all perplexed or caught in this way by motives of purity. But Surgeon is an example of the brilliant man, the man of ideas, the man who feels that it can be done, whatever it is, and it does not really matter what means are employed. He's more an example of the purely ambitious man. He does not really want to impress his wife in the way that Steward wants to. He wants to get her out of the way – he thinks of her as in the way – of his drive of doing.

KENT: Isn't Pinteados a kind of chorus in the book?

LAMMING: Yes. He is a man through whose observations you sort of see the others in relation to themselves. This brings us back to the business of the two worlds and the two times. The world of the late 16th-early 17th century, and our present world. These two worlds working together.

Pinteados is the stranger. He is the pilot on this ship, but he is also – and this would have been illegal at the time – a man from a foreign kingdom. In a way, he had no right to be on that ship, and most certainly no right to be in that position, a very crucial and very important one at the time. But what he depicts is the indispensability of the technical man in any operation. And although the officers and crew hate the peculiarly intimate relation existing between the Commandant and Pinteados, the stranger, he has the Commandant's ear in a way that none of the other officers have.

They hate him. In one sense, Surgeon was actually contemplating murdering him. He cannot be murdered, because without Pinteados, there is no pilot on that ship. This is like modern situations, where the technical agents in what are called developing societies are usually foreigners who, however much resented in certain situations, cannot be removed because there is a commitment or operation that rests on their technical capacity. You see the link. You can't kill him because there is no other pilot. This ship couldn't move without him.

Now there is another parallel between Pinteados at that time and his equivalent today. It is the particular importance of the foreigner in the affairs of people's lives. Pinteados enjoys the privilege accorded a man believed to have no interest in your affairs or in the destiny of your operation.

He's concerned with his job, whether it is a bridge, a dam, or some hydroelectric plant.

This kind of man often shares the confidence of the leader, because of his lack of involvement. If he were a native to the country, and saw some conflict between the technical operation and the philosophy of the society, his natural involvement might force him to find an alternative and thus collide with the leadership. But an outsider not concerned with such internal matters – only with a technical operation – is more trusted. This is one of the parallels.

KENT: Now to other relationships between the book and the Black experience, particularly in the slave trade and in your representation of the so-called natives of the areas. What were you trying to portray in them? We don't see them, of course, as individual persons. As I recall, Jan Carew mentioned the whites and blacks meeting as phantoms, in a kind of a phantom world, in his *New York Times* review of the book.

LAMMING: Let's put it this way. In this stage of the book, where the men have reached the African coast, in a normal, conventional way what might have happened next is that the narrative would have continued with the Middle Passage that is with the passage of Africans being taken over. Now I depart from that in order to suggest that the Europeans had a middle passage, too, one that is now going to be seen on the interior of their lives.

I think you may notice in the book that it is only when they are making the journey from Africa to the Isles of the Black Rock that we follow the history of the Europeans' domestic lives, and they are then made to go through all the spiritual torture, the spiritual brutality that characterised their own homes. That is the middle passage that they are going through on their way to the Isles of the Black Rock.

In a sense, you might say that what I have done here is to leave the Middle Passage of the Blacks as a known factor which is already part of our historical experience and imagination, and to provide what I think had not been covered before – the symbolic middle passage of the European man involved in that journey from the Coast to the Isle of Black Rock. It is during that passage that we see all the disorder, all the corruption,

155

all the chaos of his own spiritual life. Now, the other aspect of that, and I think it is a point about phantoms, is that that slave coast is already – and has been for some time – an important part in the psychology of these Europeans; therefore, it can be there as background as Carew says, as a phantom. That coast has a very special meaning, not only for the men on the ship, but for the kingdom from which they came, and the meaning of that coast is so deeply a part of the total European adventure that no journey he makes can ever be the same again.

Now, one of the things I am getting at here is that when I speak of the colonial experience, which is a theme running through my books, I am speaking about something more than what is normally called a political/colonial situation. The colonial experience is not just the experience of colonised people, but a very deep psychic experience of the coloniser himself. And the coloniser is imprisoned in that experience no less than the colonised. One of the difficulties for the commander, one of the reasons why there is going to be a failure to set up a new world and a new order, is because the real psychic meaning of that colonial experience has never been faced by him, and no new order could be set up by a man who did not come to terms in some way with the meaning of that experience.

KENT: Again, with the Black side, I get also the feeling that in the collision between the two – the colonised native and the psychically disordered European coloniser – there emerges a certain kind of ironic strength and humanness shown by the natives, both in their power of resistance and their power of spirit and sometimes in their cohesiveness.

LAMMING: Yes. I think an aspect of irony comes up. One sees it perhaps most clearly in Pierre, the young carpenter, when he experiences for the first time what it means to chase these people, to hunt them down. We see a people who are together, a people who have had some kind of social organisation, who are insisting on having some ritual. We see the whole meaning of the mother, the tremendous disturbance she creates when the sons are taken away. And while we are seeing this human spiritual response to loss on the part of the Blacks, you see in the European, Pierre, a total blindness – that he is in fact convinced the voyage has given him an opportunity to learn, to expand himself, to develop his sensibility. A central blindness does not allow him to see that his learning and the expanding of his sensibility are in fact negated, completely negated by the encounter.

KENT: He retreats into a kind of standard religious response, doesn't he?

LAMMING: He does. He is a good example in the book of the slow, gradual process of indoctrination. When he begins the voyage, he is thought to be a rather frivolous chap who likes the idea of getting out of the kingdom for a voyage of adventure. He is not particularly in awe of authority and tends to be very irreverent. But as he moves farther and farther into this journey, its process of education begins to turn him into an imperialist. We see a man who has always thought of himself as an ordinary, anonymous carpenter, having no importance whatsoever in the kingdom, blossoming very slowly into a man who sees himself as a great builder of his kingdom's enterprise. By the end of the journey, he completely identifies with the officers and with the imperial enterprise of the kingdom.

KENT: And now, the Priest also goes through a spiritual corruption from the sheer power that he gets from the Word, doesn't he?

LAMMING: The Priest, I think, really represents two sides of the role. On the one hand, the Priest is a man interested in the material benefits of this enterprise, very interested in that. There is really no separation of Church from State in this matter, but a complete marriage. The Priest is also haunted by a certain intellectual curiosity; he cannot see the Blacks merely as cargo. In order to satisfy what he thinks is his own spirituality and his own spiritual mission, he has to give an explanation for what he is doing: that there is a better chance to bring this creature of nature out of nature and into some possible enlightenment if he is transplanted from his own landscape, which is identified in the Priest's mind as a landscape of nature. He justifies it in that way.

I think there was at one time a prevailing notion that there wasn't anything so wrong with the slave trade because the

Africans transported into the new world received a privilege, the possibility of seeing the light, etc. – from which they would have been permanently excluded if left in what was conventionally thought of as the darkness of their world.

KENT: To switch to a minor character, Ivan, the painter, is a man of vision. Is he in contact with a bigger reality than the other men are?

LAMMING: Ivan functions there as the artist, and I think that in a sense he carries forward to another level, a theme that is running through my other books, a kind of side theme. You get it in *The Emigrants, Of Age and Innocence* and *Season of Adventure:* the particular predicament of the artist, of the creative imagination, in that kind of dramatic – in that kind of political situation. Ivan is a man who has some capacity, not easily explained, for predicting, foreseeing, but he sees it in forms that are not immediately communicable to people. They sometimes catch on to what he's saying, but when they do catch on, it has the ring of the impossible. He functions within that role as the artist. He portrays in some sense what I suppose Keats meant by negative capability. That is, he is a man who, while recognising the necessity for a certain act, is also very aware of the innumerable consequences of pain that go with that act, and who tries to hold these two things together. In the last scenes, for example, when they are deciding to desert the ship, he is completely with Baptiste about deserting, but, at the same time, he has a great compassion for the men who are in doubt, for the men who see this as a terrible, dangerous thing to do.

KENT: What sort of research did you conduct for this book? In his review, Carew mentions that your Commandant resembles one of the Spanish conquerors.

LAMMING: No. I intended more of a composite. A man like Hawkins would have been very much in my mind – a composite of Hawkins, a composite of Drake, of any of these very oversized figures of the period. I was sort of putting elements of them together. Speaking of sources, one of the things that has had a great effect on me over a long period of time is my reading of the *Hakluyt Voyages.*

KENT: I remember your mentioning those.

LAMMING: Yes, in *The Pleasures of Exile*. Hakluyt presents these voyages tremendously, in each page of the nine volumes, as examples of the splendour, the glory, the indescribable achievements of 'our sons.' And in a sense, what he is doing at the particular time is saying, 'Look, it would be a terrible thing if this generation of Englishmen did not take up from where this marvellous work has gone on.' This is the irony: that when it comes to questions of Black studies, sometimes there are few sources which are more rewarding for understanding how black men saw whites than in the reports of whites about what whites thought was actually happening. Quite often, a Hakluyt, or any of those men reporting those voyages, never realised how ironic that exercise would be to a later reader.

KENT: So if you can read the irony, they'll tell you something very elaborate?

LAMMING: Yes. And sometimes all you have to do is just switch over and say, 'I see you think that was a glorious moment; now let me show you how that moment was being seen from the other side.'

KENT: That's a considerable description of the performance of the total book, I think. Are there other sources that you've found useful?

LAMMING: I've always been very interested in that whole period of the late 16th–early 17th century. It's always fascinated me because, as I said earlier, it's a period which contains all the stresses that go with an emergent nationalism. It's also the period, and this raises the question of the House of Trade and Justice, where there's a great gray path forming. That is, the feudal world is collapsing. And what we are really seeing in these merchant adventurers is the beginning of that great capitalist enterprise. An argument is going on inside society between these very aggressive, individual types, who have broken away from the previous feudal structure and are slowly building up a class of men like themselves who, in fact, will set the decisive tone and direction of history for the next four or five hundred years.

KENT: The House of Trade and Justice becomes a character almost like the village in your *In the Castle of My Skin*.

LAMMING: Yes. This is an example of how one takes historical moments and historical institutions and shifts them about to create one's own mosaic. For example, the House of Trade and Justice, which is situated in Limestone and can be seen as England, actually represents a very important Spanish institution of the time: the great House of Seville, which had absolute control over all voyages, was an absolutely authoritarian structure with volumes of regulations governing all aspects of voyages. Here again is this business of working in the context of two sets of times simultaneously.

I was thinking of the House as a symbol of our contemporary situation, of the post-colonial world like that of San Cristobal. Today, it is the international corporation. That is the stupendous body that now rises above what ordinary people and their leaders imagine to be the domestic authority of the land. A country becomes what is called 'independent,' attempts, like the Reconnaissance to set out on a journey of very serious breaking away, but discovers instead the international corporation – that gigantic arrangement of modern life that has the capacity to control or redirect decisions democratically decided by people and their leaders.

KENT: That is what practically every African country confronts today.

LAMMING: Yes. The leaders, when they come to power, find themselves in a position where negotiation with that House of Trade and Justice is more crucial to them than any kind of exchange, any kind of participation, any kind of consultation between them and the community whose mandate they have.

KENT: The situation at the novel's end, where the attempt by the Commandant has come to nought – do we simply now have a dramatisation of the inevitable failure of this type of venture by the human spirit?

LAMMING: No, I wouldn't say 'inevitable failure.' I would say that what we have there is what occurs in all my previous books – what I call 'the open end.' There is really no closing of the drama. This experience will be a creative legacy, the soil of some other movement in life.

KENT: Let's swing over a bit now to *Water With Berries*, which takes its title from William Shakepeare's *The Tempest*. Maybe we can start by connecting the title more with the characters. I recall that in *The Tempest*, the 'native' Caliban states that when Prospero first arrived on Caliban's island, he gave Caliban water with berries to eat. At that point in the play, I think Caliban is experiencing a good deal of Prospero's mistreatment. So the water with berries was the kind treatment.

LAMMING: Yes, but Caliban's complaint is stronger than that. He's in a state of rage by this time, that he welcomed Prospero, educated him about the island, and, in a way, also welcomed the exchange that went on between them. The peculiar kinds of gifts that Prospero was supposed to be bringing to him – Caliban speaks not only of water with berries, etc., but also of being taught to see the greater light, and in that, the whole question has always been raised for me of the role of language as gift.

KENT: You have a statement on this in *Pleasures of Exile.*

LAMMING: Yes. In this encounter, Caliban received not just words, but language as symbolic interpretation, as instrument of the exploring consciousness. Once he had accepted language as such, the future of his development, however independent it was, would always be in some way inextricably tied up with that pioneering aspect of Prospero. Caliban at some stage would have to find a way of breaking that contract, which got sealed by language, in order to restructure some alternative reality for himself.

KENT: So, then, the characters in the book have first been on an island presumably in the West Indies, in *Water With Berries*?

LAMMING: What is happening here is that I am in a way attempting to reverse the journeys. In Shakespeare's *Tempest*, it was Prospero in the role of visitor to Caliban's island. In *Water With Berries*, it's reversed. The three characters really represent three aspects of Caliban making his journey to Prospero's ancestral home – a journey which was, at the beginning, a logical kind of development because of the relation to Prospero's language. They then discovered the reality of Prospero's home – not from a distance, not filtered through Prospero's explanation or record of his home, but through their own immediate and direct experience.

KENT: That means, doesn't it, that Teeton (the painter in *Water with Berries*), having gone through certain revolutionary experiences on the island and having come to England to find a new life discovers that Prospero's home is a reality that he must still break through in order to get to a central reality within himself?

LAMMING: Yes. One purpose or function of that voyage for Teeton and people like that, is for them in fact to test the fiction of England by its reality. For there have been men who grew up, not with a knowledge of Prospero's background and world, but with an idea of that world. And what is happening to them now is that they are experiencing in their consciousness the disintegration of that idea. The irrelevance and the falsity of that idea beside the hitherto obscured reality.

KENT: Teeton gives up painting, presumably through a discovery that either what he has been constrained to paint or the reality that he reaches through painting has nothing to do with the central rhythms of his life?

LAMMING: The paintings only have to do with a stage of life which he really wants to move beyond. Teeton is another example of this theme of the artist situated in political change. He recognises that the whole conception of the role of imagination in the creation of the people, in the direction of the society, has absolutely no meaning in the England he is living in.

KENT: What is the most concrete evidence of that?

LAMMING: The novelist, the poet, the painter is very conscious of doing with the imagination something more than creating so-called works of art. In other words, there is a sense in which he is undertaking a public task as distinct from the situation in contemporary England where the writer is a law unto himself. There, he is not a man who works under the pressures, who works with the immediacy, of what Kierkegaard called 'that immediate neighbourhood.' The society is not for him what Nigeria is to novelist Achebe or the Caribbean is to people concerned with the shaping of national consciousness, giving alternative directions to society, etc. In contemporary England the world of the creative imagination is very atomised. The literary imagination is concerned with exploring and explaining – as, say, in the breakup of a marriage – the disintegration of an individual and it goes on in a very restricted world of a few rooms and a few bars, but with no direct informing influence from the subsoil of life outside. It's a private exercise at worst, a masturbatory kind of exercise.

KENT: So Teeton's last contact with the soil as a kind of metaphor was really his relationship with his wife, Randy, and his revolutionary comrades.

LAMMING: Yes. The relationships between them in a way are really the only way they have left now of holding together the world they have left behind. They keep reliving the San Cristobal that they have left behind. The whole island is with them, and Teeton is convinced at this stage that any forward movement of these developments demands a return in some way into that world.

KENT. On the other hand, he's working out something with the character, the Old Dowager, getting into relationships with her that give him a sense of discovery. Is she part of the Prospero influence?

LAMMING: That's right. She's sort of taken over the role of Prospero, with this difference: whereas Prospero in *The Tempest* is a male force because the world from which he is operating is aggressive, expansionist and conquering, by the time we get to *Water With Berries*, that world has now contracted in a way. It has now retreated; it has aged. And what we see in the Old Dowager is the age, the remoteness, in some ways the impotence of the earlier Prospero. That power – that imperial power, that spirit of adventure, that extraordinary obsession with mastering reality, with turning the earth into one's private garden – is now gone; there is only the Old Dowager there with memories of a great past, of a great ancestral root. Now, Teeton lives as a tenant in her house, which is only another way of describing how he and people like him live in that country. He develops a very strong relationship to her. She exhibits a tremendous material concern toward him. She is careful about his health, very protective of him against the intrusions and injustices that might come from outside. There is the suggestion that in some part of her she is carrying on Prospero's role, for she does see in Teeton some aspect of her own responsibility. Now, he responds to her in a human way of care and concern; from time to time, images of his mother come to mind. But he also realises that he is permanently condemned if he does not find the way of breaking this kind of response, of breaking this kind of relationship to her. Finally, he does it by killing her.

KENT: Does that parallel what the so-called natives have to do on the island when they rape the daughter of the former controller of the island?

LAMMING: The rage inflicted on her is really that intended for Prospero, for she cannot in the minds of Prospero's victims be separated from his privilege and his history.

KENT: It's something like Fanon's saying that the ejection of the coloniser is a complete taking over and reordering of whatever's there?

LAMMING: There may be a connection, but the rape scene seems to me to be working as almost a way of exorcising that part of their lives. I think that this is where there may be a connection if at all. I believe that it is against all experience that a history which held men together in that way can come to an end in a cordial manner. That we can say, 'Here is the parting of the ways; we will meet up here and continue as though nothing had ever happened; we can put all this horror, all this brutality behind; we are now equal in a new enterprise of human liberation.' That horror and that brutality have a price, which has to be paid by the man who inflicted it – just as the man who suffered it has to find a way of exorcising that demon. It seems to me that there is almost a therapeutic need for a certain kind of violence in the breaking. There cannot be a parting of the ways. There has to be a smashing.

KENT: As [James] Baldwin would say, 'The dues have been accumulated, and they have to be paid.'

LAMMING: But there is a view, you see, that is continuing these days, which is why I make the distinction between colonial experience and the colonial situation, and I notice it sometimes in English critics of these books who say, 'Oh, God, is he coming with this again?' I mean, okay, the places have independence, etc. The colonial situation is a matter of historical record. What I'm saying is that the colonial experience is a *living* experience in the consciousness of these people. And just because the so-called colonial situation and its institutions may have been transferred into something else, it is a fallacy to think that the human-lived content of those situations are automatically transferred into something else, too. The experience is a continuing psychic experience that has to be dealt with and will have to be dealt with long after the actual colonial situation formally ends.

KENT: Swinging back a little bit to the character situation, Teeton seems almost to gain his deepest sense aliveness in his interview with Jeremy, the consul.

LAMMING: His relation to Jeremy is an aspect of the class situation. He really detests Jeremy. He detests the function which Jeremy performs. Jeremy is a bureaucrat. He works as a sort of diplomat. He therefore represents an authority Teeton was earlier imprisoned for helping to try to overthrow, one which, indeed, he's on his way back, he hopes, to San Cristobal to join forces for overthrowing. There is a part of him which feels that even to be sitting talking with Jeremy is to be involving himself in a pollution which he had put behind. At the same time, because he had shared a kind of experience of class with Jeremy – as men who had gone to school together – there always remains with him this peculiar curiosity to see what Jeremy looks like, what he is up to. Sometimes, he's even tempted to get engaged in argument with him. He tries to avoid it all the time, but a part of him in a sense has not completely exorcised Jeremy's world. He has this curiosity to look at it, though he's never likely to join it.

KENT: Well, there's something also in him that makes him the person to whom Nicole comes, isn't it? Nicole, Roger's wife.

LAMMING: Yes. He's a man who doesn't say too much; he's very reflective. And he has the sort of posture that people in difficulty gravitate towards, because he has this air of being able to listen and in some way participate by the act of listening. But they're all attracted to him in that way, not just Nicole.

KENT: In the relationship between Nicole and Roger, the musician, Roger's accusation of infidelity is a tool of evading a direct commitment to life on her terms?

165

LAMMING: It's that, but it's something else. The difference between Roger and Teeton is that, whereas Teeton always felt a certain root in his original society, Roger never felt it. From very early, he always felt this distance between him and his society. Incidentally Roger is the Indian – in this group of three. Now, there is an element of him that is very much concerned with purity, and it takes form in his work.

KENT: Prospero's false conception of purity?

LAMMING: No. I think that has to do more with Roger himself. Look at his situation, which includes marriage to this white girl who, in the normal human terms, is everything a 'conventional' wife could be. But, the one thing he does not want is children and the one thing she does want is children. What he has against the business of the child, which is not very different from what he had against the island where he was born, is a horror of the half-caste, of the impure. One of the reasons he can never accept the society that produced him is that it was made up of this cultural half-caste situation. There was no clear, clean, pure ancestral cultural life, and although he has this tremendous attachment to Nicole, he does not believe that that is worth fathering an example of what he would call the impure.

KENT: Derek seems to represent a different type of purity, in that he advocates, almost to the point of viciousness, that Roger and Nicole be completely honest with each other.

LAMMING: Derek is the type of character who, unlike Roger and certainly unlike Teeton, is the actor, a man who's never really been given to much self-scrutiny. In a different way, but not unlike Steward, he is a guy who has always believed in the purity of motive. His friendships are not investments. They result from an immediate human response towards another human being. And it is only when he finds himself in crisis that he comes to realise that perhaps there is no such innocence in a human being.

KENT: We see nothing of Nicole except her commitment to Roger, and nothing of her but a kind of gentle femininity, somewhat like Desdemona in Shakespeare's *Othello*.

LAMMING: There are aspects of that. One thing about Nicole, too, is that she is not English, she's American. She stands in relation to the place as really a stranger – as transient. That is perhaps her most central function.

KENT: Now, there is an aspect of the 'ceremony of souls' in the book. Would you refresh us generally on that ceremony as it relates to the book itself?

LAMMING: It's a ceremony in which the dead returned to speak to the living about important events in their lives – that is, before the dead passed on – and I interpret it as an example of the theme of redemption, the theme of coming to terms with the past. For example, in the traditional mythology of that ceremony, when you die, the dead soul is supposed to be locked in water and in fact cannot be released from the water into a freer element until that ceremony has taken place! Thus, in a sense, the whole journey of these Caliban-like figures rests on this necessity for whatever is dead, whatever has passed on, to be summoned back for some kind of dialogue. If this past is to be mastered, if the factors which create it are to be healed, this past must be gone into. In ways, this is the key thing about the coming back of the dead in the ceremony – that they have to go into matters which they did not, for one reason or another, when alive.

KENT: You actually saw this 'ceremony of souls' in Haiti, didn't you?

LAMMING: Yes. This actually used to happen. It's in the late '50s that I remember.

KENT: From the number of references to it, and some direct descriptions of it in your work, it seems obvious that it has become for you sort of fundamental.

LAMMING: It's very central to me in the sense that the world in which one lives is not just inhabited by the living. It is a world which is also the creation of the dead. And any architecture of the future cannot really take place without that continuing dialogue between the living and the dead. I think that theme will always be running through my books.

KENT: Dramatically, in *Natives of My Person*, isn't there such a confrontation, not with the actual dead, but with a past that will not be reconciled?

LAMMING: Yes, it is there as well.

KENT: Now, directly, in *Water With Berries*, I feel it when the woman comes out on the Heath – at that time an anonymous woman

– and she is somehow trying to confront the past through a person whom she does not know. She is putting Teeton almost in the position of a priest, although he has no Priestly powers, when she thus confronts him. She can be very frank with him because she does not know him.

LAMMING: Yes. And the other reason for the frankness, which works both ways, is that they don't see each other.

KENT: So it really is a setting for the 'ceremony of souls.' It's very powerful.

LAMMING: Yes. It is a setting for the ceremony.

KENT: Are we to assume that – there's that open-end business again – that there is left open the possibility that these revolutionary men will return, these plotters who wish to come back to the island, who seem to have so much confidence that Teeton is going to make it back through to them?

LAMMING: I think no. I didn't want to close that way. They are not going to return. What they will have to deal with now is the new reality in the experience – that is, the world – the increasing world of Blacks in England, rather than what they propose to do about the world on the island. The transformations of their 'homes' would have passed onto another generation.

KENT: You have said also that your fiction – your entire work – is really an unfolding of one work.

LAMMING: Yes. You can see, first of all. If you take *In The Castle of My Skin*, where the realisation of the world is seen through boys – this is the growing-up; and then the next book, *The Emigrants*, with these men moving out to England. The emigrants on that ship can be seen as the extensions of the boys of *In The Castle of My Skin*. This was in a way the logic of development. Society made up with people who always saw their fulfillment elsewhere, outside of the society. That aspect of migration is going to be very central to the psychology of that whole generation of people. The question was not so much 'what am I going to do here,' but 'when will the opportunity arrive for me to leave?' And this is how we see the journey of the men who, in a sense, could be said to be the boys, except that where the boys of *In The Castle* are held to one particular territory, the men are drawn from all the territories of the

Caribbean. Then, in the third book, we see that, after the special disillusionments of that voyage, after these men, too, have put the idea of where they're going beside the reality of where they are, the next logical step was for their return, which was in *Of Age and Innocence*. What we see there is the society of *In The Castle of My Skin* now extended to be the whole area in its last stages of colonialism. When *Of Age* ends, we are on the eve of the independence arrangements, and when we move into *Season of Adventure*, we have a study in the fall of the first independent republic. That is that line of backing. Now, there was at that moment no further point for me to go to without in a sense going beyond what has actually happened in the society. So, the next stage, *Natives of My Person*, was a way of going forward by making a complete return to the beginnings; it's actually the whole etiology of *In the Castle of My Skin*, *The Emigrants* and *Season of Adventure*. I think it might be possible to find in *Natives of My Person* elements, parallels and so forth in each of the preceding volumes.

KENT: You have mentioned in our conversations several writers you've responded to. Are there any Black writers who've jarred your perception or imagination?

LAMMING: I think it came later. I think Wright was perhaps the major of all Black writers. And something I must say is that the Black writing from the United States was a very, very small part of the experience for myself and people like me in the Caribbean. This is an example of one of the most interesting developments in recent times. It was not really a part of our world at all. In 1953, Blyden Jackson told me that when he read *In The Castle of My Skin*, it was the first time he had read a book by a Black man outside of the United States.

Speaking of Wright, the other day I came across an exercise book I used as a young boy to jot down things that struck me about writers of books, etc. I would in fact copy – not just make notes to return to – passages out of them. I was looking through this exercise book, which would probably have a date like 1948, and I found pages and pages of *Black Boy* written out in ink. I remember very well this very long section where Wright is reflecting about leaving for the North.

KENT: You have mentioned such writers as Melville and particularly Whitman, as some of the American writers who might be influencing West Indian writers. Of course, I guess everybody comes by James Joyce.

LAMMING: I think his influence was there. But 'influence,' I find, is always a very tricky thing in this context. Reading, in a way, is kind of like eating: foods are going in and things are happening to the metabolism that you are not consciously aware of; so, as you read, things are entering which remain lodged there, that you may not be aware of. Now, I would think that a kind of influence in that way – later a conscious influence – was Conrad. I have never forgotten the echoes which Conrad's writing produced in me.

| *Martin Carter: A Poet of the Americas: An Interview with Stewart Brown*[*]

BROWN: Do you recall when you first became aware of Martin Carter's poetry?

LAMMING: I am vague about the place and time, but it was certainly some time between my leaving Trinidad in 1950 and the early years in London. And it would have to have been via *Kyk-Over-Al*, I don't remember Carter as having been a very early contributor to *Bim* so it probably was in *Kyk* but what is more vivid is the early selection, the *Poems of Resistance*, I think that is the first real awareness of him as a voice and someone who I had not then met.

BROWN: Do you recall what your reactions were to the poems when you first encountered them?

LAMMING: Only it was a very authentic voice, and all the more so because it was linked to the events taking place in Guyana. Guyana in the 1950s and especially around 1952/53, a little before the suspension of the constitution, was in fact, I would say, politically the most advanced in consciousness of all the Caribbean territories and it was the one that was targeted as the most dangerous because of this definition – self definition sometimes – of the Peoples Progressive Party as Marxist or Leninist. So Guyana was always in the news and voices coming out of Guyana had a special significance. What I think was unusual and very striking was that the English-speaking Caribbean was not used to having poets who were so directly involved with active political movements, as Carter was, or who put poetry in the service of such a movement. I am not aware of any precedent within the English-speaking Caribbean. That

[*] This was published in the journal *Kyk-Over-Al* (49/50), June 2000. Stewart Brown is a poet, critic and editor of several anthologies of Caribbean Writing.

kind of engagement was more a feature of Hispanic writing within the region, so he stood out for that reason. And then his work had this remarkable sweep. There was something about Carter's early poems that had an echo of Whitman, that sweep, that freedom of line, so one tended to think of him as a poet of the Americas rather than of the Islands.

BROWN: Do you remember when you first met Martin?

LAMMING: Yes, very very well, very vividly. I met him on my return visit to the Caribbean and what was my first visit to Guyana, in 1955. I had been in the United States as a Guggenheim Fellow and then I had an assignment to do an article for *Holiday* on the Caribbean, which took me through all the territories, and I ended up in Guyana. I found a Guyana that was still in a state of emergency, after the suspension of the constitution and the imprisonment of the Ministers. Carter had been in prison and when I met him he was still under a kind of house arrest really, he could not go beyond a radius of about half a mile from the house and there were regulations restricting the number of people who could visit the house at one time. This had been going on for some time. He was very drawn but amazingly cheerful, he had a way of describing horror as though there were some sort of comic element in it. He was, on the surface, without any sign of bitterness, although I am reasonably sure that there was a lot of pain and hurt and resentment going on inside him. Resentment at the notion that a little Governor – as I think he would have imagined the Governor to be – could in fact come into what he regarded as his land, Carter's land, and dictate where he could go and where he could not go. I think he felt a kind of humiliation, personal and collective, about that predicament. I remember that very well, I was very moved by that.

I remember being invited out one evening and going to ask him whether we should all go out together – there was some well known place, I've forgotten the area in Georgetown – but he said he couldn't, it was beyond the radius of his 'licence'. But he said Phyllis might like to go and I took her out with three or four friends, I had the impression that she hadn't gone out, herself, for a long time. It was just one of these little Saturday evening places with music and people dancing and so on...I remember that very vividly and then going back to see Martin at their home. When I left Guyana, after three months, that situation still hadn't come to an end. Another very interesting occasion I recall from that period was a remarkable party held just before I left Guyana. I was producing some radio programmes presenting the literature of the region through radio. I think it was called 'New World of the Caribbean' or something like that, and we discovered that the Governor, a man called Rennison, listened to these programmes regularly, and was very interested in them. So when, at the end of the series, I asked a friend of mine, Frank Williams, a doctor, who had been very helpful, to let us have a party in his house for all the people involved in the programmes somebody suggested we send an invitation to Rennison. So we did, or that is, Dr Williams sent it, very quietly and discreetly. And Rennison sent back, in that kind of protocol way, saying that yes he would come. Now that was a big secret, negotiating, not letting anyone know that he was coming, because we had already invited Cheddi Jagan who had been involved in the programmes, commenting, you know. So Jagan was there with his wife, and then Rennison came and people were astonished. This was a very very remarkable evening. I mention that because I remember that I introduced Rennison to Carter and they got to talking. But Rennison wasn't fully aware of whom he was talking to – in the sense of the total circumstances of Carter's situation – and he was telling Martin about the quality of the light on the skyline when he drove around a certain area of the city in the early evening and he asks Carter 'had he been around there recently?' and of course Martin said 'No, it wouldn't be legal for me to do that,' and Rennison just stopped immediately, realising that he had entered territory for which he hadn't fully prepared himself. But Carter didn't pursue that any further.

BROWN: You worked with Carter in 1965, I think, on co-editing the Guyana Independence issue of *New World Quarterly*. What do you recall of that collaboration?

LAMMING: The *New World* group was a special group that had mainly come out of the university and was pioneered by Lloyd Best, a political economist. The editorial board was mostly made up of Mona and St Augustine people. *New World* was a very fine quarterly. They had the idea that they would do a special issue to celebrate the independence of Guyana and they brought me out, (I was living in London then), to edit the issue and Carter would assist me. Martin, who is very good at reading and editing and so on is not so good at any kind of organised activity and I had some difficulty because most of the time I couldn't find him. I didn't know where he was and nobody knew where he was at that time. I think that was a very bad time for him because after moving from that revolutionary, anti-imperialist, anti-capitalist period he was unemployed for some time until he was rescued, in an odd kind of way, by Bookers – the company that most obviously represented the continuation of that old social order. He edited some kind of in-house paper for the company and I think that he was rather burdened by his predicament of having to do such things in order to support his family – because Martin had a pretty large family, I don't remember how many children there are but there were a lot of children around at the time, all dependent, at school or whatever.

However I remember that he was extremely good in a particular situation we had to resolve. We wanted the 'Independence Issue' of the journal to cut across all the party lines but that was very difficult because we had to ask Burnham, who was then in power, if he would help in facilitating an order for the journal. We didn't want any money from him directly but we knew that the journal would be of a quality that it should be circulated among the schools and if we could just get an order to help with the printing cost that would make things possible. But it was to be a sale and a purchase, not a subsidy. Well Burnham said 'yes' automatically, because he liked the idea of being associated with that kind of product and especially with the names of the people at a regional level who were associated with it. But we also wanted Jagan. However, the polarisation of the parties in Guyana at that time, along ideological and racial lines, was so intense that the very mention of Burnham to Jagan, or vice versa would normally put an end to any further conversation. So getting the two of them to agree to appear in the same issue of the journal would be a real scoop.

I particularly wanted Jagan because I had got hold of the first chapter – though it wasn't published yet, of what became his autobiography, *The West on Trial*. And that's the best chapter in the whole book; it's the chapter in which he speaks about growing up in the Corentyne, as a boy without shoes until he came into Georgetown. It is a very very moving chapter. I asked Martin to join me and we went to see Cheddi early in the morning, at about half past five or six or so in his office, to ask him whether we could open the journal with his chapter. We didn't tell him about the government purchase but what we told him was that since the journal was a celebration of independence, as a matter of courtesy we were going to ask Burnham to just write a preface for the issue. Eventually, after a long discussion, when we had told him what our real intentions were for the journal and after I had described in detail item by item, what would be in it, like the famous essay by C.L.R. James on Khanai etc., marvellous stuff, Cheddi agreed. I think the success of that mission to persuade Cheddi to let us use his work really had to do with the lingering – in a way – affection that Jagan had for Carter, and that the feeling was mutual. What is very interesting here is the respect for Carter as a personality. Although he had broken with Jagan – he had broken with all of them in a way – at a party level, he had never broken at the level of personal friendships. It was very extraordinary, although the break was so decisive, and caused so much bitterness, one had a sense of Carter being deeply valued, respected and loved, at a personal level and as a citizen, by Jagan.

BROWN: Did you keep in touch with Carter after that period?

LAMMING: Yes, we met at intervals because I then became very attached to Guyana and made several visits when I was in the Caribbean. And Carter then came once to Barbados, he had a daughter who was married there. And then I did a TV programme with him in Barbados; Michael Gilkes did some kind of programme on Carter in which I read the poems and Carter was interviewed, etc. And then we met in Havana on various occasions, so it was that kind of friendship, whenever we were in the same country somehow or other we made a point of meeting up, having a chat etc.

BROWN: You didn't correspond?

LAMMING: No, I didn't. I don't know who might have letters from Martin, but I never corresponded with him. I don't know that he was much of a correspondent, I don't know any friends who have letters from Martin.

BROWN: Do you have favourite poems of Carter's, particular poems you value, that seem to you to stand out in his work?

LAMMING: I always return to 'University of Hunger', a wonderfully sustained kind of ballad, and I find 'I Come from the Nigger Yard' a very very fine poem, which used to blow peoples minds at one time but the more I read it I come to understand that there is much more in that poem than just protest noise. This is the interesting thing about Carter, when you re-read the early Carter, the poems that are in appearance political poems have a dimension that is not usually inherent in ordinary political poems. You see that 'I Come from the Nigger Yard' and 'University of Hunger' and other poems from *Poems of Resistance* secrete or conceal a particular vision of a society that is threatened by abortion, Carter is always having that vision. You see it then when you move away from the overtly political poems in the *Poems of Shape and Motion*, that attempt to describe a coming into being, a wanting to be other than what is. And so I don't really see a break in Carter at all, I see a change in tone and modalities of expression but I think there is a continuity of vision right through to the very hermetic *Poems of Affinity*. And even in those later poems you see that when there is an occasion which as you might say 'triggers' him – a poem like 'Assassins of the Voice' which I use a lot in speaking of the fear and terror and cowardice of that new plantation bourgeoisie – you see again, one may say the old Carter but it's the same, the same Carter vision. And always with a great concern for craft. Carter is much more concerned than people normally understand, about the shape and texture of the poem. Whatever he may be writing about, 'craft' is very high on his list of requirements for the poem. That is not a quality that one normally associates with writers of political protest poetry.

BROWN: No, and he was an intellectual too, in ways that don't fit with that stereotype of the emotional poet of protest. I remember when I first met him, in Guyana in 1988, just after Burnham had died and Guyana was a 'closed' enclave, very few influences from contemporary academic thought for example had penetrated the society, but Carter seemed both very interested in and very knowledgeable about current issues in critical theory and philosophy.

LAMMING: Yes, well the thing about Carter, unlike many Caribbean writers of my acquaintance, was that Carter was also a very great reader, a voluminous reader, and he read under the compulsion of what I would call a very philosophic turn of mind. Carter thinks very much in the way that the philosopher would think, and he brings that philosophic turn of mind to all details, however minimal, of the society. So that he has a way sometimes, even in normal conversation, of talking in metaphors about very ordinary things that had not really struck him as all that ordinary at all.

BROWN: You were talking yesterday about your own work and the sense you have of it being involved in the intellectual wing, as it were, of the anti-colonial struggle. Would you locate Carter's work alongside your own in that movement through those years?

LAMMING: I think there would be parallels. I think we would share a view that it wasn't just a question of being anti-colonial, because behind what appears to be the anti-colonial statement there is an appeal for the creation of an alternative society. It's not a question of getting rid of people – foreigners, white rule and so on, though that is there and has to be stated, but inside that appeal there is also the critique – which runs through my work – the critique of that delinquent, emergent middle class that is just waiting to take over and who really represent nothing different from the people they are trying to replace. Its really an attempt to call into being an order of society and a state of social relations which we imagine to be potential in the society and to be capable of realisation. Only if...only if.

BROWN: Carter was unusual in that he moved from expressing his views about social injustice and the social order to actually becoming a practising politician at one point in his career, a move which drew various kinds of comment, some of it negative, at the time. I wondered if you remember him in that period of his life and how you felt about what he had done.

LAMMING: I didn't pay too much attention to it, though I may have talked to him about it at times. I don't think anyone ever doubted Carter's integrity. Whatever he entered, whatever the strains were he could offer a moral and valid reason for it, even if the there were things he took no pleasure in doing. I am absolutely sure he took no pleasure in being a member of the government. He wasn't the kind of person to whom that had much appeal. He took no pleasure in representing the country at the United Nations for example, that 'status' would not appeal to him as something, in itself, worth having. He wasn't that type at all. Why then would you get committed in that way? I think the reason that he might offer, not even verbally but to himself, was that he saw himself as being used in a positive way. He represented something that could not be found in other members of the government. And therefore he was there on behalf of Guyana, he was not there on behalf of Burnham, if you see what I mean, he was not speaking on behalf of Burnham, he was not intervening on behalf of Burnham, rather he was intervening on behalf of whatever is decent in Guyana. And that is why he never held these positions for very long. He was very much 'in transit' in those kinds of positions.

BROWN: You've said that you don't really see that division that others have noticed, stylistically, between his early and his later work.

LAMMING: No, its the continuity of vision that I see, but there is a difference in the style, certainly. The rhetorical resonance of '... Nigger Yard' and 'University of Hunger' for example, a lot of that is reduced, almost weeded out in the later work. But it happens in stages really, the *Poems of Shape and Motion* sequence seems to act as a kind of bridge between the early poems and the later. You get to *Shape and Motion* and he's moving deeper and deeper inside himself as distinct from articulating the external world. Going inside. Then I think he reaches the point in the *Poems of Affinity*, which are autobiographically very exact, that there was a tragedy at work in Guyana that went beyond utterance, you had to stumble or speak in syllables. He senses a monster, a demon, something, which could no longer just be reported on or analysed, you had to stammer when you approached it. And there is that sense, in the later poems of cutting language down, very bare, very spare. And I think that what he was looking at in *Poems of Affinity* is also what he is fearing might happen in the earlier poems, but that vision of potential, in the Angela Davis poem for example, is still there, but there is a tension in him between that and an increasing pessimism, really, about the possibility of his ever seeing it fulfilled.

BROWN: So would you go along with that view of Carter's work over time, that the poetry charts a movement from optimism to despair almost, and that he chronicles not only his own process of disillusion but that of a whole generation whose post-colonial ambition, as one might call it, was progressively shattered by the unfolding events in Guyana, indeed across the whole Caribbean?

LAMMING: Yes I think that vision and that critique was shared by certain writers. It's very strong – though it may seem surprising to put together – it's a very strong concern in Walcott's work, that he is very pained by the emergence of that delinquent new chap with the briefcase and the cigar and you know, who is really the new ruler.

BROWN: Both as a man and as a poet Martin Carter seems to have been almost universally respected, almost revered, within Guyana and right across the Caribbean. Why do you think that was?

LAMMING: Carter has a stature in the collective consciousness of Guyana that is quite unique among writers in the English-speaking Caribbean. I mean in Guyana the name Martin Carter had a resonance as something authentically Guyanese, as one of the Guyanese institutions, one of the institutions of which they are most proud. I was very struck by that. It is very much like the way people respond to the name Nicolás Guillén in Cuba; 'Nicolás' can only be one Nicolás, it's Guillén. I think that has a lot to do with the marriage of the poet and the activist in struggle in the early 1950s, that he is remembered in that way. And at that time Carter's speeches would quite often take the form of the reading of those poems. A number of those poems in *Poems of Resistance* would be read at those political meetings and those memories of the poet inside that kind of struggle, and of that kind of struggle taken to another level by the poet, those memories went very deep in the consciousness of a generation. And they got transmitted to succeeding generations. He once told me a very interesting story – that one of the things which gave him the most solace was that he was once walking somewhere and there was a little girl, who must have been maybe six years old or something like that, who saw him and called out to her mother, 'Mummy Mummy look, that look like the poems man there'. And that business of being identified by a six-year-old as 'the poems man' gave him the joy that went beyond any critical analysis.

BROWN: In fact he wrote that poem about it, called 'The Poems Man'

LAMMING: Yes, well this actually happened.

BROWN: And do you think the fact that he stayed in Guyana more or less throughout his life contributed to that sense of identification the Guyanese people felt with him and his work?

LAMMING: I'm not too sure that is so. He is unlike all the other Caribbean writers who have become known beyond the Caribbean, who have had their reputations made outside the region. We would not have been known nor accepted in that way, had we not been accepted outside. Carter is one of the few, if not the only one, whose reputation was made inside the region and validated inside it, that did not require external validation. For most of the other writers their constituencies, in terms of their readers, required the validation as to whether it was a great book from the *Observer* or the *Statesman* or *The Times* or *The New York Times* whatever. That validation was necessary in terms of putting the seal of approval, 'yes this is worthwhile, ours...' on the work. And he never had that external validation, in a way it came from within and that is very unusual.

About the remaining home, I never understood that, in that as far as I know he is the only one of the family, that is the brothers and so on, all of whom went abroad to study or what have you, but Martin didn't and I've never been quite clear why that happened. Whether it was early marriage or whatever, I'm not sure. I'm inclined to think, sometimes, that it was a pity he didn't get a break from Guyana because I think that his staying put in Guyana did great damage to him and forced him to do great damage to himself in a variety of ways. He might have experienced some kind of relief if there was a certain distance for a while, I mean away. Whenever he went out it was for very brief spells.

BROWN: One curious, perhaps negative, thing comes out of his being so much validated from within the Caribbean. Though various, well-connected people have tried over the years, no one has been able to persuade a major publisher to take Carter's work on. Do you think there is anything in the notion of his work being too deeply rooted in the Guyanese experience to easily transcend its time and place? And if not, how to explain his relative obscurity when so many other, less accomplished Caribbean poets seem to have impressed international publishers?

LAMMING: I don't know...I would have thought that his quality as a poet is so good, I mean in my view he is one of the best, much better than some of the more prominent poets who are the most promoted. But if he is that good a poet and is that authentic to the Caribbean, he really ought to have some kind of appeal outside, because the two things go together. I don't think the one goes without the other although it is quite true that the relation to the Caribbean may help in the promotion of certain writers rather than others.

One reason is partly that he has been (sometimes literally) locked inside the Caribbean, he's not been out much, he's not been a man given to conferencing and being engaged in the kind of networking that takes place, you know, in these kind of gatherings. And I've always felt, with Martin, whether it was about poetry or anything else, that he has no gifts at all for self-promotion. Anything that is going to happen, in a positive way for Martin, somebody else is going to have to organise that. Carter is wholly and totally without that instinct for self-promotion and I have a feeling that that may explain, not the neglect really but the overlooking of his work, he just didn't engage at all in any kind of self-promotion.

BROWN: When I spoke to him about it he seemed completely indifferent to that kind of idea of success.

LAMMING: Yes, and my impression of him always has been that he is without any sense of competing with others, you know he has a very firm sense of his value and what it is he set out to do and he feels no need of arguing whether he is better than or not as good as anyone, he's not disturbed in the slightest.

BROWN: Yes, he had a kind of faith that time would do all the sorting out.

LAMMING: Yes, that's right.

BROWN: Finally, just looking back over his career as a whole, looking back from the end of the twentieth century over the last 50 years and the emergence of Caribbean writing as a significant body of literature, where would you put Carter's work in that story?

LAMMING: Well I think that if you are looking at the literature he will remain among the greatest of the writers of that period. I think if we explore what is there we have a very major statement about the region. I think it's a pity that we didn't have more of his prose, for he wrote with a remarkable lucidity when he's trying to get his vision across in prose, like his piece on the role of the artist that we published in that independence edition of *New World*. But I think that his place as such is very secure and I think that with time, when they are looking to see what kinds of utterance came from the corners of these Americas then Carter will stand in the very first ranks of the writers of the Americas.

19

*The Aesthetics of Decolonisation
Conversation between Anthony
Bogues and George Lamming*[*]

BOGUES: George I want to begin by thanking you very much for agreeing to do these interviews.

LAMMING: You are welcome.

BOGUES: Let's begin by talking about Caribbean English literature and criticism, and talk about a debate that seems to have been stirred again by a recent book by Louis James about the inauguration of Caribbean literature or English-speaking Caribbean literature and criticism. You have a position as, I read it, which says that Caribbean Literature really begins in the post Second World War period. Other people would argue that depending on the island, it began somewhere sometime in the late 19th and early 20th century. How would you respond to the various positions of this debate?

LAMMING: I think I would now modify the post-war statement, not fundamentally change it but I would modify. And you can go back and choose whatever marker you want according to how you are defining the literature, but if you're thinking of the creative literature, say the novel for example, I would say a reasonable good marker for me would be DeLisser and particularly *Jane's Career* which is about 1914. And I use that because, although you may have a negative view of it, the way he resolves the tensions and so on, it's an example of how I would define the literature.

It's an example of an attempt to return the society to itself; to show the society how it saw itself, how it imagined itself and also from DeLisser's point of view how he would like it to think about itself. That doesn't alter my speculation about the post-

---

*   These conversations were conducted over the past three years with George Lamming in Barbados during Winter 2006 and Summer 2009.

war because what is happening is although by then the angle of vision has shifted very sharply there's a sense in which DeLisser is taking up a position in relation to that experience which will not engage the sympathies of the writers who would come in the post-1949 period. But he is talking about a real Jamaica and nonetheless a real Caribbean and the difference between DeLisser and those writers I have in mind after 1945, would be in the emphasis of these writers in how they saw the terms of that returning the society to itself.

BOGUES: What do you think were the specific differences in the emphasis, in the angles of vision that you have in mind.

LAMMING: I think that what is happening as a result also perhaps of the Second World War that the seeds of decolonisation have started. This would not have been a part of the orientation of DeLisser. He would have been an empire man and a man who completely identified with that structure as it was in Jamaica after the First World War. The years 1937/38 are key markers in Caribbean literature. The societies of the region have an increasing awareness of their potential for consummation in a way I don't think that they would have seen in say the first two decades and so on of the 20th century. From 1936–38 ending up in Jamaica, you get a situation where people on a mass level have come into confrontation with the state, and they bypass many of the normal colonial governmental arrangements. And this is going to be, it seems to me, the kind of chapter one in terms of the modernising of the Caribbean, the legalising of unions, the formation of parties. So there's a sense of shift in the societies' consciousness of itself between DeLisser's time and the time before the war. And you can sense this shift in the emergence of journals; there is *Focus* in Jamaica and *Kyk-Over-Al* in Guyana and *Bim* in Barbados, journals out of which the post '45 writers mostly were to come out. So by the late '40s, '48 and then from '50, from '50 to '60 you get a literature that is very, very steeped in a sense of national consciousness. Shaping this literature whether the writers are conscious of it or not, are the events of the 1930s. In a way, I think the politics of the 1930s have shaped the imagination of the novels of the late '40s and the 1930s right up to the period of political independence.

BOGUES: So are you saying George that in the post Second World War period the writers, novelists, created an imagination of the English-speaking Caribbean which operates at the level of imagining the nation while in the period before that even if DeLisser was trying to have a gaze on the nation, it wasn't really a gaze on the nation since he was an 'empire man,' to use your words?

LAMMING: Yes. Yes, if you like to imagine the nation in the sense that people are conscious of, and of being on the way to becoming in charge of affairs and accepting responsibility for their affairs and so on in way that I don't think existed, certainly not to that extent, before. Imagining the nation, yes, remember also that from about 1945/46 right across the region there is a debate and there was consensus on the federation of the Anglophone Caribbean. And that by '47 or so there is the conference in Jamaica.

BOGUES: The Montego Bay Conference?

LAMMING: The Montego Bay conference in Jamaica, and a certain ethos is created by this. As a matter of fact, there's a certain consensus about federation including Jamaica at the Montego Bay conference and everybody is more or less agreed, that this is what should be. But you should note even under this heading I do have reservations about defining the nation. But there is the embryonic growth of a consciousness of nations. And then if you like, I think that certain writers, in a very conscious way, not all, but certain writers in a very conscious way thought of themselves as being an essential part of this building of this consciousness.

BOGUES: Could you name some of those writers?

LAMMING: Yes, I mean, I would think that I was very conscious in that way. I would say that Selvon without exception, in his own way was a writer who was very conscious of writing not only just about Trinidad but about a West Indian style and region which he was contributing to. And, certainly Vic Reid would have been very conscious of that. And in a way, although he did not perhaps share the enthusiasms of these others, I would put John Hearne on this list.

BOGUES: Why would you place John Hearne on this list?

LAMMING: John Hearne's *Voices Under the Window* is very conscious of contributing to the making of something that is new; very consciousness of being a part of something, just larger than Jamaica and very conscious of increasing the conscious of something in the area of where literature is new.

BOGUES: You are talking about writers who also seem to operate outside of the region.

LAMMING: Yes and I think for some time that is going to be the situation.

BOGUES: Could you say a little more about why these writers operated from outside of the region. Why does exile become so important in the early period of Caribbean literature?

LAMMING: I can't think of any major Caribbean writer who came to our attention who didn't operate outside the region. That is where they were published. But I think that this statement has to be qualified because these writers who were operating from outside didn't start to write from outside. I mean, a man like Vic Reid or Samuel Selvon had been working away long before they set foot on any boat. And of course Reid is an exception because he didn't go outside. It's very interesting that Reid was on his way to being outside and then all kinds of domestic things came up and it stopped him. But I don't sometimes make the kind of emphasis on that outside, if by outside you mean away from where you started. Rather this is a feature of, I think, of most creative people except that instead of the outside being the metropole centre of an empire and so on, the outside is moving from the province to the centre.

BOGUES: Explain that a bit more George.

LAMMING: You know if you live in South Dakota you're going to try to get to New York or Chicago. There is that pull away from where you started to where you think a certain climate, a certain kind of activity is taking place that provides you with a more fertile soil than where you are. And in the case of the very significant writers of the United States and so on, not so much of England but of the United States, there was the obligatory journey to Paris. You know, that you are unfinished unless you move to where there is fertile soil, so the phenomenon of being outside is not a uniquely Caribbean thing. There's always that gravitational pull towards a centre, usually a very developed urban centre of intellectual activity which will take you away from where you started which would be the province.

BOGUES: But is that not very complicated in the colonial context?

LAMMING: Yes

BOGUES: Complicated in the sense that the writer, the imaginary of the writer, and here I am recalling Derek Walcott's essay 'The Muse of History' in which he says that snow and daffodils were more real than heat and the oleander because they lived in the imagination and therefore in memory so is this situation not more complicated for the writer who lives in the colony?

LAMMING: Yes, I mean there's a tendency to move from where you started to some point, but of course ours is a much more complex move than that. And quite often we're also moving to this centre which will validate what we're doing. That is very critical because that activity that you call writing has not yet acquired status where you are. I mean it may be a hobby, it may be a part-time thing, but it's an activity which has not the status of vocation. It is not yet on the agenda of the general population including on the agenda of the educated classes. So there were some adventurers really, some of the people who picked up and left for London and these places in the late 1940s and 1950s. I'm not so sure that it's not really also an extreme example of the move from province to urban because I think that the writer moving from a small town in the southern states of the United States to New York is looking for validation. I mean this – they need to be reviewed, to be taken notice of in the *New York Times*. It is of course an infinitely more serious matter moving from a Caribbean village. But I think we're just an extreme case of this gravitational pull that takes place with people who are living, if you like in the periphery. We of course know there's a certain inequality in the distribution of knowledge and the distribution of access to facilities.

BOGUES: I'm coming back at you about this so let me put this more concretely. Someone moving from South Dakota to New York is a huge move; but somebody moving from Barbados to London during the period of colonialism to write makes a different move – the relationships are vastly different given the iniquities in all forms of distribution from economic to culture and knowledge matters. In other words, that there is a way in which if I move from South Dakota to New York and I'm an American novelist, my subject is still American, it is one part of the American imaginary. But what happens when I'm a Caribbean writer who moves to London? Do I still write about the Caribbean? And if I do, how do I write about the Caribbean or do I write about London? What about the impact and influence of colonial power upon the imaginary. In London I am a colonial exile; in New York if I am from South Dakota I am not. So does this not create huge differences between the two?

LAMMING: Let us take the people who leave about 1948. There were one or two people you would not have heard very much of in 1948/49. Willie Richardson was a very fine short story writer and so was Sam Selvon. There was a case, a very special kind of case about going to Oxford at around 1951 and these names are known. And in a very odd kind of way it may sound strange today but given the informing influences of the past that had produced and the weight of the colonising force that had produced you, that journey to what I call, that *journey to an expectation* – did not strike you as going necessarily to a foreign place. You were going to a more elaborate extension of something you thought you knew. And on arrival you discovered that you were living with the idea of this place as somewhere you knew. So there's a sense in which the fellow from South Dakota going to New York for the first time might have been travelling even more as a stranger to New York than the guy going from Barbados to London. You know, the thing in your head did not place that kind of distance and separation between you and that. It then becomes complicated when you discover that there is an idea of the place that you have dealt with. But what I wanted to add to that was that each of those people that I had mentioned, however much they differ and so on and whatever their relation to England, their main subject remained the Caribbean and not England. I mean, England may come into their books sometimes as a background to situations but even including Naipaul who is perhaps the one exception, all the major work is going to be about where I had left which I hadn't really left. That sense of belonging to a particular place which through the act of writing you were now discovering, that remained through the careers of all of these people and the people make great controversies around that point.

BOGUES: Could you amplify that point?

LAMMING: Well, the style is what I would want to focus on. One of the things about Trinidad that's unlike Jamaica or Barbados, is this. In Trinidad you play an old mas which you go out in last year's costumes and you're dirty and so on and then you will go and embrace people and make a mess of their clothes. So every move you make is a move to provoke and you know the result of this. But this is a play of old mas of pricking, a way of provoking anger and resentment whether it is African or whether it is Muslim or whatever. This is a very, very Trinidadian thing. And in the early work of particularly say Naipaul there is a tone in the language that is shaped entirely by the urban speech of Trinidad. Although in Naipaul there is a kind of pose of having nothing to do with the place he's never escaped the place. Every book of Naipaul is really about the way he sees Trinidad.

BOGUES: Ok, let me ask you this. We are actually circling around a question which is how would you define, Anglophone Caribbean literature in the 1940s and 1950s? What is it to you that makes it Caribbean – makes it different from say Irish Literature, from English Literature.

LAMMING: It's different from say Irish literature. Irish literature would bear the same relation to Ireland that Caribbean literature bears to the Caribbean. You make a very interesting choice because Irish literature is going to take the form of migrations as well. But always the informing influence is going to be back there whether you're dealing with James Joyce or whoever it is, it's travelling with this place that has claimed you as belonging here wherever you may be.

The Caribbean Novel

BOGUES: So how then would you define the Caribbean novel? Is the framing definition a matter of location and place?

LAMMING: No. I think you could define the literature – I mean that continuing body of work, which expresses a sensibility that has been fundamentally shaped by experience of the Caribbean. And that means the dominant forces there would mean that they are likely to be born in that place and nurtured by it for a very significant period of your life. And nurtured by it in a way that did not allow escape from it. Even if you were absent from it you did not escape the meanings of it. And therefore the literature is an attempt to understand this claim that the place has upon you whether you make a reciprocal claim on it or not. I once came across a passage that I found very interesting; it says that we really have no way of decolonising memory, since memory exercises a tremendous force on the behaviour long after you've left the scene and occasion of what had actually happened. So Wilson Harris has never left Guyana, like Naipaul has never really left Trinidad. There's a sense in which I never really left Barbados. My situation is a little different from theirs in the sense that a lot of my own shaping was also in Trinidad not just Barbados. The period I lived in Trinidad was a very, very extraordinarily redefining period for me and my writing comes out of a sensibility that has actually been shaped by that origin. And with all the values both negative and positive this shaping constitutes that origin. With that definition you can then choose who belonged to the body of writing called Caribbean literature. In this definition, we establish a clear distinction between a book being Caribbean literature and a book about the Caribbean. Because you may even live in the Caribbean and write about the Caribbean without producing a book that could be regarded in terms of it's texture; in terms of it's resonance's it is not necessarily Caribbean.

BOGUES: C.L.R. James has a statement in which he says that in the 20th century the most important Literature to occur in the English language occurs outside of England. He talks about the Irish and he talks about the Caribbean. Why do you think that is so? Do you agree with that statement? James talks about Joyce obviously, he talks about your work, Harris and so on. What is it in the experience of people for whom English is part of the colonising process which then produces a series of literatures in the 20th century that redefines English Literature itself?

LAMMING: I don't know that it's only the 20th century, I mean Swift is not in the 20th century. But, let us say why in English as distinct from what? Why is English? Are you saying it's in English as distinct from French? Or it's distinct from German as well as distinct from some other thing? I'm not too sure about this. I'm not too sure because if one is familiar with what happened with the French language in colonised territories there might be some reservation about giving English that kind of claim. Although, one might also be on reasonably sound ground because as I further reflect now, particularly about the United States.

There is something which linguists will have to deal with. There is something about the waywardness, the openness, the flexibility of English as a language that lends itself to the conversation into situations where it did not begin. And I would say that the good example to start off with is not so much the Caribbean but with the United States and Mark Twain and *Huckleberry Finn*.

I don't believe that you could have had a *Huckleberry Finn* in French, or in German. But then when you get into what is the Anglophone Caribbean, English as a language had a way of lending itself to being extended, transformed, to the point where it was no longer the language of England and became a variety of Englishes. I don't think that the linguistic structure of French probably allowed that. And England never had an academy that gave rules about how this thing was to be done. So there is something in the nature of the language itself that doesn't stop evolving and being transformed. And therefore you get on the one hand – because more than one language is going on in that United States at the same time – You get those New England people, the Hawthornes and that lot and then you get Walt Whitman. And the language is lending itself to these kind of contesting sort of sensibilities. So my answer to this is that I think there is something special about it, maybe in the nature of the language that lends itself because the other people had empires whose language did not perhaps allow this process to happen.

BOGUES: That's a fascinating answer but let us return to Caribbean Literature specifically. What do you think were some of the preoccupations of the novelists and writers in the '40s and '50s? We talked about them feeling that they are part of a nation but were there other set of preoccupations; how did they fasten upon these?

LAMMING: Well, I think in my own case I moved from Barbados to Trinidad. In Barbados, the Caribbean as a reality did not really exist for me. And this is the importance of Trinidad. It was in Trinidad that I became aware of the reality of something that was West Indian in a way that was very vague in Barbados. Jamaica had no meaning for me outside of the name George Headly. But when I went to Trinidad and very quickly within the first year or so of being introduced, going into homes and so on I found that nearly every house I went into the only Trinidadians by birth were the children, their parents were not. Lloyd Braithwaite for example who was the Vice-Chancellor at St Augustine, is a very good example. Every Trinidad house I went to, father Grenada, mother St Vincent, one grandfather from Barbados – so you are actually dealing with a family of islands. Then it dawned on me, not immediately but later and it occurred to me that this West Indian thing was not only an idea but that we were actually West Indian by blood. What had happened and still continues to happen is that we had not found a way of institutionalising what was an existential reality – Of your aunt, your grandmother, whenever you felt it out it stretched outside of the island where you were. And then, this is very important, I met Eric Williams; not Eric Williams the politician, but Williams the historian and scholar. I got to Trinidad in '46 and Williams arrived I think about 1948 for the Anglo-American Caribbean Commission and we used to meet as young people. Remember Williams was the first person who introduced to me the names of Nicolás Guillén and Aimé Césaire. And he told me if you were going to be a writer, a writer of this region you will have to know the works of these writers. And that was the opening of my consciousness – a chord was struck; a personal chord because I went to Trinidad to teach. I was recruited from Barbados to teach in a Spanish boarding school. This was an enterprise set up by a man called Negron. There were some Colombians but mainly Venezuelans. The school was for children of very well to do parents. And the idea was that these boys – it was a boys' school – would learn English and because of the oil industry that was starting up in the '40s they were being prepared for highly paid jobs in the refinery. I mentioned that because the school had to carry out the curriculum of Caracas and the exams were set by Caracas. So when Williams was talking to me about Guillén back at the school I was looking through the syllabus I noticed that Guillén was one of the texts but without Williams telling me the name would have had no meaning for me. It was just another name. But when Williams told me that I was related to Guillén in some kind of way that I then had to discover. So my experiences in Trinidad become a very re-defining moment for me. This experience had a tremendous influence on me and I became very conscious of being engaged in the discovery of the Caribbean. So after *In The Castle of My Skin* no book of mine is set in Barbados. That is where the San Cristobal comes out although every territory is in San Cristobal so there's something very conscious about that. I never returned to Barbados as a physical landscape although Barbados is in every book in some kind of way. So I would say that that orientation deepened and became stronger and stronger. So over the years there's probably no territory in the region now that I have not been in for one reason or another over some period of time. So that's my situation. If I think of Selvon as I knew him and in his work, though he was not a writer to discuss himself in terms of purpose and intention but if you look at the recurring themes and if you look at *A Brighter Sun, Turn Again Tiger,* all the early works that – before he gets to Moses and so on, is very preoccupied with what could be called the theme of Creolisation. For Selvon, creolisation means that all of we are Trinidadians. You know, Selvon was not into any Indian thing and African thing. I would say that this was going on in him all the time and it's very much there in how he's always setting up scenes in which there's nothing to choose between these people in terms of their style, in terms of what they don't like, what they like; the way they quarrel with each other and so on. I would say that's a major preoccupation of Selvon. Now, the negative side of that is not being into any creolisation but having some notion of being universal. In other words being located as not necessarily a Caribbean writer. I think Edgar Mittelholzer was like this. Yes you are Caribbean because you have to write out of a particular experience but I do not think that he wanted it validated by being Caribbean. And yet when you read his novels you don't leave the region that much. I mean, he's into that slave history and post-slave history of Guyana and then in a book on Trinidad that's remarkable. What's the title? *Morning at the Office. Morning at the Office* talks about the action of the ethnic groups and so on. Not with a view to Selvon creolising British – but with an exposure of the frigidity and the absurdity.

BOGUES: You talk a lot about Edgar but you seem to have had an ambiguous relationship to him?

LAMMING: Ambiguous only in the sense that I didn't particularly like him, I mean that was mutual and very strange. I admired his work. I had a great admiration for his work. That is, when I got to Trinidad he was the first West Indian writer who assumed that vocation totally even though he had from time to time to take jobs. On one occasion I met him there in Trinidad and went to his house and discovered then that he had reversed all the roles. He had stopped conventional jobs and so on and his wife went out to work but he worked 8–4 at home writing. And then he did the housework: shopping and preparing things and so on. At about 4 o'clock even though he was an atheist he used to sit right outside the palace of the Roman Catholic Archbishop. (Laughter)

I remember seeing him sitting there. What he invoked in me was this tremendous admiration for the toughness because Trinidad was a place that would have reduced him into a joke. You know, a man with a basket going to market and he would have had to live through all of that. I've written a piece on this, because there were only two West Indians at his funeral Salkey and I. Now the other side which was difficult was that he had pathological fear, contempt – I don't know why it is – of being in anyway thought to be black.

He would give an inventory of ancestors and there was no African. There was Swiss, German, Dutch, Aboriginal, the lot, but there was something about this African that he didn't want to have anything to do with. In his mind Africa would have been synonymous with 'bush' and 'jumbo' and all of that. I think there was a kind of nervous disorder there. The behaviour was very strange so ideologically then, much later when we met in England there was never any friendliness. But we very rarely met. The man who was very, very good at making sure we all stayed together in London was Andrew Salkey; he was a real midwife. Most of the writers who normally might not see each other or had good reasons for not seeing each other met in Andrew's flat. Whenever Andrew asked you to come nobody ever said no, whoever was coming. So, the only occasions I met Edgar was at Andrew's who had this magnificent relation and held people together. Andrew was special. If you wanted to know where so and so address was and who was out of London, if you were in Australia, Andrew knew where you were. If you were in Ghana, Andrew knew where you were: address, phone number. So he had made this a collective responsibility of his about Caribbean writers. They were to him a kind of family in which he was the person who held us together.

BOGUES: Did anybody ever ask him why he did it?

LAMMING: Not that I'm aware of. After a while we just accepted it as that's how Andrew was. You see this again is another example of maybe in a sense of innocence but Andrew is also one of those people who saw his own activity as a writer as an activity that was critical in the making of this Caribbean world, this Caribbean reality, highly conscious of that. And that everybody who was in that constituted a family and whatever their differences you had to try to hold this family together. I think that he was one of the few who maintained a regular consistent relationship with Naipaul. In fact I think he was the person who sent Naipaul's very first manuscript and negotiated its publishing. Both of them had a remarkably close kind of relationship. That is part of what you're saying, I think about who the key ones are. I just had to find the key ones and so on. He did not go away but Vic Reid. Vic Reid's writing is not just storytelling at all. Vic Reid is very, very conscious of being part, of building something; something you call a civilisation, something you call a culture. So I think in all of that generation there is this legacy: that they were a very important part of the making of something that was not only new to the world outside but also new to the world inside.

BOGUES: I want to strike a discordant note to what you are saying because one of the criticisms that I think is important about these narratives of Caribbean literature is that what is missed in general by this group of West Indian early writers, is that they were essentially creating and imaging a masculine nation, which sometimes was very Victorian. How would you respond to that as a member of that generation?

LAMMING: I don't know about the Victorianisms at all I don't think....

BOGUES: Well, some people would argue that the way in which people saw themselves functioning as novelists and writers that this was done within the mould that drew from Matthew Arnold. But even if we could put that comment aside I think it is clear that essentially what these writers were doing was constructing a masculine Caribbean nation.

LAMMING: I see. If you say the thing of the Arnold, I'm not too sure about that. You don't know how the influences were, but some of the people I have in mind may not have been influenced in that way. I do not think Selvon was, but what would be quite true was that, I thought that what you were going to say is that – we were all really products of and in this we were not alone, we're all products of an intensely patriarchal society. We were all products of a society in which women had shaped us, women had fashioned us in many ways as mothers and women were there in our lives and in the societies it was inescapable but in some way they did not occupy the same liberating and nurturing role in our literature as they actually did in our lives. So that, for example it took a long time before I was even aware of this fact. It took someone to say to me in a classroom 'but there are no girls in *In the Castle of My Skin*'. That's what the person said, there were no girls in *In the Castle of My Skin*. No, I'm sure there were girls in *In the Castle of My Skin* but what was their position? In that sense that patriarchal legacy was there. But there was a period in the development of the education of this whole region when I think literature and the book as literature took precedence over any other source of knowledge; including that of an engineer or a doctor or whoever. He may have more money and so on but the guy with the book who knew literature, who knew how to quote Shakespeare and so on occupied a very special position in the esteem of ordinary people. But we, the writers aren't any different from other occupations. We did think and we lived by that influence of the book and no matter how bright we were there was something wrong with us if we were not reading people. But I don't know that we set out to do that. It's simply that this was reflected in what was a legacy. You could of course link it to Arnold but only in the sense that it was not just Arnold. Arnold is the figure who's going to feature most in that but that is because the language itself became the major instrument of imperial expansion and of the consolidation of empire wherever it reached. That the language – wherever English went there then, this was very interesting that in a way it may come back to what I was saying earlier about the French. Ok, what did the French do? There's a very interesting thing when you look at curricular between France and England and when you look at the difference in their intellectual traditions. The French came to regard philosophy as the foundation of reason and reason articulated itself through philosophy. The English gave to literature the role that the French gave to philosophy. So instead of Descartes and Rousseau, it was Shakespeare and John

Milton which was exported. So that if you go to Martinique and look at what they're doing in the secondary school, the child in the secondary school does philosophy very early while in the English school there is Shakespeare. So I think that is not really just an Arnoldian thing. I mean whether Arnold used it given his relation and bias is of course important but it is also tied up with this, fundamental difference in the two traditions where the French tradition which regarded philosophy as its oxygen and a British intellectual tradition whose oxygen was literature.

The Caribbean Intellectual Tradition

BOGUES: You have mentioned traditions and their various oxygens. Let me ask you immediately what would you say is the oxygen of the Caribbean intellectual tradition?

LAMMING: In the same way I would say that there are things about the English and French I would say for the Caribbean that the major components are history and politics. The generating forces that lead to thinking, whatever direction you go, have been the history of the region and the politics of the place. The history that records and presents you with our purposes, beginning with the plantation and its meaning and the politics as the instrument of escape and liberation that has been the foundation of this tradition, whether it is C.L.R. James you are talking about or Eric Williams or Derek Walcott. Take *Ruins of a Great House*, Walcott may not see himself as a political man but he is informed all the time by this combination of political culture whose major components are history and politics. That's the oxygen, yes. I mean other things may be added later but these are the generative elements of our tradition.

BOGUES: In thinking about the Caribbean intellectual tradition and its literary expression, you have made the argument, that one of the defining features of Caribbean Literature is a preoccupation with the so-called peasant.

LAMMING: Yes. I did.

BOGUES: Do you still hold that position?

LAMMING: Remember that I am speaking primarily of the literature of a period. From the '70s onwards there are all kinds of changes, but I'm not so sure about that. I would hold to my original position in the sense that my modification would be to explain that I was giving a rather extended and perhaps too extended application to the word peasant. But what I meant really is peasant plus. I didn't mean literally peasant man living on the land and only land clearly, I didn't mean that. But I meant that there were formations that could be called an urban village. If you're in town, the peasant formations that are called urban villages came about through what I usually call the internal journey. There is, I would argue, about three or four journeys in Caribbean Literature: there is the journey from the outside, the journey coming in and so on, the inter-regional journey and then we have this important journey of that move that you would experience. This is a move which is very sharp and devastating, that move from country to town; that gradual and then rapid move. But I'm saying that even when you are dealing with an urban village, one has to see its relationship to the land and how it retains to a large extent what I would call the sensibility of the man on the land. So a peculiar thing used to happen. I was explaining this the other day to some people, this fantastic thing about terrain or territory. Where I grew up, we had roads, you know. There is a whole area, what could be called a village and you had this road, that road and so on. And I lived on this road. People who lived in this road belonged to this road. If you lived in this road and was seen in another road you would be asked what you were doing there. What I mean is that this sense of belonging to a plot somewhere travelled with you. That sensibility of belonging to a terrain, a piece of terrain was very important. So the very interesting thing in *In the Castle of My Skin* is a scene where it looked like there was the possibility that this landlord may be killed; then ambiguities emerge because certain elements of the village said these people from this other place come in here to interfere in our business. So I was using peasant in that sense of a sensibility – I can't even say urbanised really because at that time the urban is something we did not really have. There was no big city. And what I am saying here is that whether we were aware of it or not when you look at each of those early books the major characters in those books are not so much individuals. The major characters are composite and collective characters of place. I know that you are aware that Naipual's major character in *Miguel Street* acts through stories which are about place. *Miguel Street* is about a village not a particular individual. And what I'm saying is that this was the force that constituted that history component that became the oxygen of the intellectual tradition. That force that moved against the state and created a rupture in the society. It came from below. So all the institutions, all the democratising institutions, unions, party and so on, came from below. And therefore when you were going to deal with your society you would have to start from below. You couldn't start anywhere else but below and find out who really were below because quite often we had not looked at below seriously and this is what I meant by the novel restoring personality from down below.

BOGUES: You make a very extraordinary statement that there is one element of this person sensibility if you want to call it that, a feeling of belonging. And when you say, for example, this is my street, this is your street; you don't move there; I'm here thinking about how ordinary people in the Caribbean, begin to identify themselves; what do they belong to? Sure we belong to a nation, to an island, but there is a belonging which is linked oftentimes to the very narrow and microcosmic spaces in which we live through our experience. Is that something that we need to think about in the Caribbean? I am particularly thinking about this because of my experiences in Jamaican inner cities.

LAMMING: I think we need to think about the concept which I have used, what I have called a 'lived experience of belonging'. I think we need to not only think about it but we need to articulate it and we need to cultivate 'the Where'. 'The Where' changes so at one stage I'm talking of a period of my life, boyhood and so on with this road but that road extends itself. But if outside of this village you ask a man or a woman 'Who are you?' It's Barbados he belongs to. That is the key marker not the village. However quite often I have jokes with this where I meet somebody from Jamaica and I ask 'Where are you from?' and they know I'm from the West Indies and they say 'Kingston.' I would then say 'No, but where are you really from? I mean, you live in Kingston but where are you really from?' And then we will get back to Manchester or something. But Kingston would mean Jamaica. So there's that strong sense of belonging and outside when you go to England, the Jamaica and the Trinidad and the Barbados in dealing with the outside we become West Indian. And what I noticed that's happening now and this is fairly recent even amongst people who are not thinking in those terms at all that increasingly, the West Indies is giving way to Caribbean. This is new but what remains fixed for me and this is what I'm getting at is that whether you move from Barbados or Jamaica to West Indies to Caribbean there has been created within the historical context of this archipelago a particular kind of sensibility that links you to place in a very special kind of way. And that sense of belonging there whether it's at that point of the Caribbean or this point, or that point, I think that sense has to be reinforced, has to be propagandised. If there's one bit of propaganda in the best sense of gospel that we have to undertake is that that sense of belonging is not erased, is not jettisoned, is not lost, especially at a time when they're saying that the world has no boundaries any longer. OK. If the world has no boundaries in terms of power structures we will make sure that the boundaries of sensibility are not destroyed and which brings us to the point of the imagination. It is the imagination which maintains the boundaries of sensibility. Whatever else around may appear to crumble, the boundary of that sensibility is my imagination.

BOGUES: That is your 'sovereignty of the imagination'?

LAMMING: That is my sovereignty and then because those boundaries are of the imagination that sensibility is no longer exclusively located in Jamaica or in the archipelago. That sensibility has also taken location in New York; it has taken location in Amsterdam, it has taken location in London, it has taken location wherever migration has chosen a particular destination for the time being. What it will be with in those locations 50 or 100 years from now I don't know but I know for now and for a foreseeable future that the sensibility that I call Caribbean, that I was speaking about is to be found not only within the archipelago but it is to be found in that external frontier.

BOGUES: One of the criticisms that may be levelled at you in holding this position is that you are essentialising the Caribbean so the question I have to ask is 'What do you mean by Caribbean?' 'What is this "essential" Caribbean sensibility?' 'What exactly is it?' Are you not guilty of certain reductionism to position a Caribbean sensibility that has the power to be in Amsterdam, to be New York, in Miami or wherever.

LAMMING: I'm not essentialising. I'm saying that this particular sensibility is also shaped and given meaning not by any inherent essential essence. It is shaped and given meaning by the peculiarities of it's historical formula. That we in the Caribbean have this very extraordinary situation that there's a point in time, roughly say the end of the 15th century where we are going to find the most extraordinary enterprise leads to the peopling of this region in a way which was not perhaps intended at all. It began with the horror of genocide in which the indigenous population, very different from the mainland, within this archipelago are reduced to a fragment in a matter of 50 or 60 years. And then over a period of time, from Europe, from Africa, Asia different groups would enter in very different circumstances. But my key point is that all the branches of the human family would meet in this archipelago. And they would meet in this archipelago for the same reason. And what was the extraordinary project they met for? A method of production that would be a major marker in the formation of the modern world. Now I'm saying that we grew up taking for granted that we were doing that. This is why quite often, many years later, I used to be very struck with certain things. I went to England in 1950 when there were hardly any black people in London. I left to go to the States in 1955/56 as a Guggenheim Fellow and I was out for about two years. This was my first return. And then one of the things that really struck me when I went back to England which was not there when I left in 1955/56 was this. I went into the underground and I saw this Jamaican man directing the traffic at a station. It was the most extraordinary thing. The man had recently left Jamaica and had got the whole map of London in his hand and could be heard telling English people where their trains were and what train you take to go here and there as though he grew up with that. I am saying that we had that capacity for adaptation and it had to do with the peculiar formation of his world. He was in a peculiar sense in touch with the world inside of his archipelago in a way that his equivalent somewhere in India, or in Africa might not have been. Now that also has to do with the geography of our politics as an island people. We were never all that removed from what might be the centre of activity. Wherever you were, Kingston might be within reach somehow, it might take a week, but you would be there. There's something about an island and the sense of space and the sense of proximity, which also gives that sense of identification. So it's not any essentialism at all. I'm saying that there's nothing wrong with claiming that you tend to see the world differently. You don't see the world differently because it was God given, you see the world differently because there are forces that make you see it differently. These forces are a history and a certain kind of politics and political discourse that that history generated.

BOGUES: Since we have moved into ways of seeing the world differently, how would you define elements of the Caribbean aesthetics?

LAMMING: Well, first of all you have to begin with the notion that there is an aesthetic, not only a Caribbean aesthetic but an aesthetic of wherever you are. Sometimes the way one approaches the issues is with the negative of it. If you think of aesthetic first of all as something which produces feeling then you forget that your aesthetic really is the way in which feeling operates. The way in which feeling registers experience that is, in other words you're beginning in a sense with the body, with the material fact of the body and of the senses registering your immediate environment and therefore a way in which you harmoniously respond. So the way in which collectively there is a consensus of response to the same kind of experience would constitute the aesthetic of that place. It may not be the aesthetic of another place but it's the aesthetic of that place and it comes again out of the experience of the way feeling records and interprets experience and always to the location of the body in a particular kind of space. Let me give some examples. If you take the Caribbean novel, if you take *Castle*, if you take Reid's *New Day*, if you take Selvon and so on, a remarkable if not overwhelming mark of those novels is that they are set outdoors. They're not indoors in closed spaces and rooms. Rather they are outdoors and it seems quite correct in terms of how we live because actually most of our time is spent outdoors. When we're not working we are on the step talking or cricket is played in the road which is not enclosed, that is one of the things I was noticing in town yesterday. But I was thinking also of that movement, that being out of doors has something to do with the tone and pitch of voice so that sometimes you would think that there's a fight going on out there – there's no fight. But somehow the voice takes on the requirements of being outdoors, I mean, the man is next door but they're talking about something in a voice that sounds very much as though, in another context, you would wonder whether there is a fight. Therefore it is becoming authentically its own voice that it would be informed by an aesthetic that is shaped again by the material historical circumstances that have produced that kind of sensibility. And that may also have been true for a particular Englishman living at a particular time in England or in some particular part of England, it is not an essence. It is a combination of a historical gift too and then your feeling interprets your experience of it in a certain kind of way. The particular faculty which I know you call the imagination gives order to the disorder of those experiences. And wherever they seem in collision the imagination decides to make them coherent in a way that they would not ordinarily be coherent.

BOGUES: Could you say some more about that George?

LAMMING: Yes, it comes back again to the body and we were talking yesterday about the picture I had seen of a very stylish thing. Here we have people going to receive awards, music awards, and this lady is there in these African cornrows of a certain style. Now this is very interesting because as a matter of fact the target so to speak, by which I mean style, the targets or styles for aesthetic approval may change. These don't remain the same. So what I was very struck by was that the hair was faked. I mean what they called natural or was fixed with great care to look a certain way and it looked very much like hairstyles which some African women wear. Not so long ago in Barbados nobody would have thought of going out looking like that on a grand state occasion. You wouldn't have thought of going out like that at all. So, what I'm saying is there's a component of history returning in some kind of way that is an aesthetic response. There is something about Africa and the legacy of Africa which is either surfacing or returning, whichever you want. Either surfacing or returning in the society and you're seeing this express itself everyday in an aesthetic approval of either the style of hair or an aesthetic approval of the particular garments. But I said surfacing or return because I think I remember telling you that I remember as a boy particularly girls, schoolgirls' hair was done up like that.

BOGUES: A question that writers are not normally asked but I want to ask you because you are also a critical intellectual who operates very much within the Caribbean intellectual tradition. There have been many different theories on Caribbean societies, Creolisation, plantation society, social stratification models, and the cultural pluralist model. Did any of these models influence you at all in your writing of statements, critical essays or in your imaginative work? In addition did you take part in any of those debates in the 1950s, '60s, and '70s when these theories were being formulated?

LAMMING: I don't recall taking part in debates and as far as influence is concerned, I'm not aware of, in my work writing under any conscious influence. Influence is very, very difficult sometimes to locate and phrase. But I have read, I would say back in the '60s, I would have read M.G. Smith. I would have read Lloyd Brathwaite, and of course I am probably most familiar with Lloyd Best and plantation society. And then much later still with Kamau Brathwaite's intervention with the Creolisation theory. I am aware of them but I'm not conscious of being particularly influenced by them. What I was conscious of is of whatever I'm doing I'm deliberately trying to contribute in some way to the realisation that is the collective realisation of this ethos that I call Caribbean literature. This realisation would be made up of all the circumstances that gave rise to these models. So, there is going to be, if you're in *Castle*, you're in plantation, and if you are in *Of Age and Innocence*, you are in some kind of plantation and if you are in *Season of Adventure*, you are also in Creolisation. There is also social stratification in *Season of Adventure*. So I would say that the models, if you like, they may turn up in the work but they are not in the work because I am conscious of them. They turn up in the work because I am in a way feeling the society through all the phases that are theorised. And I think that however you name them each carries a truth within it and each carries a limitation within it. I see for example that M.G. Smith gives a kind of closure that is not acceptable although when you break down how he's looking at the distances that are created by difference you can say yes. And if for example you think of the kind of crisis that may arise as the imperial power removes itself it may look that is how it is and how it will be done. Closure doesn't make sense to me at all. An interesting thing about Lloyd Brathwaite although I haven't looked at it in a long time, but the thing that always struck me when I first read his work on social stratification was how accurate he was except for the total omission of the Indian presence. I've always wondered how it was possible and yet it was possible because when I lived in Trinidad I realised how communities moved around each other. However what has been happening is the emergence if you like, and I would place this just in the last 25, 30 to 35 years ago of a highly schooled Indo-Trinidad intelligentsia. There is now a very sharp and contested interaction. When I went to Trinidad in 1946 it would have been a very rare thing to seen an Indian in the civil service. We then reached a stage where somewhere in the 1990s about 40 per cent or more of the cabinet was Indian. And if today you go into banks and other places of work you will see that the Indian presence has entered the workplace in a way it had not say in 1940s. So the societies, wherever that happens, are discovering themselves in way that they didn't know themselves before. And since they're discovering themselves in a context of scarcity, and under the pressure of forces that insist on controlling them, the interactions become fiercely competitive in way that they may not have been if they were so to speak left on their own. But I find Trinidad extraordinarily exciting more so than most of the other places that have that kind of multi-ethnic set up. I think it has something to do with the degree that it is so urbanised as distinct from say Guyana. And what one would have hoped for is that this is where the collapse of the federation would have been mitigated. Just think of the combination of Trinidad and Guyana within the context of one Caribbean. The potential would have been enormous.

BOGUES: Let me turn for a bit to something you said earlier. You talk about ways of feeling in the sense of your feeling the Caribbean, but also in *Pleasures of Exile* you talk about ways of seeing. As you introduce the text you say and I am paraphrasing here, this is a report of one man's way of seeing. What are the distinctions you wish to make here?

LAMMING: What I'm saying is that I see the language as function in two different ways. I see what I call the language of statement, which would be *Pleasures of Exile*, the lecture, and other forms of that kind. But the organisation of the message, how it is to be organised is very different, from how it is in the fiction, which I call the language of feeling. What the language is aiming at in fiction is to get the feeling to think. And what language is doing in the statement is to get the mind to feel, but actually the subject doesn't change. And so within the novel one uses the devices of fiction.

BOGUES: What makes you practise one form of language as opposed to another?

LAMMING: I think I really began with public speaking in a serious way when I first returned to the Caribbean. I was never into that in England. But when I first returned to the Caribbean, in the late '50s out of the blue, the then General Secretary of Barbados Workers Union Frank Walcott, who was a very interesting man, working class, self-educated, powerful force in Barbados; He asked me would I come and give a talk to the union. I was not too sure of this and then I said yes, I think I will. So I went and it began my thinking about language of statement. All this is coming before *Pleasures of Exile* in the late '50s. It was a very strange event and there was a most extraordinary crowd including some white people who never went into the union meetings before. Two factors were at work there, one was the fact that many people came out to see the boy whose name they had heard from abroad and they wanted to know what he would look and sound like, and then there was the police because the lecture was advertised as 'The Black Man in the Modern World'. (Laughter) This, as far as I know, was the very first time that the word black had ever appeared in the title of a lecture in Barbados. This was about 1956/57 or something like that. I think the black thing was what got everybody going. *(Laughter from both Anthony Bogues and George Lamming)*

LAMMING: Now I'm trying to get the ideology and practice of this and I'm saying that it started there. After that I spoke often to them over the years and always from the union, I never spoke from a party platform. Always from the union platform in the knowledge that the union contained both or all the parties. And then I realised that the language that I used in the novels was not likely to be the same because they were not, most of the union audience were not going to read these novels. And therefore I set about thinking deliberately about these two sets of language. How to find a way of getting that kind of audience to know what was happening in the books. And quite often I would use excerpts as illustrations from the books. That is how that came about so that always the language of statement must be different. The novel is about the unfolding of all kinds of layers of feeling, making the invisible visible. So the other level of language is always intended for somebody out there who might not be dealing with the books but who will listen; who will listen to you although what you're saying is more or less what is in the novels.

BOGUES: So therefore your public, let's put it this way, your public persona, your public speeches then become what for you? Another function of you being a writer but in a different way?

LAMMING: Oh, yes. Very much so. But I don't want the novels to get into the didactic posture of the statement. I try to avoid that as far as one can but the intention is the same.

BOGUES: In *Pleasures of Exile* you make the statement that you are not an engineer of theories. And I get the sense sometimes when I read your work you seem to draw back from theories. But at the same time the way in which you see things, particularly your language of statements demonstrate a highly developed and sophisticated theoretical approach to questions of language itself, to issues which face the Caribbean; How would you respond to these observations?

LAMMING: When I say I am not an engineer of theory what I mean is that I am not into doing theorising myself. But I am, I'm not too sure whether this true of only my generation, I am a voracious reader. I read across many fields but most of my reading is history actually, history and philosophy.

BOGUES: History and philosophy, that is interesting.

LAMMING: Yes. I do more of that than I read fiction. I'll tell you how that started. That started way back with the philosophy side in England, but not with the English. From around about 1952/53. I got very, very interested in the French writers. And the French writers that I got interested in because they were very much, on the agenda of argument and discourse at that moment. I read and re-read two writers, Sartre and Malruax. I lived with them which meant I read them in a way that I wouldn't read any English novel. There was no English novelist that had for me the attraction of the French. But I was very fascinated by the way the ideas were incorporated into a novel of Sartre or a Malreaux novel. Both these writers wrote novels which were very much in a sense 'novel of ideas'. Now, a book that I read and which influenced me somewhat as I read it more than once because it seemed to link with something so natural for me to be linked to from the Caribbean point of view, not from the French, and that book was Sartre's *What is Literature?* In particular I had to read the sections that had to deal with the nature of choice and the obligation of a writer. This I would say if I could trace a conscious influence on how you were working your way through your own thinking, this I'd say was very key: the concept of the obligation of a writer and choice. And I then started to re-think my colonial situation of the Caribbean. How could you be articulating something called fiction, predicaments and so on of a society without in some way being committed to what should happen to that society? And if you were going to be committed to it in some way you had to choose. And it is from there also that, more and more a political position of myself in relation to directorates and so on as the Caribbean took place and increased. Now there is a funny story associated with my preoccupation with French philosophy and literature at the time. I always refer to money as 'christmas paper' (Laughter) and I used the money of my first contract to stop in a bookshop, a very famous bookshop.

BOGUES: What's the name of it?

LAMMING: Zwemmers. But before the contract I could only look and now after this contract I thought that there are books I would really like to get my hands on. So when I left the publisher the afternoon a voice said 'Go to Zwemmers and see if they will take this cheque'. So I went to Zwemmers and I remember very well the things I bought. I bought two books, I bought Freud's *The Interpretation of Dreams*. I was interested in Freud because I had read about him from the French writers I was reading, and then I told the man he used to see me come in and look and I asked him, I want these, would this be all right? And he said well let us see. Now I don't know whether he phoned Michael Joseph the publisher to find out but he was a long time coming back and he came back and said ok you can use the cheque and he gave me change. What is interesting in this story is that I immediately went for books which I had become interested in through my reading of French writers. I used to read English novels because one ought to be in touch with what was happening around them, but I never really got into them in the way that I got into French. So that also explained the interest in French philosophy and it also explained the way why in part of *In Age and Innocence* there is the beginnings of coming to grips with the existentialist mode of perceiving my reality.

BOGUES: That's my next question: some people call you an existentialist writer. Would you say, you hold to that or it doesn't really matter you?

LAMMING: No, not really. You know that word has a variety of applications. At the time I read that there was a fantastic book, it's very small, which was a debate between Sartre and M. Naville, I think was his name. He was a leading Marxist intellectual in France and the French would have this kind of thing – Sartre and Naville were brought together in public sessions, and I have it somewhere in my books, it then came out, the exchanges came out in a thing called *existentialism and humanism*.

BOGUES: Yes, I know of this work.

LAMMING: That debate between them was very interesting. Sartre, the existentialist and Naville. There was then a reply, he was not in the debate, but he was replying to Sartre to both of them, but mainly to Sartre, from a man called Jacques Maritain who was Catholic philosopher. And I got caught up in that kind of fascinating crossfire which then led me to Kierkegaard. I mean each would claim some portion of an existentialist mode of thought without being described as existentialist. So if you had asked me what I mean by existentialism there's a statement I think it's the Kierkegaard where he says a man must live each day as if it were his last.

Radical Caribbean Thought

BOGUES: You are very keen on choice and commitment. I would say that the commitments of the radical Caribbean intellectuals up to say 1960s and 1970s are fairly clear.

LAMMING: Yes, I agree.

BOGUES: What do you think of radical Caribbean intellectual life now? In particular post the collapse of the Grenadian Revolution and in the period of general neoliberalism?

LAMMING: Well, let me say that there probably is a certain amount of intellectual work that is being done that people are not aware of. One of the problems and you know this better than I do is that we don't have a sufficiently strong infrastructure for a certain kind of publishing house, the kind of printing facilities that would make journals regular although there is for example the *Trinidad and Tobago Review* which can have difficulty getting readership. But despite that I'm saying there probably is a considerable body of thinking and writing that we are not aware of because it's not in print. It is handed around between friends. Then there are the things that come out from Jamaica, from the Centre for Caribbean Thought and there is the journal *Small Axe*. Then there is work of yourself, Paget Henry, the late Lloyd Best and David Scott. But these come heavily within the social sciences, and history. And I was trying to think where do other forms of work appear say in the areas of literature and cultural matters and the person who springs to mind would be Gordon Rohlehr. There is Kamau Brathwaite of course, but I am very interested in Rohlehr. I don't think Rohler is recognised for the weight that he has in thinking through these societies. And what I am seeing is this. What they share with the people of the '60s and '70s is, they share a sense, a very, very strong sense of being Caribbean. Now they may define that in their own kind of way, but when they are engaged in argument with themselves or with others the terrain over which the argument is usually conducted is the experience of the Caribbean. So even if it is about Africa, it is an Africa seen through the filter of that Caribbean reality. In this way they belong along with what was going on with the '60s and '70s. The difference between then and now is that the intellectuals of the '60s and '70s had an absolute conviction that they could shape Caribbean society according to their modes of thinking and according to the will which they had. Whether they were in Jamaica or wherever and whatever differences in ideological posture they had the equipment and the capacity to mobilise for moving this region in a particular direction. That's the difference between the intellectuals of that period and today. Today there is a block, in part, because of the casualties of some serious defeats. It seems to me on the whole, from the texture of the thinking and the vocabulary of the thinking that there has been a temporary suspension of the political. The political in an immediate and activist intervention sense has been suspended as being futile. And what has taken its place is what I call this retreat into theory. In this retreat they are trying to find ways of understanding why collapses took place without any promise of getting out of that. We're just looking back to see how errors were made and to theorise those errors. And what to me has happened there is that I'm back to my language problem that I raised in *The Pleasures of Exile*; that in the process of theorising I find that the tools of analysis require a vocabulary that is not native to their actual experience. It's as though there's a kind of bottled vocabulary to investigate and to re-think a certain kind of intellectual and political experience, so that they are having in a way, language problems in articulating a mode of thought that is not too different from the problem that the poets had in an earlier period. We recall that the early Caribbean poets had to find a way of getting out of the romantic diction and into a native voice. I would say that the novelists found, after some time, ways of holding on to this voice so by the time you get to Lovelace a native voice has been found for the most complex problems. That voice is not there with this generation of the theorists and I would assume, but I do not know, that they are aware of it. And this is what I mean by a retreat. Quite often I find this disturbing. Sometimes it also happens with the French people you get the feeling that the authenticity of the theory becomes the very essence of the theory as distinct from theory helping to clarify and liberate. So these theorists will then get into a kind of exchange with themselves about the accuracy of the tools, when the only function of the tools really is to illuminate and liberate. That is my contention.

BOGUES: We have a disagreement here George, because I think a lot of these theorists, myself, and others included would say that what some of us are trying to do is actually work through a language – yes to work through understanding 'errors' and 'collapses' if you wish to use those words but yet to do so while finding a language in history and social science, a native language that speaks in idiom of the population of the geographical area we come from and to do so while engaging in thinking critically about the region.

LAMMING: But when you say that it still makes me think of retreat and how the political has been suspended because the language that is being used is totally inaccessible and would be totally incapable of mobilising anything outside of that immediate frontier. It's a frontier that is established there by that language. I find for example that Rohlehr is not too burdened with that, although Rohlehr is involved in complexities. You know, he may intend to use a vocabulary that has to do with the folk and music and so on but he's never really too outside of access. I'm thinking of other examples and I found that in Walter Rodney. Rodney managed not to strain himself. And of course the perfect model, the man who remained lucid is James. I mean so lucid that many people accuse James of over-simplification. But James had a way of speaking and writing and I think if you're going to do that, if you're going to get engaged in mobilising a collective mind so to speak there has to be some over-simplification. You cannot introduce the volume of complexity and so on if you're mobilising an idea. And I always thought James had a very over-simplified idea about the Greek city states but what you are doing there is that you are leaving a very clear idea of what you are talking about which will then be discussed.

BOGUES: But is it not part of the explanation for what you are calling the suspension of the political in the way you describe occurs because the political is no longer simple? It is not simply about taking power, that the political resides in the everyday forms of culture? So are we not into two different situations. And are there not today different configurations of power?

LAMMING: I don't think that there is any situation where there would really be a call for the suspension of the political. I said the political because I don't mean that they're not in parties and so on, I don't mean that. I mean the political almost as a way of making theory prescriptive if you like. That is not there. I don't get the feeling that they are addressing the society. They're addressing somebody above the society but they're not addressing the society and that brings me back to my old complaint long ago before they started social theory, of this enormous distance between the head and the belly of society

– this failure to find that language that would communicate. This was to some extent really a problem with Lloyd Best; very sharp ideas and very complex but then it varies, sometimes he manages to do this but sometimes it has an opaque capacity which would be extremely difficult for that world down below to deal with. But to repeat what I said earlier, my main thing, I don't get a sense that a society is being addressed. I get a sense that colleagues are being addressed.

BOGUES: Oh, so it's a shift of audience?

LAMMING: Yes. And a shift of audience would also imply a shift of concerns. So what was the original concern of what does this thing out there do, what do you do with it is lost. Now there may be lots of other circumstances contributing to that but that is very, very real and it is a difficulty.

BOGUES: Let me ask you what is perhaps a problematic question. As somebody who belongs to the generation that we in my generation think very highly of, do you think that my generation has not lived up to what you think are expectations? In other words, are we not standing sufficiently on the shoulders of the people like yourself?

LAMMING: I would be careful about making those comparisons because one is very conscious of the kinds of change that has taken place in our situation. I don't know about the living up to, but I think that a way has to be found to narrow the distance between yourselves and the community. That distance is much too wide. Even the people whom you might identify as being in active politics may have some problems even with how the theorists are saying what they are saying because they also have had no opportunity to exercise the mind in that kind of way. What I am concerned with really is the disconnection between the community and the intellectual.

BOGUES: Let us return to something you have written a lot about, the imagination and sovereignty. I want to ask whether or not the way in which you deploy the relationship between these terms, sovereignty and imagination, is it not really a counter hegemonic weapon against domination? Are you not trying to find an imaginative space where alternative language is possible?

LAMMING: When I use the terms – really I'm using sovereignty as almost synonymous with imagination. I'm thinking of the imagination as, I can't put it better, as faculty which is not subject to the determinations and so on of the material life although it has its origin in the material life. And that, as I said earlier, it is also a faculty which brings order; it brings order and coherence to what may be the fragmentary feeling and so on of a particular experience. And its function therefore is to make intelligible the kind of evidence that could not be communicated by a pure didactic statement. So, in a way 'sovereignty of the imagination' is related to what you say in that whatever the external constraints of material life that the area of rescue that we have is the possibility that the imagination continues to exercise that autonomy which it has. So that if I use it more frequently now than before it's also because, I am very conscious of the continuing threat of what is called globalisation – the continuing menace of forces that are utterly beyond your actual physical control. However you have a shield in the imagination, you have a particular shield, a kind of defence for making sense of your world whose sense is negated by those external forces.

BOGUES: That's remarkable George because there's a passage in *In the Castle of My Skin* which I have used frequently over the last year in talks that I have given about empire and the ways in which neoconservatism and neoliberalism attempt to shut down all alternative imaginings of a different world. Every time I read this passage there's a visible and audible gasp from the audience. The passage is one where the schoolboys are discussing the possibility of slavery after they met the older woman. You wrote: 'they couldn't get the garden out of their minds and the more they thought of the garden the more ashamed they became and the more they repented. They were all slaves and they made us slaves too.' And then you go on and say 'The Empire and the garden. We are to speak of them the same way. They belong to the same person, they belong to God. The garden is God's own garden and the empire is God's own empire. They work together for us. That's all we have to think about now, the empire and the garden.' And there's a way when one thinks about this passage in conversation, between the schoolboys, that you are eloquently describing what you have called 'a terror of the mind'. So I wanted to ask you about this passage and it's relationship between sovereignty and the imagination?

LAMMING: I think that the particular passage you cite is making one aware of the function of the school which was a kind of external prescription for erasure. This erasure takes the form of mystifying the relationship between the empire and the garden. Empire on the one hand, of what the school represents; garden, biblical garden and so on, what the school is preparing you for and both of these are God's. But what the imagination does with that is to restore your autonomy through a kind of heavy satirising of the experience. This is in fact literally what the teacher might be telling you either between Sunday school and classroom and it is being offered in a way that imagination decides to give that a sense that is utterly unacceptable. And the other way you do it is a satirical presentation of it. So that although you may not be able to escape the teacher and laugh you are in the context of the character made to feel fairly safe from these constraints.

BOGUES: I am coming back to the idea of counter-hegemony here. Is that notion influenced at all by Gramsci or not? I ask because you have said you read Marxist literature while you first lived in Trinidad.

LAMMING: Not that I am aware of. I mean I'm thinking of synonymous imagination and sovereignty – in that context. The aspect of the Gramsci is there – but I wouldn't have read Gramsci when I wrote *Castle*. That would have come much later, although I could see where the school as institution assumes that hegemonic authority that he would be speaking of in his work.

BOGUES: Are you influenced at all by Gramsci and by extension Marx?

LAMMING: As I say, it's difficult to trace. I read Gramsci's *Prison Notebooks* and I feel a kind of identification with that concept of hegemony – the way in which power exercises itself through institutions in such a way that it normalises what is even most abnormal in your life. I felt a certain identification with that. I'm conscious of Marx in areas of my thinking but that has to do more with my own Caribbean life. I have had repeating conversations in Grenada about this. I have always said that I'd never met a Marxist baby. So I am not really concerned with definitions of me as a Marxist. What really interested me was how you got there. What was the journey that led you to that. So I was saying that in order to say what I recognised about reading Marx as an aspect of Marx is that I had lived what Marx was actually talking about. I didn't learn what Marx was saying from reading Marx. When Marx is speaking about the material base of authority, the material base of the authority of institutions, I mean I had grown up in the society where it was very clear to me where power was located. And it was clear to me what were the agencies of that power and where one was located in relation to all that. And that brings back in this sense when you're asking about models the overwhelming force of the plantation in the shaping life of any Barbadian of my generation in Barbados. I mean, wherever you moved there no appointment which could really be made of say the rector of a parish church without the planter not knowing who he was and approved it. So even the church in terms of its personnel required the authority of the plantation and of course the relation of the church to the school, the headmaster of that kind of school could not be appointed without the approval of the rector who may have been involved in the appointment himself. I saw those gradations of authority working through these various institutions and that the foundation upon which all this rested was that man in the field. So I'd lived that. When I came to Marx and social formations and how these come about, I mean he's really talking about something I had actually lived.

BOGUES: Was there a text of Marx which you admired?

LAMMING: Well, the one that I was rather very struck by and today I've been re-reading and this brings me back to my early view about this current generation of Caribbean theorists, is the extraordinary power and lucidity and complexity of the *Communist Manifesto*. What you have there is an absolute stroke of genius because you have to go back and read it and read it again. It only makes more and more sense as you acquaint yourself with a historical background against which he's writing

– but that he should in one stroke try to encapsulate this vast volume of historical movement across that period of time. Which brings me back to the necessity for oversimplification because remember the *Communist Manifesto* is addressed specifically and directly to workers. He's not talking to Marxists, and this is what I mean, the clarity of the target is quite there and he's made sure that the language is going to be accessible to that kind of literate worker who will find his way through that, but then later if he's so inclined will then have to go and check out the history behind. I'm always very struck by *The German Ideology*. In particular with that sense of the role of class and the shaping power of class in social relations, remains very strong and in an extraordinary kind of way you see that in its most extreme and farcical ways in a place like Barbados.

BOGUES: I understand you once made a brief attempt to join the Communist Party of England?

LAMMING: Oh, yes but that was not my first exposure to Marx. I was exposed to Marx in Trinidad not England. In Trinidad there were a few very close friends that met around literature, around writing, and one was absolutely brilliant, called Clifford Sealy. He had a rare bookshop called the Clifford Sealy's bookshop. Clifford and I were very, very close. He was very much influenced by a man called Jack Kelshall who was a Marxist. And Cliff lived in Belmont, the same place I was telling you about. And we used to meet at Cliff's basement place in Belmont to read Marx. But some of these things were in Russian. *(Laughter)* These fellows were so dedicated that anything on Marx we read. But we also had some translations, so that was the first. But my relation then was purely a literary relation to that writing which then turned into something that allowed me to connections with some kind of English intellectual. And it was a very innocent kind of thing really when I decided to join the Communist party in England. I went to join because I thought I would get this kind of discussion that I had in Trinidad and because it would help me clarify the Marx thing as well. But I didn't know you don't join the party like that. *(Laughter)* I went down to them thinking this in the morning. When I got there they asked me who I was and so on, what interests I have politically and took my name and I never heard from them again. *(Laughter)* And that was it.

BOGUES: Did you make any attempt to join any other political organisations?

LAMMING: No. I've never really joined in that sense but I have on many occasions supported movements that I felt I identified with. I always supported where I thought the organisation corresponded to ways in which I was thinking and whether they failed or not, whether they were keys to liberation they always got my support. My other explicit attempt at organisational life was when I came back from England. In 1956 I felt a tremendous transformation going on with Eric Williams. He had asked me to speak and I spoke in Woodford Square on the night that he was introducing the candidates to the first election.

BOGUES: What did you speak about?

LAMMING: I don't remember the details now but I was speaking about largely the power and the importance of the kind of public education because that was something quite extraordinary to have been taking on a most sophisticated level but absolutely lucid and so on to five or six thousand people on Woodford Square in which politics became a school. And all kinds of people who might have been doing all kinds of nonsense and so on at night would not fail to be at Woodford Square. So it was in a way my head – belly theme, where the head had really re-attached itself to the belly. Williams in Woodford Square was absolutely brilliant, and I was struck by the way people reacted. Because he was always citing with this research power and would tell them, if you go in the library in the *Guardian* of 1902 and all that, it caused a lot of trouble. The people who worked in the library who used to just lend out books said that people after the meeting would come and say the doctor says that this happened in 1920. They were never involved in finding anything for anybody. So that meant a man who normally would be loitering had found meaningful activity. This is what I mean and – that that has got lost. In fact it got lost five years later when the University of Woodford Square ceased to be the University of Woodford Square. But it was along those lines that

I spoke. All this is of course tied up with my experiences with Cliff and then the Communist Party. I never joined the PNM but I spoke in the very early days. In Barbados, I avoided the party thing because this was a kind of tribal family wars, but whenever I was back I spoke. In fact this is very interesting; there's a Barbados, a world down below in Barbados that knows me, they don't know the books, but they know me from these speeches and they'll quote them sometimes. They will stop you and say you may not remember but... and they'll tell me something 15 years ago that took place.

Eric Williams

BOGUES: I get the sense, and you can tell me if I'm wrong, that you have a deep appreciation for Eric Williams?

LAMMING: Yes.

BOGUES: A very complex appreciation.

LAMMING: Yes, and disappointments also at the same time. But great appreciation.

BOGUES: When I hear you speak of Eric Williams and the way you do is of course different from my generation who see him as a neocolonial politician through the lenses of the 1970 Trinidadian Rebellion.

LAMMING: Yes.

BOGUES: But I always get a sense from you that there's another Williams.

LAMMING: But there is. If you look at some of the speeches sometimes there is a Williams that people have almost forgotten. When you read Williams on Education and the kind of University, Williams wanted that is the Williams which I think your generation would have hooked into, because he had a conception of the University as actually a moral force mobilising the entire society. And I think he got that because of American experience, not the Oxford thing. He'd gone through Oxford and decided that was not for us because he was totally against anything about residential Universities. He wanted the University in the middle of Kingston and the residences were to be made – just as they are made all over in the cities all over the United States – proper residences would be made for students who stayed with families and so on. Can you imagine what 50 years later what Kingston would have been if Mona was in the middle of Kingston? I mean, you would have had an intellectual working class in Kingston. For a period, the Woodford Square with outdoor lectures, this is what he was getting at. That is the Williams I'm talking about. I don't know if you know my little pamphlet on him, I think I have some copies there, when they had a conference on him in Trinidad a few years ago? I came across it the other day, I must send it to you. They brought out a book that they had sent me and it had actually been published in it. This is much later now, I'm looking back on him today and we must realise he was always regional. He made it his business to know every territory. He knew people like Césaire very well. Whenever he spoke, he never spoke about Trinidad and Tobago except within the context of the region. And then all that got whittled down to where it became just nationalist PNM Trinidad and Tobago and so on. There was really a decline in Williams. But there is a Williams who still has to be presented as a person with a conception of the region with its own shipping service and food programme. And that's the Williams I'm thinking about.

BOGUES: Why do you think he became so disappointed and was himself a disappointment? What happened?

LAMMING: I don't know how to answer that except that there is something very complex about Williams. There was a part of Williams that never recovered from whatever empire had done to him. There was that part of him. And there was a part of him which, whatever his hostilities and his prejudices and so on, still had some reverence for all that Oxford meant. And the other side of that I think, which may come nearer to answering your question, is to remember that he was man of his period. Remember Williams was winning the scholarship in 1931 or '32 or something like that – very advanced in a way. If you imagine a boy in 1929 or something winning a scholarship when the only thing that a black man could be is a lawyer or a doctor, to have talked about doing history, to me that is a part of him too that I think had to be very unusual. Remember he was poor. His family had no connections. In fact, I think his father was upset with what he considered this foolishness to study history. He was the one who was to have rescued the family, everything was invested in him and now he had come back to be an ordinary teacher. So there was that kind of mark on him. Williams was never really a man of the people – never. I mean, he was a man for the people if you wanted to address the people but he was not, and he never pretended to be a man of the people. As well I think this is what has happened: that after he only had say a minor defeat or something like that he would retreat into a kind of sulking which meant that there was a part of Williams that probably felt that society was unworthy of him. And I think with that Oxford and that coming back and tremendous doctoral authority, this is what Lloyd Best means when he talks about the doctor – anything the doctor say 'then is so'. This means that the doctor couldn't take any kind of loss, any kind of deviation from anyone. There was another aspect that I now recall. Williams and the PNM are unique in our world as a type of political personality. The PNM is the only national political movement in the Caribbean and Williams the only leader of a movement that came to power without any association with labour. From Barbados to Jamaica, the Party and the Union were twins. Williams had absolutely nothing to do with the unions. The nearest he came to it was with the teachers; it was the teachers who pulled him out. Now, that had a lot of repercussions because it also meant, his distancing himself from labour. It also meant that he had also distanced himself from dealing with the Indian problems because you could only deal with the Indian problem by identifying with labour. You couldn't deal with the problem of Afro and Indo-Trinidadian society by hand-picking Indians and so on. That was the ambivalence in him coming back and putting his bucket down. That was a side of him, you know, that created the complexities. And I think in a way while he enjoyed the power, I feel he regretted very much that it took him away from the historian that he was or could be because after a while then he started writing a different kind of history from his famous *Capitalism and Slavery*.

BOGUES: What about his other political contributions?

LAMMING: Oh. Very important, very important and tremendous and unquestionable contribution to the political development of Trinidad and Tobago. You also have to see that all his major critics of another generation are his products. When you hear people like Susan Craig speak about how her father took her by the hand, when she was 11 or 12, and dragged her down to Woodford Square, there's a whole generation, which I thought you would have been proud of that. This generation then starts to use the very tools that Williams had given them to analyse what he was doing and attack it. So in a way his contribution to a generation is beyond question and remains and it is a generation that then put more and more distance between him and them. But the fact is that he was the shaping influence in the kind of people they became. I don't think you can erase that and it cannot be forgotten. The other thing that he did was this; until he came to the scene, Trinidad never had an experience of coherent party politics. If you had six elected men, they belonged to six different parties. The first national, serious national party that Trinidad had was the PNM. Now what I thought was most unfortunate probably for Williams and the party was that he'd never had any experience of being in Opposition. I was in Trinidad fairly early at the first election and nobody expected him to win. Williams himself did not. I mean he was just known as the scholar who had no record of any corruption or of any kind – clean, straight and so on. He was not liked by the traditional black middle class, they had no use for him, they did not like this anti-imperialist talk. Then there was his constitutional views about governors that he spoke about in a sarcastic way saying to people look at the mess that they'd done. So there was a class of people who were against him and then there was the white bias which was quite clear. Of course there was as well the Catholic Church. The Catholic priests in the confessional used to warn and threaten things if Williams came to power. So all the established forces were combining against him. And the only thing that he had – he couldn't depend on any labour through unions – was a very, very solid constituency occupationally, with the teachers.

Wherever they were, whether primary school teacher, an intermediate school teacher, I'm not sure about the top ones at the elite high schools, but he had the teachers and levels of the police. He won by a very narrow margin. But you know, looking back when we discussed sometimes we felt that it's a great pity that he won because we thought that for the first time Trinidad would have gotten a serious and coherent Opposition in which he would have concentrated on building movement for about four years or something like that. And then he would have come into power with that kind of structure. He did not have these structures. I mean, theoretically he says it has to be there and constitutionally it has to be there but he paid them no attention at all. So that's a big complexity in Williams and I think the biographies are going to require this combination of you know that kind of psycho-historian to get it right.

BOGUES: Ok. Let us leave politics for a while and come back to literature. Let me ask you a question about Joseph Conrad before we return to your novels. You often speak of Conrad as being the first major political novelist. You have talked about Conrad's concreteness in his writing. How do you think of Conrad in relationship to literature in general and in relationship to your own work?

The Politics of the Novel

LAMMING: Conrad is probably the first Third World novelist, in the sense of the novelist who first dealt with what we call the challenge for Imperialism posed by what we call the Third World. You will find a number of people who come out of a colonial background, Rhohler for example, who would have done their major work on Conrad. And the reason is that Conrad has a very special appeal for people who have come out of a colonial background because he wrote from the 19th Century and saw Africa and all of that through that filter. He's also perhaps the most severe critic of the project of imperialism. What I mean by concreteness? For me the two key books of Conrad and the ones that I return to often is of course *Heart of Darkness* and the greater book is *Nostromo*. In each case he is looking at the hypocrisy, and delinquency of men who say they are on a mission that represents the highest ideals and in the case of *Heart of Darkness* the concreteness is ivory – what he calls the material interests. And that is at the source of their corruption, the source of their destabilisation of something that they call civilisation. In this Conrad is very concrete, he doesn't get abstract. They're looking for ivory and it's the ivory, and how much ivory! And in *Nostromo* it's the silver, and what he does in *Nostromo* is introduce the American factor, the old British thing now has to contend with the new ascending, in a way, juvenile but soon to be very adult imperial rival. It's the silver and the material interests which I mean by the concreteness of his writing. I am also struck by his life. He's born in Poland when Poland is a colony of Czarist Russian. He is 8 or 9 when his father, who would be today what we would call an anti-colonial freedom fighter was captured and did a lot of detention jail time. When his father died, he was only about 8 or 9. As a little boy he was made to leave the quarters and the mother was ill most of the time. And then we know of the extraordinary torture of the wife as the spouse of a political revolutionary man. And what you notice in Conrad is this strange ambiguity. The severest critic of this imperial enterprise and also an extremely hostile to its ending. There is a deep paradox in him.

BOGUES: However many African writers do not share your position on Conrad at all as an anti-colonial figure so how do you reconcile your admiration for him?

LAMMING: I know, and that it started with the Chinua Achebe essay. There is truth in Achebe's essay in the sense that when Conrad describes Africans, when Marlow describes the Africans, Marlow is in fact looking through the eyes of that 19th century 'civilised' man – that's how he saw Africans. And Conrad may not have been all that different in that respect. When Achebe writes the first novel *Things Fall Apart* it's almost like a reply. Because it's the same time period and he's saying, you know, look, you've done this – so this is the civilisation that he is reconstructing in Africa. So you had the man who is looking through this blind eye, this blind Eurocentric eye at this African thing and this blind eye can only present one kind of view about Africa. But I think you have to see this other very lucid, penetrating thing. I don't take the critique of imperialism as sentimentality.

BOGUES: But wasn't he also, Mr Kurtz – the figure Marlow becomes entranced with; isn't he, this fellow person who goes after the ivory, isn't he also trying to say that there is a way in which not only if you pursue, ivory, but if you mix with these so called 'uncivilised people' then what will happen is that the constraints of your civilisation will then collapse and you will become a certain kind of figure?

LAMMING: Yes. But there's another reading of that. You could say that, yes, but you could also say that what he's saying is that the area of darkness is not just a place, the area of darkness is to be found, in that human thing which if, not subject to the constraints that are created then by society would become something else. What rescues Marlow is work. This is a Conrad theme the redeeming power of work; if you remove work in the sense of justification for existence you're left with Kurtz. And, in this reading, if you look at Kurtz, he gives Kurtz his ancestry, of all of Europe. Well, I mean, I don't agree with Achebe about the banning of the book or else everybody shouldn't be read. As a matter of fact, I think it should be read for precisely those reasons that Achebe thinks it shouldn't be, because you do want people to see. It is important to let white kids see how a world called the white world looked at themselves in a relation to other people, I don't think they should be spared that. You can take away a lot of readings, but what Achebe is doing is making sure and exposing the academic writing in which Conrad's racism does not come up at all. Which tells you something about that. Although they go into all kinds of psychology that's caused by this and that, there is nothing about Conrad's attitudes to blacks. This is what Achebe was angry about.

BOGUES: Would you call yourself a political novelist?

LAMMING: Yes but I don't remember defining myself in that way? I know that I'm usually defined in that way.

BOGUES: How would you define yourself then? In your own self-reflection what kind of novelist are you?

LAMMING: Well, usually what I've said is that when you look at the books, that I have always seen the kind of novel I write as dramatic poem. Because it doesn't satisfy or try to satisfy what would be the requirements of the orthodox traditional kind of novel. So it is a kind of prose narrative in which a number of the different genres are employed. So in *Castle*, you know it had diaries, it had letters and sometime narration takes the form of a sort of dialogue you would get for a play. And that goes through all of my novels, that kind of breaking up of the form. I don't shy away from the term political and this is my difficulty with a certain school of Caribbean critics. I am very opposed to the notion that politics and the political is a polluting factor when it is brought into the novel. There is a whole view about this and it comes out of a certain kind of school which says that this something called a text has to be looked at in relation to whatever are the laws governing this particular form. I don't believe this. On the contrary and this is where the aesthetics come in, I believe in the political centrality, or that the political as very central to the organisation of a narrative that is coming out of the kind of experience that I'm sharing. Now that is not quite the same thing as writing a political novel. But I want to point to how important writing a novel that makes you very conscious of how central politics has been as a shaping influence in the lives of the people that we are talking about. It's not marginal. There is nothing to hide, it's there and the question is how do you let the imagination use it in a way that makes it an organic part of the daily lives of the people you're talking about. As opposed to the view that somehow it must be erased, kept at a distance.

BOGUES: Are there any Caribbean authors writing what you would consider political novels using the subtle difference you just stated?

LAMMING: I'm trying to think. I'm not too sure. I was going to say really whether they are writing or not nearly all Caribbean novels are very much influenced by the centrality of politics in the situations that they are talking about. I mean, I would not necessarily call them political novels. Although John Hearne comes very near in his novel *Stranger at the Gate*. And I don't know that politics is not at work in all Caribbean writers. I mean, who would not declare themselves as political. Politics as I understand it is very, strong in much of Walcott. So I regard politics as for us, inescapable. We have not reached the stage – I hope we don't reach the stage – where the novel or any form of our writing becomes exclusively preoccupied with the investigation of an individual consciousness. And then the terrain is two or three people within some suburban context like most of the contemporary American and British novels in fact – a very circumscribed kind of investigating, I don't know all the complexities of some kind of recurring relationship that is usually found – betrayal, infidelity and that kind of thing. In fact that is the case where, in most of the contemporary fiction, with the exception of people like Roth. Which is why Mark Twain was very strong and why *Huckleberry Finn* is so remarkable.

BOGUES: Let me ask you about history because critics have actually said that your work is very historical. And I want to begin by talking about Wilson Harris's notion of hidden history, hidden or submerged history which resides in what he calls the 'arts of the imagination.' In making this point Harris makes muted but sharp criticism of C.L.R. James and his historical work. How does history function in your novels?

LAMMING: I'm not too keen on Harris, because I think in a way not unlike today's theorists there is a kind of mystification that he does. I've read his thing about the 'arts of imagination.' However I am not quite clear how you would write that kind of history and call it history. One of the criticisms he's making about some of the history written, and I'm not too sure this would be true of all Caribbean history, is I think a kind of historical writing which is descriptive and statistical and written in ways where you don't feel that the imagination as a liberating force is there. The material is there put together for example in Williams's book, *Capitalism and Slavery*. But it is done in such a way where the people as persons disappear behind the weight of the statistics. So I think, yes that there is a valid criticism about some historical writing in the Caribbean, with the one exception of course – where the imagination is at work in the organisation of the material and that really is C.L.R. James and the *Black Jacobins*. I can understand a complaint that says we don't get very much of that kind of history, but I still don't know exactly what Harris means.

BOGUES: Well, what about history and your work?

LAMMING: It is always there and very strong. And it's always there in all the books. But it's perhaps strongest in the book that I'm most proud of, *Natives of My Person*. And that is the one book in which, with the exception of *Pleasures* which is non-fiction, but of the fiction books *Natives of My Person* is the one in which I read everything that I thought you had to read about ships in the 16th and 17th century. And I spent a lot of time going through what that was about and how they worked and so on. And I must say that when I was doing this book I found Williams's book about the documents of West Indian history very useful.

BOGUES: I am aware of Williams's book.

LAMMING: But he never did other volumes. You never saw any other volumes. I once had a talk with him about this. I think that this book is one of the most rewarding things to read, I always travel with it. If you look at how it is organised, you get a clear view of how that European mind worked. There were to be, I think, five volumes or something, I only saw volume one. And what I think happened was that all the material was there and he collapsed the material into *From Columbus to Castro* as one. But by then he'd come into office, I think he was working his way through writing a kind of history that was in the best sense regional and political but it never happened and besides, *From Columbus to Castro*, what we get is *The History of Trinidad and Tobago* where he's really trying to plant the kind nationalist spirit.

Caliban and Language

BOGUES: Caliban is one of the central themes in your critical essays, but I have always felt that your thinking about Caliban tends to be a bit ambiguous. Like many anti-colonial writers you pay attention to Caliban and Shakespeare but that your attention is a complex one because you are very preoccupied that Caliban is caught into a prison house of language. And you don't see him as coming out of that easily or at all.

LAMMING: Not really, because, if you look at *Pleasures* again, there's not a closure with Caliban. Sometimes, I think Roberto Retamar was wrong, there was not a closure with Caliban; the Caliban theme was left open. Caliban is also to be understood at the stage in relation to the chapter that follows. The chapter that follows in the text is 'Caliban Orders History'. *Pleasures* was written in 1959 in six or seven weeks. It was written very, very fast. But why did I do the James chapter in that way? You know it's very difficult for you to believe this. But in 1959 it was very difficult to meet people in any significant numbers who'd ever heard of *Black Jacobins*. I don't think you could find *Black Jacobins* in most libraries anywhere in the Caribbean up to 1959. So, in a way one had almost to re-write the story of the *Black Jacobins*. A lot of people came to *Black Jacobins* for the first time through *Pleasures Of Exile* because you know one of the scandals is that is was published in 1938, so we don't know what happened to it between 1939 and 1940 when London is bombed. I don't know what happened to copies. One or two would be in the British Museum and so on. But there was not a publication of *Black Jacobins* in England again until about the 1960s. So that's why it's presented in that way. But the title of the chapter and that it should come immediately was clear indication that no closure had been brought to Caliban. Now this links to Fanon, because the reason no closure was brought is that Caliban had to take freedom by violence and that's where the Haitian Toussaint L'Ouverture comes in. There was no alternative to it. So that would raise the question of an imperative violence in this certain kind of situation. I'm going to maintain this point because this is where Caliban as

Toussaint takes the sword. Toussaint takes the sword and by the sword he creates a kind of new dispensation. But we were still now, after the territory had been possessed we were still with the problems of how we would define this territory and that has not been resolved. So the story of Caliban is still open. It has not been resolved.

BOGUES: Ok – go on.

LAMMING: And I'm saying that this is also the problem that the theorists are into. So my thing about the language is that the tool of analysis still remains somehow a tool not totally possessed because all of its defining powers are coming from a source that is other than source which we were scrutinising. In that sense I still think the language question is unresolved.

BOGUES: What happens now?

LAMMING: And it remains unresolved. I mean the problem with Haiti, of how would you define the new structures and what would they be and so on? Of course there was also the external factor but there was that internal thing of when you close the language of the plantation off, then how to deal with the world that was plantation orientated and today remains plantation orientated. You know tourism is a plantation stage two. Tourism filters through the plantation. I'm using language now in the sense that we're *still battling with* getting it clear. We're so tied up in all this Westminster and a whole set of, even when you see it's a defect, afraid to say look, let's see how we can put an end to this. When you say this people say you're fascist or something if you start to question the function and validity of all this two party business. Is there some form of organising our social relations and arriving at some social consensus without that paraphernalia that we have inherited and we have not got rid of? And that is why in spite of all the practice of the sharpness and so on, we have brilliant lawyers but we don't have an independent jurisprudence. And that has to do with in what language would we do this? In what language would I now put the will of the people? Because that is what a constitution would be and that would be the problem of your courts, your final court that would be the people's court you're still looking for. What is the jurisprudence that would inform the court?

So I'm saying that my question raised about the language, to me, that remains unresolved.

BOGUES: Is this question about language the final act of decolonisation?

LAMMING: It is. It would be. And that is the sense in which the language becomes a liberating power because the day you found a language that was minted by you it would render all the concepts that you used irrelevant.

BOGUES: How does that language become minted by you, George?

LAMMING: It could only become minted by you first of all I think by paying closer and more minute attention to the people you're taking about and for. And I don't think we've done that. We know the people we're talking about in some distant and abstract way but we don't often really know them on the inside. And sometimes our institutions have created that kind of distance and that is where we would begin. You know sometimes the people from below have a peculiar kind of language and have more clarity and freshness and so. (*Laughter by Lamming*). That aside, my language thing remains, there's still hope in there and to be worked on.

BOGUES: I wanted to talk to you about what to me is one of the most extraordinary pieces of your writing that I return to again and again. It's a conversation between Crim and Powell in *Season of Adventure* where there is a discussion about freedom and in the conversation you talk about man, language and beast. This is what you wrote:

> 'Is words make a note with you said Powell, 'like how you beat your drum till it shape a tune, 'words bent your brain till it language your tongue?
> 'Is what that got to do with man?
> 'Everything. Till then you ain't nothin' but a beast'
> 'Some beasts does talk'
> 'But talk ain't nothin' till it ask' said Powell.
> 'This is a question the beast ask itself'

I get the sense that in this novel and in others that there are two things which you do. You are of course an anti-colonial writer and some would say a post-colonial novelist and that is fine. But I also think that there is a way in which your fiction raises the fundamental questions about human generically speaking, while raising fundamental questions about what freedom can look like. You are looking at freedom from the optic of where you are located, i.e. therefore in the Caribbean, and using that to raise a whole set of large questions. It is why I think you're writing is, if you wish philosophical, that they are novels of ideas which cannot be contained in conventional form. How would you respond to these issues?

LAMMING: That will take us into areas that I could not answer definitively. I conceive of what you call the human as in a sense almost a kind of project. And that where we are now, and I don't mean Caribbean I mean generally, in a kind of transition period between what I would call a pre-human and human; that the great struggle now is how to work one's way towards being human. This is the problem wherever you are. That this species has found itself with you might call it a kind of gift. If you're religious you've settled that question and so I can't settle that question in a way. The gift of a capacity, a potential for self-realisation that is very conscious of something to be realised that is if not frustrated, aborted, left in some way unfulfilled, by all the various journeys that it does take on. And it is still looking for the way towards that kind of self-freedom. This kind of freedom I think of as the experience of a self-fruition of that self-realisation. The realisation of the self, that would be, and that is, the drive towards that is there from the beginning. The freedom is there from the beginning. I think what I'm trying to get Powell to say is that this is the road. Powell tells you what road to take. But nobody can take that road for you or build that road for you. The freedom is how you start meaning in a sense you're on freedom road and you mustn't get off freedom road at anybody's request or be put on any road that somebody else is calling for you. But it is the realisation of the potential for realising self and however that self is to be elaborated.

Some Concluding Issues

BOGUES: George I want ask a few last questions. How do you look
at Haiti and the meaning of Haiti today for the Caribbean?

LAMMING: If you go back and look at what happened to Haiti
immediately after the Revolution, you would see that Haiti
would have to stand alone. I don't mean only alone in relation
to the rest of the world but alone also in relation to its own
brothers and sisters in its own neighbourhood as it took a
direction that was an affront to all ruling powers at the time.
The plantation slave system was brought to an end in Haiti;
deliberately brought to an end. And that mass of people
seemed to have made a choice that it wasn't to be restored.
That is the only part of this region where that had happened,
in which you bring the plantation to an end by the sword. And
then with the mass thing because some of the leaders might
have restored it if given the chance, but the mass thing said
no, that is not coming back. And in a way they had been made
to pay a price for that kind of defiance because it's a defiance
of all the imperatives of rule and of the powers that we lived
by. So Haiti was punished, left alone to carry that. We never
had a Caribbean sense of coming to the support of Haiti.
And this brings us back to the language in the sense of how
you would organise. The Haitians never succeeded in finding
or throwing up a leadership which would help to provide an
alternative language to the language of the plantation and
that – by language now I just don't mean words and so on. I
mean the language of how would you organise your society
from beginning with its own culture and so on. But what I
find when I meet Haitians, people who are living there who
migrated, that in spite of all the horrors and calamities, of
all the Caribbean peoples I meet, the Haitians still remain
to me, on my encounters with the ones I know, the ones who
have the strongest sense of self, you know, of who I am. I find
that is stronger in the Haitian than in any other part of the
Caribbean and there's some way in which the sensibility was
an extraordinary kind of dignity. And these things go together
with the horrors and a certain kind of dignity, you know. The

other thing that we don't have is that there is an extraordinary vitality. *(Lamming Laughter)* You never get any sense of the death of the vibrancy of a people, you know. It's sad how that vibrancy is directed and they have remained the target of predators. I don't know. I don't like transferring things; you can't transfer your responsibilities, but I think one of the major problems too has been the extraordinary force of corporate capital from the mainland that determines the direction of Haiti. And whenever there has been an attempt from within Haiti to make a break, that has always gotten thwarted.

BOGUES: We were talking about Sylvia Wynter's work over breakfast this morning. Do you want to say anything about her?

LAMMING: Yes, I was saying that you know when I was mentioning the names of people I did not mention Sylvia Wynter and it's very interesting because I don't think of Sylvia as belonging to my generation. There's something about Sylvia Wynter's engagement which makes her as contemporary as a generation who would come later. But what I was saying about her was tied up also with the language problem. I think that Sylvia has very, very important insights but somehow these insights get entangled in a vocabulary that makes them more obscure than I think they need to be. And I'm comparing some of her current work with some of the most rewarding things that she had written in the *Jamaica Journal*. I mean, when you go back to *Jamaica Journal* and read some of her things on looking at how to read Caribbean literature or looking at her interpretation of some of the debates at the time these are very complex issues but rendered with great lucidity and with great point. However, I think even though her writing today has a quality of what I call persistent abstraction, again part of my language issue; you're very aware that there is something of very great importance seen and being said.

BOGUES: What do you think of the Caribbean writing today? Particularly of the female writers that have emerged in the last decade or so; because it can be argued that women are the most important writers in the region today.

LAMMING: Well I cannot go through all the things, I was trying to think when I saw your question. The way in which I think both in terms of volume and in terms of quality was that there was a shift from what was a kind of male dominating voice to the female. In many areas, not only in the fiction but also in the critical works as well. And I think that has been an immensely rich contribution to the literature. Now, about the ones that stay with me. Let me say the development that is in a sense the most startling and the very fascinating within the field of Caribbean fiction is women's writing that is coming from the Indo-Caribbean. That is because this was at one stage the most silent of all voices. Normally women were not supposed to talk but there was a view of the Indian woman that she had no voice, not only was she not to talk but she had no voice. And what is fascinating is what this voice is now articulating.

BOGUES: Are you talking about anyone in particular?

LAMMING: Yes, I'm thinking *Cereus Blooms at Night* by Shani Mootoo, a Trinidadian but who is outside. Then there is a very interesting writer, Lakshmi Persaud the author of *Raise the Lanterns High*. Now, what is very interesting about this is there's a sense in which Persaud is like the opposite of Selvon. In Persaud's, *Raise the Lanterns High*, she seems to be very preoccupied with the restoration of a kind of Hindu ethos, but a Hindu ethos that would also be able to accommodate to the liberation of the internal mind. I was reading that with some students and they picked up very quickly. It is very strange that no other ethnic group appears in the novel at all. It is held as a very workable piece of our region but its held strictly within the Hindu world. In the novel, she has a kind of in-dream, as flashback to, she goes right to the ancient tradition in Indian and deals with the widow burning. And she uses the widow burning in a very interesting way to draw the parallels to the three queens who have to make the decision when the king dies. Everybody is waiting for the widow burning and one of them says no. Now the story of this is the Trinidad side of the story of this girl who when she's about 12 on her way home going through a canefield, witnesses a rape and screams. She has some kind of binoculars and it was dangerous for her to be heard and seen so she never got a chance to see the man but she saw that the man's hands had a ring. Something like 12 years later when she has gone out and become educated, out to the University and back home, so she's very different from the rest of the family, but not broken completely, very much subject to the will of the mother and the father who are dead and so on, there is almost like a kind of arranged marriage with a doctor and so she's engaged to be married. And she goes out looking for some jewellery in a jeweller's shop, very special jewellery and she's looking through and then she sees this ring. Of course the ring is very scary, she says that's kind of evil. And she was trying to look at it and the man says oh be careful don't. And then he tells her we just keep it there because it was specially made for this man. And then it turns out that it was specially made for the man she's engaged to. It creates a whole stir in her and she goes into all kinds of states, nervous collapse and so on. Should this marriage go through or shouldn't it? And then in this state that she goes in, she has very coma-like unconscious state, she goes back and then starts to equate the situations of the widows; whether the widows should concede to the burning. Because one really came from the south where this was not the practice and she said the king had told her that if he died that she didn't have to, she was free from all that. Then she said that we would have better things to do like setting up a school or something. But the way it is presented is a tremendous thing. These crowds have gathered from a widow burning. So what she does is to equate to burn or not to burn, to marry or not to marry. And in a very interesting way when she was trying to interpret why she does it there are all kinds of extraordinary get aways. The widows don't burn. Which was the sharpest kind of violation of the tradition, but she marries. So where you thought the traditional thing would have yielded to the weight the tradition, no, the traditional thing broke loose and the advanced thing that had even been abroad come back and marries. The other aspect of that that is very interesting where when the widows break loose, the question now is that they have no future again in that place and so Indenture comes into play. So in a way you begin then to see a moment in which indenture was a moment of liberation, not exclusively oppression. That the fleeing was into whatever was out there. The reservation is if you were Trinidadian reading this you would have to have a sense of – how come only in this sums to their limit. There is no interaction But there is a boldness of that presentation. There's not concealing it and her early work, to misrepresent her but there's a strong kind of, ethno-centric bias there. But she writes with grace and it's a very powerful kind. And she is one of many. So there is an Indo female voice which has established itself quite clearly. This is a voice that's very interesting but how will it evolve? However I should note that I do not see a Guyanese equivalent of this.

BOGUES: What are you working on now George?

LAMMING: I'm still battling with *(Laughter)* my philosophers.

BOGUES: But are you not also battling with the 'beginning' of the Caribbean and Columbus.

LAMMING: Yes, but I'm bringing it right down to this trial. I think I'm going to bring a closure to that. But sometimes my travels in and out and so on breaks things and when I break things getting back to it is not always easy. I wanted to do something which is a little unusual that would take the form of a lot of different forms as the novels and I have chunks of it here and there.

BOGUES: Are you playing around with different structures of dramatic writing?

LAMMING: It's everything. A lot of it would take the form of a play. I mean it could be sheltered in that reading with voices and so on. The idea is really this: I created the ceremony of souls and in fact now what happens is instead of the male priest, it's a woman who has the power of the ceremony to summon the dead. In that ceremony the dead come and they have to give account to the living about what happened. So she summoned them. Columbus, La Casas, they come back to the ceremony.

BOGUES: Go on.

LAMMING: And as they come, the Tonelle moves around. One chapter with the Tonelle is in Jamaica, another chapter with Tonelle is in Barbados and then there is a shift in time sequence. We then have the tourist, that Tonelle is in Barbados and we're dealing with what has happened since Columbus last left. So it moves around and when Tonelle is in Trinidad it's the contestation with the Afro-Indo. All of this is set up in some peculiar kind of way. But the last thing is this. There's a thing when he, Columbus, is in Haiti first of all with talking about the priest, and that is a mixture of description and then sometimes I lift completely the debates of Las Casas and then the mambo will intervene to comment. And then that would take a prose narrative so it's a kind of mix up thing. But again its very, rich in historical events but bringing Columbus right down, right to today. And how it's set up is that the mambo is mythology but she is an ordinary woman in the day, that is, an ordinary person that would be selling things and so, but in the ceremony she becomes something else. There's also an aspect to that she has a cross-examination of Columbus. And she's asking him what really happened at La Navidad where there were slaughtered and why? And what happened, she goes through the whole thing though he defends himself. Now, I structured it in such a way that in the myth she's had more than one life.

BOGUES: Ah

LAMMING: And she was present on every occasion that she's now asking him questions about. So she was...

BOGUES: She was a witness-

LAMMING: She was a witness, yes, so a lot of the questions are rhetorical. So she will come back and say if that is so why then did you do this?

BOGUES: Thanks very, very much George. Really, thanks very much.

LAMMING: All right that's fine, yes. I think we should go for lunch don't you?

SECTION 3

Reflective Notes: The Past and Present

20 | *After a Decade**

When we say that we can always recognise a person's voice, I think we are referring to the particular kind of music that it makes in our heads. In a similar way, if two countries share the same language, we learn to recognise a difference in their rhythms of speech. As a boy, who had never left his island, I could tell in a matter of minutes whether the film was British or American. The words had a common meaning, but they made an entirely different kind of noise.

All this seemed perfectly natural; but I didn't know, until I got to England, that ordinary speech could have a meaning other than words. I hadn't suspected that the simple request for a glass of water, or a pint of bitter, could tell me more about a man than he might want me to know. Those syllables worked like a guide to tell me that a producer's secretary in the BBC will not ask for water in the way a factory girl does.

They might have started life in the same street; they might have been casualties of the same kind of education, but those tongues obeyed different orders when the words, 'glass' and 'water', had to be spoken. And if the factory girl learned to type, her skill didn't necessarily lead to a new kind of job until her tongue had learnt a new kind of music. As convicts may be recognised by their uniform, so the English, it seemed, could be classified by their vowel sounds. They were branded on the tongue.

I might have let the matter rest there if it didn't lead to a second observation. I had called on a West Indian who lived with a family in Chiswick. The English husband worked in a tyre factory, and repaired clocks in his spare time. That evening they invited us to tea. We talked for hours; and I kept thinking that if this house were an example of the country's hospitality, I had no need to worry what would happen in the future.

---

*   This article was published in the *West Indian Gazette* Vol. 4 No. 14, 1962.

Then I asked the husband what radio programmes he liked best, and he said that they never listened to more than one. This seemed very strange, since my friend had told me that the family usually spent all evening listening to the radio. We had obviously misunderstood each other. I was thinking of individual broadcasts while he was referring exclusively to the Light Programme. For years they had fiddled with one switch. The radio was turned on, and after that, it was simply a matter of making it louder or turning it off.

'Don't you ever wonder what's happening on one of the other services?' I said, and his reply was my first lesson in living with the English. He said: 'I'm not interested in Richard II and all that.' I saw no reason why he should be interested in this particular dead king; nor would I have thought any less of him if he found this play of Shakespeare to be a bore, for it was not taste or intelligence which was revealed in his reply.

It was a conviction which had nothing to do with history or literature, but rather with the BBC. He was convinced that what happened on the Home Service was not intended for him. Richard II and all that – whether all that was a talk about trade unions, a discussion about England and the colonies or a performance of English folk music.

He listened to programmes on the Light not because they required less attention, or gave more amusement, but because he was convinced that they were his special ration of fun. He belonged to the Light as a black man belongs to a race, called Negro. Here was a fascinating contrast in the expectations of two men. My West Indian friend had finished school at about 12 or 13. He also worked in the tyre factory. He wasn't interested either in Richard II and all that; but he had been telling me about a programme which he had heard on the Home Service the night before. Was this a difference in their ambition, a difference in their need for culture? It was not. The West Indian's freedom to switch from the Light to the Home was the result of his ignorance.

He was ignorant of the special relation which the Englishman had felt between these two services. To the West Indian, Home and Light were simply the names of stations like ZFY or ABX. You turned to one if you didn't care for what was happening on the other; and that was that. To the Englishman, they were like foreign territories, with equally foreign habits. And it seemed to me at the same time that there was some connection between the music of this Englishman's tongue, and the music which he had learnt to anticipate from the radio.

So the word class, which was not new, became a monument with a stature I had not known before. It left its signature on the tongue; it explained the sporting language of professional and amateur; it was a code which partitioned the bars of the public house; it was the principle that authorised how and where culture was to be distributed. It was a way of life.

England which had played such a large part in my past now became an even more vital experience for my future. When I reflected on the authority which that Chiswick family, and all like them, had invested in the agents of power who organised their entertainment, I realised that almost two thirds of the population of this country were in a colonial relation to the culture and traditions which were called English. And it was at this point that my own process of decolonisation began.

But how is it that life could go on obeying this formula of class; for class, in this sense, is a kind of formula. And the formula, to my surprise was applied when people of the same dominant class were together. I shall give an example of life as I saw it at the other extreme of the Chiswick family.

A senior Fellow at Cambridge had invited me to have dinner in his college. This was an atmosphere of complete serenity; the voices were gentle as doves! Impossible to imagine the police intruding here to ask any questions about last night's burglary. Only God or a bomb could rebuke this sacred routine. And yet you felt that such serenity didn't just happen. It was the result of a certain collective restraint.

The stranger is expected to fall into line, although no one will commit the impertinence of telling him in so many words, how the line works. He must keep one eye on his plate while the other travels, without notice, over the details of this ritual. The undergraduates had dispersed and dinner was over.

A waiter arrived with a magnificent silver jug which was placed before the Dean. I thought this contained some special brew, and wondered why they hadn't changed the glasses. But it was only water. And suddenly it seemed that the words, 'tribe' and 'ceremony' were written everywhere. The Dean had dipped his napkin into the jug, and was scrubbing his ears with an impatient index finger. The jug was then passed to the man on his left; the napkin was soaked and our man lifted his spectacles and soothed the scar on his nose. So it continued, from one to the next, until everyone had performed this after-dinner ablution at table. Then the Dean got up, and Fellows and guests followed in the order of their seniority to the Senior Common room where dinner would end with conversation and port.

It was here that I learnt my second lesson, and what now strikes me as the secret of this triumphant formula. Everyone remained standing until the Dean had spoken. And it went on like this. A wave of the hand then his voice: 'Colson...Saintsbury'; and the two men took their seats together. Another couple were named to keep each other's company; and then another. Here were men, advanced in years and full of scholarship, who accepted that no one, except the Dean, had any choice as to whom he should talk with.

I would always remember this evening when, much later, I noticed that on every level of life in England, people had acquired, by habit or calculation, some particular technique of endurance. You would complain about everything: the weather, transport and the cost of living; but the complaint was negligible besides your capacity to endure what offended you. And it seemed to have created a characteristic that is unique in the English. Everyone has some degree of patriotism; but English patriotism contains a surprising paradox. It leaves the impression that no man could ever feel as strongly about his country as the Englishman does, and at the same time, it allows any foreigner to abuse the country as he pleases; and this abuse is accepted in the most amiable spirit of agreement. I have spent much time trying to work out the source of this attitude. And what remains so far is a question. Is it due to an invulnerable self-assurance? Or is it a highly perfected camouflage for hiding a collective fear; the fear of exposure?

The last decade does not provide me with any experience of revolutionary change in England; but during the second half of the 1950s I became aware of a new emphasis in people's preoccupations. The hydrogen bomb increased its hold on the popular imagination; and the loudest and most indignant voices were those of the young. Also, race ceased to be a liberal speculation about life in America or South Africa, and became, instead, a fact like the milk on your doorstep. People who were ashamed of the conduct of their army in Kenya or the Caribbean found themselves unprepared for a black stranger, whose skin made class irrelevant, and who had read that there was a room within which he would like to rent. Could he have it? You knew that the answer had to be given right then and there. And the answer was often long, circuitous, a marathon of courtesies that ended with a regret that the room, like a bird, had just gone. Of course, it was still there, and empty, too.

It is in such circumstances that one sees the role of conscience in the English imagination. The vice which foreigners call hypocrisy is diluted and transformed by habit into a question of conscience. Its logic takes simple form. 'It was wrong not to let the black man have the room, but my method of refusal avoided an even greater wrong. I didn't hurt his feelings.' Of course, he knows that the room is free, and you know that he knows. You're both in the know. But it is a knowledge which has no weight until you tell the truth. The truth will hurt his feelings, and this is the one error which conscience will not allow. Sometimes the man is hurt-proof. It is the rain that really worries him. He may lose his temper, and call you names. And at last the score is even. Anyone who talked like that was bound to give trouble.

But this kind of ambiguity can produce the most disastrous consequences; and its worst example, in my experience, was the racial violence of Notting Hill. Here all the niceties of cricket came to an end. I don't think that we have heard the last word from Notting Hill.

In America or South Africa, race assumes the proportions of an open war. The enemy and his weapons are common knowledge. But in England it works like an underground movement, an invisible Fifth Column. Sometimes it is almost impossible to tell whether your accusations were truly justified. I had a classic example of this one Sunday morning. I had gone into the local pub in a very bad mood, unprepared for any kind of intercourse. So I spread my newspaper wide, and worked up a furious concentration in my reading. Soon I felt a peculiar movement. It was a huge black dog pawing my leg.

I tried not to pay attention but it didn't work. So I turned, and with vindictive care I lifted the dog's paw and set it down very gently on the floor. It was a slow, delicate, and very conspicuous operation. The owner had seen, and we both understood. Red with embarrassment she walked across and seized the dog by the collar, and two slaps on its backside followed a sad warning that it wouldn't be taken out again.

I thought it was all over, and was about to return to my paper when I saw her leading the dog towards me. And in the most confidential voice, she told it: 'Now, would you say sorry to uncle?' A young man who overheard her was absolutely furious that she should add insult to injury by regarding me, too, as a dog.

But I knew he was wrong. It was her way of bringing me within the family circle.

21 | *We Mourn Her to Celebrate Example!**

You ask me how I remember Claudia. The answer is simple. I shall think of her as a person, a superior person. Not so much superior to others as superior in the quality of her response to living. And I speak carefully when I say that she was lucky.

In spite of illness? In spite of the recorded adversities which attended such a career as hers?

Yes, in spite of all that. She had found in her work a reason for living, and work discovered in her a servant with infinite capacity to serve. The citizen is lucky in whom such a marriage takes place and lasts until the very end of breathing.

Politics resided in every nerve of Claudia's body. That I learnt about her, and a little more. Militant for her cause, she was also gracious in her relationships. The lioness could disagree like an angel. Here was a great source of her strength: a certain flexibility of mind and a generous heart.

She has left her signature on the lives of all who knew her, comrades and friends, here and in every land where people continue Claudia's struggle to help rescue men from the barbarism of greed and the savage exploitation which bleeds and brutalises the poor of every race.

If we mourn her loss, it is only to celebrate her example.

---

*   Published in *West Indian Gazette & Afro-Asian-Caribbean News* Vol. 8 No. 2, 1965. This was written on the death of Claudia Jones. For a recent biography of Claudia Jones see Carol Boyce Davies, *Left of Karl Marx*. (Duke University Press, 2007).

22 | *The Legacy of Eric Williams**

Dr Eric Williams started in a way which to my mind is unique in the history of Caribbean politics. He started with an intensive and quite exhausting campaign of popular education. He turned history, the history of the Caribbean, into gossip so that the story of a people's predicament seemed no longer the infinite barren track of documents, dates and texts. Everything became news: slavery, colonisation, the forgivable deception of metropolitan rule, the sad and inevitable unawareness of native production. His lectures retained always the character of whisper which everyone was allowed to hear, a rumor which experience had established as truth. And whatever misgivings we may have about the ultimate value of popular education, this undertaking, it seems to me, has become an achievement of genius on the part of a teacher.

No other British West Indian politician has exposed himself so consistently to the gravest of all political risks: the risk of refusing to talk down to an electorate. He distinguished very early and quite clearly between formal education which is often wasteful, and native intelligence; and having done that, he worked on the native intelligence by demanding at all times an adult attention and response to his lectures. This was an example, probably the first of its kind in our part of the world, of the teacher, in the noblest sense of teacher, turned politician, and of the politician, in the truly moral sense of politician, turned teacher...

So when he visited Jamaica shortly after the formation of the PNM to consult with Norman Manley, the Manleys were astonished and amused by the authority of tone with which he spoke about his plans for Trinidad and Tobago. One member of the Manley family told me: 'We thought him a bit cracked to be talking as a Government with a party

---

*   Published in *Callaloo* Vol. 20. #4 Fall 1997 pp. 731–736.

of a few months old and about to face its first election. In Jamaica it took the PNP some 12 years before we won our first election.'

In the euphoria of success which had marked his sojourn in Oxford, Williams made no distinction between dream and reality; indeed he may have unconsciously embraced the belief that dream was the foundation of all reality.

The PNM won its first election eight months after it was founded. In my recollection of the period it was thought they would do well and provide the country with its first coherent and critical parliamentary Opposition. But victory was beyond the expectations of his most ardent admirers. It was a victory which also contradicted the history of party evolution in other territories, for Williams had maintained a strategic distance from the organised working class which was the twin of the political party in Barbados, Jamaica, Guyana and elsewhere. Nor was he favoured by the old Trinidad traditional coloured middle class whose ambition for imperial honours would have made them uncomfortable with the doctor's language of colonial and imperialist and letting down my bucket, which was not a vessel of high repute. His constituency was the aspiring lower middle class, a generation who were just a leap away from the cane patch, and struggling with belligerent pride to redeem their humble origin. Education was the only weapon that could rescue them from the multiple humiliations of the past.

This was the critical importance of Woodford Square. But paradox was at the heart of everything Williams did. His reputation as a man of learning carried a certain mystique in a society where scarcity of education was an imperative of colonial rule. He attracted vast crowds. Men travelled with their children to make sure no member of the family would be deprived of the feast of knowledge. But Williams was not himself a man with a taste for crowds. This proximity to the ordinary man by hand shake and pat on the back was a difficult exercise for him to simulate; and he made no effort to overcome what would have been a fatal deficiency in the normal politician. He was not the normal politician; and that was his first essential gift to the political culture of Trinidad and Tobago.

The poor often make the finest candidates for aristocratic elevation; and Dr Williams had come to see himself as the scion of an intellectual aristocracy that was old and exempt from the customary indignities that go with national and racial difference. QRC had cultivated this illusion in its wards; Oxford with a sadistic grace exploded it. But it would take the abrasive racist culture of the United States and the tutelage of Howard University to radicalise Williams's relation to his scholarship. In a sense it was Howard that really returned him to his roots. It would be at Howard that he would learn the communication skills of lecturing to hundreds of students (a long way from the selective intimacy of the Oxford tutorial), skills that would prepare him for the sustained triumph of Woodford Square. The Woodford Square of Eric Williams has had no precedent or successor in any part of the English-speaking Caribbean.

The paradox of this achievement would be experienced a decade or so later when the fiercest and most sophisticated of his critics would have been among the earliest and most adoring graduates of the university of Woodford Square. Here we get a glimpse of the chemistry of success at work. Dr Williams's overwhelming self-confidence carried with it the seed of an irreversible self-alienation. The senior Caribbean historian neither had nor encouraged any collaborative contact with the younger generation of Caribbean historians who had been profoundly influenced by his initiatives. The continuity he advocated was in fact made unworkable by his own tendency of sullen withdrawal. The story is told (and never denied) that he once asked a senior public servant: 'Who is this Elsa Goveia?' Dr Goveia was in fact the finest Caribbean historian her peers had come to venerate since the publication of *Capitalism and Slavery*.

But all these inadequacies wither away beside the monumental effort which Eric Williams made on behalf of this region. From 1948 when he first arrived in Trinidad to take up his post with the Commission, his influence on me and my generation was profound and enduring. He taught us to see the history of any part of the Caribbean as the history of all; and he thought the task of the historian, in our particular context, was to break down particularism and parochialism in each territory. Here his appeal for regional perspective was brilliantly demonstrated by his own example.

He was an activist scholar, and he made no apology for the intention of commitment which informed his work as an historian and intellectual. Since the Caribbean was his terrain he made it his duty to travel and establish direct contact with the territories he studied, exploring their major archives. 'I spent eight weeks in Havana in the

National Archive and the Biblioteca Nacional, about the most valuable weeks in my career.' The full meaning of this sentence can only be appreciated when we study Volume I of his *Documents in West Indian History 1492-1655*.

On the same visit he would meet with the great Cuban ethnographer Fernando Ortiz, discussing the African origins of Cuban music and folklore.

He would undertake a similar journey to Haiti with the great historian Jean Price-Mars as his major target. The same experience would be extended to Puerto Rico and later Martinique where he discovered Moreau de Saint-Méry's six volumes of laws, a unique publication in Caribbean historiography. It is here we learn that there were 128 gradations of 'blood' in varying parts white or black which would define the status of free coloureds. Not being white or how to avoid being black has been a most complicated predicament for those with an appetite for social recognition. It is the regional thrust and character of his mission as an historian and intellectual that put me forever in his debt. Every novel of mine carries some trace of his research.

Dr Williams didn't just travel. He set an example which was never built on by generations which succeeded him. Williams worked hard at cultivating the languages of the territories whose peoples were his concern. He read and spoke the major languages of the region. He could undertake his own translations from the French and Spanish sources as he went about the business of digging up and storing every item of evidence relevant for his purpose. The generation of historians and other academics who followed Williams offer by comparison an example of linguistic illiteracy. The majority can only function in one language, and the terrain of investigation is invariably confined to the territory where they were born. There is, I suspect, a much greater language flexibility among the women vendors who trade in vegetables and garments across the Caribbean than you are likely to find in the average academic on any of the university's three campuses. And I don't think it is an exaggeration to say that the Williams passion for scholarship has now given way to a persistent management of individual careers, and a new entrepreneurial skill in a vague and expanding industry in consultancies.

Nor is there much evidence that his capacity for unrelenting intellectual labour has been emulated. When he left the Commission in 1955 in spite of the turbulence and hurt of his tenure, Williams had drafted 40 chapters of a *History of the Caribbean* and collected 2000 documents for the series that should have been *Documents in West Indian History*. This work was planned in 5 volumes ending with the period 1942–1962, a work I mostly treasure and not least because it defined an appetite and curiosity I couldn't claim before I arrived in Trinidad.

'Its goal', he wrote, 'is the cultural integration of the entire area, a synthesis of existing knowledge, as the essential foundation of the great need of our time, a closer collabouration among the various countries of the Caribbean with their common heritage of subordination to and dictation by outside interests.'

The series never got beyond Volume I, and I suspect that the pressure of active politics had now made impossible the meticulous organisation of such abundant sources; for it is the brilliant narrative organisation of the material that makes Volume I a work of such compelling fascination. I believe Williams, in these circumstances, decided to collapse all the remaining documents into a different kind of narrative which became *From Columbus to Castro*.

It is not possible to separate his intellectual legacy from his political stewardship over the affairs of Trinidad and Tobago for some 25 years. The inventory of failure and achievement will undergo great variations according to the angle of vision and sectoral interests which are being reflected. For a quarter of a century he would have been at the centre of the most controversial exchanges at both the national and regional level: Federation, Chaguaramas, Independence, the University of the West Indies, Caricom, Cuba, Grenada and his own February rebellion of 1970. But there are only two aspects of this astonishing career that I feel inclined to reflect on.

Williams begins his autobiography *Inward Hunger* with a portrait of the society in the year he was born, 1911. It is a searing account of general human degradation; but the focus of attention here is the extremities of the horror which afflicted one sector of the population:

> Bad as social conditions were generally, they were most deplorable among the Indian immigrants, the lowest paid, the most poorly fed and the worst housed section of the population ... There was no question that the Indian occupied the lowest rung of the ladder

in Trinidad. Cribb'd, cabin'd, and confin'd in the sugar plantation economy, from which other racial groups had succeeded in a large part in escaping, the few who did escape to the Mecca of Port-of-Spain were concentrated on the outskirts of the town in a sort of ghetto popularly known as "Coolie-Town" – today St James, a bustling suburb of the capital – which tourists interested in Oriental scenes and ceremonies were advised to visit in order to see 'the Son of India in all his phases of Oriental primitiveness'.

Half a century later there would be an astonishing transformation in achievement and potential of the entire population. Yet it is the Indian success that arouses most alarm, even though a substantial portion of the Indian population have remained cribb'd, cabin'd and confin'd. What is the source of this alarm? Why are the Indians so frightened by the just demands of Black Power? Why does a largely Indian Government with an Indian Prime Minister cause such a sharp rise in the temperature of racial feeling? All these questions generate a fearful potency after 30 years of PNM rule with Dr Williams as the singular authoritative agent of policy, strategy and implementation.

Statistics are no guide to an answer which has to be sought in the complex relations which link the concepts of nation, race and culture: a family of constructs of largely European origin which served to orchestrate the attitudes we should adopt to any encounter with difference. European racism was a form of ethnic nationalism that invested the colour line with a power of definition which neither African nor Asian colonised could have escaped. There is no Trinidadian of African or Asian descent who is free from the nurturing influences of a racial consciousness. This is not to be confused with racism although the line is thin which distinguishes an inherited way of feeling from the cultivation of an ethnic nationalism as the foundation of one particular group's claim to political supremacy.

It is difficult to deny the charge of ethnic nationalism which had been consistently directed against the various stages of PNM rule; but it would be no less difficult to support the voices which reiterate these charges, because there is a resistance to genuine dialogue about the reciprocal responsibilities which both groups share in reducing political discourse to the grossest level of electoral combat, and the concealed agendas of carving out material interests according to the vagaries of ethnic alliance and identification. This is the peril which now threatens Mr Panday. It is dues collecting time.

Where is Dr Williams to be located in these conflicts of sectoral interests and national sovereignty? It may be argued that there is no necessary correspondence between what a man says and the contradictory instances of discrimination which derived from directives his party agents or public functionaries carried out in his name. Dr Williams was seen as the indisputable source of the party's authority, and carried therefore the burden of its moral delinquency. And this was precisely the essence of C.L.R. James's warning and prediction. The party, as the heart and pulse of a national movement whose democratic organs would nourish and quicken the conscience of all layers of its leadership, had gone into decay. Democracy wasn't given a chance to take root in a soil which had not yet recovered from the Massa Day tradition which Dr Williams himself had so mercilessly exposed. The Party had become the Government's yard fowl; and it is a matter of some speculation what was the status of Dr Williams's authority in the later stage of his stewardship.

But it is his intellectual profile which concerns me now and how this relates to the conflict of ethnicity in a 'multi-cultural' society like Trinidad and Tobago. His speech to the children at the Independence Youth Rally is more complex than the simplicity of its appeal would suggest:

> Some of you have ancestors who came from one country. Some of you profess one religion, some another, others a third or fourth. You in your schools have, like the nation in general, only two alternatives – You learn to live together in peace or you fight it out and destroy one another. The second alternative makes no sense and is sheer barbarism. The first alternative is civilised and is simple common sense. You, the children, yours is the greatest responsibility to educate your parents...

Williams's entire intellectual career was an unrelenting struggle against racism which for him had its roots in the economics of imperial expansion. He was a secular humanist, with all the limitations of that specific western mode of thought, which had conferred on its great intellectual achievements a universalising authority that regarded the

Other, in any of its forms, as an eccentricity which could be normalised by patient observation, study and interpretation.

With such an orientation it is not always easy to distinguish between national unity and national dilution. The Other's refusal to be diluted quickly becomes an example of recalcitrance; and recalcitrance soon becomes synonymous with disloyalty. Williams's critical intelligence made him alert to the complexity of what he was involved in. This difference in religion, this difference in modes of cultural affirmation, required a new agenda of perspectives, a wholly new way of looking at the concept of nation and the cliché of national unity.

We would have to educate feeling to respect the autonomy of the Other's difference, to negotiate the cultural spaces which were the legitimate claim of the Other; and to work towards an environment which could manage stability as a state of creative conflict. He recognised at a late stage a truth about the great challenge of diversity and the diasporic adventure which should have been the fertilising soil, the crusading rhetoric of the Party he had founded.

It may not be a coincidence that in his last address to the PNM convention he should have consoled himself with the epigram: 'What God hath put asunder let no man bring together. That is the law of Caribbean society.' He knew what he had failed to do; and that too may be a great virtue. All his life he had flown in the face of God.

23 | *Caribbean Thought: History, Pedagogy and Archive**

Pro-Vice Chancellor, Professor Beckles, Ambassador Kellman, Senator Taitt, Sheryl Farnum, the Minister of Culture, Ladies and Gentleman, and Attendees. I don't get a response from attendees, do you recognise the word 'attendees'? I came across it for the first time this morning in the paper announcing this event, and it says 'attendees can obtain copies of Lamming's latest publication.' I'm not in very good voice, I had intended to be, in a way, lighthearted this evening. It went on to say about Lamming that he went to school at the Roebuck school from which he won a scholarship to Combermere. Now I don't know if there are any Combermere people in here, but I'd like to tell them that since I am the living example, that if you get to Combermere at the right time, and if you leave Combermere with the right equipment you will not have to go to any other place in order to get to many other places. I called this morning to communicate a message to the former Prime Minister, and he wasn't there but I got hold of his aide who said, 'Oh Mr Lamming, I am glad to hear your voice, you know, I read your first book, I never got around to any of the others.' I want to say something briefly about that, not getting around to any of the others. *In the Castle of My Skin* has been a great nuisance of a book, there are a lot of people who stop there and never get around to any of the others. But I want to raise a serious matter around that, particularly when I hear the press and people applauding individuals, like you applaud someone who gets the Nobel Prize. We applaud some individual winner of prizes, and this is what I want to say about that. It appears in a lecture essay which I gave called 'Western Education and the Caribbean Intellectual':

> The sovereignty of a literature cannot be guaranteed by the
> excellence of individual works of the imagination or the ingenuity

---

*   Talk given June 2009 at the Errol Barrow Centre for Creative Imagination, University of the West Indies, Cave Hill Campus, Barbados.

of discourse between writers and their critics. The sovereignty of literature depends on the possession of the text by the total society over the most varied terrain of mediation. The text has to become familiar and an ordinary part of daily conversation. Books stay alive when they are talked about in a variety of situations by people who recognize that the book is talking about them and may have originated with them. This is all that is meant by the term 'classic' in reference to any national literature. And every literature is a national literature. It does not endure exclusively by virtue of the gifts of the writers, but rather through the persistence of those mediators, intellectuals who persist in extending the terrain of mediation.

The point I want to make about that, speaking particularly on behalf of another generation of writers, it's extremely difficult to argue that you have a literature if your writers do not have a reading class. The literature cannot be made exclusively by writers. And so the aide gave me something to talk about. And now I am very interested in the building that is named after me. I was very struck by the word 'pedagogy' – I have an interest in words. It has a very long and curious history, this word. Originally to the Greeks, a pedagogue was the slave who took a boy to and from school, they called him a pedagogue. It was a very interesting role the Greeks had of the role of a slave, to take the boy to and from school. Then the word, about in the 15th century, got elevated to mean a schoolmaster. And then later there is a further elevation which comes a little nearer to us, pedagogy which is the science of instruction, or the science of introductory training, and that is about where we are here. It is with this concept of pedagogy as the science or method of training that makes me remember now, if you will allow me, the late Richard Alsopp. I met Alsopp first in the 1950s, in Guyana, I had an extremely strange confrontation with him. And then over the years his name would come up from time to time, but I got to know him in later years. And what I was very struck by, as I run into academics, was that he was a very rare example of a man who had a genuine passion for scholarship. And in spite of the various controversies that have gone on about how long he took on a particular work, I think now with my interests in language, when I look at *The Dictionary of Caribbean English Usage*, I am very glad to say that I have known him, and I think that Cave Hill should be very proud that the legacy he has left with that work is one of the rare productions of knowledge that this university can claim. Also pedagogy takes one to what is the question that I think is, or should be, at the centre of all university activity: the question of epistemology, that is, the production of knowledge. How, and what grounds of assumption do we come by this knowledge, this was the question which always haunted the members of the New World Group – a group who had always tried to establish the foundations of an independent Caribbean thought. And if there is no such thing, as a Caribbean thought, then there can be no such species as a Caribbean man, and any talk of Caribbean civilisation would be a misuse of language. I am sure that there is an identifiable body of Caribbean thought. Now, I had asked one of the members of the campus staff to find for me for this occasion, a copy of a graduation address. I was asked to give a graduation address here, I think it was 1980...but it could not be found. For weeks they looked around and there is no video of a graduation address.

And that brings me to the question of archival power. Who keeps and preserves ordered evidence, or who decides not to, and why? Every history book which you read is a challenge of archival power, because historians can only function with the archive that is available to them. And then whenever you are reading history you want to find out the origins of the archive. On whose interests was the archive preserved? And if you suspect that this archive is incomplete, where can we probably find it? This power of archive explains why (I do not know if the History Department of this university investigates this matter) one of the greatest scandals of western historiography, is the erasure of Haiti and the Haitian War of Independence from western historiography. The Haitian War of Independence was the most radical political revolution in the age of revolutions. And when you read a historian like Eric Hobsbawm, perhaps one of the greatest British historians of his time, in his magisterial work *The Age of Revolution 1789-1843*, there are three references to Haiti and Toussaint, and one of the three is a footnote. Hobsbawm is not only the leading historian on the period in which he is dealing, but Hobsbawm is also a Marxist historian. So this omission cannot even be assigned to conservative fraudulence, and if you get a chance to look at *The Penguin Dictionary of Modern History* beginning at much the same time and coming down into the 1940s, there is perhaps one mention of Haiti and of the

Haitian Revolution. And yet Hobsbawm would say in the same book that L'Ouverture was the first great liberator in the Americas – but not a page on the Haitian War of Independence. This is an example of the weight of archival power. And I want to not only ask, but to challenge the University of the West Indies to think about the question of archival power and where they themselves are located in dealing with the dynamics of that power. To what extent the university may be the casualty of another's archival power.

Recently I was asked to come to speak at the opening of a school which was named after me, and this is causing me some inconvenience. Once a week I get a phone call asking to speak to the headmistress. I say I am not an administrator, I do not know the number of the school, would you ask the operator to find the school for you. But I went to speak to the school and I went deliberately, and there's a sense in much of what I'm saying to you is influenced by what I had to say to the school. I was telling them, as I'm telling you now, that in happier times, the year 2008 would have been, and should have been, the fiftieth anniversary of a genuinely sovereign West Indian nation. That is how we should have been celebrating 2008. But after four years of petty insular disputes and recriminations, the experiment was abandoned. And that moment was lost. We have avoided calling this event by its real name, because it was indeed the betrayal of a people by a political leadership, which comprised the brightest and most distinguished products of our colonial education. The most prominent of them were Oxford graduates. We have never recovered from that failure. And two generations later, it now appears we are about to repeat it. I want to bring to your attention Arthur Lewis's reflection on that moment. He describes this failure, his word is 'odd,' and it was very odd since these three heads of government, despite their unquestioned allegiance to the cause, ultimately wrecked the federation. I want you for a moment to draw a parallel between that moment and two generations later, when a similar proclaimed allegiance to a cause is about to wreck the entire regional enterprise. Lewis continues, and I'm going to quote him exactly,

> Adams, Manley, and Williams were all men of the highest quality
> on any definition of the word. Their talents were outstanding and
> their education the envy of mankind. They were men of immaculate
> integrity and selfless devotion to the public service. Each was at

the top of his profession before entering the public life, and gained neither prestige nor money for entering politics. Each would have been recognized in any country of the world as a public servant of the highest caliber.

I want you to draw another parallel: let us draw the parallel between that moment and those men and our contemporary situation. For the last 20 years, or so, the political leadership, that is the prime ministers and their technocrats from Jamaica to Barbados, have been the products of the University of the West Indies. I attended the Conference of Caribbean Studies in Jamaica recently, and when a charge was made at the conference, that we were witnessing now a political failure, the question was asked, is that not therefore an institutional failure? For we are not at Oxford now, we are on home ground. I want you to grasp with that point, we're on home ground now. There's a period when nearly every prime minister within this territory was a product of the University of the West Indies whose mandate in 1944 was in fact to produce a cadre of leaders that would realise the fruition of the regional enterprise. These are not the casualties of Oxford, they are whatever you want to choose, of the University of the West Indies. And we must consider the meaning of that question. Lewis asks how did these highly intelligent men come to make so many errors in so short a period? And he says, 'clearly the leadership was awful.' I have tried, in a lecture 'The Sovereignty of Imagination' and which appears in the second volume of the *Bim* magazine, if you can find it, and I'm trying to answer Lewis in that essay. Lewis's judgement carries weight, but it is possible that although he saw with great clarity the situation he describes and laments, he may have been looking in the wrong direction. The answer to his question or some portion of that answer may be found in the cultural displacement of the men involved. They were the brilliant products of an epistemological formation which was in profound discord with the concrete and novel realties that now challenge the imagination. They were the casualties of an inherited tutelage, colonial in essence, and thereby placing an overwhelming constraint on the concept of liberation. It had happened before, and it had been articulated with remarkable candour and I quote here the Argentinean philosopher, Ezequiel Martínez Estrada, he's referring to this situation, that is the crisis in leadership of Latin American liberation struggles that had in great agony, won their release from the political domination of a colonising European power. And this is what Estrada has to say:

> neither here nor elsewhere is there any public awareness of the fact that cultural emancipation is not any easier, although it may be less bloody than political liberty. And a great part of the failure of our independence movements was due to the fact that our liberation and our liberators were never liberated from themselves. Mentally free, they were subconsciously in chains because they continued to accept the structure of European cultures, changing only their forms and a small part of their content in the same way that they had done with their political institutions.

And it is on the note of culture and the case for cultural liberation that this university must think. For it is that concept of cultural liberation which is linked to the font of archival power, and which is also linked the commitment to epistemological insurrection. There are two words used everyday by politicians, and they are now subject to a consensus of abuse. One is culture and the other is development. Everyday I hear this word, and then when I listen to the various stations, you hear the word in practice and realise that culture is reduced to a synonym of popular entertainment. Speakers are not always aware that they insult large elements of young people by regarding them as incapable of any intellectual activity beyond reggae on the hill. It is a mode of perception that has allowed the market to kidnap this society, convert the society into a service station, and evaluate every human activity as a commodity for sale.

Because I do not draw any sharp distinction between the political and the aesthetic, it is proper for me to speak of the dysfunctional nature of our political culture. The most toxic force which alienates political thought is the political party. A generation will have to reflect seriously on democratic ways of removing the party from the electoral process, making it a constitutional requirement that no citizen could contest a national election as the member of a political party. You are quite mistaken if you think that this system is the only system that would allow democratic practice in the area of politics; you are quite mistaken about that. The late social scientist, Carl Stone, made some very fascinating observations on this question in Jamaica. He was describing what he calls the 'clientelist' relation between the party and its members. If the party wins you have to look after the people who support the party. I think it was in 1992, I don't have the text with me, the former Prime Minister Owen Arthur addressing an audience in Mona, Jamaica, made an extraordinary statement, not to me extraordinary, but remarkable coming from a man holding office. He said that because of this system of winner take all, at the end of the election about 50 per cent of the electorate are disenfranchised. What he's saying is, if we win, those that voted the wrong way may have to wait five years, or whatever you want to give. It locates the party as a toxic force in the electorate. Stone, very insightful social scientist, was looking at the territories to try to transform this arrangement. What he complained about was the way in which, he said, the tendency to personalise power at the expense of institutional machinery. He went on further to suggest that one of the great problems was that the politicians while offering their promises and so on, had never worked out, and this is his phrase 'no commanding vision of the new society to be created.'

I think that is a just evaluation, but I think that it is based in a way on a mistaken assumption, because we should not assume that the political man is always suitably equipped to articulate a commanding vision of a new society. The politician is overwhelmed by concrete tasks to be performed, decisions to be taken urgently, often without any pause for reflection. He or she is haunted by the failure to deliver and their working orders are spent in a permanent state of emergency. The shadow of parliamentary Opposition where it exists, blurs their sense of priorities. They live with intrigue or the constant threat of betrayal, even within their own ranks. It is, I suspect, a feverish atmosphere, and hardly conducive to that state of reflective self-consciousness from which a vision of new society is born. It's asking too much of the politician. But, and this is my suggestion, where the concept of archive and epistemology come together; it is possible, that the political leader could arrive at such a vision if he enjoyed a certain measure of collaborative support from other modes of thought and perception; from the historian, the poet, the student of philosophy, and the social scientist, the economist, the theater director who recreates the cultural history of the nation. It is the collective dialogue between these different categories of sensibility which ultimately gives voice to a commanding vision of a new society. But it is precisely this voice which has withdrawn its service from any form of political engagement. There is a large category of intellectual workers of integrity, who view such involvement with misgiving. The risks, they think, are too great. And the risk is the party. They are very cautious about what will be the consequences of their party affiliation. The party of as a toxic force, annihilating political thought, should be at the top of the agenda for those who congregate at the pedagogical centre.

I'm going to conclude by telling you what I was telling the teachers and students at the primary school. I was trying to communicate to them, particularly to the students, that what they now know as independent Barbados, and independent St Lucia, and independent Guyana and Jamaica, would have been, and could have been, a family of islands sharing the same national house, and it would have been a more triumphant cultural and political achievement than anything we have so far known. The primary school is not only the first but the most important foundation on which the entire edifice of learning is constructed. It is here at this level of initiation that we must engage in an area of education that is very casually neglected. It is the education of feeling, the nurturing of consciousness, to respond sympathetically to a world of persons and custom, that are momentarily different from those we have known. To discover your landscape as a livable home, will depend not so much on the vagaries of our political directors, important as these are, but on the kind of education that takes place in all schools on this level of initiation. For it is on the base of the primary school that we must nurture this feeling, that the regional unification of our institutions is the only reliable guarantee of achieving a political status that could be defined as sovereign.

24 | *Reflections on Writing*
The Pleasures of Exile*

I always feel like a man in bad faith when I hear some of these introductions because they're not any part of the agenda of my expectations and what I sometimes might have to say about the books may not be too consistent with the claims made about them. However before I proceed, I want to say two things. One has to do with omissions, which occurred in my first lecture yesterday when I was talking about Caribbean literature. I did something that was in order but was incomplete: the examples I used were nearly exclusively from the Anglophone Caribbean. And the Anglophone Caribbean is not the Caribbean. When I say the Caribbean, I do mean the Archipelago. And so there is a considerable dimension that I did not really refer to. So I just wanted you to bear that in mind that when we are speaking of the Caribbean I am thinking really of those voices that come from Haiti and Martinique and also from the mainland of Surinam and the other territories. I wanted to just read a very short extract from a poem by Nicolás Guillén. Yesterday I was going to begin with this poem, which is called 'My Last Name':

> Well then I asked you now:
> Don't you see these drums in my eyes?
> Don't you see these drums, tightened and
> beaten with two dried-up tears?
> Don't I have, perhaps,
> a nocturnal grandfather
> with a great black scar
> (darker still than this skin)
> a great scar made by a whip?
> Have I not, then,
> a grandfather who's Mandingo, Dahoman, Congolese?

---

* Talk given at the University of Pittsburgh at a seminar on Caribbean literature organised by the journal *boundary2* in October 2009.

What is his name? Oh yes, give me his name!
Andrés? Francisco? Amable?
How do you say Andrés in Congolese?
How have you always said
Franscisco in Dahonman?
In Mandingo, how do you say Amable?
No? Were they, then, other last names?

'My Last Name,' speaks of that name which has been omitted, not only from person but that name that comes from that continent that has also been erased in the construction of the history. Yesterday that was going to be the opening, followed by a poem from a different generation, almost two generations after Guillén, but moving now from Cuba to Guyana, and moving from that mixture of Europe and Africa which is Guillén to Asia. It's a very touching poem. It's by a woman by the name of Mahadai Das, of Guyana, and I would say 25 to 30 years younger than Guillén. And it's called 'If I came to India,'

If I came to India, shall I be on a broken pilgrimage to Mahatma?
Resigned or rebellious, a street corner hunger?
Shall I wear a penitence, a saffron robe,
wooden beads of my days cast about my breast?
Should I be Methuselah in my tradition, a foreign vine grafted to the Deccan peninsula?
Shall I find a poet naked in the mountain,
Shall I discover philosophy in mountain caves where Everest reigns?
Near the Tibetan border where monks levitate, is the secret of being written on a parched leaf?
If I come will I find myself?

This inward search for that external ancestral kingdom, in one case Guillén, asking where is the name from the place you have left out, and Das a little nearer to the ancestral source, wondering what risk would this journey back mean for me? My second omission yesterday was that I made no reference to the immense contribution of women to Caribbean literature, and that is because most of the books that you're reading and most of the literature that drew your attention to the Caribbean, say beginning from the late 1940s, those 20 years, 1948–1968, is what they would call this extraordinary explosion of publication and so on is almost an exclusively male presentation of the voice of the Caribbean. It's only somewhere in the late '60s, and by the time you get in the '70s and '80s, that you find the female voice becoming more and more dominant, not only numerically but also in quality.

I will now try to follow the title 'Reflections on *The Pleasures of Exile*'. If you notice *The Pleasures of Exile* was written in, about five or six weeks. I'd just finished writing what I'd thought was, and which I still feel, is really the most seminal of my books, *Season of Adventure*, but it was not published yet, there was some delay, and while that was happening, *Pleasures of Exile* was not on my agenda. But this is what happened. I am waiting to find out when Michael Joseph, a very prominent publisher, would publish the novel. At the time, I think the delay had to do with the report. British publishers keep a special retainer, a critic, who deals with certain books and so on, and my book was being read by a man who was almost the equivalent of Pritchett, a man called Walter Allen. Walter Allen and Victor Pritchett were the leading reviewers.

Now there is a background to this very peculiar story, I had written *In the Castle of My Skin* and was now trying to live as a writer and I'd had the immense ambition never to be employed. At whatever costs, in spite of whatever adversities, I was not to be employed I had to find my way. In this respect the BBC was very helpful in giving you little things to read and reviews to do. But I'd started *In the Castle of My Skin* and there was an English novelist by the name of Arthur Calder-Marshall, very well-known in the '30s, he belongs to that guild of Christopher Isherwood, and was very prominent, and they used to use him as a critic on the programme that I was on. I once asked his opinion and I said: Look, I have three chapters of this book, do you think I should submit it, because I need some money? And Arthur Calder-Marshall said: Well, you could, but it's not a good idea because you don't know whose hand it's going to fall into and, you know, after three chapters... you know if I'm not impressed with three chapters I will tell them not to bother with this. So you might be doing a great disservice to the three chapters if they don't really read the whole book. But, he said, if you feel so strongly about it, I would send them to Michael Joseph. So in desperation I sent them, these three chapters, to Michael Joseph.

About ten days later I got a letter from Michael Joseph, and this letter said we'd received this report from Walter Allen and we'd like it if you could come into the office to discuss this with us. So I went to 'discuss this with us' and Allen had written up his impression of the three chapters and added in a postscript which they didn't let me see, I heard that later, the postscript said 'I don't think you should lose this.' There was a man called Robert Lusty now Sir Robert Lusty, he was the man who dealt with contracts and the money, he didn't read anything, he deals with the contracts. So he said 'We will give you a contract for it and we just want you to think about it and so on' and I said 'No the contract's okay' so he pressed a bell and a lady arrived with this contract and he asked me 'Will you take it home and go it through, it's pretty standard, but I wouldn't want to do business now,' so I said 'No, no, I want to sign now I won't take this thing anywhere, if you say it's standard it's okay by me' and I looked through the contract, it has this whole page until it comes to the advance; there's an advance they give, and they give half, and the other half, on delivery of the whole manuscript. And the advance for that first half was £100. Which was to me in the 1950s like telephone numbers: I couldn't quite imagine that amount, I didn't even have a bank account then. And I saw this and I said that I would sign, and he was very reluctant, he said 'Are you sure?' and I said 'Yes' and I signed it and he said farewell, but I wanted to find out if I could get a cheque now. And he pressed a button and I got the cheque.

And so that is the extraordinary story of things always happen that one was not expecting. But with *Season*, there was this delay. Allen wrote back to say that it was, you know, 'characteristic Lamming,' it was what I think people would regard as a difficult book to read but it is 'one of the books that will last.' It was very brief. And I think that that was the delay. Now the delay then made me very anxious, I wanted a book to come out quickly. In this writing period, I had a telephone call from Toronto, there was an interesting magazine called *Tamarack*, a Canadian magazine, edited by a very remarkable man, the late Bob Weaver, who was head of CBC talks. Bob Weaver wanted to bring out a special issue on the Caribbean writers, all of whom were now living in England. For this magazine, I wrote what became the chapter, 'The Occasion for Speaking.' So *The Pleasures of Exile* started with writing this article for Bob Weaver on why West Indians were in England. And as it went through, one idea germinated the other idea, and so on. Everything that happens after came out of 'The Occasion for Speaking' – what is the meaning of exile and what is the nature of colonial experience. That is how this book came about.

Now there are really two themes running through the book, which you all speculate on in your different ways. One is power, and the way power, the role that power plays in the actual organisation of knowledge; there are forces at work which determine what will be validated as knowledge, as E. H. Carr says in *What is History:* what is a fact. Evidence becomes a fact when historians say it's a fact. And so you get this way in which the organisation of knowledge, how it will be organised and how you identify it – there's always a force of power, which directs this. I was thinking of that in relation to an interesting book, *The Social Mission of English Studies*, really worth looking at. We speak now of a Department of English Literature, and there was a time when the Department of English Literature was a very prestigious department, there was no university, certainly within United Kingdom – Oxford, Cambridge, and so on – that was very prestigious, the Department of English Literature. And now what is remarkable about that is it's an example of what we are speaking of here, about power organising knowledge. What is a discipline? If you look for a dictionary definition, a discipline is a branch of knowledge, that's a discipline. But not every branch of knowledge is regarded as a discipline. How then does a branch of knowledge get elevated to the status of a discipline? That's the story of English Literature, because there was a period, a very long period, when no respectable old university would consider what you call English to be, a discipline, or a subject worthy of academic study. That was completely out of the question, and the only way that that got in was when it was being presented as philology. Philology was respected as a discipline which justified a department, and I gather that philology was respected in that way because philology was held in very high regard by the Germans and the German tradition was regarded really as the peak of intellectual inquiry. Both the Germans and philology lost status after 1914, and you're going to find that there's a decline in any study of philology after 1914–18, which is still having some problems. The first attempt to make it something of a study, is not in universities, it is the remarkable suggestion that we know it would be useful to introduce this to workers in technical schools, as a way, and this is Matthew Arnold's phrase, it would be a way of softening the coarseness of the lower classes. That's the journey that English takes; it begins first of all for technical, manual workers. This is what is meant by English as the social mission. English studies begins as a social mission and it makes me think too that when as a boy they presented us with Shakespeare, how Shakespeare was being used too, as a social mission and not having to do much with Literature. An example of this role that power plays, and if all of you here would know or if you would want to check it would be very interesting, how none of the disciplines which you now have were elevated to departments. There certainly was a time when there was no such discipline as sociology, you may trace that history right back to almost everything you now call a discipline and realise that there was a time when this did not earn the right to be called a discipline although it was a branch of knowledge. And it would be interesting to investigate what were the forces and who really were the authoritative voices that said 'yes' it could be, and so it became.

Now, given that role of power, the other aspect of that as a theme here is the power of naming, the absolute control which goes with naming. You want to bring something within the orbit of your understanding the first thing you do is to give it a name. And then you examine it in relation to what the name you give it is supposed to have. This morning it occurred to me when I was reading *Black Jacobins,* you know this word Negro comes up all through, and that's a word that I would not use today, I would not write that word today in any text, and yet it's on nearly every page of *Black Jacobins* and on nearly every page of *The Pleasures of Exile.* When, and by what force was this change of name? When did Negro give way to whatever it has given way to? If you read James Baldwin, if you read Richard Wright, Negro was going to be pretty standard and pretty dignified. And then somehow it loses its potency and its validity and it becomes a negative type of classification. Whenever I said Caribbean in *Pleasures of Exile* it's West Indies. And I'm accepting that because we have somehow decided that's not the correct naming for this. And we have to ask ourselves when did this shift take place, there is some power at work there, whether it's personal or institutional, there is a situational power at work which is determining that.

And now for the last one, I asked my students to research this at Brown University. My generation and generations before me who went to school, grew up doing something called geography, and there is a whole area which we knew as North America and South America. I am not clear when, or why, or by whom, 'south' gave way to 'latin.' What I want you to help me, particularly people, in that strange concoction called Latin America, is to tell me when did south give way to latin, when did South America stop being South America and become Latin America, and why? Is it something to do with language? Is it that they speak Spanish and therefore we will make it consistent with the name in the sense that they speak a language that is a derivative of Latin and is it that? And if you are so preoccupied, with linguistic origins and so on, then why didn't you change the North to 'Anglo' if the South becomes Latin? If it is linguistics you are interested in, why does the North stay North and not Anglo America? I would like you to tell me, either this morning or when we meet again, that somebody knows or somebody is going to tell us, but it is very interesting to pursue that. But it is one of the examples I'm offering for what I call that role of power and the force of power and nature of power relations, which condition that power to name, and that way in which the name then becomes like your history, and not only your history, the name becomes almost like your flesh, to haunt you in the way in which your flesh, the skin, cannot then be removed.

Power and Knowledge

Which brings me to the other theme, that third role of power in the organising of knowledge. The other theme, linked to that really, is this persistence, the persistence of influence; the way we can be influenced, the way influence works, the way an influence will retain its potency to affect behaviour, long after the event or the occasion which gave rise to the influence has withered away. No one even remembers the event that gave rise to the influence, but the legacy of the influence retains a certain potency which is never quite shaken off. So that quite often your behaviour will manifest certain characteristics that at first even surprise you, because you are not aware that this particular influence was still so strongly at work. There are a lot of things that we do which we thought we had stopped doing a long long time ago. Influence, the persistence of influence, sticks on you in that kind of way. The most fundamental of those influences, which is naming now, and what really has been I would say the theme running through all of my books.

This theme is really the pursuit of freedom and the liberation from a certain influence. That influence I'm referring to is the colonial influence. We sometimes use the colonial a little too lightly, but it has an extraordinary depth, in the way I understand it.

In a way I think that there is no one who has not had a colonial experience, because sometimes I think of the world of childhood as the first lesson in a colonial experience. This person you call the child, whose survival becomes totally dependent on others who carry names like Mother or Father or Guardian and so on. You can't feed yourself and then when you can you are told what you can or cannot, should or should not, eat. You say no, but you learn very quickly how to say yes, because no is a painful experience, and so on. That power outside you, in that world of childhood...and I was reading to my class a few days ago at Brown, and there's a very amusing book called *The Buddha of Suburbia* by Hanif Kureishi. He has an interesting page there in which there's this confrontation with his father, he's always quarrelling with his father, Kureishi is an interesting man, and he says: this man is a nuisance, but I can't say so because there's this extraordinary influence, you know, that people called parents have, you know whenever I'm in a quarrel with this man I find myself back in the role of the eight-year old having to censor what I say, long after I have left the eight-year old. And what has happened there is that this reveals a real political drama when you leave that world of childhood, which is the first step. And the statistic I want to use here is that at the turn of the twentieth century, 80 per cent of the world's population lived in some state of colonial subjugation. So that it's a very global experience, and it's therefore and I've begun to follow that with what may seem a very unorthodox way of looking at history, eighty percent at the turn of the twentieth century, 80 per cent across Asia and Africa, and in parts of the Americas were in colonial relationships. And that is why I sometimes think, that when you look at the major events of the twentieth century, there are two civil wars, they are known as the First World War and the Second World War, I regard them as European civil wars, there were two European civil wars. How did they come to be called World Wars? They come to be world wars because the civil wars were being fought by the powers that controlled all the rest of the world and if they were at war, you were ordered to be at war too, although the war may have had nothing to do with you. So that we had the two European civil wars, and that's where history focuses on the horrors and so on of the twentieth century. But as Walter Benjamin says, you know every chapter in dominance has a corresponding chapter in liberation or freedom.

To me then the central moment or the critical moment of that twentieth century, coming out of the civil wars, is after the Second World War. From 1945 and escalating, it is the thrust of decolonisation, the process of decolonisation, by which we enter the beginning of the reshaping of how the world will have to look at itself. The empires have collapsed. India, in '47 becomes free, Africa, Nkrumah in '57 and within 20 years, things escalate. Up to 1948 – later, but before 1958 – there is no independent country south of the Sahara, none. I'm going to forget Liberia which is supposed to be an exception but it's difficult to see it as such. This was the iconic importance of Nkrumah, who was in that kind of pioneer role, that decentralising, that decolonisation, and that is the process through which we move.

I've said that the books, in a way – and I've always thought when I look back on them – that each book is really an instalment. *The Emigrants* is Chapter Two, you know. *Castle* with these boys on the beach, you know doing the extraordinary kind of philosophising about sky, and village and so on. In *The Emigrants* they're the men on the ship going out to England. And *Of Age and Innocence,* Chapter three is the return voyage, you know of the migrant who has seen the centre of corporations and now comes back with political ideas of transformations and so on. *Of Age and Innocence* is the last and dying stages of the colonial regime. In *Season of Adventure* we then leap into what you call independence with the almost inevitable result that the first republic will collapse. In *The Natives of My Person* it's as though I end with my beginning and I go back to what would be in a way the prologue to *In the Castle of My Skin*. I go back to the seventeenth century and I reconstruct a voyage of adventure of men now going out. This is a way of completing that cycle, and I see these as really the instalments of one book, so to speak, this pursuit of freedom which is engaged always with this battle that goes on for decolonisation of the mind.

I think I will pause there and maybe get back to some of the notes that I made, but there are probably some questions which you'd probably like to ask, I've brought the texts from yesterday if you'd like to refer back to them.

Questions

Q1:   Thank you Professor Lamming. I wonder if you might be able to talk about, just a little bit about the colonial influence on conceptions of the land and the natural world...

GL: The land?

Q1:   Yes, I know you mention, Selvon specifically, that his prose created a kind of organic music of the earth, and you talk about the soil as a large part of what the West Indian novel brought back to reading and these lumps of earth. And I wondered how from the perspective of today you saw maybe Caribbean writers potentially resisting the colonial influence on how the land is seen, or interacted with or named?

GL: When I'm using the land and the soil in that context and when I'm talking about the peasant...that is not necessarily connected to the experience or fact of colonial...it has to do with the kind of relation that the writer may have to the human experience that he's talking about, and what I mean by peasant is this. There are people whose style of life have remained not too far removed from the style of life that you get in an agricultural kind of community. And I mean also as well, less formally schooled people. Many of these people, their formal schooling, not their learning, but their formal schooling which had stopped much earlier than the middle class because the class thing comes in here – however, you will find that their capacity for speech is not in a way curtailed or interrupted by the sophistication of the book. There's a sense in which the book comes between you and how you feel, although it is giving you a guide, print comes between you, and their language. The language of the person from 'down below' is a language which expresses itself quite often in metaphor, and the richest kind of images come out. They do not see it as metaphor and images, but whenever you say something, you liken it to something in order to clarify what you are saying, and I'm saying also that with that there is a certain rhythm of the speech. Selvon, because he kept nearer to that which means he was in the drinking bouts for example with these people, he was not just reading about them and so on, he moved about with them. Selvon was the kind of guy who would go and help some guy cut some grass. He was that sort, and not because he was investigating anything, but that was his natural instinctive pose, and that is what I mean by being close to the soil. I do feel that some of the strength in Shakespeare in that period comes from the agricultural strength of the language where reporting on life had not removed you very much, from what you call the rhythms of an agricultural life. It's what I meant by land. So that need not be tied to the concept of colonial. Where the colonial matter comes up is if you were then speaking about ownership, then, yes they would nearly always be working land that might not have been their land. Although in the case of Selvon if you were dealing with Trinidad and the Indian population they were probably and very likely working land that was their own plots of ground.

Q2: Professor Lamming, you said that one of the key things that drives you is the pursuit of freedom. The liberation from colonial influence…I want to ask you to respond to the comment that this pursuit has made you a political writer – has made you a writer that is perhaps difficult to read. In your writing matters of aesthetics seem to play a secondary mode to the ways in which you try to make a more meticulous historical or political point.

GL: It may surprise you that the answer is in two parts. I do not think that there is any writer of significance whose experience of exploring his reality escapes what I call the political. So there is essentially the mark of influence of a context whose decisive ingredients is politics. At the same time I've never really thought of myself as a political novelist, at all, although this is a term put on me. What I do know is that what happens in my books is that what you call politics, that is the way people go about organising their lives together, that politics is central to the exploration of the experiences that I am looking at, it's central, it's not peripheral. I've always regarded my books more as what you might call dramatic poems, rather than actual political novels. If you like, the politics is a character in the books, it's not that the books are political books but politics is a character in the books, and I think that it's unavoidable.

I know there are writers and critics who raise this complaint about the politics in the books and so on. But you know where that is coming from, it's coming from a particular school. There was a notion that it was in some way indecent to allow a marriage of these two, that the function and expression which you called aesthetic should be so sanctified that at no time should it be polluted by the disorder of what you call the political. And whenever you say creative and the imagination and so on, you were dealing with the realm of the aesthetic and that was an autonomous realm, that was not in any way connected to, nor should you allow any obvious connection, with the realm of politics. And there's a whole lot of literature and theory and so on built up around that kind of formalism. I.A. Richards carried out an experiment with his students at Cambridge. He gave them a number of poems, but he removed the title and he removed the authors' names, and just asked for views. And then he got the most extraordinary responses, some of these poems were thought to be great works, some of the students were saying this is nonsense. Had they known the title, and had they realised who the authors were, they were saying something else. What he was getting was that it was possible, if you would learn to read in a certain way, it was possible to come to an interpretation of a poem without any reference at all about the biographical information about the author, historical information about the period, or whatever, that the relations of words to each other in the formation of sentences constituted a logic that could in fact be analysed and deciphered without any of those other references. It is a very kind of formalism, a very structuralist kind of thinking and so on. And as well a very aesthetic kind of thinking. To me it carries no weight whatsoever, it's almost like saying the poem could write itself. As a matter of fact this has even gone in another direction now, because there's another group of people whom I call the deforestation people, that have removed the right of author altogether, the right: oh, you wrote the book, but you only thought so, no – you were only a channel through which and I will show you the forces that were working through you that produced it – but don't get any illusions that you yourself produced it. So we're having books now with author-less authors, they're there but they're not there. I don't know that those of you who are in English departments will know how much that is so. It probably is intensified in a way now with what one may call, I try to speak very respectfully, the tyranny of theory, in which theory has evolved into an autonomous industry, in which the book is now called the text. The text is only the occasion for a whole set of critical combat. The text disappears, and then the theorists are in combat with one another about what they mean. It is quite extraordinary when you are reading some of these things, I have to read them when students send things to me to read. But when these things come to me I have to ask 'will you please tell me what you want to say, instead of this, I'm not saying that you shouldn't write this, but tell me what you really want to say.' It's as though the academic industry has dictated that a certain language is required in order to validate your presence, and so on, in that particular space.

Q3:   I'd like to ask a question that links the two lectures, because there are two triplicities that are at work in both lectures. Yesterday the triplicity was Africa, Asia (India, specifically) and Europe in relation to the infrastructure of black colonial labour, and in your account of the BBC there's a triplicity which transposes class into the equivalent in the prior model, both are theoretical models of the role played by an infrastructure of exploitable power. The difference between the two lectures has to do with the status of the term belonging, and specifically your capacity, when you were in England after you had been authorised by Walter Allen as a writer. The language you used was 'this was a book that would last,' and in between the publication which would give you your status as an author, empowered by colonising subject, you wrote this book in six weeks, which was *The Pleasures of Exile*, in which you did not, in a sense, belong to any of the triplicities, but you belonged instead, if I understand what you're saying, to the movement of language, to the movement of language that allowed you in both presentations to create what I would describe as openings between already existing locales, peoples, places, that let something else enter the world that was the outcome of an imaginative practice. The difference between the two lectures also seems to call attention to the something that the second lecture in particular is asking to be formulated: what was it that allowed you as a writer to shift in your self-representation, your self-naming, from a writer in England under the tutelary power of the BBC, who depended upon the influence of a critic with the power of Walter Allen to even get acknowledged as a name? What shifted your self-naming, a figure who belonged to a discipline that didn't include either Caribbean writers or West Indian writers, the discipline of the Commonwealth or British Literature broadly understood? What relations of power produced the discipline that allows yourself to represent what you now do as a form of writing that yesterday you connected with Trinidad in particular, and today you associate with the Caribbean as opposed to West Indies? Don't all of those moves require theoretical reflection, haven't you tacitly produced or enacted a theory that requires the activity of mind that you've associated with deforestation to describe? In a sense weren't you author-less before you became an author, authorised by Walter Allen, and as you wrote *The Pleasures of Exile* weren't you author-less moving within the realm of language as such?

GL: The last one reminds me of a famous saying, you know, that 'A writer without a book is like a cowboy without his horse and pistol.' You can't walk around saying, I'm a cowboy, when you have no horse, and you have no pistol. I just remembered that when you said that. The thing about theory: I distance myself sometimes from being the author of theories, I understand theory as the reflection on experience and you articulate the meaning and the nature of that experience. But what I miss when I'm speaking about how *Pleasures* was written in six weeks. I had been, in that period...I had a 1955–56, very important experiences that you've mentioned there, because some very, I would say critical, things happened in my life. I had never been a man too much connected to any formal religions and so on, but my mother, who was what I think would now be called a fundamentalist, and she had very clear ideas about me, and she had a copy of *In the Castle of My Skin* and would say to me. You see this? and speaking about author-less she says 'God never sends a bird without a branch' and so I have nothing to do with this, I am only a vessel through which the Lord is speaking. So there's a sense in which the experience of authorlessness came to me by another voice altogether. But the critical experiences now you raise it, if you take *Pleasures* as I said, 1960, 1959, '60 was *Of Age and Innocence,* books were coming close, and there's some significant journeys that I made. In 1955–56 I got what was then called the Somerset Maugham Award, it was a British award, and that was for *Castle,* and the condition was that you had to spend that money out of England and I went to Ghana. And yes when I arrived, you know, in fact I see a reflection of me right there, it's very interesting. This body and this skin and so on and there was this boy who looked exactly like what I would be doing at that age, I saw these boys and it was like looking at me at that age, until suddenly the nearer I got to them I realised I couldn't understand one word they were saying. They were speaking either Fante or Twi. Then I became aware of how you can experience continuity and discontinuity in the same moment. I was a Guggenheim Fellow in 1956. I came to the United States for the first time. That was a tremendous experience. I'd come from London where I'd been living for about six years, and I came to New York and I used to spend nights walking up and down looking at buildings that looked so unreal but magnificently unreal. There was no night, there was so much light. I go up to Harlem and back there was then a very famous restaurant named the Red Rooster, and I have never seen so much wool, I think all of the lambs were killed, all these women in wool, wool, all kinds. Keep in mind that when I had left London, the city was recovering from the war. And then a meal was served to a woman, and they had something called a T-bone steak that was brought on a dish, which in London was a meal for four people on a Sunday. And I wondered if this one woman was going to eat it, and I asked a man next to me if she'd eat all that and he said, oh yes and she'll have a snack after as well. And all the while I was putting together a lot of words being in some peculiar way an insider and peripheral. Then there is the journey through the Caribbean, the connection with the journey to Africa, that gives me a third or fourth eye and all of my experience. There is also the experience I am feeling. The critics of the novels, the English critics of the novels and even when the novels are spoken of in an affirmative way I don't think they understand what is happening. *The Pleasures of Exile* was written fast in that way, because I was saying: Look, this is how I want you to read *Season of Adventure* when it comes. It was in a way notes for whoever was going to read *Season of Adventure*. It wrapped up everything I was doing, it comes up there. And about theory and opening up, this was the problem: many of them, even the ones who were supposed to be very advanced, retained, it's quite right for them, a certain notion of the form of the novel, in which the nineteenth century and later into the twentieth in spite of Joyce and so on, there is a notion, you have essential character, and it is through the consciousness of this character that you investigate the subjectivities. And I am not into that, and in *In The Castle of My Skin* I keep saying that the central character is the village, my central character is not an individual, my central character is a collectivity, and it is through the window of the collectivity that I will look at the individual presences. So it's enormously reverse of the other way, and that's why you got criticism like: the only feeling of this novel was its episodic nature. It doesn't have this causal continuity and so on which they expect. I didn't want the novel to have that. I wanted it to have a fundamental pattern of associations, not a causal continuity looking through a central character. I was always very struck that *Castle* is not only read now but it's becoming a text for theorists about form. This I think opens up the notion that what may appear to be episodic may not really be episodic. The other thing about *Castle* is the unpredictable shifting of what you might call the angle of vision. We open with an I and then the personal I disappears and the novel will move from a first person perspective into a generalised, they, we, and so on. That also caused confusion among critics who were very good critics working according to their own criteria and their own methods. In *Pleasures of Exile*, I was in a sense trying to send a message to potential readers as to how I think you should start looking at a book like *Season of Adventure,* and of course I had a lot of trouble, the Caribbean critics were sometimes more hostile, than the English critics for different kinds of reasons. *Of Age and Innocence* but particularly *Season of Adventure* became a sort of *persona non grata* among the middle layers of the population.

Q4: Mine is going to be short. I also was fascinated by the point you made about the three levels of BBC programming as a social allegory. It made me think...your illustrious predecessor at the BBC, George Orwell, when he was working some years earlier at the BBC was fascinated with the problem...whether it was possible to create solidarity...in India in particular and elsewhere. So my question for you is where would the overseas service fit on your allegory of the three levels? Is there some way of belonging?

Q5: I had an overseas question too. This is a question about regional namings that are colonising. You started with the two poems, one connected to Africa across the ocean, one connected to India across the ocean. And in the Pacific there's a lot of movement by writers to decolonise themselves from South Pacific, Pacific Islands, or Asia-Pacific, and the preferred term becomes Oceanian, and that's the container that allows for linkages that have been there all along, and I'm wondering if you would be comfortable with something that would push the Caribbean towards an Oceanic framework, to open up the region in ways that you've kind of suggested.

GL: My answer is no to that. There's a man called Paul Gilroy, who has written a book called *The Black Atlantic*. But *The Black Atlantic* is the equivalent, instead of staying within your region and so on, the Atlantic now becomes the arena. But the point is that my folks don't live in the sea, my folks are on land. The question there about the Overseas Services, the thinking there really was, remember the thinking is empire and the way empire is scattered, that overseas service is really intended for that expatriate all around the world, the English in Kenya, in Barbados, in all kinds of colonial services and running banks and all of that. It's for the English overseas really that the Overseas Service is concerned with mainly. The expatriate overseas, to keep them in touch…and also in a way to reinforce authority where they are functioning in those particular roles.

SECTION 4

Critical Reflections on the Politics, Arts and Aesthetics of George Lamming

25 | *George Lamming and the Epistemology of Exile: Ways of Seeing, Singularity and Colonialism*

Clevis Headley

The motivation for this brief essay is George Lamming's classic *The Pleasures of Exile*, a text that installed exile as a historically situated but yet transcendental condition of both Caribbean identity and the modern Caribbean literary tradition. Indeed, some thinkers have confidently proclaimed that 'for Lamming, the concept of a West Indian identity is entirely the consequence of the experience of exile.'[1] And Lamming writes that, 'no islander from the West Indies sees himself as a West Indian until he encounters another islander in a foreign territory...in this sense, most of the West Indians of my generation were born in England.'[2] Here I do not seek to develop a general theory of exile nor an epistemology unique to Lamming but, rather, to probe some of the attendant epistemological implications of exile[3] in the Caribbean intellectual tradition, invigorated both by Lamming's inspiring example and brilliant work.

The wedding of exile and epistemology may unfortunately encourage the false but enticing idea of the existence of a neutral and objective framework to study and revise conceptual schemes. But, sadly enough, there is no 'cosmic exile.'[4] There is no god's eye perspective available to human beings. That human beings are denied the pleasures of cosmic exile, denied a god-like view from nowhere, and are forced to experience the world and their relationships with others from where they stand, undermines enthusiastic a priori searches for 'transcendental homelessness'.[5] Human positionality is hostile to the idea of axiological invariance, characteristic of colonialism and all other totalising schemes. Lamming was no stranger to the subtleties of positionality, for he 'called for the writer to accept his or her human responsibility as an individual in a particular social situation.'[6]

Unfortunately, this message has not yet reached writers such as V. S. Naipaul,[7] for Naipaul has exploited and continues to exploit the cultural equivalence of cosmic exile, namely, a construction of exile and displacement as providing the colonial writer with the opportunity to become a true individual who, uncorrupted by cultural, racial and national interests, functions as an ideal observer, as 'a reasonable and objective commentator on colonial and post colonial societies.'[8]

Despite the impossibility of cosmic exile, there is a certain metaphorical exile pregnant with epistemic relevance.[9] Here I will exploit the semantic density of 'exile' by unreservingly appropriating the metaphor of exile to reconfigure the activities of Caribbean writers away from home. I shall execute this task by summarily bolstering the thesis that a specific structuring of exile yields a space conducive to epistemological mischief, a space from which to raid colonialism's dialectical web. Colonialism, masquerading as the material manifestation of Hegel's all-encompassing dialectic, truly exploits the idea of containing its opposite within itself.

Defining Exile

Focusing on the idea of the epistemological resourcefulness of exile presupposes being clear about exile precisely because of its contestability. This contestability is obvious in the following intriguing definition by Arnold Eisen: Exile, he tells us, is 'the awareness of being somewhere else than where God is and humanity should be.'[10] This sense of exile as alienation, a sense of distance from God, must be untangled from the more common notion of secular exile. Of course there is also the sense of ontological or existential exile, the sense of the individual being separated form him/herself, other human beings and also from nature.

But despite the heterology of exile, meaning its multiple referents, understanding exile for purposes of this essay requires semantic clarity to illuminate the differences among the expatriate, the émigré or immigrant, and the refugee. This semantic strategy follows Zeleza's analytical typology of exile in the following terms: 'exile as cultural alienation, exile as political angst, and exile as cosmopolitan affiliation.'[11] The expatriate is the individual who voluntarily leaves his/her native land in search of a place more conducive to his or her interests and pursuits. The expatriate is also the individual, the seeker of the exotic in some instances, who temporarily leaves home to work abroad. Since he or she voluntarily leaves home, and does not suffer from the nostalgia for home, the expatriate can return at anytime. Émigrés or immigrants, being highly motivated by economic considerations or the search for educational opportunities, voluntarily leave home in search of a better life, seeking to better their lot in life. And, finally, refugees are persons who, because of war or famine or some other political disaster, become unrepresentative individuals, asylum-seekers and, in crossing borders for safety, become the wards of international relief agencies.

Traditionally speaking, the exile, from a literal perspective, designates the individual forced to leave home because of political banishment or similarly, who, because of political reasons, must leave in order to avoid suffering some unfortunate circumstance.[12] Exile connotes some punitive act of state, an act which forces an individual to leave his own country. And the condition of exile is all the more extreme precisely because of the desire to return home. Here exile connotes 'political punishment', banishment, and the stigma of being an outsider.

It is my contention that the experience of West Indian writers and other West Indians who left home for Europe is not a determinate case of exile, exile specifically in the literal sense of having suffered a punitive act of banishment or displacement. Nevertheless, the impossibility of framing the West Indian situation as literal exile, as an uncontested exilic condition, offers the possibility of construing the West Indian condition metaphorically, among other things, as epistemological and existential exile. Indeed, Paul Tiyambe Zeleza frames 'Exile as an existential and epistemological condition, as a spatial and temporal state of being, belonging, and becoming....'[13] Hence, the epistemological grounding of exile captures the sense of normative exclusion from participating in the process of configuring, in dramatic terms, the dramatic saga of human existence. It also captures the struggle involving critically engaging the norms of colonialism. Indeed, the connection among exile, epistemology and colonialism is the more obvious when once we acknowledge that 'Colonial knowledge both enabled conquest and was produced by it; in a certain important ways, knowledge was what colonialism was all about.'[14]

Perhaps it would not be too much of an exaggeration to claim that West Indian writers who journeyed to the metropole also suffered literary exile. Andrew Gurr, viewing exile as an escape from colonial provincialism and marginality states that, 'An artist born in a colony is made consciousness of the culturally subservient status of his home and is forced to go into exile in the metropolis as a means of compensating for that sense of cultural subservience.'[15] For the West Indian writer, this compensation did not necessarily entail a complete and total rejection of the local condition and the sweet embrace of metropolitan culture. Consequently, if exile, as stated by Chancy is 'productive contradiction',[16] it certainly need not imply that the West Indian writer sought to escape from his or her positionality within culture and tradition. 'Exile is not a subjective quest...to escape....'[17] Nor is exile the unadvisable urge to flee from responsibility. Lamming, in his 1983 introduction to *In the Castle of My Skin*, describes the condition that led West Indians to leave for London as follows:

> It was not a physical cruelty. Indeed, the colonial experience of my generation was almost wholly without violence. No torture, no concentration camp, no mysterious disappearance of hostile natives, no army encamped with order to kill. The Caribbean endured a different kind of subjugation. It was a terror of the mind; a daily exercise in self-mutilation. Black versus Black in a battle for self-improvement.[18]

Lamming, nevertheless, clearly acknowledges the peculiarity of Caribbean writers away from home – the uniqueness of exile as it pertains to Caribbean writers. While he intimates that exile may seem universal, particularly in a situation where residing in a strange society produces experiences of being excluded, he warns, however, about the ease with which this situation can give rise to complacency. According to Lamming, 'We are made to feel a sense of exile by our inadequacy and our irrelevance of function in a society whose past we can't alter, and whose future is always beyond us. Idleness can easily guide us into accepting this as a condition. Sooner or later, in silence or with rhetoric, we sign a contract whose epitaph reads: "To be an exile is to be alive."'[19] Lamming, forever perceptive, quickly tempers this observation by underscoring the distinctiveness of the Caribbean writer and his involvement with the question of exile.

Spatial sameness can aggravate exile by imposing a double burden on the Caribbean writer. As Lamming writes, 'When the exile is a man of colonial orientation, and his chosen residence is the country which colonised his own history, then there are certain complications. For each exile has not only got to prove his worth to the other, he has to win the approval of Headquarters, meaning in the case of the West Indian writer, England.'[20] Instead of experiencing exile as displacement and wandering, the Caribbean writer, as it were, finds himself/herself located at the zero point of abstract universality, at the heart of empire.

Before bringing this section to a close, it bears noting that the heterology of exile is not only present in its referential multiplicity but is also evident when approached from the perspective of social positionality. Many authors have called attention to the fact that men and women may very well experience exile differently. Whereas men often seek exile because of perceived 'objective' reasons, for example, being in conflict with political authority, women's experience of exile is more personal or private in that women seek exile in order to escape cultural structures that make them prisoners in their daily existence. According to Alena Heitlinger, 'the decision to become an exile could also be motivated by the politics of gender. Women who choose exile often do so in order to escape from oppressive nationalist, religious, and patriarchal discourses and laws.'[21] And in her study of Afro-Caribbean women writers, Myriam Chancy has charged that the discourse of exile produced by African and Caribbean writers has 'by and large failed to encompass the realities of women of African descent.'[22] Chancy singles out Lamming for criticism, referring to 'his exclusion of the female Caribbean exile from his theorisation on that state of alienation.'[23] But Chancy's point is more general. According to her, 'if we have come to know the condition of exile through literature, we have come to know it primarily through a male prism.'[24]

On the Psychology of Exile

Obviously, our focus in this essay will primarily centre on those West Indians who journeyed to England to 'make a career as a writer' and not exclusively on those who migrated because of economic or political ambitions. Consequently, this endeavour precludes the tendency to read the experience of these respective groups in terms of a psychological and traumatic disability, the idea of exile as 'physical disconnection and psychic disorientation.'[25] So, even if exile can be psychologically volatile, my intention is to banish 'exile' from the realm of the psychology so that by 'exile' we 'do not mean something sad or deprived.'[26] Exile need not be construed as an incubator of psychological volatility. Rather than pathologise the condition of those who suffer exile, it is more constructive to focus on the epistemological resources of exile. Of course, this development need not prohibit using relevant psychological concepts to illuminate certain aspect of the condition of exile. So, even if West Indians writers were not banished from their home countries, it is still possible to recruit abjection, the phenomenon of the rejected and the excluded, being treated as undesirable, as filth, to describe the attitudes of some West Indians who regarded home (the Caribbean) as unbearable, and as something to be despised. So that exile, as social abjection, is the phenomenon of separation from home, namely one's native homeland, such that the foreign land threatens to obliterate home. But, as is characteristic of abjection, what is defiled is at the same time both horrible and fascinating. So, from the perspective of exile, home is both horrible and fascinating.

Indeed, instead of the common tendency to interpret exile, whether literally or metaphorically, as the equivalence of severe cultural shock, a generic situation always attendant to travel and relocation, I prefer to interpret the unique experience of West Indian writers as an epistemological rupture. Yet, again, I want to distance this notion of epistemological rupture from psychological frames of interpretation.

From another perspective we can talk in terms of the phenomenology of exile, not a pure phenomenology in the sense of seeking to ascertain the basic features of exile totally independently of any presuppositions or prejudice, but an existential phenomenology of exile which would frame exile as the condition of embodied individuals that are variously located in situations marked by class, gender, cultural, and religious, etc., determinations. Such an existential phenomenology seeking to describe the lived reality of exile would focus on exile as that kind of highly contested and uncertain existence that is a 'condition of consistent, continual displacement;…the radical uprooting of all that one is and stands for, in a communal context, without loss of know ledge of those roots.'[27]

But the fact remains that the seductive attractiveness of the psychological interpretation proves so irresistible that even when the epistemological consequences are mentioned, many thinkers still immediately recruit psychological imagery as their basic model of interpretation. Gikandi writes:

> [T]here is a vital epistemological consequence to the condition of exile: it forces an earlier generation of Caribbean writers ... to an irreversible cognizance of their cultural schizophrenia; in turn, this awareness of division comes with what Walcott has aptly called 'a gradual sense of a loss of innocence about history.'[28]

In another context, Jan Carew has similarly imposed a psychologistic gloss on the relation between exile and Caribbean writers. He contends that the Caribbean writer is 'a creature balanced between limbo and nothingness, exile abroad and homelessness at home, between the people on the one hand and the coloniser on the other.'[29] Partial escape from this dishevelled existential condition is, according to Carew, contingent on embracing the European fragment of the many inherited cultural fragments. But even here the situation of the Caribbean writer is not completely resolved precisely because, according to Carew, 'Hiding behind the screen of this European fragment, the Caribbean writer oscillates in and out of sunlight and shadows, exile abroad and homelessness at home.'[30]

Most recently, Caryl Phillips 'suggests in *The Final Passage* that the confrontation by West Indians with their former colonial power cannot but be a shattering experience because they are cognitively ill-equipped to understand their ambivalent relation to England, and hence to fend for themselves.'[31] Here, once again, are traces of a psychologically impaired Caribbean subject.

In another context, Aimé Césaire has flirted with the psychological appeal of exile, attributing psychic damage to Caribbean peoples. According to him:

> Throughout their history, people in the Caribbean...have suffered a great deal. But I think that what they have suffered from the most are not the scourges known to the rest of the world-hunger, misery, and the like-which exist in a real way. What we have suffered from the most, more than any other people, is really alienation, in other

words, lack of knowledge of oneself. This seems fundamental to me. The [Caribbean] being is a human being who is deprived of his own self, of his history, of his traditions, and his beliefs. In a nutshell. he is an abandoned being.[32]

Unlike Carew and Phillips, and to lesser extent Césaire, Lamming unsettles rigid psychological construals of Caribbean exile by placing distance between himself and such interpretations of exile, specifically the idea that the individual in exile longs for home and suffers from melancholy due to separation from the object of his desire or love. He writes:

This may be the dilemma of the West Indian writer abroad: that he hungers for nourishment from a soil which he (as an ordinary citizen) could not at present endure. The pleasure and paradox of my own exile is that I belong wherever I am. My role, it seems, has rather to do with time and change than with geography of circumstances; and yet there is always an acre of ground in the New World which keeps growing echoes in my head. I can only hope that these echoes do not die before my work comes to an end.[33]

In order to avoid being misunderstood, I am not suggesting that it is totally impossible to justify reading Lamming as being concerned with exile in the psychological sense of focusing on the isolation an individual can experience, the sense of being exiled from others and, as it were, living in a solipsistic world. Brathwaite addresses this sense of exile as personal isolation in the work of Lamming. Brathwaite writes:

Reading the later books [*The Emigrants and Of Age and Innocence*] as an extension of the experience of the first, one comes to realise that *In the Castle of My Skin* has for the author, a deeper more personal significance. As Lamming's work goes forward, we come to understand that the title of that book is not a signature of colour, but a symbol of personal isolation. Standing alone in his isolation, the individual, Lamming says in *The Emigrants* is unable to communicate with his fellow man. The harder he tries, the more completely is he misunderstood. Misunderstanding is the theme of *The Emigrants*.[34]

Clearly, Brathwaite, as a consequent of his reading of Lamming's work, attributes a certain individualistic bias to him. But Braithwaite's actions should not be interpreted as a casual gloss but, rather, as exposing, as it were, a deep-seated 'metaphysical prejudice.' Indeed, Brathwaite was not deterred from describing Lamming's later novels as signifying the "the logical conclusion to the journey of the self-regarding mind."[35] In his discussion of *Of Age and Innocence*, Brathwaite denounces the egocentric enterprise he attributes to Lamming. But Braithwaite's point is ontological and ethical and not necessarily psychological. He writes:

> The dilemma of the characters in *Of Age and Innocence* is how to coexist in a world of several of these special individualities. The resolution of the dilemma ends in failure because it seems to me that the premise is all wrong. For mind to be truly itself it cannot only be self-regarding, introspective and selfish, it must be out-going: aware of its responsibilities to others in society.[36]

It is possible, however, to escape the trap of psychologising exile if we were to view exile as defying certain principles that many believe provide a firm basis for knowledge, the principles of identity and sameness and the concept of identity-in-difference. This interpretive change allows for the possible construal of exile as creating the conditions for openness to difference. Edward Said writes:

> For an exile, habits of life, expression, or activity in the new environment inevitably occur against the memory of these things in another environment. Thus both the new and the old environments are vivid, actual, occurring together contrapuntally. There is a unique pleasure in this sort of apprehension, especially if the exile is conscious of other contrapuntal juxtapositions that diminish orthodox judgement and elevate appreciative sympathy. There is also a particular sense of achievement in acting as if one were at home wherever one happens to be.[37]

Caribbean writers, although strangers in the metropolitan centres of colonialism, were not simply forced to taste 'the bitterness of physical and psychological exile,'[38] but found themselves strategically situated to construct alternative narratives of self and community in the epistemological space offered by exile; they were well-positioned to counter the teleological narratives of the West. Far from simply imparting to Caribbean writers an isolated subjectivity and individuality, an 'objectless inwardness,'[39] exile conferred epistemological credential on Caribbean writers. C.L.R. James commenting upon the situation of the West Indian writer abroad writes, 'It is when you are outside, but can take part as a member, that you see differently from the ways they see, and you are able to write independently.'[40]

Before continuing I will qualify my earlier point about distancing exile from psychologistic interpretations There is a sense in which exile can be linked to trauma. But this linkage is not primarily psychological in the sense of rendering the victim of trauma psychically compromised and existentially incapacitated. Cathy Caruth uses trauma to interrupt the Western linear conception of history and its assumption about the referentiality of language. Caruth argues that the Western conception of history is referentially-based. namely history is seen as requiring a direct connection between experience and some referent. Caruth rejects the demand for referentiality as complicit with totalising; trauma, however, breaks the assumed innocent link between language and reality and, she concludes that if there are no metanarratives that can ground history, we can permit 'history to arise where immediate understanding may not'[41]

Obviously, then, the ambivalence and ambiguity attendant to exile need not be reduced or translated into a threat to ego integrity-specifically tagged as a psychological problem. It would not be too much of an exaggeration to hold that the West Indian, because of exile, is seen by many as an example of Hegel's unhappy consciousness, a consciousnesses 'inwardly divided in two, disunited consciousness.'[42] So, instead of invoking cultural schizophrenia, hence, exploiting the notion of split personality or split consciousness and all the attending disabling connotations, perhaps it would be more constructive to talk about the biculturality, pluriculturality or tansculturality of Caribbean writers.

Exile and the Possibility of Caribbean Writing

There is no escaping the fact that exilic texts are material examples of the fictional status of concepts, that is, that all concepts are subject to both construction as well as deconstruction. The dialectical existence of exile itself is mirrored in exile texts. Accordingly, exile and home are not stable and absolute opposites but, in certain cases, are interchangeable. Sophia McClennen aptly captures the Hegelian drama of exile writing. She writes:

> [E]xile writing often contains the following unity of opposites: the condition of exile is depicted as physical and mental; exile is a state that both liberates and confines the writers; writing is both the cause of exile and the way to supersede it; exile is both spiritual/abstract and material; exile is personal/individual and political/collective; exile writing recuperates the past and re-imagines it; exiles write about the past and also about the future; the experience of exile is both unique and universal; exile improves and also restricts the writer's work; exile heightens both regionalism and cosmopolitanism, both nationalism and globalisation. These interpenetrating oppositions are only a few of the most salient dialectical tensions found in exile writing. These tensions track in a variety of different ways in each particular case, but these tensions are a common feature of exile writing.[43]

With regard to the West Indian situation, exile provided the occasion for speaking, for a speech emergent from the realisation that established narratives of self and community failed to provide the intelligibility and coherence needed by West Indians abroad to make sense of their existence. Interestingly enough, then, the epistemological rupture of exile is characteristic of the Caribbean context precisely because, instead of rendering the West Indian condition of exile pathological, exile became the occasion for a new epistemology of self and community. Exile need not be interpreted as necessarily disabling the West Indian writer; rather, it facilitated a narrative of liberation, an epistemology of freedom. Exile made possible '[t]he capacity to reject epistemological fixations' and to deliver the imagination of West Indian writers 'to other temporal and spatial possibilities.'[44] For it comes as no surprise that many canonical texts of West Indian literature and intellectual tradition were authored in exile. Here I am thinking of Aimé Césaire's *Cahier*, Frantz Fanon's *Black Skin, White Masks*, C. L. R. James's *Black Jacobins*, V. S. Naipaul's *A House for Mr Biswas*, and George Lamming's *In the Castle of My Skin*. This fact underscores the crucial significance of 'the phenomenon of exile as a historical and existential condition' to the development of a tradition of Caribbean writing.[45] As stated earlier, there is no exaggeration in viewing exile as historically contingent, yet paradoxically serving as the quasi-transcendental ground of West Indian literature. It should be clear by now why exile need not be construed as historical exile,[46] namely, the idea that slavery displaced Afro-Caribbean peoples from their respective African cultures and cursed them with natal alienation. Furthermore, that they now suffer the common fate of collective exile. Hence, having been consigned to infinite exile, West Indians inevitably suffer from chronic psychic wounds that are not amenable to therapeutic resolution.

It merits noting here that there is indeed a relation between exile and history in the Caribbean. What is not clear is the extent to which it would be correct to interpret exile exclusively in terms of natal alienation. Kamau Brathwaite acknowledges a relation between exile and history but he does not view this relationship pathologically. According to him, the metaphors of rootlessness or restlessness invoked to frame the experience of Afro-Caribbean peoples must be interpreted in conjunction with the presence of an immaterial anthropological reality. Brathwaite writes:

> The dichotomy, I think, is still there. It is a permanent part of our heritage. It comes, in a way, as an almost physical inheritance from Africa where in nature, drought and lushness, the flower and the desert, lie side by side. It is a spiritual inheritance from slavery and the long story before that of the migrant African moving from the lower Nile across the desert to the Western ocean only to meet the Portuguese and a history that was to mean the middle passage, America, and a rootless sojourn in the Caribbean Sea.

This dichotomy expresses itself in the West Indian through a certain psychic tension, an excitability, a definite feeling of having no past, of not really belonging (which some prefer to call 'adaptability'); and finds relief in laughter and (more seriously) in movement-dance, cricket, carnival, emigration.[47]

But again, we must insist that exile is neither a psychological condition nor an ontological structure of the human condition. Hence, consistent with the idea of exile as an epistemological phenomenon, I find the following statement by Glissant troubling. He writes:

The truth is that exile is within us from the outset, and is even more corrosive because we have not managed to drive it into the open with our precarious assurances nor have we succeeded all together in dislodging it. All Caribbean poetry is a witness to this.[48]

However, most recently, Glissant has exposed a nuanced notion of exile, exile as contrary to totality, hence moving away from his earlier psychological tainted notion of exile. In exile, he writes 'roots are lacking.'[49] And he adds the following in commenting on Gilles Deluze and Felix Guattari notions of the root:

The root is unique, a stock taking all upon itself and killing all around it. In opposition to this [Deluze and Guattari] propose the rhizome, an enmeshed toot system, a network spreading either in the ground or in the air, with no predatory rootstock taking over permanently. The notion of the rhizome maintains, therefore, the idea of rootedness but challenges that of a totalitarian root. Rhizomatic thought is the principle behind what I call the Poetics of Relation, in which each and every identity is extended through a relationship with the Other.[50]

So, if being rooted involves the predatory displacing of the Other, exile, lacking roots, is a matter of resisting totalitarian designs and embracing a posture of affirmating the Other. If this latter sense of exile is a departure from any psychological underpinning, Glissant's earlier construal is not.

Hence, instead of viewing exile as a condition to be expelled, Caribbean writers use exile as a epistemic space, as a zone of knowing distanced from the hegemony of colonialism in order to engage in the imaginative dismantling of the for-structures of colonialism, as well as the unthought of colonialism, what has remained unasked about Colonialism.

Epistemology

The idea of the epistemology of exile need not be theoretically committed to a model of epistemology as representative of the natural sciences. This counter-epistemology does not seek to develop an account of how knowledge of the external physical world is possible nor attempt to establish the conditions of knowledge, as well as the criteria of knowledge. Similarly, it does not assume that there is any advanced theoretical foundation or justification for ways of living, meaning that '[t]here is no transcendental basis, no non-question begging deduction or procedural commitment, no final, binding empirical proof.'[51] What is truly sought, in this context, is creative imagination and not necessarily being held captive to the rigid demands and constraints of any artificially contrived abstract and formalistic mode of argumentation. Epistemology, in this existential setting, while not giving comfort to naive relativism, is not a matter of one seeking disinterested and objective reasons to ground or justify knowledge. Knowledge, to an appreciable degree of confidence, is what Lamming calls, one's way of seeing, the courageous attempt to seek deep insights into one's state of being by reflecting on one's own interests and concerns. One pursues or rather suffers the truth, which facilitates openness to others and to other cultures, while refusing to sanction any self-sameness or absolutising of the ego.

Let me frame this epistemological difference within Kierkegaardian language (noting that Patrick Taylor, in another context, acknowledges striking similarities between Lamming and Kierkegaard).[52] Kierkegaard wrote that 'To be a stranger, to be in exile is precisely the characteristic suffering of the religious man.'[53] Building upon this insight, I firmly identify exile as a site of knowledge, specifically as a defining possibility for existential knowledge. Reflection in exile is not objective reflection in the pursuit of truth as an object divorced from an existing thinking subject; similarly, there is no appeal to an objective notion of the truth, truth as independent and not embedded in a particular historical context or cultural context. Following Kierkegaard, we can state that objective reflection 'turns existence into an indifferent, vanishing something.' And truth also becomes something 'indifferent'. Alternatively, subjective reflection, unlike objective reflection, is passionately engaged reflection, not 'apathetic and disengaged.'[54] Subjective reflection 'leads to action and decision, while objective reflection leads to inactivity, indecision, and indolence.'[55] Subjective reflection also means that the individual relates to truth 'subjectively by making it an issue for *him or her*, he or she then critically questions the efficacy and merits of the prevailing "universal" [claims] in the names of those individual subjects whom the law [political principles, cultural assumptions] does not accommodate.'[56] Donald Hinds, for example, effectively describes the experience of the journey to Britain from the Caribbean as a 'journey to an illusion'.[57] In this context, Hinds is not appealing to the Freudian notion of illusion as wish fulfilment but, rather, the debunking of colonial discourses experienced by subjects of empire when they became acquainted with the ugly realities of empire for the first time. So the illusion of European 'ontological superiority' characteristic of colonial ideologies was summarily dismissed as the colonial immigrants encountered life in the Motherland. It is no wonder that Caribbean thinkers engaged in the most radical questioning of colonialism while in exile.

Exile also bears upon the notion of subjective truth from another perspective. Exile can serve as a means of unsettling the complacency of location. In a home environment, one may complacently take certain things for granted; one may come to perceive and think of the world as given, as natural kind with its own independent structure and immune to the constitutive powers of human consciousness. Exile transports one to an unfamiliar spatiality where one's consciousness becomes saturated with the aching awareness of one's subject position, namely one's location in a physical environment. Furthermore, one must also make habitable an unfamiliar discursive space. In this new subject position, the objectivity emergent from one's prior complacent mode of being is displaced by a new subjective awareness. This displacing or interruption of the objective by the subjective is aptly captured by Patricia Williams. She writes:

> One of the most important results of reconceptualizing from 'objective truth' to rhetorical event will be a more nuanced sense of...social responsibility. This will be so because much of what is spoken in so-called objective, unmediated voices is in fact mired in hidden subjectivities and unexamined claims that make property of others beyond self, all the while denying such conditions.[58]

In this essay, the operative notion of truth is that of the subjectivity of truth. According to this idea of truth as subjectivity, we are, once again, instructed that "truth does not have any transcendental or objective basis, but is something whose functioning is predicated upon the existence of flesh-and-blood human beings who are subject to [an] endless tide of becoming."[59]

Regarding Lamming, I share Patrick Taylor's observation that he (Lamming) belongs to the tradition of liberating narrative. Taylor writes, 'The challenge of liberating narrative is to transform the sociopolitical totality so that lived history becomes open possibility. This is the challenge of Lamming's novels.'[60] Lamming announces, in *The Pleasures of Exile*, that he has no intention of pursuing objective reflection. He declares no desire to construct theories, to engineer ideas, but rather seeks to express the complexities of the truth he suffers as an existing human being; he intends to remain faithful to the etiology of his subjectivity. I prefer to describe his activity as subjective reflection, for as he states: 'I shall have failed to communicate my meaning if I leave the impression that I am constructing theories. I haven't got the kind of equipment which is required of men who engineer ideas; but I do believe that what a person thinks is very much determined by the way that person sees. This book is really no more than a report on one man's way of seeing, using certain facts of experience as evidence and a guide.'[61]

On another occasion, while commenting upon his original interpretation of *The Tempest*, Lamming underscores the significance of reading the play through the lens of his being-in-the-world and not being burdened with a formalist reading of the play, a reading that views it as a totality whose meaning is detached from lived reality. Lamming states, "It will not help to say that I am wrong in the parallels which I have set out to interpret; for I shall reply that my mistake, lived and deeply felt by millions of men like me – proves the positive value of error. It is a value which you must learn.[62]

Lamming, being keenly aware of the asymmetries of exile, reinforces the connection between subjectivity and truth. On his view, truth, also construed as subjective engagement, is a matter of one's way of seeing. In response to the tendency to dismiss any reference to racism as a case of one having a chip on one's shoulders, Lamming states that this strategy of closure is an attempt to erase the subjective truth of one's lived reality. The complacency of a familiar space leads many individuals to execute this cynical ploy through an appeal to universality, namely invoking a formal and abstract notion of equality. In direct response to this dismissal, Lamming writes: 'It does not occur to him that he is making me an offer of equality, or reminding me of his original disposition to grant me that much. He is horrified if I say that his equality, on the evidence of his charge, is an abstract equality. It does not grow from a felt recognition of my capacity for experience, my particular way of seeing.'[63] Here I want to reinforce Lamming's position and directly connect it to the relation between epistemology and exile. Perhaps, what Lamming is intimating is that 'universal categories cannot express radical singularity and therefore are impotent to repress the anarchy of difference.'[64]

Subjectively existing, intimately connected with subjective reflection, also assumes the mode of self-awareness. This self-awareness can be epistemologically grounded in exile so that one re-evaluates one's former beliefs about oneself and one's relationship with others. In exile, this revaluation requires a critical engagement of colonialism by Caribbean writers. 'Awareness,' according to Lamming, 'is a minimum condition for attaining freedom.'[65] Indeed, there is greater depth to the epistemological awareness of exile. Lamming himself has described this awareness using the trope of 'levels of consciousness': Self, community (being-with-others), and human existence. Gordon Rohlehr offers the following description of Lamming's position:

> The artist's first loyalty, according to Lamming, was to the self revealed after descent into the private desolation of the soul, and after struggle to rescue experience from inner chaos and invest it with verbal shape. His second loyalty was to 'the world in which he moves among other men', since society was the origin of part of his consciousness. Lamming then noted the burden of living in a society where one major issue such as race predominated. This burden might prove so overwhelming to the writer that he might forget his third responsibility: to the wider community of all mankind, whose common fate he shared, and in whose name and on whose behalf he had embarked 'upon a definition of himself.[66]

Obviously, then, for the Caribbean writer, the epistemological challenges which exile poses require a struggle against the colonialism of being. Epistemic courage renders Caribbean intellectual activity as partly an ethical obligation to prevent Western society, in the form of colonialism, from absolutising itself, rending itself normative, constituting both the standard and the realisation of human perfectibility. Here there is a refusal to view Western culture as the unfolding of a 'metaphysical telos.'

Joyce Jonas's apt description of Lamming captures the thrust of the epistemological and ethical urgency of Caribbean intellectual activity. She writes:

> His task as a creative West Indian writer is to mount a perpetual assault on the word of assumed Eurocentric authority, to resist any and every world view that colonises him and to assert, in place or the sacred 'shrines' of Western cultural imperialism, an ongoing narrative activity that invites us to step outside the 'given' into a limbo where imaginative new connections call be made, and where acts of reconstituting reality hold infinite possibilities.[67]

Jonas perceptively captures a significant aspect of the epistemological matrix of exile: The importance of eternal hostility to colonialism and to all systems of totality, frames of interpretation, and narrative schemes that do violence to the other – that assassinate singularity. Consistently with Jonas's position, the Caribbean writer [must] first resists colonial authority, [must] devalorizes European cultural "shrines"; second, 'his or her discourse [must] invites us to step outside of a world of given meanings and identities'; third, '...by establishing a new semiotic and ideological connection between the coloniser and the colonised, [the Caribbean writer must] sets out to reorder the narrative of history.'[68] Caribbean writers, in attacking colonialism, forcefully intimate a conception of 'truth [as] not the expression of the divine design of *Geist*...'[69] Their focus on countering Eurocentric authority and reconfiguring history entails the reconstruction of tradition, hence marking one major difference in the exilic condition of the Caribbean writer and the modernist idea that exile is essentially the occasion for the rejection of tradition and community.

In another context, Blanchot also declares that exile demands an infinite hostility to any metaphysics courting Totality, Unity and Identity. While embracing the nomadic truth of exile, he writes: 'There is a truth of exile, a vocation of exile, and if to be Jewish is to be destined to dispersion, then this dispersion, just as it calls to a dwelling without place, and just as it destroys all fixed relationships of power with an individual, a group, or a State, also brings out in the face of the exigency of Totality, another exigency, and prohibits finally the temptation of Unity-Identity.'[70]

The idea of the epistemology of exile can also be connected to Kierkegaard's notion of the teleological suspension of the ethical. Indeed, here, there is a fusion of the ethical and the epistemological for, as in Kierkegaard's own work, the teleological suspension of the ethical does not entail a rejection of ethics but represents a radical attempt to establish a relation with the Other by rejecting the artificiality and formalism of the reigning order. The idea is that 'The aim of the teleological suspension of the ethical is to reinforce the fact that our ethical codes are ineluctably open to revision, since they are the formulations of existing individuals who are always in the process of becoming, forever subject to the vagaries of time and contingency.'[71] So an obvious parallel emerges between the idea of the teleological suspension of the ethical and the epistemology of exile, once we come to understand the former as 'a means by which both the laws of the state and those fundamental ethical principles that govern our actions are sufficiently loosened up so as to prevent them from becoming dogmatic, rigid, and insensitive....'[72] Exile, consequently, resembles 'the teleological suspension of the ethical' precisely because it leads, at least epistemologically, to a loosening up of the principles, and presuppositions of colonialism. If the ethical represents the universal, colonialism has similarly presented itself as the universal. But the categories of exile, existence, becoming, and contingency enable us to keep the dominant codes of culture open to revision. This revisioning takes the form of a renaming of things or, put differently, a rebirth of language. The project of renaming, the infinite newness of language, shatters the old, fossilised language of colonialism. Indeed, thoroughly infused with an imperative of liberation, a new language emerges which violates both the syntax and semantic of colonial discourse, making room for new styles of thinking.

Exile also summons singularity through the auspices of responsibility. If exile offers the space to initiate an epistemological raid on the universalism of colonialism, the knowledge gained in this process should lead one to welcome and celebrate the singularity repressed by universality of colonialism. Here responsibility can, although not necessarily, take the form of both an "obligation to the singular other that overrides one's obligation to the universality of the law," as well as of an obligation to the singular other of colonialism, one's own cultural tradition.

Clearly, then, one unfortunate limitation of colonialism, as observed from exile, is its failure to sustain a genuine sense of community; at most it accommodates a certain 'meaningless externality',[73] a situation where individuals are supposed to regulate their lives in accordance with an already predetermined set of rules and codes. Lamming hinted at the transformation which takes place during exile. Lamming in *The Emigrants* hints about the possibility of a transformation taking place that would deny any familiar object 'of its history, making it a new thing, almost unknown, since all the attributes of presence would be destroyed, leaving what was once a thing with certain fixed references, a kind of blank.'[74] David Ellis offers the following commentary on this passage: 'At this point, the emigrants enter a new perceptual field which would see them become immigrants. In crossing this discursive/ideological line, they fell prey to a new set of social determinants and find themselves cut off from any previous certainties.'[75] It is exile that makes possible this release from dogmatic slumber and the arrival into an altered epistemological plane of existence.

Conclusion

My effort to connect epistemology and exile bears some similarity to the work of Nikos Papastergiadis. Papastergiadis also appreciates the link between epistemology and exile, since he claims that 'exile is often a crucial component in the methodology of critical thinking.'[76] By critical thinking he does not entail regimenting one's thinking in accordance with the technical formalisms of logic. Rather, he describes the critical thinking associated with exile as 'metaphorical' because it is the 'process which discovers validation through the association of contraries.'[77] Further more, critical thinking is otherwise manifested as the crossing back and forth 'between distance and detachment on the one hand and empathy or involvement on the other.'[78] Here the pleasures of exile blend with the epistemic benefits of exile such that one enjoys a 'bifocal perspective' which, in turn, makes possible a third constituent between 'self-defeating binarisms.'[79] Papastergiadis rejects the romantic view of exile 'as providing a detached and hence insightful view of the country of origin,'[80] but embraces the idea that the 'dynamic of displacement' is not compatible with an either/or approach but rather a complementarian both/and perspectives.[81]

To conclude, whereas traditional epistemology articulates knowledge as identity of subject and object or as identity of thought and object, the epistemology of exile is not antagonistic to difference but encourages a spatial and relational revisioning of things. With exile, spatial distance is not the contradictory of cognitive proximity. This point establishes why exile, among other things, can provide a space for knowledge. Traditional epistemology can court the worst of fanaticism, a self enclosed egology, an imperial subjectivity, and a deficient imagination, a servant of sameness and identity. Exile propagates perspectivism, contingency and the pleasures of uncertainty. Exile may create spatial distance, but not necessarily a separation in consciousness; in exile there is the opportunity of pursuing new possibilities while crossing borders of thought, transgressing the limits of thought and imagination, and violating boundaries of conventional intelligibility. Exile offers the privilege of knowing that the same borders of thought that offer metaphysical comfort can also become prisons of the imagination. It is the pleasures of these truths that Lamming's own subjective existence, his tenure in exile, summons us to experience and to enjoy.

Notes

1. David Ellis, "'Transatlantic Passages': Lamming, Phillips, and the Course of Black Writing in Britain," *Obsidian* III (Fall/Winter 2004), Volume 5, Number 2, p. 72.
2. George Lamming, *The Pleasures of Exile* (Ann Arbor: University of Michigan Press, 1992), 214.
3. For an intriguing discussion of the connection between exile and epistemology in the thought of Levinas and Derrida, see Martin Srajek's "Apocalypse: Epistemological Exile vis-á-vis Truth," in Martin Srajek, *In the Margins of Deconstruction: Jewish Conceptions of Ethics in Emmanuel Levinas and Jacques Derrida* (Pittsburgh, PA: Duquesne University Press, 2000), 189-90.
4. This phrase is taken from Quine. See Williard Van Orman Quine, *Word & Object* (The M. I. T. Press, Cambridge, 1960), 275.
5. Edward Said, *Reflections on Exile and Other Essays* (Cambridge: Harvard University Press, 2002), 18.
6. Patrick Taylor, *Narrative of Liberation: Perspectives on Afro-Caribbean Literature, Popular Culture, and Politics* (Ithaca: Cornell University Press, 1989), 184. See George Lamming, "The Negro Writer and his World," *Présence Africaine*, (June–November 1956).
7. For a good critical discussion or Naipaul's relation to exile, see Rob Nixon, "London Calling: V. S. Naipaul and the License of Exile", *The South Atlantic Quarterly*, 87:1 (Winter 1988), 1–37.
8. Simon Gikandi, *Writing in Limbo. Modernism and Caribbean Literature* (Ithaca: Cornell University Press, 1992), 34.

9.   Paul Tiyambe Zeleza writes that. "[E]xile can also be metaphorical, referring to aristic representations of alienation from familiar traditions. This is to suggest that exile, in its literary dimensions, comes in three forms: the exile of the writers themselves, exile as a theme in literary work, and the existence of a corpus of exile literature or literature of exile". Paul Tiyambe Zeleza, "The Politics and Poetics of Exile: Edward Said In Africa," *Research In African Literatures*, Fall 2005, Volume 36. Number 3, p.11.

10. Arnold Eisen, "Exile," *Contemporary Jewish Religious Thought: Original Essays on Critical Concepts, Movements and Thoughts*, edited by Arthur A. Cohen and Paul Mendes-Flohr (New York: MacMillian, 1987), 225.

11. Paul Tiyambe Zeleza, (2005), 16.

12. Martin Srajek offers the following description of exile. 'What does it mean to be in exile? In all cases being in exile points towards a situation of removal or distance from what once used to be familiar. One is away from one's homeland, possibly also away from one's family. In almost every case exile involves at least a partial, surrender of one's own language in favor of the language that is spoken by the majority of the people into whose land one has been brought. This would indicate that exile also implies being under the control and rule of another people. Consequently, one has to live under constant surveillance and observation.' Martin Srajek, *In the Margins of Deconstruction: Jewish Conceptions of Ethics in Emmanuel Levinas and Jacques Derrida* (Pittsburgh, PA: Duquesne University Press, 2000), 189–90.)

13. Paul Tiyambe Zeleza, (2005), 2.

14. This statement comes from Nicholas Dirks in his Foreword to Bernard Cohn, *Colonialism and Its Forms of Knowledge: The British in India* (Princeton, NJ: Princeton University Press 1996), ix.

15. Andrew Gurr, *Writers in Exile: The Identity of Home in Modern Literature* (Sussex; Harvester, 1981), 8.

16. Myriam Chancy, Searching for Safe Spaces: Afro-Caribbean Women Writers in Exile (Philadelphia; Temple University Press, 1997), 14.

17. Simon Gikandi (1992), 26.

18. George Lamming, *In the Castle of My Skin* (Ann Arbor, Michigan: University of Michigan Press, 1994), xxxix.

19. George Lamming, (1992), 24.

20. Ibid., 24.

21. Alena Heitlinger, Émigré Feminism: Transnational Perspectives (Toronto: University of Toronto Press, 1999), 5.

22. Myriam Chancy, *Searching for Sale Spaces: Afro-Caribbean Women Writers in Exile* (Philadelphia; Temple University Press, 1997), 23.

23. Ibid., 24.

24. Ibid., 2.

25. Margaret Joseph, *Caliban In Exile: The Outsider in Caribbean Fiction* (Westport, Ct: Greenwood Press, 1992) 52.

26. Edward Said, *Culture and Imperialism* (New York: Alfred A. Knopf, 1993) xxvii.

27. Myriam Chancy, (1997), 1.

28. Simon Gikandi, (1992), 26.

29. Jan Carew, 'The Caribbean Writer and Exile," in *Fulcrums of Change: Origins of Racism in the Americas and Other Essays* (Trenton, N. J.: Africa World Press, 198), 91.

30. Ibid., 92.

31. Bénédicte Ledent, *Caryl Phillips* (Manchester: Manchester University Press, 2002), 27.

32. Ex-Iles: Essays on Caribbean Cinema, edited by Mbye Cham (Trenton, NJ: Africa World Press, 1992,), 360.
33. George Lamming (1992), 50.
34. Edward Brathwaite, "The New West Indian Novelists," Part II, *Bim* VIII, no. 32, (January–June 1961), p. 273.
35. Ibid., 274.
36. Ibid.
37. Edward Said (2002), 186.
38. Margaret Joseph (1992), 61.
39. Theodore Adorno, Kierkegaard. *Construction of the Aesthetic*, trans. Robert Hullot-Kentor (Minneapolis: University of Minnesota Press, 1989), 24–46.
40. Quoted in Caryl Phillips, "Living and Writing in the Caribbean: An Experiment", *Kunapipi*, volume 11, number 2 (1989), 50.
41. Cathy Caruth, *Unclaimed Experience: Trauma, Narrative, and History* (Baltimore: Johns Hopkins University Press, 1996), 11.
42. G. W. F. Hegel, *Phenomenology of Spirit*, trans. A. V. Miller (New York: Oxford University Press, 1971), 126.
43. Sophia McClennen, *The Dialectics of Exile: Nation, Time, Language, and Space in Hispanic Literatures* (West Lafayette, IN: Purdue University Press, 2004), 30.
44. Simon Gikandi (1992), 13.
45. Simon Gikandi (1992), 33.
46. Ngũgĩ wa Thiongo, "Home From Exile: George Lamming and the Colonial Situation", *The Pan-Africanist*, 1 (1971), 3.
47. Edward Kamau Brathwaite, "Sir Galahad and the Islands," *Bim*, 25 (July–December 1957), 32.
48. Édouard Glissant, *Caribbean Discourse: Selected Essays*, trans. J. Michael Dash (Charlottesville: University of Virginia Press, 1989), 153–54.
49. Édouard Glissant, *Poetics of Relation*, translated by Betsy Wing (Ann Arbor, MI: The University of Michigan Press, 1997), 11.
50. Ibid.
51. John Stuhr, *Pragmatism, Postmodernism and the Future of Philosophy* (New York: Routledge, 2002), 59.
52. Patrick Taylor, (1989).
53. *Søren Kierkegaard's Journals and Papers*, Volume 4, trans. H. V. Hong and E. H. Hong Bloomington: Indiana University Press, 1967–68), 4650.
54. Mark Dooley, *The Politics of Exodus: Søren Kierkegaard's Ethics of Responsibility* (New York: Fordham University Press, 2001), 5.
55. Ibid., 5.
56. Ibid., 5.
57. Donald Hinds, *Journey to an Illusion: The West Indian in Britian* (London: Heinemann, 1966).
58. Patricia Williams, *The Alchemy of Race and Rights* (Cambridge: Harvard University Press, 1991), 11.
59. Mark Dooley (2001), 168.
60. Patrick Taylor (1989), 189.
61. George Lamming (1992), 56.
62. George Lamming (1992), 13.
63. Ibid., 74.
64. Mark Taylor, *Altarity* (Chicago University of Chicago Press, 1987), 206.
65. George Lamming (1992),12.
66. Gordon Rohlehr, *Pathfinder: Black Awakening in the Arrivants of Edward Kamau Brathwaite (Carapichaima, Trinidad: HEM Printers, 1981*), p. 14.

67. Joyce Jonas, "Carnival Strategies in Lamming's *In the Castle of My Skin*," *Callaloo* 11 (spring 1988), 359.
68. Simon Gikandi (1992), 58.
69. Mark Dooly (2001), 168.
70. Quoted in Gary Mole, *Levinas. Blachot, Jabés: Figures of Estrangement* (Gainesville: University Press of Florida, 1997), 41.
71. Mark Dooley (2001), xviii.
72. Ibid.
73. Ibid., 5.
74. George Lamming, *The Emigrants* (London: Allison and Busby, 1980),83.
75. David Ellis (2004), 71.
76. Nikos Papastergiadis, *Modernity and Exile: The Stranger in John Berger's Writings* (Manchester: Manchester University Press, 1993), 14.
77. Ibid., 18.
78. Benedicte Ledent (2002), 52–53.
79. Nikos Papastergiadis (1993), 26.
80. Bénédicte Ledent (2002), 53.
81. Vernon Dixon and Badi G. Foster, *Beyond Black or White An Alternative America* (Boson: Little Brown, 1971), 64.

26 | *Lamming's Critique of Imperialist Discourse*

Glyne Griffith

Russian formalist critics such as Victor Shlovsky have argued that literature's *modus operandi* is denaturalisation, or defamiliarisation. As a consequence of presenting readers with the commonplace and the ordinary in extraordinary ways, literature encourages us to see old situations in new ways. It asks us to think critically about that which we have perhaps taken for granted. In doing so, literature assists us in imaginatively transcending the status quo so that we might envision how we and the world could be. George Lamming's novels and essays artistically employ the strategy of defamiliarisation to assist us in imagining a world beyond the colonialist and imperialist vision. His literary and critical works achieve this transcendent quality not only because of their explicitly political and ideological content, but also as a result of Lamming's subtle subversion of traditional narrative form. His consistent engagement with political and ideological content, combined with a sophisticated subversion of narrative and other structural forms produces Lamming's critique of imperialist discourse.

The term 'discourse' as I use it here refers, of course, not simply to a narrative, but to a whole way of understanding the world and oneself in it; discourse represents a coherent interdependence of epistemology and ontology. The historical legacies of modern, that is to say post-Columbian, imperialism have produced a particular set of discourses that naturalise the colonial and imperial experience for the coloniser, as well as the colonised. This process and legacy of naturalisation is what I refer to as imperialist discourse, and it is this discourse, or 'way of seeing' as Lamming might say, that his literary and critical writing denaturalises.

To say that Lamming's fiction denaturalises imperialist discourse, and to claim that his novels are mainly concerned with the human experience of colonialism and empire might appear to suggest that his oeuvre is less concerned with aesthetic matters, but this is not so.

Lamming's fiction is no less concerned with aesthetic matters than it is with a content rooted substantially in ideological and political thought. His fiction consistently draws together the aesthetic and political because Lamming understands these modes of thinking and being in the world as interdependent rather than as antagonistic or mutually exclusive paradigms of existence. As a consequence, his fiction demonstrates considerable care with narrative structure, and his authorial engagement with novelistic form is no less scrupulous than his analyses of the ideology and politics of empire.

Lamming's novels demonstrate that he is at least as concerned with the politics of language as he is with the language of politics. He is as careful with the manner of the telling of his tales as he is insistent with the polemic that characterises his content. Indeed, one might say that Lamming's art gives polemic a good name. His polemic is not a by-product of his art, but is his art's *raison d'être*. We can take it for granted that the content of Lamming's fiction is political and polemical. This is quite well documented. What is perhaps less well featured is Lamming's aesthetic. This imbalance is not merely an issue of emphasis or focus, but has consequences for a nuanced exegesis of Lamming's fiction. It is difficult to fully appreciate Lamming's aesthetic achievement as a novelist if we pay insufficient attention to the ways in which his experimentation with structure subverts many of the expectations consolidated by the 19th century English novel.

Lamming employs the novel to subvert, by making strange, traditional novelistic expectations such as consolidation of character, the dominance and authority of the narrative voice, and the typical discursive demarcation between fiction and autobiography. In addition, his fiction uses intertextuality and heterogeneous genres to occlude the usual distinctions between creative and critical writing, fiction and non-fiction. Such narrative and structural heterogeneity denaturalises the reader's unselfconscious regard of tradition novel structures. Several critics have drawn our attention to Lamming's penchant for such experimentation. In her analysis of *In the Castle of My Skin*, Sandra Pouchet-Paquet observes that:

> The novel is unsatisfactory as autobiography because Lamming pays little attention to the conventions of this genre in his organisation of the narrative. The finely executed balance between first person and omniscient narrative, between G's personal history and the

description of village life, augments the novel's political concerns rather than its autobiographical character.[1]

And in his critique of *Season of Adventure*, Ken Ramchand states:

The reader approaching *Season of Adventure* with set principles about what the art of the novel is or ought to be will find many of the work's best effects achieved at times when the principles are most blatantly flouted.[2]

Such critical observations recognise that Lamming is resisting structural conventions as he develops his novels, and as Pouchet-Paquet suggests, his authorial resistance against structural and stylistic conventions augments the political concerns addressed by his novels. Lamming's experimentation with novelistic form and content bespeaks his understanding that traditional novelistic conventions have been implicated in imperialism's way of seeing the world, and representing the world. Thus, Edward Said tells us that:

Without empire ... there is no European novel as we know it, and indeed if we study the impulses giving rise to it, we shall see the far from accidental convergence between the patterns of narrative authority constitutive of the novel on the one hand, and, on the other, a complex ideological configuration underlying the tendency to imperialism.

Every novelist and every critic or theorist of the European novel notes its institutional character. The novel is fundamentally tied to bourgeois society; in Charles Moraze's phrase, it accompanies and indeed is a part of the conquest of Western society by what he calls *les bourgeois conquerants*. No less significantly, the novel is inaugurated in England by *Robinson Crusoe*, a work whose protagonist is the founder of a new world, which he rules and reclaims for Christianity and England.[3]

Scrutiny of Lamming's experimentation with the novel's form and content reveals his implicit recognition of the genre's indebtedness to imperialist ideology. In the attempt to subvert our conventional expectations – expectations that tend to obscure the connections between the bourgeois novel and imperialist ideology – Lamming relies upon several atypical strategies. Let us take them in turn.

The decentralised protagonist in *Season of Adventure* and *In the Castle of My Skin*

In *Season of Adventure*, the quasi-central character, Fola shares the 'spotlight' typically reserved for the protagonist with several other characters such as Gort, Chiki, and Powell. This group or composite protagonist is set against the larger identity and political struggles that are examined in the novel. *Season of Adventure* demonstrates an awareness of the problem of identity politics set against a background of imperialist ideology, and it explores the interconnectedness of ontology and epistemology without falling victim to traditional novelistic notions of character consolidation and egocentric individuality. Throughout the novel, the narrative refers to Fola's other selves or facets of identity by employing the phrase 'other than' to name that which is not Fola's individuality and yet makes her sense of self possible. Lamming embarked on this strategy of subverting the reader's expectations of a consolidated, egocentric protagonist as early as his first novel, *In the Castle of My Skin*. As Sandra Pouchet-Paquet reminds us:

> The central figure, though vividly present in the first person narrative, emerges as a figure whose personal experience crystallizes the experience of the entire community. In a sense he is the village ... he is a collective character.[4]

We recognise that as early as 1953 when *In the Castle of My Skin* was first published, Lamming was concerned with subverting the traditional novelistic notion of character as unitary and comprehensible as an ego-centred self. Indeed, in Lamming's first novel we are provided with signposts for rationalising the narrative's experimentation with character. In the novel there are consistent references to the interchangeability of persons and numbers so that the idea of individuality and separateness are deemphasised. We read, for example:

> Miss Forster. My mother. Bob's mother. It seemed they were three pieces in a pattern which remained constant. The flow of its history was undisturbed by any difference in the pieces, nor was its evenness affected by any likeness. There was a difference and there was no difference.[5]

Later, in a narrative section that describes boys from Creighton village placing nails on the railroad tracks to have them flattened into crude knives by the passing train, we read:

Three. Thirteen, Thirty. Boys. Three. Thirteen.

Thirty. Knives ... Three, Thirteen, Thirty. It does not matter. They come and go to perpetuate the custom of this corner. Once a week, black pudding and souse. The pattern has absorbed them, and in the wood where the night is thickest it has embraced another two in intimate intercourse.[6]

Such narrative sections imaginatively convey the profound depersonalisation experienced by the masses of colonised peoples as a consequence of the coloniser's view of the colonised. The colonised become a condition, a problem, a series of statistics, mere numbers. At the same time, Lamming is using these sections of narrative to challenge us to recognise that this apparent interchangeability of persons and statistics, a people and a condition, is part of a *doppleganger* effect produced by imperialist ideology, part of an ideological configuration that is essential to the coloniser's view of himself.

In a section of *In the Castle of My Skin*, several schoolboys are discussing the status of royalty in England and, more specifically, the reality of the king's existence:

There was a shadow king who did whatever a king should do. It was the shadow king who went to parades, took the salute and did those things with which we associated the king. The shadow king was a part of the English tradition. The English, the boy said, were fond of shadows. They never did anything in the open. Everything was done in shadow, and even the king, the greatest of them, worked through his shadow. Somebody asked if you were ever talking to a real man or a shadow when you talked to an Englishman, and the boy said yes. Some of them were the man and the shadow at the same time, but more shadow than man. But you had to be careful when you had anything to do with English people. It was always difficult to distinguish between the man and the shadow, and sometimes it was all shadow.[7]

This rather elaborate discussion of the *doppleganger* effect, placed into the consciousness of a young village schoolboy hardly serves the effect of verisimilitude in the novel. What an intellectually precocious and insightful boy he would have to be to convincingly provide his schoolmates, and by extension ourselves as readers, with such ironic commentary on the coloniser's paradoxical presence and absence in the colonial world. It is far more likely that narrative sections such as this are hermeneutic signposts to help us contextualise Lamming's experimentation with character construction in the context of imperialist ideology. In other words, the colonised subject believes that the coloniser is indispensable to his existence, and to the extent that he believes this he is unable to recognise that he is essential to the coloniser's sense of self and reason for being. The colonised subject is that unacknowledged 'other' or shadow that is indispensable to the coloniser's imperialist ontology.

In the interstices of the ironic distance between the schoolboy's comment and any possibility of verisimilitude, and in the representational spaces between G and Boy Blue, Trumper and George Lamming, Fola and 'other than Fola,' readers of Lamming's fiction, that is to say, the formerly colonised and the former coloniser alike are challenged to recognise themselves in each other and, in so doing, to recognise their equal capacity to transcend the limitations of imperialist ideology. This mutual recognition of human capacity and potential is critical to the coloniser's (or former coloniser's) recognition of himself as only a man, rather than a mythical giant or demi-god, and simultaneously critical to the colonised (or formerly colonised) person's view of himself as truly a man rather than a condition.

Lamming presents us with this assertion in several guises. Two that we might consider here are culled, respectively, from the scene in *In the Castle of My Skin* where Boy Blue is rescued by a fisherman from drowning, and from the section in *The Pleasures of Exile* where the author is contemplating the condition of the colonial subject living and writing in the 'mother country.' First, we are privy to the thoughts of G, Trumper, and Boy Blue regarding the fisherman after Boy Blue's rescue:

Some hours ago we had discovered a giant. Now we had discovered a man. The giant was the man, but being a man he could no longer be a giant. The man had undermined the giant. We did not say that because we had no words with which to say it ... He was stronger than all of us put together.

Perhaps he was stronger than all the village. It made no difference. He was only big and strong, as we would say in the village, but he was like one of us, just like one of us. A man.[8]

Next, we are offered the following observation in *The Pleasures of Exile*:

> When the exile is a man of colonial orientation, and his chosen residence is the country which colonised his own history, then there are certain complications ... [A]lthough the new circumstances are quite different, and even more favourable than those he left in the West Indies, his reservations, his psychology, his whole sense of cultural expectation have not greatly changed ... On more than one occasion I have seen a West Indian writer pleased by compliments which should have been recognised and accepted as simple truths about himself and his work.[9]

Here is Lamming's analysis of imperialist discourse at work; here is his skillful negotiation of the politics of language.

Intertextuality and parallelism: Fictional fact and factual fiction

Lamming employs Shakespeare's *The Tempest* as a thematic element in much of his work, but it is important to recognise that such intertextuality is not indicative of a filial relationship between Shakespeare's text and Lamming's discourse. Lamming's critique is concerned with the rehabilitation of Prospero and Caliban. This rehabilitation is a simultaneous ontological and epistemological exercise so that Lamming's rewriting of *The Tempest* is not merely a conventional referencing of literary precedent. It is a revisioning of precedent, the establishment of an alternative precedent. Lamming's oeuvre is at pains to remind us of the dialectical relationship between conceptual and material realities. As a result, in *The Pleasures of Exile* he indicates that there are, for him, just three important events in British Caribbean history, and he lists these in chronological order as Columbus's voyages to the Americas, the abolition of slavery, and the arrival of India and China in the Caribbean. The definitive regional response to these historical events, Lamming suggests, was '...the discovery of the novel by West Indians as a way of investigating and projecting the inner experience of the West Indian community.'[10] This sense of the intersection of material and conceptual experiences is germane to Lamming's practice of intertextuality.

In *In the Castle of My Skin*, we are presented with the scene of white men entertaining themselves by tossing coins into the sea to watch young black boys dive for them:

> The white men who invariably were tourists tossed the coins in all directions from the club, and the boys hustled below the water. There the sea was deeper, and the pennies never reached the sand for the boys could see them all the way sagging down to the sand. If the white men were enjoying themselves they would order the boys not to leap before the coins had settled. The boys dived and the white men watched the sprawling black limbs in their scramble ... The white men laughed, and later decided to settle the dispute [among the boys] by tossing more coins. If the dispute went on after their return the white men would tell them to fight it out, and the boys fought.[11]

We might usefully compare this scene in Lamming's novel to a somewhat similar scene in Ralph Ellison's *Invisible Man*, first published in 1952, just one year before *In the Castle of My Skin* appeared. In this scene, white men in the southern United States are also entertaining themselves by offering coins to black boys:

> I lunged for a yellow coin lying on the blue design of the carpet, touching it and sending a surprised shriek to join those around me. I tried frantically to remove my hand but could not let go. A hot, violent force tore through my body, shaking me like a wet rat. The rug was electrified. The hair bristled up on my head as I shook myself free. My muscles jumped, my nerves jangled, writhed. But I saw this was not stopping the other boys. Laughing in fear and embarrassment, some were holding back and scooping up the coins knocked off by the painful contortions of others. The men roared above us as we struggled.[12]

The parallelism between these two scenes, one set in the British Caribbean and the other in the southern United States, is striking. Despite emanating from different geographical and cultural locations, these two novels reproduce parallel fictional scenes as a consequence of the shared material experience of racism, a racism that is rooted in imperialist ideology, and a racism that undergirds colonialist practices in the British Caribbean and 'Jim Crow' apartheid in the southern United States. This material intertextuality reminds us of the global nature of imperialist ideology and the contorted ontologies such ideology reproduces. It effects a subtle effacement of the author, any author, as the sole owner of the property that is otherwise recognised in the world of private property as his, or her, work. It recuperates the echo of a pre-capitalist world that understood authorship as a communal enterprise and, as a result, parallels the sort of composite characterisation with which Lamming's oeuvre is associated. Thus, even in his relationship to his own literary production, George Lamming appears to be reminding us of the role of capitalist and imperialist ideologies in shaping our view of the world and ourselves in it. His writing self-consciously reminds us of formalism's comprehension that the best art is a process of defamiliarisation, resonating at all levels of human endeavour.

Notes

1. Sandra Pouchet-Paquet, *The Novels of George Lamming* (London: Heinemann, 1983) 14.
2. Kenneth Ramchand, *The West Indian Novel and Its Background* (revised ed. Kingston: Ian Randle Publishers, 2003).
3. Edward W Said, *Culture and Imperialism* (New York: Vintage Books, 1994) 82–83.
4. Pouchet-Paquet 14.
5. George Lamming, *In the Castle of My Skin* (New York: McGraw Hill, 1954) 24.
6. Lamming, *Castle* 32.
7. Lamming, *Castle* 54–55.
8. Lamming, *Castle* 152–153.
9. George Lamming, *The Pleasures of Exile* (London: Michael Joseph, 1960) 24–25.
10. Lamming, *Pleasures* 37.
11. Lamming, *Castle* 115–116.
12. Ralph Ellison, *Invisible Man* (New York: Vintage Books, 1995) 27.

27 | The Historic Centrality of Mr Slime: Lamming's Pursuit of Class Betrayal in Novels and Speeches

Andaiye

Introduction and Acknowledgement

Like everyone I know who writes for political rather than academic purposes, I never write a major presentation or article except in consultation with my closest political colleagues, who always include Eusi Kwayana, Karen de Souza, and Selma James.[1] Since we were active together in organised left politics in Guyana and the Caribbean from 1979 until recently, Eusi Kwayana and Karen de Souza responded to the drafts out of that shared experience. With Selma James the collaboration was broader and deeper: we worked on the presentation together. She saw Mr Slime as a major contribution, the defeat in the very seed of the movement, anticipating a theme in the literature that was to follow from the newly 'independent' countries. I proposed this theme be characterised as class betrayal, starting with *In the Castle of my Skin*, then widened the scope of the presentation to include the speeches, realising with excitement that the theme of class betrayal runs through them. Mr Slime is a great metaphor for betrayal, intentionally unsubtle. His unnamed presence in the speeches is not subtle either: a person like Mr Slime or his opposite is at the centre of many of them. Yet I had not seen this until then: working with Selma James I often discover what I know. In the end, I had what I wanted to say about the relationship between Lamming's work and the failure of organised Caribbean politics since Federation, including its 'progressive' politics – a failure at the heart of which is the repeated betrayal of the people whom Lamming had made the heroes and heroines of his fiction.

Entry Point: On the Murder of Rodney

On June 13, 1980, Walter Rodney was assassinated in Georgetown, Guyana. Ten days later, Lamming delivered the first of his 1980–1983 speeches at the memorial service held in Georgetown.[2] In the Foreword to *Conversations* which I wrote in 1990/1991, I recorded what I thought about the speech:

> June 21, 1980: Although the date had been announced, the authorities had not released the body. The mood in the church was bleak, bleakest among those of us who had worked with Walter in the WPA.[3] WPA youth were all, it seemed, at the back of the church, in the church at all only out of respect for the wishes of Pat, Walter's wife, but unable to enter more fully into what felt so weak a response to atrocity.
>
> The eulogies made before George spoke could not meet the need. The need was for revenge; what was happening was a funeral service with Walter, as it were, twice absent.
>
> When George began, the youth were suspicious: both appearance and manner were at first alienating. "A white-hair man with a accent," one said later.
>
> But when he ended there was first, from the back a single, sharp handclap, which became, almost in the same instant, perhaps one hundred; until the wave of WPA youth applauding moved forward and spread up through the church; and for the first time in my experience, a eulogy in a Guyanese church provoked a standing ovation.
>
> Afterwards, I asked some of the youth what had happened. They said the ovation was not for George, it was for Walter. George had brought Walter into the church, had made possible a Ceremony of Souls with '(its) drama of redemption, (its) drama of returning, (its) drama of cleansing for a commitment towards the future'[4] (*Conversations*, 8).

Nearly 23 years after that speech was made, I asked one of those youth, now 45 years old,[5] how long it had lasted. She thought for a few moments, then answered, 'Close to one hour. Perhaps a little under.'

In fact, the speech could not have lasted more than 15 minutes; in printed form, it is three pages long.

Why does its impact remain literally larger than life so many years later? I understand that better now than I did in 1990/1991. Once you place the speech in Lamming's whole work and you see his pursuit of betrayal all through that work, you see that what the audience was feeling – or as he explains the function of his speeches what he was making the collective mind of the crowd feel – was the size of his and their outrage and sorrow at the loss of a man who was the antithesis of Mr Slime, a man with whom they were as familiar as he was, from their lives. Part 1 was the outrage:

> Today we meet in a dangerous land, and at the most dangerous of times. The danger may be that supreme authority, the supervising conscience of the nation, has ceased to be answerable to any moral law, has ceased to recognise or respect any minimum requirement of ordinary human decency...('On the Murder of Rodney', *Conversations*, 184)

In Part 2 the tone changed: since Rodney was the antithesis of Mr Slime, a tribute to him that expressed who he truly was had to be in language that was the antithesis of the inflated language of Caribbean (and other) eulogies. So he said that Rodney was a man who was 'serious', who was 'not smart', 'not bright', who 'did not seek to score points for the sake of argument'. Who, instead, was 'an intellectual worker among those who had been deprived of his advantages', who 'had a rare gift of intellect to which he felt a special duty...(as) a tool, a reservoir of power which could only justify itself if it were put into service, and on behalf of social need'(*Conversations*, 184). He ended his tribute with the poem Martin Carter had written for Rodney, 'Assassins of Conversation', whose very name was an acknowledgement of the Rodney who used to sit before a handful of working people under a bottom house, or stand before thousands at a street corner, telling them what they made happen.[6]

Although I would say now that my entry point into Lamming's pursuit of betrayal was not the novels but the 1980–1983 speeches, the word betrayal is not mentioned once in the Foreword to *Conversations* since at that time I did not see that betrayal was central to the speeches. I cannot explain this inability or refusal to see what is now so clear by claiming that I was distant from the politics in and about which the speeches were made: in the period between 1980 when Rodney was assassinated and 1983 when Maurice Bishop, Jacqueline Creft and their colleagues were assassinated, I was an Executive member of the WPA, was centrally engaged in the political struggle in Guyana, and for more than two of those years, involved in meetings of Caribbean Left organisations in Grenada. Now that I have seen that Mr Slime is everywhere in the speeches, I believe that I was unable or unwilling to see this until I had come out of what Lamming calls 'the political Left' – because seeing it would raise doubts about my politics that I was not prepared to face, still less, to act upon. And yet the experience of the Left in the English-speaking Caribbean – not only elsewhere – shows that the interpretation of the world which begins (and usually ends) with the so-called 'point of production' is really about a belief in the management and control of people, and not about the revolutionising of human relations – including the relations of production.

Admitting that Lamming was pursuing betrayal in the speeches led me directly back to the novels, in particular, to *In the Castle of my Skin* (*Castle*), the novel that launched his pursuit and *Season of Adventure* (*Season*), the novel that underlined the deadly serious implications of what was being pursued.

While betrayal is by definition a blow from an unexpected place ('Something startles where I thought I was safest' – the epigraph to *Castle*), the betrayal Lamming is concerned with is of course betrayal of a class, rather than as a purely personal act. In *Castle*, betrayal comes from someone – Mr Slime – who has deserted his roots in the working class for what Lamming calls in *Season* 'a derivative middle-class' (362)[7] – someone who is the enemy of what Trumper knows he and his boyhood community must now live by: '...this world is a world o' camps, an' you got to find out which camp you're in. And above everything else keep that camp clean' (*Season*, 280).

In the Castle of my Skin: In Slime is the Fury of the Class

We know that *Castle* broke new ground by making the community, the village, the 'hero'. But what precisely does that determine?

The function of the hero/heroine in most novels is to make an experience and change through it. Succeed or fail, there is an individual transformation, a new self-consciousness: the heroine or hero finally understands what is going on in her/his life and/or her/his society. The situation and characters may move on and change, but none besides the main character transform themselves or us.

It is fundamentally an elitist framework. Though the novel's content may be anti-elitist, the fact is that only one or two people learn the hidden truth and teach us or bring others to it. But if the village is the hero, the reader is invited to appreciate the contribution to laying out the truth of every unique individual usually hidden behind the 'ordinary' non-hero or heroine. Then the progress of each is dependent on the collective wisdom and progress of all. G is all the things that Ma and Pa and his long-suffering mother and his experience of Empire Day have taught all of them, all the boys trying to figure out what it is they are living through. It is a collective enterprise and learning and revelation.

That is a very typical working class process, an important part of how the movement moves, of which academics who 'think' are rarely aware. Working class people collectively compare and digest experience, debate their meaning and reach collective decisions about what action should and should not be taken. Change is individual but it is also collective. The whole community makes its points of reference, who in turn incite other individuals who give direction to the making of history. This direction, as given in *Castle* by G, has been shaped by the collective. The collectivity ensures that we are less likely to get stuck by taking a moment of time as a fixed reality (what Hegel calls a fixed category), which leads us to actions that suit an earlier moment. It is always the danger with individuals, but the collectivity pulls us all into our future: the next historical stage, At the end of *Castle*, this is where we – villager as well as reader – know we have reached.

Acts of rebellion in a novel based on an 'individual hero' are uniquely individual, rarely a manifestation of the general will. But what G learns he brings back to those same mutually-craving-for-understanding boys, now young men who hear him.

So that treating the village as the hero gives a chance to reveal all the collective history and torment for *every* individual that goes into the novel's time span. No one is less an individual; every one has more dimensions, and her/his individuality is not an end in itself quite different from the Freudian century that made every social trauma an individual's responsibility to right individually. In this sense *Castle* is a novel which in structure and intention is describing a working class process.[8]

Given this, it is not surprising that it tackles the fundamental political question of class betrayal.

'Well there's something that I want to know If this council business bound to be so', sang Sparrow in 'No, Doctor, No', one of his earliest calypsos, after the first election victory of the People's National Movement (PNM). Are politicians bound to sell out? While Lamming does not address exactly this question in *Castle*, he is already claiming that the leadership of the movement to independence is corrupt and available to the colonial power before they get into government, at the beginning of the movement rather than at its apex. In this very early case, it was the promise of power, rather than power itself, that was enough to corrupt. The betrayal is signaled long before it is committed: the character and the name Slime enter the novel early.

And here in Mr Slime is the fury of the class not only against the colonial power but even more, against the traitors within the working class. The name Slime is a poetic evocation of the filth of betrayal (compare Trumper's 'keep that camp clean'). When the villagers are reading the bill which the overseer has posted on the lamppost to announce that the land has been sold and that information should be sought from Mr Slime, they don't know yet that they have been betrayed, but the stench of betrayal comes up from the way the words echo in their minds: 'It say we got to see Mr. Slime. See Mr. Slime. Mr. Slime. Mr. Slime. Mr. Slime' (*Castle*, 259). It is also a signal for us to take note that a fundamental political reality is being penetrated and exposed.

It is not only early in the novel. It is the first in the English-speaking anti-imperialist body of creative work where the enemy within the movement is fingered. Five years after Mr Slime saw the light of day, Chinua Achebe told us that *Things Fall Apart* not because of 'a foreign conscience called imperialist' but because those we nurture and sacrifice into power help not us but our enemies.

Season of Adventure: 'I also am Mr Slime'

In *Season*, as we know, the pursuit of betrayal turns (partly) inward and goes for its roots. The central statement on betrayal in the novel is the Author's Note, which Lamming has called 'a shock tactic of intervention' offering a 'definition of failure with full recognition of the responsibility involved' (*Conversations*, 261–62).

This use of the author's voice in a work of fiction was probably unprecedented at the time. It is not that Lamming took himself as author into the fiction; what he did was to take a character in a novel, Powell, and bring him out of the fiction as his half-brother:

> ...Believe it or not: Powell was my brother; my half brother by a different mother.

> Until the age of ten Powell and I had lived together, equal in the affection of two mothers. Powell had made my dreams; and I had lived his passions. Identical in years, and stage by stage, Powell and I were taught in the same primary school.

> And then the division came (*Season*, 331–332).

The corruption begins early, with the scholarship to secondary school.

Lamming explained the purpose of the Author's Note in a 2002 interview in *Small Axe*:

> The Author's Note came naturally as part of the narrative...I felt now that I wanted to *personalize* that total statement, to say that it is me also that I am talking about, not me as any author but me as a man called 'Lamming' who is caught up in that ambivalence about directions, and who daily has to question himself about the value of his relationships ... (*Small Axe*, 100).

I – middle class by virtue of the privilege of education – am Mr Slime.

If the device of the Author's Note was *probably* unprecedented, the use to which Lamming puts it was undoubtedly so: it was an acknowledgement of personal responsibility for the desperation that betrayal imposed.

> I believe deep in my bones that the mad impulse that drove Powell to his criminal defeat was largely my doing. I will not have this explained away by talk about the environment; nor can I allow my own moral infirmity to be transferred to a foreign conscience called

imperialist. I shall go beyond my grave in the knowledge that I am responsible for what happened to my brother (*Conversations*, 332).

Underscoring that the betrayal was his, the novel refuses to locate it in Chiki, to whom Powell says as Chiki leaves the Forest Reserve to go to high school: 'it aint you alone what goin' up, is all the boys who have no scholarship, Chick...Remember all the boys waitin' to hear' (*Season*, 229). And Chiki returns, as he says, 'not only to live, but to be where I belong' (*Season*, 237).

Nor does the fact that the 'foreign conscience called imperialist' creates the conditions in which he, Lamming, was trained – educated – into betrayal absolve him of responsibility for scabbing.

Pursuing Betrayal in the Speeches: 'The Honourable Member'

When creative writing is sustained through an umbilical cord to the movement, it can suffer withdrawal symptoms from that movement's decline. In the English-speaking Caribbean this happened in the sixties after the death of Federation, when politicians gave the macho (and disastrous) brag that they were 'going it alone'. Lamming's history after the movement's decline tells us how political *Castle* was: how much the impulse for it had come from the movement. When Lamming said 'I didn't write that book; I couldn't write that book; that book wrote itself,'[9] he was conveying that it was the movement that had energised and empowered his imagination and liberated his own perceptions to write that rarity, a great novel. But when the movement was betrayed and defeated, his ability to write fiction was undermined. Instead, he made himself into a superb non-party political commentator. This is how he explains the shift:

> ...at some stage I had come to feel that if I had anything of relevance and value to say that could be immediately effective in however minimal a way, it would be more effectively done by that statement, by that lecture-form, than by the novel-form

> ...whenever I am asked to give a public address on some major occasion, I am also doing it with a view that it would play the role the fiction would have played if they were able to read the fiction, or if the fiction were made available to them (*Small Axe*, 198).

He ascribes different functions to the novels and speeches: the speeches 'making the collective mind of the crowd feel', the novels; 'making the feeling think' (*Conversations*, 28–29). Yet as we've seen, whatever the difference in their function, novels and speeches are part of the same project: recording the painful but also life-affirming history of the Caribbean, beginning with the working class, and therefore, addressing the fundamental issue of the whole period from the 1930s to the 1980s, class betrayal leading to defeat.

As statements which translate the themes of his novels, the speeches quote often from the novels. Lamming explains this in *Small Axe*:

> Now as to statement/fiction/lecture/novel, what quite often I am doing – and if you look through *Conversations*, the extracts from the novels are used quite a lot – is spelling out in the lectures the themes raised in the fiction…when I give a lecture about the honourable member, and trace the history of this parliamentarian, from the great-grandfather in the canefield, right through to the schoolmaster whose son is now a lawyer, that is very clear. They're (union members) hearing that very clear. But I am telling them what *Season* and *Of Age and Innocence* is (sic) about (197).

He is saying that 'The Honourable Member' which, as we shall see, is all about betrayal by the political elite, is what *Season of Adventure*, *Of Age and Innocence* – and first, I would add, *In the Castle of my Skin* – are about.

While *Castle* and *Season* deal with betrayal as novels can ('The novel does not only depict aspects of social reality. It explodes it. It ploughs it up' *Conversations*, 29), 'The Honourable Member' deals with betrayal stripped of its complexity. This is an address Lamming gave to the fortieth Annual Conference of the Barbados Workers' Union, which describes a 40-year-old lawyer/politician trained at university abroad, returning to work as a lawyer before entering politics. Today he is rich: 'His known assets are estimated to be in the region of a figure, not under three quarters of a million'. His house is pretentious. His taste is suspect: 'The walls, on all sides, are disfigured by juvenile souvenirs of illuminated nights in New York, eating out along the Bay of San Francisco, racially mixed couples at play around a kidney-shaped swimming pool in Miami.' He appears not to read, except for magazines: 'There are no books anywhere'.

The Honourable Member is not unique; he is of the class whose members had 'a privilege of schooling'. It is a class whose members 'now embrace as the most desirable reward of their efforts in this life: social power and material wealth', and which, 'putting its own self-interest above and beyond social incentives, is so eager to separate itself, by lifestyle and the hunger for status, from the working class from which it derived'.

The process of social evolution which has brought the Honourable Member to this criterion of success began with a great-grandfather who was a labourer on the estate from age nine, died at forty (the Honourable Member's age) and continues through a grandfather who was an independent artisan of great skill, whose view of education 'as the only possible means of rescuing his offspring from the humiliations his ancestors had endured' made him push for his son, the Honourable Member's father, to become a teacher. The Honourable Member's children have carried the social distance from their roots still further: he has 'a girl who went to St Winifred's from a junior school called St Gabriel's and a son who, after problems at home, was placed in a minor public school in the South of England'. Neither child can remember travelling by bus in Barbados. While the Honourable Member's great-grandfather was a man who, himself exploited, was attracted to stories he had heard in his childhood of workers who had risen up against the merchant/planter class, he himself belongs to the category of men whose major appeal 'in what is thought to be an honest election' is that struggle against exploitation is the work of communist agitators.

The audience for this speech would have included women and men who had never read *Castle*, and others who, on reading it, would have pretended not to see themselves in Mr Slime. The speech is therefore of value for two reasons: it introduced a new audience among waged workers to Lamming's indictment of the political elite, and it brought the indictment unambiguously to their bosses.

'I Can Smell the Middle Class Everywhere'

Lamming's 1980–1983 speeches should be analysed in two groups – those, like 'The Honourable Member', which he made between 1980 and mid-1982, and the three he made from late 1982 to the end of 1983. To remind ourselves of the events and feeling of the first of these periods: in 1980, in spite of Rodney's assassination in June of that year, there was strong optimism that the region was in a new stage of rebellion. This had started in March 1979 when Gairy was overthrown in Grenada; four months later, in July, Somoza was overthrown in Nicaragua. The removal of Gairy from power fed into the multi-racial rebellion against the Burnham regime in Guyana, led by Rodney and the WPA; overnight, posters appeared on the walls of the capital proclaiming 'De Shah [of Iran] gone! Gairy gone! Who next?' Inside Grenada, women, men, children were energised by their belief that the 'revo' was theirs and could therefore transform their lives.[10] West Indian people from across the English-speaking Caribbean were working inside Grenada to support the revolution. Cultural workers were organised in its defence. Grenada was also a pole around which the Left in CARICOM gathered strength. Adding to existing Left parties, there was a growth in the number and militancy of small, Left groups. Meetings of Left parties and trade unions were frequent. Closer ties were being created with Cuba and to lesser degree, Nicaragua.[11] As Lamming has said, 'the *region* was in a moment of resistance in Grenada' (*Small Axe*, 188).

Of course, this resistance was only part of what was happening in the region: the 'loss' of Grenada and Nicaragua meant that the United States was on the attack, actively supported by many CARICOM governments. The 'war against communism' continued to have Cuba as a main target, along with Nicaragua and Grenada, but pro-US CARICOM governments demonstrated a particular hysteria towards Grenada: they feared it like a virus which would spread till it infected them. Thus, between 1980 and mid-1982, Lamming was in part responding to what he identified as the betrayal of the Grenadian people by these Caribbean governments, similar to the betrayal of the Guyanese people in 1953 by the same strata but not yet in government.

But where was he smelling betrayal in late 1982 when he made the speech, 'A Visit to Carriacou'? This speech, addressed to members of NJM, teachers and other working people on that island, is more informal than any other in the period, and reads like a response to something in the immediate environment that the reader does not know about:

I have spent a lot of my life in association with Marxists of a variety of colours. But I have never in my life met a Marxist baby. Never. Never. ... When a man tells me he is a Marxist, ... I want to know how he got there. I want to know what was the particular journey that led him from wherever he was to that point of perception and conviction and redemption which he calls Marxist. It is that journey ... that allows me to see his connection with what he is calling himself (*Conversations*, 24).

What man calling himself a Marxist is he speaking to and about? At the moment of listening or reading, we only know that he is contrasting where he came from with where an unnamed man who calls himself a Marxist, comes from.[12] In other words, we know that the middle class person he is smelling is part of the Caribbean Left.

...when I hear people discussing class, I did not discover that from Marx. I lived with class....I did not discover how class society deforms human relations from Marx. I lived it. And so I developed an extraordinary nose. I can smell middle class people everywhere (*Conversations*, 26).

Also in 1982, for the first time he clearly identifies the leadership of the trade union movement as suspect, a group the working class must be on guard against:

The problem for us here is that these tendencies we identify in what is called the middle class emerge in the leadership of organised labour. And that is what the rank and file of the working people have got to keep their eyes on: the compromise, the ambivalence of leadership throughout the trade unions of this region ('Nationalism and Nation', *Conversations*, 230).

It is true that by 1982 divisions in the Left had widened, as those who defined themselves as Marxist-Leninists pushed for an ever-narrowing concentration of power in the NJM, and in those members of the party imbued with 'the science' presumably of revolution, in the name of 'securing the revolution'. But these were not divisions that Lamming would have known about from the inside. The cultural workers Lamming coordinated to work in and for Grenada were not universally welcomed in Grenada: while for Lamming culture could never be 'decoration of daily life' or, in the crude sense, a tool, for the Grenada government their job was simply to mobilise support for the revolution, and for the orthodox Marxist-Leninists inside the party, he was simply a 'social democrat'. He could not know what was happening on the inside; and yet, this small incident in Carriacou in which men of the Left shut out working class people carried him immediately to the pursuit of betrayal.

'The Tragedy of a Whole Region'

Situating Mr Slime in the Left is never explicit until after Bishop's murder, following which he indicts the political elite of both Right and Left.

'The Plantation Mongrel' targets the Right. Delivered at the Guild of Undergraduates, UWI, Cave Hill one month after Bishop's death, it is a speech of uncontrolled rage. We recall the environment – the witch-hunting of critics of the US invasion of Grenada and of the complicity of Caribbean governments in it; prominent among these critics was Rickey Singh, a Guyanese journalist based in Barbados, which threatened to deport him. Here was Lamming's answer:

> In recent times, we have heard one notable Black voice, which represents a tradition of the plantation mongrel, howling for the deportation of aliens who infest this island. It is you who are also his target.
>
> So let us ask our plantation mongrel this question: 'How many Barbadians infest Guyana?' 'How many Barbadians infest St Lucia?' 'How many Barbadians infest Trinidad and Tobago?'" (*Conversations*, 244–45).

At the close of the speech he tells the students that they have a choice between the two traditions: 'You may take the road through Garvey and James to Fanon and Rodney and Bishop. Or you may choose the other tradition which leads you down the defecated tracks of the Black plantation mongrel' (*Conversations*, 250).

In 'The Tragedy of a Whole Region', the tribute delivered at the memorial service for Bishop in Trinidad and Tobago in December 1983, he indicts politicians across their claimed ideologcal differences as equally colonised: 'The colonial legacy is deep and pervasive; *and it has afflicted the political Left, no less than the Right*, with a psychology of dependence which has crippled the imagination and makes it inoperative in moments of crisis' (*Conversations*, 247; my emphasis).

Here again, he pairs Rodney and Bishop, describing them as men of the same generation with the same 'privilege of education' who could have had access to 'that minority kingdom' and carry out the function of their class 'to reinforce and stabilize [the] ... social division of labour and status' (*Conversations*, 239):

> But Rodney and Bishop gave the word 'ambition' a new virtue, by making the central ambition of their lives a commitment to break, in a decisive way, with the tradition which had trained them to approve and supervise over the intellectual enslavement of their own people. They broke away; and they became subversive traitors to that tradition which could so easily have bestowed on them the blessings of those who proudly identify themselves as affluent consumers. It was this betrayal which ultimately cost them their lives (*Conversations*, 239–40).

Honouring Bishop on his own, he chooses words that draw the sharpest possible contrast between him and those who had opposed him, speaking of him as a man 'who required no textbook, no sterile list of abstract principles, to recognize where his duty lay. His head found a home in the hearts of his people at mass level; and he tried to move forward from the concrete experience of the reality' (*Conversations*, 238–39).

The colonised Left, on the other hand, required textbooks. Following the US invasion copies of NJM Central Committee minutes were 'discovered' in which members are recorded as analysing the Grenada situation via the most abstract use of Lenin textbooks: they were virtual caricatures of what Lamming said in the *Small Axe* interview about the Left:

> ...even in the better types...I always saw...[the leaders of the Left] in the role of people who had the text...and on whom had been conferred the privilege to interpret and explain this text for the others, but who really had no organic connection or direct connection with the daily lives of that other...(*Small Axe*, 176).

The Historic Centrality of Mr Slime

Lamming is not a political activist; he need not meet, nor does he meet the standards we set ourselves. No quantity of speeches of quality changes his novelist status. When he ventures into politics, as he occasionally does in some of the speeches, the step is not always as imaginative and deeply truthful as in his 'real' work. For example, when he locates the leadership of the movement in organised labour he is retreating from his own recognition of the unwaged caring labour of women. In 'The Tragedy of a Whole Region' he finds the continuing struggle for a 'human world' in Trinidad and Tobago not only 'on sugar estates, [and] in the oilfields', but also 'among the most determined workers in the public and *domestic* services of the land' [*Conversations*, 238; my emphasis], while in 'The Honourable Member', he indicts the politician for his betrayal not only of his male ancestors, but of 'the women who fathered many a household, nursed man and child without a wage and have remained to this day the last surviving example of legalized slave-labour' [*Conversations*, 220]. They do the work but they will not lead since they are not part of organised, waged labour. *Castle* has a more truthful foundation. Ma and Pa, for example, are hardly excluded from leadership!

As we have seen, Lamming's achievement is that in *Castle, Season,* and 'A Visit to Carriacou', he is pursuing betrayal when no one else is. Here is his later explanation of the appearance of Mr Slime in *Castle*:

> I think there is planted in the change, and what seemed the inevitability of the change, also the question of great doubt about where this will go. In some way I am already very sceptical of the authenticity of what would be the leadership in the form of Mr Slime...I am in some way conscious of the kinds of compromise in which this leadership will be involved...I am going to see '37 and '38 in fact *kidnapped*...by a leadership that had little or nothing to do with the makings of it. And by leaders who are very decent but saw themselves as the natural heirs to the departing imperial power. Not necessarily the natural leaders of the people who become their constituency...they chose themselves as the leaders, by virtue of education, by virtue also of the mythology which the school has played in shaping our social relations (*Small Axe*, 113).

The novel itself is clearer than this quote suggests when it speaks of 'leaders who are very decent'. It is true that G says in *Castle* that when Mr Slime taught him 'he seemed perfectly decent', but Lamming did not choose the name Slime as a metaphor for decent men. Later in the same interview, he underscores this when he speaks of Grantley Adams ensuring that working class men with great organising skill 'would be erased in some way'. He may be referring here to rumours of murders of strugglers by those ambitious for the movement to choose them over more worthy and more working class points of reference.

In *Season of Adventure* 'the great doubt' is about where independence will go. Early in the novel Crim and Powell are talking about how education has 'wiped out everything from middle class memory except what they've learned'.

> 'I was thinkin','' he (Crim) said, 'how the Independence would change all that wipin' out, change everything that confuse.'
>
> Powell's pride had been aroused. His voice came loud and fretful.
>
> 'Change my arse,' he shouted, 'is independence what it is? One day in July you say you want to be that there thing, an' one day in a next July the law say, all right, from now you's what you askin' for. What change that can change...? (*Season*, 17).

In his talk 'Politics and Culture', Lamming says that the warnings against betrayal that he makes to the graduates at the UWI graduation ceremony where he is to receive an honorary doctorate 'have their origin in my novel, *Season of Adventure*, in which I offered the prediction that the new independence arrangements would inevitably, fail....'(*Conversations*, 79).

The explanation for his ability to sense betrayal before anyone else lies in the experience of childhood which he says made him able to 'smell the middle class everywhere'; this experience 'is penetrating, moving through me all the time', he explains, and 'is in *Season of Adventure*' (*Conversations*, 26):

> ...I was in a situation in which I lived in two worlds. This high school was intended for people to go into the Civil Service, the professional classes and so on. But I was alright there: I was a good cricketer, I redeemed myself in that way; my football was very good.

But, and this is the one that hit the vein, if I left that school at ten after three in the afternoon, and that labouratory of democracy was still going on, and we were walking down the main street and without warning I saw my mother coming towards me – that was very serious – should I acknowledge her or not? And in those situations she just caught my eye and I caught hers and as we come nearer to each other we are both thinking about the same thing because I am not too sure that I want to be identified there. And in a curious kind of way she does not mind if I don't because of who I am with now – Dr Some body's son.

He finds different varieties of traitor, in different places, but most have their roots in colonial education. For G, High School was 'the instrument that tore and kept us (G from Trumper, Boy Blue and Bob) apart' (*Castle*, 208). In *Season*, Lamming's betrayal of Powell had its origins in his 'migration into another world' after a scholarship to secondary school: 'And then the division came' (*Season*, 332). In 'Politics and Culture', he asks the graduates what they will do with their education: 'Whom does your labour serve? And towards what vision of mankind?' (*Conversations*, 81). 'Where shall you stand in relation to that system which will offer you a marketplace for the highest bidder for your skills?' (*Conversations*, 79) – questions which are at once a warning to the graduates and an indictment of those faculty in the audience who have used their education to achieve social distance from their community:

> You are a minority; and you are a minority because education is scarce; and was intended to be a scarcity so that it might serve as an instrument of a continuing social stratification, an index of privilege and status, a deformed habit of material self-improvement (*Conversations*, 80).

In his lecture 'The Imperial Encirclement' he makes the point that the problem is not only that a man's education gives him a claim to leadership cut off from the class he claims to lead, but that this separation makes him at best useless to the class:

> By virtue of its uniqueness, that is as a minority, by virtue of its training and skill, which in certain areas were superior to those of the masses of the population, it (the educated minority) assumed as

a right the status of leadership. It would have seen itself as the head of the society, unaware that a head cannot move without its belly, for it is the belly which feeds the head ... And it is the ancient neglect of the belly that has made for the continuing impoverishment of the head (*Conversations*, 207).

In *Season*, the point is sharpened by Crim in the exchange with Powell referred to earlier: 'You can call it forget,' said Crim, 'was a complete wipin' out from his memory. Is like how education wipe out every thin' San Cristobal got except the ceremony an' the bands. To teacher an' all who well-to-do it happen. Everythin' wipe out, leavin' only what they learn.'

Powell's answer tells us that this 'wipin' out' does not only impoverish the educated; it brings danger to the rest of us: 'Is bad that wipin' out,' he (Powell) said, his voice grown feeble with contrition. 'Is murder an' confusion when it happen. It kill everything. Now an' then an' all what is to come it confuse' (*Season* 17).

Lamming ascribes Bishop's murder to our collective failure 'to make a decisive break with that old colonial legacy which left us tenants of the very ground which the hands of our ancestors have humanized and made fruitful for hostile strangers; and which, out of habit, we call home'. I am certain that, then or now, betrayal does not breed only in the colonial legacy. But it is true that the Caribbean Left did little to help the Grenadian people defend themselves against their internal or external enemies; it could not. In fact, I believe that those of us who would have defined ourselves then as part of that Left betrayed the Grenadian people and the region, at least by silence and inaction. We were part of the problem and assumed we were part of the solution. Worse: many of us thought we *were* the solution.

Since then, although the region's survival (or at least, the survival of some of its territories, and I include the 21st century revolution in Venezuela) is threatened, there is no visible movement fighting back and only isolated pockets form part of the growing global movement against war, against debt, against the International Finance Institutions (IFIs), against globalisation, against internecine tribalism – that is, racism. In all our territories there is a great deal of violence, and all of that violence is turned inward.

'He (Powell) has not been found in the book,' Lamming says in his lecture 'A Visit to Carriacou', 'and I suspect he is still alive' (*Conversations*, 16).

Class betrayal is still the fundamental issue of our time. And part of the reason we do not know that is because we have not acknowledged who Mr Slime is; we have not examined with all our learning and research all the places he does his betraying; and therefore we have not explored how the education most if not all of us here have received has in some measure betrayed the movement we often claim to be part of and even speak for. That is what happens when novels are taken to be fiction and fictitious politics are taken to be reality. Mr Slime lives, but so does brother Powell. He is in our movement, with his mother and his sister, and we know every day better the many faces of the enemy.

Notes

1. Eusi Kwayana has been a political activist in Guyana and the wider Caribbean for more than 50 years, first as a member of the original People's Progressive Party in Guyana and a Minister in the 1953 government led by Cheddi Jagan and most recently as a leader in the Working People's Alliance (WPA). Karen de Souza has been a political activist for more than 20 years, beginning in 1979 in the WPA during the heyday of the civil rebellion against dictatorship led by Walter Rodney and since 1990 as coordinator of Red Thread, an autonomous multiracial women's group which coordinates the Global Women's Strike (GWS) in Guyana. Selma James, widow of C.L.R. James, was active from 1945 in the Johnson-Forest Tendency founded by James. They were involved together in the movement for West Indian Federation 1958–62. In 1972 she founded the International Wages for Housework Campaign, which, since 2000, has co-ordinated the GWS, a network of women and autonomous women's organisations in more than 60 countries of the global South and North which campaigns for new global priorities – from investment in military spending to investment in meeting people's needs. All three were close colleagues of Walter Rodney.

2. The 1980–1983 speeches are, in chronological order, 'On the Murder of Rodney' (June 1980); 'Politics and Culture' (1980; month unknown); 'The Honourable Member' (August 1981); 'Builders of our Caribbean House' (July 1981); 'The Imperial Encirclement' (December 1981); 'Nationalism and Nation' (1982, month unknown); 'A Visit to Carriacou' (November 1982); 'The Plantation Mongrel' (November 1983); and 'The Tragedy of a Whole Region' (December 1983). They form part of *Conversations – George Lamming: Essays, Addresses and Interviews, 1953–1990*, edited by Richard Drayton and Andaiye (1992).

3. Working People's Alliance, the political party in Guyana of which Rodney was a founding member.

4. 'The West Indian People: A View from 1965', *Conversations*, 253.

5. Interview, Karen de Souza, April 12, 2003.

6. The term 'what they made happen' is adapted from something that Powell says in *Season* which is very different: '...ever I give you freedom, Crim, then all your future is mine, 'cause whatever you do in freedom is what I make happen' (18).

7. Dr Kofi James-Williams Baako, 'the latest President', in a speech to the new Parliament.

8. Working class is not used in this essay with the rigidity that led some participants in a regional Left meeting in the early '80s to conclude that one Caribbean island had only about 6–8 members of the working class (or some such number).

9. Private conversation with Selma James, April 2003.

10. This view is based on my own observations and discussions in Grenada, and those of several colleagues, including working class members of the WPA. It comes out of the visits made in 1980 and 1981, in particular.

11. There was also clearly a plan involving the WPJ and the NJM to forge a unified Left: as one small indicator of this, Lamming reports that at the beginning of his relationship with Grenada, he was approached by Bernard Coard, Deputy Prime Minister of Grenada, to use his presumed influence with the WPA to persuade its leadership to reach an accommodation with the People's Progressive Party (PPP).

12. The incident that provoked this is recounted in the *Small Axe* interview. See 'The Sovereignty of Imagination: An Interview with George Lamming.' David Scott in *Small Axe* No, 12 September 2002, pp. 72–200.

28 | *Postcolonial Negations: George Lamming's Open Future*

Thought need not be content with its own legality; without abandoning it, we can think against our own thought, and if it were possible to define dialectics, this would be a definition worth suggesting.

Theodor Adorno, *Negative Dialectics*[1]

...[W]ithin any given [moment] ... the narrative is always battling with a complexity, that in every act there is going to be a seed of its negation. And that battle is going on all the time.

George Lamming, Interview, 'The Sovereignty of the Imagination'[2]

Over half a century has passed since George Lamming's first novel *In the Castle of My Skin* was published in 1953. The autobiographical fiction quickly eclipsed his literary beginnings as a poet (as he had primarily thought of himself) and short story writer, firmly establishing him in the canon of the modern, some would say modernist, Caribbean novel.[3] Although readers of the entire corpus of his fiction might have conflicting opinions about what remains his masterpiece, the striking success of the first novel almost overshadowed his other achievements, which include the impressive breadth and range of his later fiction, his lectures, interviews, addresses, his controversial engagements in the intellectual and labour politics of the region, all of which play more than a supplementary role in his oeuvre. The first novel is probably the most commonly read of his fiction, and its emphatic focus on the dispossessed villagers, its sketch of emergent black and nationalist consciousness through the eyes and voices of the schoolboys, its critique of colonial education in the 'Little England' of Barbados, its working class sympathies and peasant ethos continue to be deeply and essentially identified with Lamming's influence on the sociology and aesthetic theory of the Caribbean novel. But his later novels go on to depict a broader anglophone Caribbean with increasingly complex renderings of ethnic, sexual, and gender relations. His interviews and lectures also address a contemporary Caribbean informed by his itinerant routes across different continents, revealing a writer who combines an occasionally uncompromising political stance with an unquestionably ethical commitment toward a humane Caribbean, even global, politics.

While it is true that writers such as Lamming attain an aura of prophetic stature and lend themselves more easily to the authorial fallacy (which goes beyond what they say or are understood to say in fiction), it is just as true that they are held to political standards not usually applicable to most writers of imaginative literature. Given the overtly political platform of much anticolonial, particularly nationalist, literature, it is not surprising that writers of this affiliation are under pressure to fictionalise their way into revolution.[4] This seems fair enough where Lamming is concerned because he makes little distinction between artistic transformation and political praxis, sometimes to his peril. Despite his complaints about the inhospitable climate of the anglophone Caribbean in the 1950s for creative writing which, according to him, compelled most writers to get out and stay out, Lamming has remained convinced that the cultural sphere should not only be autonomous, but should play an 'evangelical' role in regional politics.[5] 'The political sovereignty of a people is impossible unless it rests upon an authentic cultural base created by its working people,' he declares, reversing the usual hierarchy of culture as superstructure and implying that he is part of the 'working people' who have an 'authentic' culture, all of which are arguable for varied reasons.[6] His hyperbolic assertions in *The Pleasures of Exile* about the historic emergence of the West Indian novel are not evidence of bourgeois grandstanding, but betray a deep anxiety about a decolonised future.

Unlike African and Indian cultures, which had strong native traditions to serve as buffer and resistance to colonial onslaughts, according to Lamming, the aboriginal traditions of the West Indies were severely affected, the pre-Columbian landscape as radically transformed as the culture by the exigencies of plantation economies. What would the hybrid, contentious, almost entirely immigrant populations of the region, with its long history of violence and inhumanity toward many of them, turn to once the colonial regimes formally ended? What common ground could frequently hostile groups brought together for capitalist exploitation forge in the putative nationhood of universal suffrage? Here Lamming's voice is distinct from other writers such as Derek Walcott, Dennis Scott, and Kamau Brathwaite. For Walcott it is precisely the newness of the Americas that bears the most exciting and original promise. If, as Adorno claimed after the horrors of Auschwitz, affirmation is demonic and such genocide calls for negative Art, unspeakable historics are continually represented and recuperated in Walcott, Brathwaite, and in Wilson Harris, whose limbo theory recalls the myth of Orpheus moving his enemies with his music and continuing his exquisite performance as he is rent apart. Scott's drama, *An Echo in the Bone*, follows Walcott's tendency to play the upbeat note. As Rachel philosophically concludes after the therapeutic rite of the Nine-Nights ceremony, 'And tomorrow the sun going come up same as ever. No matter what is past, you can't stop the blood from drumming, and you can't stop the heart from hoping.'[7] Even Brathwaite's Caliban who tends to brood as much as Lamming's on the sins of the past, rises from the watery hell of the Middle Passage, out from under the limbo stick, to step with hopeful trepidation on the ground of the New World:

> *up*
> *up*
> *up*
> *and the music is saving me.*[8]

Although Brathwaite uses a structure and metaphysics of negation, his echo of Aimé Césaire in 'Tom' ultimately affirms unconditionally:

> *for we who have achieved nothing*
> *work*
> *who have not built*
> *dream*
> *who have forgotten all*
> *dance*
> *and dare to remember.*[9]

His litany of affirmative Caribbean achievement is antiphonically posed as a series of destabilising supplements, largely verbs that literally undermine the dominant colonial negations of cultural potential and creative agency in slave economies.

Despite momentary mood swings upward, Lamming's Ceremony of the Souls rarely offers complete closure. He handles the questions raised above in a paradoxical manner, never quite giving up on the potential of the Caribbean, but never fully assured that a complete break with the nightmarish past is possible. (Note the dreams, visions, hallucinations, and déjà-vu episodes in his fiction). The frequently aborted endings and enterprises in the novels, the deep foreboding about the future, including in the relatively more optimistic *Season of Adventure* and *Natives of My Person*, the uncanny and sometimes incomprehensible sequence of events, might be taken as Lamming's last word on the politics of decolonisation, his disappointing prophecy for the actual future of the Caribbean (given when he wrote his last novel, now his present). Similarly, his famous appropriation of Shakespeare's Caliban as the symbol of Caribbean resistance has led to a blind spot that many critics have discussed, the problematic portrayal of female characters in his own fiction, particularly their inability to be as politically savvy as their male counterparts (as Miranda is with Caliban) or their marginal presence (like Sycorax and Miranda's unnamed mother).

However, David Scott's question about generative vision in his interview of Lamming concedes the limits of Ma's ability to look past her present in *Castle* without the foreclosure of national or feminist potential in her ultimately conservative attitude. He sees Ma, instead, as the aged, fragile giant upon whose shoulders the youngsters in the novel and the later generation outside the novel (such as Scott) stand in order to glimpse a future unavailable to Ma herself. Scott explains that 'a generation prepares the possibility for the vision of a succeeding generation even if it cannot entirely support that vision.' 'That vision does not exist without the prior conditioning of the older generation,' he adds.[10] Agreeing with him, Lamming reads the generative moment – and here I mean both generational as well as (re)generating – as 'a seed of its negation' (see second epigraph). Both Lamming's own work and its reception reveal productive seeds of negation that define his complex, often contradictory, legacy. The fact that Lamming has not published fiction since the seventies is read as a withering of potential, his silence about a future he cannot predict, but neither Lamming's continuing interventions in nonfictional forms nor the debates his writings and lectures have stimulated support this assumption.[11] Later in this essay, I will read the Caliban trope and its implications for Lamming's work as a 'negation of the negation' which will, in turn, as Lamming foresees, germinate its own negation.

If the sense of generational negation is somewhat similar to T. S. Eliot's critique of enlightened perspectives on 'dead writers,' the 20-20 vision of hindsight ('we know so much more than they did' – but we know it in part because of them, implies Eliot), it seems rather appropriate since some of the conflicts and tensions related to Lamming are similar to those surrounding the modernist legacy in general.[12] The early responses to Euro-American high modernists were mixed, predictably including horror of the upstarts who were taking all kinds of liberties with accepted prose and poetic conventions and excitement over the revolutionary iconoclasm (quite a bit of it self professed) of the rebellious generation. Some decades later, the very high priests of unorthodoxy: James Joyce, T. S. Eliot, W. B. Yeats, D. H. Lawrence, Ezra Pound were all pilloried as racist, sexist, and proto fascist, if not downright fascist, the new generation marvelling at how aesthetic nonconformism did not automatically translate into political radicalism. Not the least of their limitations was the high modernist attitude to women, but the 'discovery' of several women writers in addition to Virginia Woolf, namely Marianne Moore, Djuna Barnes, Gertrude Stein and so on led to other controversies, some of which questioned the idealised readings of women writers and women's writing techniques as more truly egalitarian and revolutionary. Indeed, in the ideology of *ecriture feminine*, women writers could be (re)claimed as more modernist and innovative in style than the canonical male writers, who at best emulated the 'natural' convolutions of the 'mother tongue' and the unsingular, non-phallic companionship of 'women's lips.'[13] In the midst of this furor, later feminist writers deflated the radical aura of the male canon, exposing the deplorable presentation of female characters in their work, eventually leading one critic to ask despairingly, 'How useful is it to prove over and over again that Hemingway, Faulkner, or Joyce was or was not a misogynist?'[14] Reading critiques of modernism against the grain, Rita Felski applauds the insights of post-structuralist challenges to any dogmatic reading of the movement, viewing 'the modernist artwork...as a site of resistive impulses and radical indeterminacy.'[15] In poststructuralist readings of modernism, '[d]eformation, depersonalization, obscurity, dehumanization, incongruency, dissonance, and empty ideality' are negative categories that not only present an accurate picture of how the world seemed in the best and worst of times, but also not uncreative expressions of the modem condition.[16]

Locating Chinua Achebe's denunciation of Joseph Conrad's *Heart of Darkness* in 1974 as an explosive moment in postcolonial critiques of modernism, the editors of *Modernism and Empire*, Howard J. Booth and Nigel Rigby, both agree that ideologies of empire affected modernist themes but they also argue that as in Conrad himself, anticolonial critiques paradoxically coexisted with racist beliefs.[17] While modernist influence is generally perceived as radiating outward in the logic of colonial dependence, essays in this collection draw attention to the cosmopolitan contours of modernism, not just Picasso and cubist art, but Conrad and his marine voyages, Rudyard Kipling and E. M. Forster in India, Rabindranath Tagore, the Japanese haiku, and Ezra Pound, where one cannot always assume that it was the West that was the primary influence and the East the mimic echo, even if the modernists themselves would generally not have deigned to think otherwise. The modernist writers in the metropolis must have also begun meeting, however infrequently and possibly reluctantly, the immigrants from the colonies, and it would be curious to have some sense of T. S. Eliot's reaction to George Lamming.[18] What all this suggests is that if modernism of the Anglo-American variety was itself a messy and multifaceted creature, then other modernisms must offer different accounts.

Houston Baker believes that the already 'teasing semantics' of modernist terminologies and periodisations are further befuddled by his suspicion of a movement that, like the civilisation it is tied to, 'is exclusively Western, preeminently bourgeois, and optically white.'[19] His study of the Harlem Renaissance notes its internal paradoxes as a liberatory space for African Americans who found in Art one of the rare areas where the colour line of the segregated 1920s was not as rigidly drawn as in other occupations in the US But '[e]xceptional art'was still 'an illusory Afro-American goal' in the larger, intransigent context where black people were inevitably disadvantaged in the hostile economic, political, and ideological environment of polarised race. Rather than read the Harlem Renaissance as a 'failure,' however, in comparison to its presumably more robust neighbours in Anglo-American and Irish modernism, Baker implies that its very existence was a miracle, a formulation remarkably similar to Lamming's conception of the West Indian writer of the '50s.[20] If both intellectuals mark limits to the modernist projects of their choice, these are historical limits enforced by the virtually inflexible social conditions, not inherent flaws of the enterprise.

With Lamming and the anglicised context of Bajan education, and his own migration to London (although as an unemployed writer, not by the Oxbridge route), the problem of affinity with metropolitan modernism must have been complex. As Simon Gikandi points out, Caribbean writers of this period were caught between the inevitable difference of European modernism and their 'proximity to high modernism.' If alienation and exile are typical themes in European high modernist literature, they have a specific valence in the Caribbean history of continuing diasporic migration. But Gikandi insists on foregrounding such issues in his analysis, since 'any meaningful account of Caribbean literature cannot ignore the angst that has generated some of the most powerful texts on the colonial situation.'[21] Achebe's dismayed apprehension of the racial and historical gulf separating Marlow (with whom he had so far identified) and himself would probably be echoed, although differently from Achebe, by Teeton in *The Emigrants*.

Gikandi's delicate reference to 'a certain uneasiness' regarding modernist trends points to a heated debate that is not confined simply to a definition of Caribbean literature and its dominant themes, regarding which Lamming has himself offered controversial prescriptions. Gikandi's attempt to recuperate a productive space for a Caribbean modernist aesthetic is a response to Michael Thelwell's objections to the 'corrupting influence' of modernism on Caribbean fiction and its evasion of ethical, social engagement.[22] Attacks such as these probably owe some allegiance to Georg Lukacs's notorious impatience with modernist conventions such as incomprehensible fate, static temporality, solipsism, aborted potential, 'attenuation of actuality,' 'dissolution of personality,' 'obsession with morbidity,' and nihilist disintegration that he identifies as the contrived repertoire of modernist indulgences.[23] But Thelwell's attacks are made in a similar spirit, one would assume, as Ngũgĩ wa Thiongo's contemptuous dismissal of 'neo-African literature' (African literatures in European languages). 'In the process this literature created, falsely and even absurdly, an English-speaking (or French or Portuguese) African peasantry and working class, a clear negation or falsification of the historical process and reality. This European-language-speaking peasantry and working class, existing only in novels and dramas, was [sic] at times invested with the vacillating mentality, the evasive self-contemplation, the existential anguished human condition, or the man-torn-between-two-worlds-facedness of the petty-bourgeoisie.'[24]

The conflation of a class with characteristics typically identified as high modernist is too obvious to miss here, and would, by this account, set up an interesting conflict between Lamming and Ngugi, friends and comrades otherwise. Some of Lamming's peasant or working-class characters, though not sharing the specific native-language situation described by Ngugi, nevertheless come perilously close to Ngugi's caricatured portrayal. Entire passages in *In the Castle*, *Season of Adventure*, and *Of Age and Innocence*, which might be said to deal most specifically with the constituencies idealised by Ngugi, embody the sluggish pace of action, or more appropriately, the inaction heartily condemned by Ngugi. In *The Emigrants*, which is largely set in England during the '50s migration, the neurotic repetitiveness of suspended (in)animation is particularly striking: 'We were all waiting for something to happen.'[25] Many of the plots deal with paralysed inaction, stifling claustrophobia, mystifying narrative loops and coils, fragmented meanings, mental breakdowns in the best (or worst as some would have it) of modernist traditions. Most of Lamming's novels end with a sense of hushed expectancy, if not with a sense of void. One could say that the class of the characters is in the final analysis meaningless when mediated by the modernist, middle-class writer, but what is disconcerting is that Ngugi does not see Lamming as part of the tradition he despises but instead openly acknowledges his debt to the latter. Lamming himself has no doubt that he writes in the tradition of the Caribbean novel, which he once said is not middle class but peasant.[26] Ironically, Ngugi's own novels, such as *The River Between* and *A Grain of Wheat*, bear some resemblance to the radical uncertainties and painful indecisiveness of Lamming's fiction. What, then, did Ngugi find so inspiring in Lamming's novels? And are both of them deluded in their vision of novels about peasants written by no-longer-peasant intellectuals? (The category of the peasant is itself controversial in the context of Barbados).

Lamming's idealisation of peasant life and concerns and his own deliberate focus on them must be examined in the context of the 1930s, a formative period both in his young life and in the incipient nation of Barbados. His youthful migration to Trinidad and his introduction to the older Beacon group could only have reinforced his sense of a new Caribbean aesthetic more expressive of and attuned to those turbulent times. As Reinhard Sander persuasively demonstrates in *The Trinidad Awakening*, in a context of minimal book culture, magazines and journals were a godsend to writers starved of a literary community and forum.[27] The Beacon group, inspired by the postwar nationalist and peasant insurgencies sweeping through various British colonies and by Marxist attention to the proletarians, pursued a literary manifesto that stressed a focus on lower-class settings against a colonial tradition that was dominantly anglophile or anglo-oriented, predominantly negrophobic, and middle class. While it would be disingenuous to claim that all these writers and those they influenced lived as close to the soil or urban yard as their chosen subjects, Lamming's unapologetic sense of lower class roots is not dissimulating, given his own background and what being middle class and black must have meant both for him and for intellectuals such as James in the rigidly stratified class-and colour-coded world of Trinidad and Barbados, in particular, where the white plantocracy was still deeply entrenched.

Sometimes the only claim to middle class aspiration was to establish a distant and disdainful attitude to the poor, who were generally black (or perhaps the other way around). In this context, to claim any kind of solidarity with the masses was both revolutionary and self-serving, since some of these writers were bitterly aware that they belonged to neither high nor low, but certainly were not part of the establishment at the time. But it was also a more ethical choice than the one made by the Slimes of Lamming's fiction who turned their backs on their roots in order to climb the social ladder that opened up as the colonial hierarchy finally began to crack. While it is easy enough to criticise these writers for romanticising their lower class subjects, at least some credit must be given to their project against what Herbert Marcuse would call the 'affirmative character of culture.'[28] In hindsight, the hostility toward the middle classes and white minorities and the focus on black peasants in what is now a dominant Afro-Caribbean, middle class ethos may seem unproductively ethnocentric, but as a dialectical process, as Friedrich Engels argues in his antagonistic response to Eugen Duhring, it is a logic of negation, a 'law,' in Engels's strong words, that 'holds good in the animal and plant kingdoms, in geology, in mathematics, in history and in philosophy.'[29] And lest this model seem mechanistically teleological and deterministic, neither Engels nor many of the writers of the turbulent period of the dawn of independence were blissfully oblivious to variations and unravelings of context-driven acts and enunciations of negation. Nor did the seeming limits of one's history entirely dull the critical faculty that transcends temporality, and makes one ahead of one's time, so to speak. Lamming's critiques of nationalist rhetoric and his sense of gender and ethnic affiliations preceded the enlightenment of a later generation more conscious of the diverse Caribbean, but they tend to be muted by the attention paid to the Caliban motif.

Caliban himself is negation, in the sense that Antonio Gramsci means with the lower classes coming into consciousness of their role in history. And Lamming says as much in his reading of Caliban as a 'condition' wrought by Prospero through the ideology and history of the Shakespearean age. As Ranajit Guha puts it,

> Inversion was its [the insurgency's] principal modality. It was a political struggle in which the rebel appropriated and/or destroyed the insignia of his enemy's power and hoped thus to abolish the marks of his own subalternity. Inevitably, therefore, by rising in revolt the peasant involved himself in a project which was, by its very nature, negatively constituted. The 'names, battle-cries and costumes' he assumed in order to carry this out were all taken from his adversaries. It was no doubt a project predicated on power, but its terms were derived from the very structure of authority against which he had been driven to revolt. He spoke this in a 'borrowed language' – that of his enemy, for he knew none other.[30]

Setting limits upon this language and the terms of combative engagement as only borrowed is too categorical, but Guha's words bear an amazing similarity to Lamming's reflections two decades earlier on Caliban as figuration, not historical agent, dialectically thinking against his own reading of a revolutionary Caliban. In one sense, Caliban is indeed a blasphemous challenge to his (non)existence in colonial thought, the not-Man who finally identifies Prospero as the monster. The 'Lie' in the text world and real world is vehemently rejected and reformulated as a different truth. But to wallow in it, not to think against this new truth perpetuates its own set of denials and erasures. 'Caliban cannot be revealed in any relation to himself; for he has no self which is not a reaction to circumstances imposed upon his life,' Lamming warns.[31] It is no surprise, therefore, that rather than retreat to a rearguard defence following the negation of Caliban himself through gender and ethnic differences, which exposed the *other* silences ignored or imposed by Caliban's speech (or by speaking only of Caliban), Lamming has responded to the worries and promises of the contemporary Caribbean, as evident in *Coming, Coming, Coming Home*, even if his strong sense of slave history as definitive remains.

While Lamming's historic interventions into colonial and postcolonial histories began with his determination to find 'the occasion for speaking' from his perspective, he is just as capable of maintaining an anti-assertive taciturnity where readers might crave neat and uplifting solutions. His characters are often prone to silences, incomplete and incoherent thoughts, miscommunications, and deferrals that would frustrate readers who expect a better grip on the text. Not all of the conventions of narrative expectation and fulfillment are thus denied, however, and the lucid exchanges are to be noted. *Of Age and Innocence* has the familiar appearance at the end of the novel of an unknowable, probably unrecognisable 'Tomorrow,' with the occasional silences, the occasion, Lamming would say, for *not* speaking. But there is one crystal clear conversation amidst all the emphasis on doubt and mourning. Misunderstanding Bill's role in the crises that confound everyone, Thief concludes:

'As every bee is a bee, so every skin that show white qualify for the same crucifixion.'

The conversation proceeds:

'But San Cristobal can't claim no special colour,' said Rockey. 'It hold every race that woman an' man can make, an' every colour too.'

'Yet some colours more sacred than the rest,' said Thief. 'An' it going' to take a terrible, terrible crime to make them meet in a common place.'

Rockey then warns Thief, 'if you choose a murderin' evil, whatever reason you choose it make no difference, then you buildin' a tabernacle that can only house one breed, an' the sun goin' set a lastin' disgrace on the bones that help you build.'[32] I quote the passage at length in order to note the strategic clarity in an argument about multiethnic and racial politics, since the deaths and sense of mystified mourning in the novel might signal only revenge and destruction in Thief's apocalyptic vision. In such instances, silences and voids do not indicate continual tone deafness to the multitudinous voices and histories that make up the Caribbean, or advocate a future unblessed by the sun.

'True theory recognizes the misery and lack of happiness prevailing in the established order,' declares Marcuse. 'Even when it shows the way to transformation, it offers no consolation that reconciles one to the present.'[33] It is this grim scenario that has led to activist projects such as Marxism and feminism being accused of lacking a sense of humor, of being dourly focused on violence and victimisation (or conversely of vulgarly romanticising the revolutionary potential of subaltern subjects). Since the point of theory is, I would think, to be just that, theory, not dogma, I reserve judgement on Marcuse's truth claims, but I find the measured sobriety of anti-affirmative culture here not sanctimonious and holier than thou, as activist engagements are unfortunately prone to be on occasion. That is, in the context of the popular carnivalisation of Caribbean cultures in the overdeveloped world and with the islands' social structures largely set up for tourist inflow and native outflow, the memory of lived trauma that one finds so often in Caribbean literature is a necessary negation. In an early essay, Sylvia Wynter does not dismiss the Caribbean 'history of survival,' but insists also on the 'squalid and innumerable failures of the many.'[34] What has to be carefully negotiated is that neither perspective is cancelled by the other, but instead the contradictions are sublated.[35]

This is not to assume that Lamming's sense of negation sounds only a note of gloom and doom, although his novels are admittedly a heavy read as compared to his essays. His use of the seed image recalls Engels's own impatience with caricatures of negation as meaning only negativity, non-existence, and destruction. Engels invokes the grain of barley, its various incarnations as it passes from the organic stage to that of processed culture and back again into the soil to continue the cycle; and then of geological strata through the centuries in ceaseless transformation and (re)production.[36] In *Pleasures*, Lamming suggests that continual recrimination can only stall a future 'which must always remain open.'[37] He returns to this view in the epigrammatic line in *Natives*, 'we are a future they must learn.' In that novel the generational production of knowledge may be most directly related to the women. Caribbean literary production is certainly in that future as the ascendance of writers such as Paule Marshall, Jamaica Kincaid, and Michelle Cliff and the growing book-length projects and essays on women writers, genders, and sexualities demonstrate. There is a later generation of East Indian women writers, and a younger breed of second-generation migrants in metropolitan locations who have expanded the field since Lamming wrote *Pleasures*. Although conditions for indigenous writing and publishing could be improved, we may see more and more writers like Earl Lovelace not based outside the Caribbean. Whether the utopian future, in Lamming's words, when the 'No and Yes is masterless and slaveless,' will fulfil its potential is yet to be determined.[38] But the many mansions of Caribbean literature do not indicate the end of contentious or collegial dialogues.

Notes

1.   Theodor Adorno, *Negative Dialectics*, trans. E. B. Ashton (New York: Continuum, 1977), 141.
2.   George Lamming, 'The Sovereignty of the Imagination,' Interview by David Scott, *Small Axe* 12 (September 2002): 153.
3.   I use 'Caribbean' and 'West Indian' in a fairly conventional but not necessarily standard way, the former to indicate a broader, more contemporary sense of the region and the latter when I want to foreground the British colonial period and its anglophone context. Unless I specifically cite from a Lamming text, I have not provided a bibliography.
4.   Although there is a long debate about the elastic terminology of the postcolonial that is too well rehearsed to go into here, I follow for now the distinction some critics make between the *anti*colonial, which is specifically oppositional to colonial rule, and the *post*colonial, which may be so, but especially in the eyes of some Left-identified intellectuals, more often involves collusion and cooptation, generally by migrant intellectuals who have settled comfortably in the metropolitan spaces of the First World. The vocabulary of the anticolonial is thus tied to resistance, nationalism, and independence, while that of the postcolonial, at least in its dominant avatar in the UK and the US, would engage more often with subversion, mimicry, hybridity. Dissenting critics would probably find all kinds of complications with this division, but for the purpose of this passage on prescriptive expectations (what, according to demanding readers, postcolonial writers and critics ought to produce), I underline these assumptions.

5. Lamming uses 'evangelical' more than once to speak of himself specifically and of the intellectual worker generally as committed to a political education, urgently necessary, according to him, against the threat of 'recolonization' through dependency structures in the Caribbean. His weighty prose in the novels moves to a clearer, but still declamatory style in his lectures, although he is aware that the prophetic role he assumes will be unpalatable to his critics. Lamming's sense of cultural autonomy, or 'sovereignty,' as he prefers, obviously does not indicate some kind of art for art's sake revival. It foregrounds what must be a painful irony for him: despite a largely moribund public interest in historians and writers, the imagination is still the most creative aspect of the nation's future since the reality is far from sovereign for the 'decolonized' subjects.

6. Lamming, 'The Honourable Member,' in *Conversations: George Lamming, Essays, Addresses, and Interviews, 1953-1990*, ed. Richard Drayton and Andaiye (London: Karia Press, 1992), 225. His stinging portrait of a bourgeois politician is unlikely to appeal to thin-skinned members of the middle classes, but this 'type' has been similarly satirised in various postcolonial literatures. Lamming's reference to elections as a 'national cockfight' is just as applicable to the world's most glorified democracy, particularly after the Florida fiasco in 2000. The slowly increasing presence of female politicians is grounds for fresh speculations, but in 1981 Lamming argued that (dis)honorable members exploit the 'greater sacrifice of courage and will' of women in their households who enabled the education and upward mobility of the men through their unacknowledged labour (220).

7. Dennis Scott, 'An Echo in the Bone,' in *Plays for Today*, ed. Errol Hill (Essex: Longman, 1985), 136.

8. (Edward) Kamau Brathwaite, *The Arrivants: A New World Trilogy* (Oxford: Oxford University Press, 1973), 195.

9. Brathwaite, *Arrivants*, 13. Here the primacy Lamming gives to culture as base makes sense. As writing was to the slave, as Henry Louis Gates, Jr., has argued, asserting that slaves had culture was a revolutionary act. Lamming's reading of culture, though, is very broad, Gramscian in its embrace of workers not generally considered 'cultured,' and refusing the split between labour and culture.

10. David Scott, 'The Sovereignty of the Imagination,' 153.

11. See, for instance, A. J. Simoes da Silva, *The Luxury of Nationalist Despair: George Lamming's Fiction as Decolonising Project* (Amsterdam: Rodopi, 2000). He believes that Lamming's critics have let him off too easily and offers some highly provocative readings, including the extraordinary label of Lamming as 'antiCaribbean.' The work is, however, not simplistically dismissive of Lamming's contributions

12. T. S. Eliot, 'Tradition and the Individual Talent,' in *Selected Essays* (London: Faber and Faber, 1951), 16.

13. An alternative reading could mean that if modernist was defined through the narrow, pseudo-universalist confines of the male canon, then women writers of the period were anti-modernist. Similar theories could be applied to non-western writings, which were feminised in this gendered formula. I put terms identified with the work associated largely with French feminists in quotation marks in the text to indicate that I have misgivings about such essential differences dependent on biology, even if I am occasionally guilty of subscribing to these ultimately untenable gated communities. Poststructuralist negation theory has ironic consequences for such reinscriptions of women's histories, since what some feminists

have concluded is that not just black women, but 'woman' herself is unrepresentable, a category under erasure. While negation discourse has a formidable range in philosophy and logic, psychology and psychoanalysis, linguistics, and Marxist theories, one can see why its challenges to the process of reading and interpretation, its focus on absence, silence, (the not-there, the not-said), make it particularly attractive to poststructuralists who read exclusions and non-events as rich, not arid, in potential.

14. Lisa Rado, 'Lost and Found: Remembering Modernism, Rethinking Feminism,' in *Rereading Modernism: New Directions in Feminist Criticism*, ed. Lisa Rado (New York: Garland, 1994), 6. Rado hastens to add that if she finds this exercise unproductive, 'it is not out of disdain or contempt for the old,' but in order to seek varied approaches to gender (11).

15. Rita Felski, 'Modernism and Modernity: Engendering Literary History,' in *Rereading Modernism*, 195. See also Bruce Robbins, 'Modernism in History, Modernism in Power,' in *Modernism Reconsidered*, ed. Robert Kiely (Cambridge, Massachusetts: Harvard University Press, 1983), where he calls for an 'update' on Georg Lukacs (230). Rather than overturn Lukacs's accusation of modernism as a 'negation of history,' though, I am reconsidering his limited interpretation of negation.

16. Jonathan Culler, 'On the Negativity of Modern Poetry: Friedrich, Baudelaire, and the Critical Tradition,' in *Languages of the Unsayable: The Play of Negativity in Literature and Literary Theory*, ed. Sanford Budick and Wolfgang Iser (New York: Columbia University Press, 1989). Only the words in quotation marks are Culler's, the rest of the sentence expresses my views and should not be attributed to Culler.

17. See the 'Introduction' in *Modernism and Empire*, ed. Howard J. Booth and Nigel Rigby (Manchester: Manchester University Press, 2000), 2.

18. I am thinking of Lamming's amusing anecdote about T. S. Eliot in *The Pleasures of Exile* (London: Michael Joseph, 1960),65.

19. Houston A. Baker, Jr., *Modernism and the Harlem Renaissance* (Chicago: The University of Chicago Press, 1987), 6.

20. Lamming, *Pleasures*, 27.

21. Simon Gikandi, *Writing in Limbo: Modernism and Caribbean Literature* (Ithaca: Cornell University Press, 1992),25. Lamming may occupy for different critics a sliding scale of literary genealogies. Belinda Edmondson's *Making Men: Gender, Literary Authority, and Women's Writing in Caribbean Narrative* (Durham: Duke University Press, 1999) reads Lamming into a Victorian tradition. Given the style of *Natives of My Person*, as a more obvious example, others may well identify him as a postmodern writer. Then, of course, as a Caribbean writer, he may not exactly fit any of these categories as they are defined by dominant cultures. Lamming himself has expressed admiration for the prose of Joseph Conrad and Thomas Hardy, which accounts for the tone of his own prose. See *Pleasures*, p. 39. But his own manipulations of narrative conventions might also make his works 'anti-novels' in comparison to conventional nineteenth century prose fiction.

22. Gikandi, *Limbo*, 3.

23. Georg Lukacs, *Realism in Our Time: Literature and Class Struggle*, ed. Ruth Nanda Anshen (New York: Harper and Row, 1962).

24. Ngũgĩ wa Thiong'o. *Decolonising the Mind: The Politics of Language in African Literature* (London: J. Currey, 1986),22.

25. Lamming, *The Emigrants*, (1954; Ann Arbor: The University of Michigan Press, 1994), 5. The sentiment, if not the exact sentence, is repeated both throughout this novel as well as in others.

26. Lamming, *Pleasures*, 44–45.
27. Reinhard Sander, *The Trinidad Awakening: West Indian Literature of the Nineteen Thirties* (New York: Greenwood Press, 1988). Sander points out that it was this generation that enabled, however indirectly, the emergence of the novelists of the fifties, Lamming and his contemporaries: John Hearne, V. S. Naipaul, Wilson Harris, Samuel Selvon, Andrew Salkey and others.
28. Herbert Marcuse, *Negations: Essays in Critical Theory*, trans. Jeremy J. Shapiro (Boston: Beacon Press, 1969). By affirmative culture Marcuse means the beatification of suffering and the idealisation of impoverishment by a bourgeis culture that separated the mind and body from the immanent soul.
29. Friedrich Engels, *Herr Eugen Duhring's Revolution in Science: (Anti-Duhring)*, trans. Emile Burns (London: Martin Lawrence, 1943), 159.
30. Ranajit Guha, *Elementary Aspects of Peasant Insurgency in Colonial India* (Delhi: Oxford University Press, 1983), 75.
31. Lamming, *Pleasures*, 107.
32. Lamming, *Of Age and Innocence* (1958; London: Allison and Busby, 1981),394–95.
33. Marcuse, *Negations*, 118.
34. Sylvia Wynter, 'We Must Learn to Sit Down Together and Talk a Little Culture: Reflections on West Indian Writing and Criticism,' *Jamaica Journal* 2.4 (1968): 31. I am not entirely sure, though, that this tradition of negation is the same in V. S. Naipaul and George Lamming, just because both provide jeremiads about the region. If Naipaul has come in for more than his share of attacks, it is because he has been equally unsparing of the Caribbean. In *Pleasures*, Lamming reproves Naipaul for stressing the differences between Samuel Selvon and black writers, claiming that Selvon and he have far more in common than Selvon and Naipaul do, regardless of ethnic background (224).
35. The most obvious critique of negation as negativity (and it is that, but not only that) is that it focuses too much on trauma and we need to get on with life. See, for instance, Sheila Radford-Hill's coined term 'un-negation' as a counter to Michele Wallace's 'variations on negation' in Radford-Hill, *Further to Fly: Black Women and the Politics of Empowerment* (Minnesota: University of Minnesota Press, 2000); Wallace, *Invisibility Blues: From Pop to Theory* (London: Verso, 1990). But negation is about more than negativity or even anti-affirmation. It is a critical, creative process of germination, to use Lamming's seed image, that enables the condition of its negation into yet another creative form. See Engels below.
36. Engels, *Anti-Duhring*, 154, 155.
37. Lamming, *Pleasures*, 15.
38. Ibid., 158.

29 | *From Intellectual Workers for Regional Sovereignty to Culture and Sovereignty in the Caribbean and The Sovereignty of the Imagination: The Shifting Ground of a Writer and Public Intellectual*

Sandra Pouchet Paquet

This paper explores some apparent contradictions in the culture/sovereignty nexus in George Lamming's fiction, essays, addresses and lectures. The relationship between culture and sovereignty is by no means a straightforward one, and I would like to avoid hegemonic definitions of culture that control the terms of the discourse and its outcome. This includes the one cited and endorsed by Lamming in 'The Imperial Encirclement:'[1]

> If we think of culture as not a question of refinement and erudition, but the totality of processes that contribute to the understanding, the reproducing or the transformation of the social system, through the symbolic re-presentation or re-elabouration of material systems, a culture policy, then, cannot be seen as an added complement nor as a luxury task to be taken up after the economic and political changes have taken place.[2]

In this instance, the definition of culture as a totality of processes also stipulates the obligations of state government to support and manage the cultural process. I would like to explore issues arising out of the culture/sovereignty nexus in relation to the sovereignty of the imagination without such definitional hegemony. If culture is understood as a social construction that varies across time and space with multiple meanings that are redefined continually, it becomes easier to unpack some of the practices associated with it that rationalise and even mask the relations between culture, sovereignty, and imagination.

My position is that Caribbean cultural practices are antagonistic to hegemonic definition; they are constantly being modified by cultural practices within the region and outside the region, and this makes culture a subversive partner to concepts of sovereignty. Of course sovereignty is also a social construction and subject to changing practices, but one that nonetheless speaks consistently to authority, autonomy and control over what transpires within and across the borders of the nation-state.[3] Whereas sovereignty speaks to territorial boundaries and the state's exclusive authority, Caribbean cultural practices have steadily worked to undermine that authority in the dependent and independent territories of the region, and in extra-regional territories as well. Culturally, the Caribbean is trans-boundary, not merely within the region, but extending outward to the world beyond it. To link culture and sovereignty is to suggest that the two fit together very naturally in some predetermined kind of way. It seems to me that they do so only in a utopian or imagined Caribbean. The cultural communities of the Caribbean simply do not coincide with national and even regional boundaries, and to try to press Caribbean cultures, broadly or narrowly defined, into the service of nation-formation as Lamming has done, is a legitimate but nonetheless coercive proposition that conflicts with the sovereignty of the imagination that Lamming also celebrates in the body of his work.

In 'Coming, Coming, Coming Home' (1995), Lamming, who has been an outspoken champion of Caribbean sovereignty throughout his public life, remarks on the phenomenon of the transnational household as a defining feature of Caribbean life and culture.[4]

I shall use this licence of language and ask you to entertain a concept of Nation that is not defined by specific territorial boundaries, and whose peoples, scattered across a variety of latitudes within and beyond the archipelago, show their loyalty to the 'nation-state' laws of their particular location without any severance of cultural contiguity to their original worlds of childhood.

More recently, in an interview with Knolly Moses for Panmedia, Lamming responds specifically to the issue of whether Caribbean culture can resist American influence and he does so with characteristic visionary logic:

> Given our proximity to the United States and the very intimate interactions we have with the U.S., it is very difficult to find any Caribbean family that has no relations with America. So the question is not fighting off the influence, but how to develop a critical relation to that influence.[5]

This should not be interpreted as a sign that Lamming is retreating from his staunch position on regional and cultural sovereignty, but it does suggest that he remains sensitive to 'the contradictions of this imperial arrangement.'[6] The fact is that, for better and for worse, the United States like Europe plays a crucial role in Caribbean economic and cultural production. In respect to the external frontier charted by Caribbean writers, Lamming clarifies his position further:

> Our writers are dependent on external promotion. We have not worked out in the Caribbean itself a publishing infrastructure. Most major Caribbean writers have publishers outside. And where you don't have the apparatus of literature in the community itself, there is no direct exchange between the writer and the reading class that you find in the United States or England.[7]

The dilemma for Caribbean writers and artists as Lamming describes it in the *Panmedia* interview is not new. Before Americanisation, there was Europeanisation, and both European and American cultural influences have generated enormous cultural production in Caribbean populations both outside and within the Caribbean. Lamming is not alone in his estimate of the dependency of Caribbean cultural production on extra-regional technologies, for example, Maryse Condé had her say in 'Order, Disorder, Freedom, and the West Indian Writer:'

> Are we condemned to explore to saturation the resources of our narrow islands? We live in a world where, already, frontiers have ceased to exist. ... In new environments one faces new experiences which reshape the West Indian personality. For those who stay on the islands, changes occur also. As Glissant himself puts it, the Caribbean Sea, which he opposes to the Mediterranean, is not a closed area. On the contrary, it opens onto the world and its varied energetic influences.[8]

A key question here would be, what patterns of communal identity are consistent with cultural production from the Caribbean, and how do these coincide or conflict with concepts of sovereignty? That Condé should cite Édouard Glissant comes as no surprise since Glissant's *Poetics of Relations* is in part an elaborate response to this question of identification with a culture or civilisation that is not necessarily an identification with a sovereign nation.

The conceptual underpinnings of sovereignty are tied to the rights, capacities, and responsibilities of the nation-state, some of which are exclusively within the state's authority, and others that are negotiated with other states. This reminds us that sovereignty has external as well as internal dimensions, and that the sovereignty of the nation-state is also a social construction and subject to modification. It follows that degrees of autonomy, control, and authority in effect mark the boundaries of the state that may or may not coincide with actual territorial or cultural boundaries. In *Imagined Communities*, Benedict Anderson argued that the nation 'is an imagined political community – and imagined as both inherently limited and sovereign'. According to Anderson, 'the nation is imagined as *limited*' because it has finite boundaries; as sovereign because it dreams of being free; and 'as a *community*, because,...the nation is always conceived as a deep, horizontal comradeship'. It is finite, sovereign, and fraternal.

These values coincide roughly with the utopian vision that inspired three conferences on regional sovereignty with which George Lamming is associated, either as a participant or coordinator, in Cuba, Grenada, and Trinidad and Tobago in the early 1980s. The First Conference of Intellectual Workers for Regional Sovereignty of the Caribbean Peoples was held in Grenada in November 1982. A Second Conference on Culture and Sovereignty in the Caribbean was scheduled to take place in Grenada in June 1983; it was eventually held in Trinidad & Tobago in January 1984 because of the assassination of Maurice Bishop and the subsequent invasion of Grenada by the United States. Both conferences were inspired by the First Meeting of Intellectuals for the Sovereignty of the Peoples of our Americas in Havana in September 1981, and were coordinated by George Lamming. All were convened in the first years after Lamming's return to the Caribbean, which coincides roughly with the tenure of Maurice Bishop as Prime Minister of Grenada, from 15 March 1979 to 19 October 1983. The ideological underpinnings of these conferences were always quite clear, and these are reiterated in David Scott's 'The Sovereignty of the Imagination: An Interview with George Lamming:' the man of culture and the man of letters, the artist and the intellectual, have a responsibility to work with the politician, the statesman, and the political activist in the quest for regional liberation and integration through a ministry of culture, and vice versa. The emphasis then was on the pursuit of shared goals that were organised around sovereignty as bedrock in the pursuit of liberation from old and new forms of colonisation. What is clear from addresses like 'Nationalism and Nation' (1982), 'Culture and Sovereignty' (1982), and 'The National Dance Theatre of Jamaica: A Celebration' (1985), and is reiterated in the recent Scott interview, is that in Lamming's opinion the collective action he envisioned was stymied by what he describes as the philistinism of the political intelligentsia:[9]

> It is a crippling deficiency of the regional educational system that it has been reluctant to understand and accept the role of art as an intellectual discipline...

The radical political intelligentsia of the left have been victims of the same deprivation. They plan for a new society whose cultural base and perspectives are nowhere on their agenda. Because they think, in all innocence, that such matters can wait until the other structures are securely put in place. (Lamming, 'The National Dance Theatre' 173)[10]

The current emphasis on the sovereignty of the imagination appears to subordinate an earlier emphasis on shared responsibility for the development of a culture of regional liberation and integration; in fact, it privileges the subjective imagination, perhaps in an attempt to right an observed crippling educational deficiency that fails "to understand and accept the role of art as an intellectual discipline.

> The question of sovereignty, then, particularly in the light of the definition of nation as being a particular space defined in terms of politics and laws, that sovereignty is limited....But what I'm claiming that is *not* limited is another kind of sovereignty, and that is the capacity you have for *choosing* and making and remaking that self which you discover is you, is distinctly you. (*Small Axe*, 147)

I read Lamming's statement on sovereignty in part as a personal one that speaks to a reconstituted subjectivity and a re-rooting of the aesthetic self geographically and culturally in the Caribbean. By extension, it also speaks to a community's capacity for reinventing itself through a heightened consciousness of freedom that has been a preoccupation of Lamming's fiction since *In the Castle of my Skin*, and remains an open question.

Though there is an observable change in areas of performance and intervention since the publication of Lamming's last novels *Natives of My Person* and *Water with Berries* in 1971, and his subsequent return to the Caribbean. Yet, in his interview with David Scott, Lamming insists that he hasn't changed, that it was always his intention to intervene in the cultural process even though he has never been interested in political office:

> I haven't changed very much in that sense of almost seeing what I do and myself as a kind of evangelist. I'm a preacher of some kind; I am a man bringing a message of some kind. That would have been there in 1956. I am bringing my message; I don't know what you would make of it. And that is there right down to the later Carifesta addresses. (*Small Axe*, 197)

Some questions to ask at this point are where and when does the writer as evangelist enter into Lamming's self-definition as a writer and public intellectual? What does this mean in relation to his prior performance as a novelist? How is the act of reconstituting one's role from novelist to evangelist achieved? After all, in Lamming's fiction the evangelist is a suspicious and unreliable character; for example, in *In the Castle of My Skin*, the evangelist Brother Dickson is not to be trusted with the truth, and in *Of Age and Innocence*, evangelism doesn't fare much better. Yet, this is the descriptor Lamming uses, not only to describe his current role and function as writer and public intellectual, but also to characterise C.L.R. James in his eulogy at James's funeral in Trinidad in 1989. Published in *Conversations* as 'C.L.R. James, Evangelist,' in that address, the word evangelist describes a style of delivery and a certainty of purpose that, according to Lamming, 'was a source of immense strength. It was also the cause of more than one grievous error' ('C.L.R. James' 195–96). It appears that the use of evangelist allows Lamming to distinguish between 'the characteristics of what might be called his intellectual personality' ('C.L.R. James' 196) and his works – the books, the pamphlets and the public lectures' ('C.L.R.

James' 197), and to praise the interventionist role and function of this outstanding citizen of the world without endorsing all of the James corpus:[11]

> And this is, indeed, the correct word to define his role and function in our lives. C.L.R. was an evangelist. But it took me some time to realise the real nature of this kind of performance. It had nothing to do with display of knowledge, or parading the wide range of reference which supported such discourse.

> This eloquence was of a different order. He literally believed what he was saying. There was no distance between head and tongue; and each judgement established a direct and organic connection between what was said and how he felt. (Lamming, 'C.L.R. James' 195–96)

This qualified though admiring description of C.L.R. James, the public intellectual, modifies Lamming's earlier self-positioning in relation to James in *The Pleasures of Exile*, where he reads, reproduces, and links his ambitions as a writer to James's *The Black Jacobins* in an elabourately argued commitment to a Caribbean-centred, text-based discourse.[12]

Between the publication of *Castle* in 1953 and the publication of *Season of Adventure* in 1960, the public role of the writer and intellectual in Lamming's corpus does not sit well with that of the evangelist, especially when one considers the latter's associations with the fixed values of Christian dogma and even fanaticism. In 'The Negro Writer and His World,' an address delivered at the First International Congress of Black Writers and Artists in Paris, September 21, 1956, Lamming described the work of the writer in terms of a very complicated relationship between private and public worlds that is far removed from the closed rhetoric of the evangelist; it is above all "a form of self-enquiry, a clarification of his relations with other men, and a report of his own *very highly subjective* conception of the possible meaning of man's life" (*Conversations*, 41; emphasis mine). His priorities are clear: 'for the writer this private world is his one priceless possession. It is precisely from this point that everything else will proceed. And in these circumstances it cannot be sacrificed to his immediate neighbourhood (even when that neighbourhood means a group defined by an artificial misfortune which includes him)' (*Conversations*, 42).[13] If this suggests an artificial distancing of self from the problems of ordinary life, he argues that this is not really the case: 'the private world of the writer is modified, even made possible, by the world in which he moves among other men. Much as he might think it otherwise, it is through the presence of others that his own presence is given meaning' (*Conversations*, 44). And there is yet another dimension to the writer's world, the world of human beings everywhere: 'He shares in their community. What he cannot escape is the essential need to find meaning in his destiny, and every utterance he makes in this direction is an utterance made on behalf of all men' (*Conversations*, 45). The relationship between the writer and his world engages the subjective, the local, and the universal in the here and now. In this context, the subjective imagination is the lifeblood of the community; shaman-like, the artist as vehicle of his community's consciousness, speaks to that community and the world in the imagery of his native culture and the psychological experiences that bind him to that community.

In Lamming's corpus, the sacred dimension of the creative imagination of conscience is embodied in the figure of the houngan rather than the evangelist; his current emphasis on evangelism describes a different level of activism and a new relation to his artistic endeavors.

The evangelist does not so much speak for the 'people' as to them; his role is to communicate a way of seeing and understanding through an intense and committed engagement directly with his audience. So how is one to read the relationship between the parallel worlds of Lamming's fiction, lectures, essays, addresses, and edited works, all remarkably consistent until the eighties, and the self-conscious re-creation of role and function reported in the Scott interview?

In this interview, though Lamming reaffirms the artistic value of the novel as a form and the singular importance of the creative writer, he distances himself from the novel which had been his genre of choice previously: 'I don't think as a form that that is necessarily exhausted at all. As far as I personally am concerned, I don't feel a great urgency to return to it – that is, to return to a narrative that is known and recognised as the novel' (*Small Axe*, 198). There are two aspects of this distancing of the artistic self from future efforts at the novel in the Scott interview on which I'd like to focus, however briefly. One is his presumptuous if ironic surrender of the genre to women writers, and the other is an overriding sense of the inefficacy and irrelevance of his novels in a community that does not read his novels though it pays attention to his public voice as an orator and political activist.

Revisiting the artist's role as houngan, as arbiter of the region's material and spiritual history, Lamming passes the baton, so to speak, to the women writers:

> I'll give you an example of what I'm doing. It's all within the frame of the Ceremony of Souls – I'm back to the Ceremony of Souls. That comes up in each. And what I'm doing is I have the *tonelle* as the region. So one night they might be in Haiti, and one night they might be in St Lucia, and one night they might be in Barbados... The one who is in charge of that now is not the *houngan* of the earlier *Season*; it is the *mambo*. And what she's doing here is summoning from this water the major figures. (*Small Axe*, 198)

Though the genius of imagination is not contained in individual gender, it can be argued that the artist and visionary is consistently a male phenomenon in Lamming's fiction.[14] While I am mistrustful of any gender-based guilt lurking in Lamming's ironic statement of surrender, Lamming has used his creative genius before to identify the personal responsibility of the artist in the specific circumstances that shape the nature of the artist's quest for liberating truth. For example, the frequently cited 'Author's Note' which Lamming inserts into *Season of Adventure*, in which he assumes personal responsibility for the criminal career of Powell, a character in the novel who has become a murderer and rapist: 'I will not have this explained away by talk about environment; nor can I allow my own moral infirmity to be transferred to a foreign conscience, labeled imperialist. I shall go beyond the grave in the knowledge that I am responsible for what happened to my brother' (*Season*, 332). The profound relationship between memory, guilt, and the language of the imagination clarifies the writer's dilemma here in a self-confessional and self-judgemental art that collapses the insulating boundaries of the novel as genre; in effect, Lamming the author identifies himself as a character who emerges out of his own fiction with a moral intention that is in conflict with the symmetry of the novel.[15] The trope is a curious one that represents the writer's corpus in part as a mission of self-discovery/recovery, and the writing of *Season of Adventure* as an epiphany in his personal quest for liberation from the alienation from native community he endures as a professional writer and universal intellectual. In hindsight, it anticipates Teeton's abandonment of his art and dependence on the Old Dowager in *Water with Berries* in pursuit of an active role in revolutionary politics: "I'm coming; I'll be there. It was the call of the Gathering; his voice from the future".[16] At the end of that novel, the termination of his successful professional life as a painter is represented as a necessary precondition to political action. This supports the idea that Lamming's fiction not only parallels but also prepares the way for a subsequent reconstitution of self and function.

Lamming introduced the 'Ceremony of Souls' as an organising value in his relationship to his work as a writer in *The Pleasures of Exile* and in *Season of Adventure*, which were both published in 1960. But in 'A Visit to Carriacou' (1982), in one of the many references to this ceremony that run the course of his public life, Lamming describes the ceremony as a moment of epiphany that impressed on him as a Caribbean artist, 'the necessity of reconciling the past with each moment of conscious living....And in the way we work I discovered this was about my own life'(*Conversations*, 25).[17] In Lamming's corpus, the symbolic drama of this ceremony is a metaphor for the artist's visionary power and his necessary role in society. Yet not only is this exceptional novelist rejecting the idea of new contributions to the novel as a genre, he signals a change in direction, form, and vision from the writer to the reader of his own texts, and in the process ratcheting down the density of his self-reflexive creative vision in service of a more direct exchange with his target audience, and a more immediate engagement with the linear narrative of history. In this mode, 'the language of statement' intervenes and revises 'the language of fiction' (*Small Axe*, 196–97). It would seem that Lamming's achievements as a novelist do not preclude a re-imagining of the art of the novel. As A.J.M. Bundy observes of Wilson Harris's essays and lectures: 'By redrafting through verbal clues, those verbal clues permit the author to see, not merely with vision, but into vision' (5). Perhaps, this is where the *evangelist* finds a point of entry as mediator of the writer's 'own *very highly subjective* conception of the possible meaning of man's life' (*Conversations*, 41; emphasis mine). Not surprisingly, Lamming amends his previous definition of one's immediate neighbourhood to accommodate his new emphasis on political education:

> If our immediate neighbourhood is the neighbourhood of our personal relationships, of how to be with our neighbours, it seems to me that any education which equips us for how to be with each other has got to be political education. It has got to be an education, which, first of all, lets us know, helps us to understand, what is the context of power, the character of that social reality within which those individual personal relationships take place, because those personal relationships cannot be regarded as having an autonomy. (*Conversations*, 204)

Of course, it is precisely this preoccupation with the context of power and the constitution of a new politics of truth that is the hallmark of Lamming's fiction from its inception. What is different is his commitment to fiction as an ongoing quest.

Lamming is quite explicit about his changed mission as creative writer in conversation with David Scott:

> I do not expect most of you there whom I'm talking to, particularly if it's the union people, I do not expect that they're going to be reading any *Of Age and Innocence*, that they're going to be reading any *Season of Adventure*. But when I give a lecture about the honorable member, and trace the history of this parliamentarian, from the great-grandfather in the cane field, right through to the schoolmaster whose son is now a lawyer, that is very clear. They're hearing that very clear. But I am telling them what *Season* and *Of Age and Innocence* is about. In other words, the lectures are used really as statements that illustrate the theme and content of the novels. (*Small Axe*, 197)

The burden of the literate imagination and the unfinished task of probing and rehearsing the resources of conflict-ridden community, as Lamming represents it in this interview, is a burden he faced before in the early stages of his career as a writer. In fact, it prompted his emigration to the United Kingdom in 1950. There are echoes in the recent Scott interview of the pronounced sense of alienation as a colonial writer evident in *The Pleasures of Exile*:

This was the kind of atmosphere in which all of us grew up. On the one hand a mass of people who were either illiterate, or if not had no connection whatever to literature since they were too poor or too tired to read; and on the other hand a colonial middle-class educated, it seemed, for the specific purpose of sneering at anything which grew or was made on native soil. (*Pleasures*, 40)

But what Lamming identified primarily as a colonial writer's problem then, reappears in the Scott interview, not as colonial alienation and exile but as a full-blown post independence Caribbean-centred crisis of irrelevance and inefficacy that has inspired a closure of one sphere of creative enterprise and the constitution of another: 'at some stage I had come to feel that if I had anything of relevance and value to say that could be immediately effective in however minimal a way, it would be more effectively done by that statement, by that lecture-form, than by the novel-form' (*Small Axe*, 179). In this mode, Lamming abandons his role as novelist for that of teacher and evangelist of sorts, and reconstitutes the wide-ranging world of his creative genius in a more narrowly drawn role and function. In the process, he is also addressing the aesthetics of literature within the current Caribbean situation. After all, Lamming is not simply reiterating plot and subject matter of the novels in his public addresses; in each case he is creating a new text of distinct provenance that directs a reading forward and backward between the novel and its role in Caribbean culture.[18] Is Lamming in fact re-imagining the art of the novel in response to a deeply felt conflict between the alienation imposed by the form of his fiction and the moral imperative of the author?

In 'Challenges of the Struggle for Sovereignty: Changing the Word versus Writing the Stories,' Merle Hodge expressed her concern about the situation of the Caribbean writer: 'If we agree that Caribbean literature can contribute to the political process of empowering Caribbean people, then we must set about solving another problem: how do we deliver Caribbean literature to the Caribbean people?'[19] The problem as Hodge describes it is not dissimilar to what Lamming describes, and neither is her response to the marginalisation of the novel in a literate society: 'In this situation creative writing becomes, for me, a guerilla activity'.[20] Even these issues, cursorily drawn as they are, invite closer consideration of the paradoxes that beset the creative writer and public intellectual in a situation where the art of the literary imagination is under siege.

It is clear from essays, addresses, and interviews, edited works, and novels, that the role of the public intellectual and the intellectual personality engaged Lamming from the outset as a barometer of sustainable change.[21] The thematic of the artist and writer as public intellectual is a recurring one perhaps in anticipation of the current crisis of alienation he describes among the region's intellectuals in essays like 'Western Education and the Caribbean Intellectual' and 'Coming, Coming Home.'[22] A distinguishing feature of Lamming's 'coming home' to the Caribbean in 1980 has been a high profile, personal investment in the political struggles of the region. Before this, Lamming's political posture was very much that of a public intellectual of the 'left,' writer, visionary, and world traveler. His previous political engagement was carefully modulated by a life of errantry and exile. This is how he situates himself as a very young and very successful writer and intellectual in *Pleasures*:

> This may be the dilemma of the West Indian writer abroad: that he hungers for nourishment from a soil which he (as an ordinary citizen) could not at present endure.

> The pleasure and the paradox of my own exile is that I belong wherever I am. My role, it seems, has rather to do with time and change than with the geography of circumstances; and yet there is always an acre of ground in the New World which keeps growing echoes in my head. I can only hope these echoes do not die before my work comes to an end. (*Pleasures*, 50)

At this time, Lamming is very much the writer and intellectual as free subject and world traveller. He commits himself to speaking and teaching engagements as a free agent. His universal appeal is courted and sustained by his role as a brilliant writer and intellectual. His books are translated into multiple languages, and are read and taught at institutions of higher learning on every continent. His credentials are published books, his radical anti-colonial politics, and his reputation as an orator and a teacher.

Lamming's introductory chapter in *The Pleasures of Exile* marks him as in the tradition of what Michel Foucault terms the 'universal intellectual:'

It is possible to suppose that the 'universal' intellectual, as he functioned in the nineteenth and twentieth centuries was in fact derived from a quite specific historical figure: the man of justice, the man of law, who counterposes to power, despotism and the abuses and arrogance of wealth, the universality of justice and the equity of an ideal law.[23]

In his introduction, Lamming establishes moral and intellectual authority in the context of the Law, the Judge, the Jury, the Prosecutor, Caliban as a man of language and letters, a reader of cultures and societies, who can hold his own in Prospero's courts of Justice. In fact, he casts himself hypothetically in the exemplary roles of all these, laying claim to his right to be heard as universal spokesman.

Lamming is always eager to point out that beginning in the 1960s he has been in and out of the region, 'not just as a witness and observer, but in a sense as a certain kind of activist working with the New World Group' which was founded by Lloyd Best.[24] Yet when Lamming takes up residence in the Caribbean after being based abroad for 30 years, he returns to a changed social landscape that is chock full of intellectuals in the sociological as well as the political sense, Marxist and Capitalist in orientation and all the variations in between the intellectual left and the intellectual right. They are operating in a variety of professions – as teachers, doctors, lawyers, jurists, economists, sociologists, city planners and engineers, politicians, entrepreneurs, journalists, etc. The moral and political privilege of the writer as intellectual in the vanguard of cultural and social change is on the wane in the Caribbean. Power is already largely in the hands of the so-called 'specific' intellectuals who, Foucault argues, derive from the savant or expert, rather than the tradition of the jurist:

> The figure in which the functions and prestige of this new intellectual are concentrated is no longer that of the "writer of genius," but that of the "absolute savant," no longer he who bears the values of all, opposes the unjust sovereign or his ministers and makes his cry resound even beyond the grave. It is rather he who, along with a handful of others, has at his disposal, whether in the service of the State or against it, powers which can either benefit or irrevocably destroy life.[25]

It is no surprise really that premonitions about any future return to the Caribbean, expressed earlier in *Pleasures*, have acquired the ring of truth with the passage of time:

> In the Caribbean we have a glorious opportunity of making some valid and permanent contribution to man's life in this century.... The novelists have helped; yet when the new Caribbean emerges it may not be for them. It will be, like the future, an item on the list of possessions which the next generation of writers and builders will claim. I am still young by ordinary standards (thirty-two, to be exact), but already I feel that I have had it (as a writer where the British Caribbean is concerned. I have lost my place or my place has deserted me. (*Pleasures*, 50)

When Lamming returns to the region some twenty years later to claim his place, so to speak, it is to work for change as a public intellectual in the political sense on behalf of social justice, equality of opportunity for the women, minorities, the working poor, and the chronically unemployed.[26] His choice is mirrored in that of Pierre, the carpenter and visionary of *Natives of My Person*, when he abandons ship with the mutinous crew of the *Enterprise*, as well as that of Teeton the painter at the end of *Water with Berries*. In the current situation in the Caribbean, Lamming has allied himself with labour organisations of the region in a spirit of at-oneness with the predicament of the working poor, and with intellectuals and movements of the Left whenever and wherever his vision coincides with theirs. In fact, Lamming repositioned himself in local and regional terms at a time when an energetic Left appeared to be gaining political ground. Yet, the constant that Lamming encountered on his return is relentless and unanticipated change, and the subjective imagination under siege.

The essays, addresses, and interviews collected in *Conversations: George Lamming* and in *Coming, Coming Home: Conversations II* that was published in the Caribbean, chronicle a personal, cultural, and intellectual history of migration and return. In the edited volumes of Caribbean literary and cultural history, *On the Canvas of the World* and *Enterprise of the Indies*, also published in the Caribbean, Lamming assembles in a broader canvas, an account of that odyssey. Having established his mastery of the 'foreign' book, his primary audience in these publications is a Caribbean audience, and his 'motive is an evangelical one.'[27] If Lamming has not published new fiction since 1971, he has been at work intellectually and culturally in a sphere and manner of his own choosing. This is perhaps one way in which the sovereignty of the imagination asserts itself at the expense of prescribed colonial and postcolonial cultural roles and functions that beset the Caribbean writer. In *The Luxury of Nationalist Despair: George Lamming's Fiction as Decolonising Project*, Samoes Da Silva concludes: 'Having attempted throughout his work to articulate for himself a position from which he can finally speak in a voice and manner that are clearly his own, free of the angry recrimination of "writing back," Lamming retreats into silence' (201). But he has not retreated into silence, though he has not published any new fiction. One might argue that Lamming is effectively redefining an aesthetics of literature within the postcolonial Caribbean around a reconstituted subjectivity as Caribbean based political activist and public intellectual. It would appear that Lamming is about the business of recreating a nationalist imaginary through the rigors of direct and organic engagement with the cultural dynamics of the region. He breaks with the definition of the postcolonial writer 'as necessarily always also a voyeur, a user, a usurper, an "educated native" who can only presume to speak for the people' (Da Silva 31).[28] And furthermore, he breaks with the definition of the postcolonial intellectual as one who 'belongs to a social class for whom the peasant is essentially an oppositional Other, albeit also an object of desire' (Da Silva (31).

In his post novel-writing phase, Lamming presents a particular challenge to postcolonial critics and cultural theorists because he has distanced himself from his life-pattern as novelist and universal intellectual in order to reposition himself within a specific culture, language, and history, in other words, to reconnect with the everyday experience of intellectual and cultural life in the Caribbean, 'as a kind of evangelist...a preacher of some kind...a man bringing a message' (*Small Axe*, 197). This new configuration collapses the boundaries that kept the intellectual and writer separate from his chosen constituency, at least in theory. The risk for the creative writer and public intellectual who attempts this transition is of course isolation and loss of influence in spheres of power outside the Caribbean. Another risk is that of being caught up in and manipulated by local politics. Foucault has argued that it may be 'necessary to think of the political problems of intellectuals not in terms of "science" and "ideology," but in terms of "truth" and "power." And thus the question of the professionalisation of intellectuals and the division between intellectual and manual labour can be envisioned in a new way'. In an important sense, this is precisely the kind of challenge that Lamming has undertaken with such evangelistic zeal. The shift from Intellectual Workers for Regional Sovereignty to The Sovereignty of the Imagination is a shift of emphasis to the intellectual discipline of imaginative inquiry and the cultural foundations of regional sovereignty. A far more radical shift is the refocusing of his creative energies from one who dedicates himself to producing the most extraordinary fiction that the general population does not read, to one who dedicates himself to bridging the gap between artists, intellectuals, technocrats, and the population that they serve. It remains to be seen whether Lamming can accomplish this in the relative isolation of his missionary role and consciousness.

Notes

1. This address was given at the Annual Dinner of the Jamaica Press Association in Kingston, Jamaica on December 12, 1981.
2. Lamming defines culture with remarkable consistency in his essays, lectures, and addresses in the 1980s. Here he cites Garcia Canclini. See also George Lamming 'The Tragedy of a Whole Region'; 'Culture and Sovereignity'; and 'The Makers of History' in Drayton, Richard and Andaiye. Eds. *Conversations: George Lamming*. London: Karia Press, 1992
3. Janice Thomson's working definition of sovereignty in "State Sovereignty and International Relations: Bridging the Gap between Theory and Empirical Research," *International Studies Quarterly* 39.2 (June 1995): 213-233 seems universally appropriate here: 'Sovereignty is the recognition by internal and external actors that the state has the exclusive authority to intervene coercively in activities within its territory'. These appear to be values associated with sovereignty regardless of ideological bias. In 'Culture and Sovereignty,' Lamming's definition is more measured: 'Sovereignty implies freedom from external control, or from the controlling influence of external factors. Or, as I intend, sovereignty is the collective power of a people to exercise control and direction over their means of existence; and the freedom to define and to redefine all those processes, material and otherwise, which make up our social reality' (284). See also: Joseph A. Camilleri and Jim Falk, eds., *End of Sovereignty? The Politics of a Shrinking and Fragmenting World* (1992); Thomas J. Bierstecker and Cynthia Weber, eds. *State Sovereignty as Social Construct* (1966); and Janice E. Thomson, "State Sovereignty and International Relations: Bridging the Gap between Theory and Empirical Research' (1995).
4. 'Coming, Coming, Coming Home' is the title essay in George Lamming's *Coming, Coming Home: Conversations II*, St Maarten: House of Nehesi Publishers, 1995. 29–48.

5. George Lamming, 'Damning Lamming.' Interview with Knolly Moses. *Panmedia* (1998) http://panmedia.com.jmlfeatures/lamming.htm

6. In an address delivered at the graduation ceremony, University of the West Indies, Cave Hill in 1980, Lamming observes: 'such are the contradictions of this imperial arrangement, that this same power which had organised the castration of our creative energies, would be responsible for returning our names where they belonged. The enemy had rescued us from total anonymity' ('Politics and Culture' 82).

7. *Panmedia*

8. Maryse Conde, "Order, Disorder, Freedom and the West Indian Writer." *Yale French Studies* 83.2 (1993): 121–35.

9. In 'Culture and Sovereignty,' Lamming observes about contemporary Caribbean society: 'Novelists function without a substantial and continuing reading class, even among the certified graduates of the region's university. This literature has hardly aroused the active interest of many who make up the political intelligentsia. The philistinism of the Left is a source of very tragic political error' (Lamming, *Conversations* 285). It is interesting to compare this with Wilson Harris in 'Profiles of Myth and the New World' originally published in 1966: 'The danger that confronts us ... lodges in technologies that may be used to manipulate whole and entire societies, and the elites within those societies who deem themselves literate but are conscripted by linear biases and fallacious absolutes' (Bundy, A.J.M. Ed. *Selected Essays of Wilson Harris: The Unfinished Genesis of the Imagination.* London: Routledge, 1999). Subsequently, this argument about a cleavage 'between the historical convention in the Caribbean and Guianas and the arts of the imagination' was more fully fleshed out in 'History, Fable and Myth,' first published in 1970 (Bundy 156). This becomes a central argument in Paget Henry's *Caliban's Reason* published in 2000, where he differentiates between historicism and poeticism in Afro-Caribbean philosophical thought though Henry does not identify George Lamming's significant role in identifying the cleavage between these modes of thought.

10. Lamming's review of Rex Nettleford's *Dance Jamaica* in "The National Dance Theatre of Jamaica: A Celebration." *Conversations.* Eds. Drayton and Andaiye. 169–75.

11. Lamming's eulogy reflects similar observations, equally provocative, about the intellectual as a public figure by Edward Said in *Representations of the Intellectual* New York: Vintage Books, 1996. 'My argument is that intellectuals are individuals with a vocation for the art of representing, whether that is talking, writing, teaching, appearing on television....when I read Jean-Paul Sartre or Bertrand Russell it is their specific, individual voice and presence that makes an impression on me over and above their arguments because they are speaking out for their beliefs' (12–13). He explains his position as follows: 'In the outpouring of studies about intellectuals there has been far too much defining of the intellectual, and not enough stock taken of the image, the signature, the actual intervention and performance, all of which taken together constitute the very lifeblood of every real intellectual' (13).

12. *The Black Jacobins* was out of print and neglected in 1960, the year of *Pleasures'* publication. See my Foreword to the Michigan edition of *The Pleasures of Exile* (Ann Arbor: University of Michigan Press, 1992. vii–xxvii) for a fuller discussion of Lamming's intellectual investment in the cultural authority of the written word (xix).

13. In 'The Negro Writer and His World' Lamming explains exactly what he means by immediate neighborhood: 'They are what the Danish philosopher Soren Kerkegaard calls, "the immediate neighbourhood," one's family, sometimes one's enemies, and always one's friends' (42).

14. This is Wilson Harris's point in 'Apprenticeship of the Furies,' when he urges: 'Think of the human vessel in the genius of the Imagination symbolizing ingredients within itself and beyond itself which are richer and stranger than individual gender' (Bundy 227). Harris argues in his inimitable way that if the womb is 'a seminal vessel,' this implies 'the partiality of the male and the partiality of the female,' and 'such partiality tells of a deep hunger in the body of nature, it tells of an unfinished climax of body and spirit, it tells of the reach of spirit into far-flung responsibilities within essences of creation...' (227).

15. In *Representations of the Intellectual*, Edward Said searches out the basic question for the intellectual, himself among them: 'In effect I am asking the basic question for the intellectual: how does one speak the truth? What truth? For whom and where?' (88), and again, 'what truth and principles should one defend, uphold, represent? This is no Pontius Pilate question, a way of washing one's hands of a difficult case, but the necessary beginning of a survey of where today the intellectual stands and what a treacherous, uncharted minefield surrounds him or her' (89).

16. I refer to the Holt, Rinehart and Winston edition of *Water with Berries* (1972) that ends with Chapter 12 rather than with Chapter 13.

17. Published in *Conversations*, 22–31. In another address, 'The West Indian People: A View from 1965,' Lamming explained its symbolic value: 'It is not important to believe in the actual details of the ceremony. What is important is its symbolic drama, the drama of redemption, the drama of returning, the drama of cleansing for a commitment towards the future. A part of our cleansing has to take the form of the backward glance, not in a state of complaint or in a state of rancour, but the backward glance as part of the need to understand' (*Conversations* 254). The houngan's function in mediating crises in the body politic through dialogue roughly parallels the shamanic quest in Wilson Harris's 'In the Name of Liberty:' 'The shaman-from times immemorial-is a voyager into the unconscious,....The shaman carries within himself the seed of genesis...His task, in physical fact, is to recover the profoundest reality of meaning when meaning may so easily become the victim of lust and lies' (Bundy 215). Harris continues: 'The shaman needs to surrender himself to a numinous realm in search of the inimitable, apparently ungraspable body of the law of truth. What is apparently ungraspable possesses a core of numinosity or myth that may give to shamanic fiction a far-flung reality. Myth becomes a basic corrective to tyrannous or despotic immediacy' (Bundy 215).

18. In his introduction to *Selected Essays of Wilson Harris*, Andrew Bundy makes a point about the poetics of the literary essay that has direct relevance to Lamming's corpus: 'If the essay promotes a reading forward and backward between the novel and its role as dream-book of the culture, we can suppose that the essay will provide the hunches, conjectures, hypotheses for the reality of the dream-book of the culture, the essay will do this chiefly by bringing into sharp focus our own background in received ideas and how these match or are contradicted by the phenomenology of the dream-book' (17).

19. Merle Hodge, "Challenges of the Struggle for Sovereignty: Changing the World versus Writing Stories." *Caribbean Women Writers*: Essays from the

First International Conference. Edited by Selwyn R. Cudjoe. Wellesley, MA: Callaloux Publications, 1990. 202–208.

20. Ibid., 206.

21. In short, Lamming's entire corpus: in *Conversations* and in *Conversations II* (St Martin: House of Nehesi Publishers, 1995), in the special Independence issues of *The New World Group* in 1966 through 1967), in the *Enterprise of the Indies* Vols. 1 & 2 (Port of Spain: Trinidad & Tobago Institute of the West Indies, 1999), as well as in his six novels published between 1953 and 1980, and the invaluable *The Pleasures of Exile*.

22. Both essays were published in *Coming, Coming Home: Conversations II* in 1995.

23. Edward Said outlines the risks of universality as he sees them: 'Universality means taking a risk in order to go beyond the easy certainties provided by our background, language, nationality, which so often shield us from the reality of others. It also means looking for and trying to uphold a single standard for human behavior when it comes to such matters as foreign and social policy' (*Representations* xiv).

24. See for example an interview with Lamming in 1989, published in *Banyan* at http://www.pancaribbean.comlbanyanllamming.htrn

25. Foucault sees this as a post Second World War phenomenon. Michael Foucault. *Power/Knowledge: Selected Interviews and Other Writings 1972–1977*. Trans. Colin Gordon et al. New York: Pantheon Books, 1980.

26. See Lamming's 'Coming, Coming, Coming Home,' especially 37–42.

27. Editor's Note, *Enterprise of the Indies* vii.

28. In conversation with Françoise Pfaff, Maryse Condé observes with characteristic irony: 'Any literature is an attempt to portray yourself, to situate yourself in the world, to define yourself in relationship to others and to yourself. People don't write for any other reason....If people knew themselves, they would not write' (73). But the point is an interesting one in respect to Lamming's recentering of an aesthetic of literature.

30 | *Coming, Coming Home –* **Must be Read**

George Lamming's new book, *Coming, Coming Home,* is a book which must be read by every Caribbean person who wishes to be truly Caribbean.

It is not by accident, but with a clear and definite purpose, that Lamming quotes the great Italian philosopher, one of the most influential of the 20th century, Antonio Gramsci, who wrote that 'the starting point of critical elaboration is the consciousness of what one really is, and is knowing "thyself" as a product of the historical process to date which has deposited in you an infinity of traces without leaving an inventory...therefore it is imperative at the outset to compile such an inventory.'

I can say, without fear of contradiction, that Lamming's new work, perhaps his most important, is an invaluable contribution to compiling that inventory of ourselves so necessary to understanding who we are, and the elabouration of that consciousness, which will allow us to understand where we must go, as a product of the historical process to date. There is no more important task, and Lamming has approached that task using deep philosophical knowledge, a firm grasp of history, past and contemporary, and at the same time he used the poet's marvellous sense of economy so that much, very much is compressed in little. There is not a wasted word in this wonderful book, *Coming, Coming Home*.

Coming, Coming Home as the title suggests is probably an answer to some of the questions posed by Lamming in the Independence period in his *Pleasures of Exile*. And therefore this is Lamming's answer to the post-independence period, using as well his creative imagination, and the structure of the novelist in these seminal essays.

In my view, Lamming's new book ranks only in the category of Gordon Lewis's *Main Currents in Caribbean Thought*. C.L.R. James's *Modern Politics* and Jose Marti's *Our America – Writings on Latin America and the Cuban struggle for Independence*.

With that said I go straight to Lamming's all important essay 'Western Education and the Caribbean Intellectual'.

Here is Lamming in a masterpiece of economy and compression describing the essential experience of the Caribbean, the prism, as it were, through which the Caribbean must be seen as the starting point of that critical elaboration to define what and who we are as Caribbean people: Lamming writes:

> The original experience of African and Asian [in the Caribbean] is the experience of a controlled and violent alienation from the product of their labour, alienation from the meaning and purpose of human labour. And they were often *strangers to each other* even when they had derived from the same continent.

No one can learn about any Caribbean territory anywhere who does not understand the twin processes of 'alienation from the product of their labour as well as the alienation from the meaning and purpose of human labour'. Then there is the second process of estrangement. Estrangement of African from African, and of Indian from Indian, and African from Indian, and then intellectual estranged African or Indian from mass, is the essential and abiding dilemma of the Caribbean. History has deposited us here. The point is to go beyond.

African slaves were emancipated from slavery. Indian indentured labour were emancipated from indentured labour. Independence formally freed Caribbean peoples from colonialism. But, creating a community of women and men who are not alienated from the product of their labour, and who are not alienated from the meaning and purpose of human labour, by controlling the product and organisation of human labour, is a matter that has not been addressed except in one Caribbean territory. This is not to say that it has not been attempted.

Here is Lamming speaking of one such attempt: The late Walter Rodney 'had initiated in his personal and professional life [as well as his political life] a decisive break with the tradition he had been trained to serve; and died in the conviction that the only fruitful emancipation was self-emancipation; that ordinary men and women should be intellectually equipped to liberate themselves from those hostile forms of ownership that are based exclusively on the principle of material self-interest.'

Let me illustrate the point. In what I describe as an animated exchange with Prime Minister Lester Bird last Thursday night I told him that I knew him. He, in turn, agreed that 'we go back a long way, but I did not know Lester Bird now.' He missed the point. I knew him in the larger sense, as historical and social type, as opposite to Rodney. That is, Lester Bird is one who is addicted 'to those hostile forms of ownership that are based exclusively on the principle of material self-interest.' It is a tradition. A negative tradition. A negative tradition lasting some 4–500 years, and with which Lester Bird and his ilk have not and cannot break. That tradition is the ceaseless accumulation of wealth by fair and more often by foul means, while aiding and abetting others, mainly foreign to do the same, if not more ferociously so. It began with Columbus.

Let me prove that point as Lamming does. Here is Columbus describing the population of the Caribbean he met, and which people are part 'of the infinity traces' which make up the Caribbean inventory, in both existence and essence. Wrote Columbus about the population of the Caribbean he met:

> brought us parrots, balls of cotton thread, spears and many other things...that they exchanged for glass beads...they do not bear arms.

Columbus continued as Lamming notes, with a chorus of other voices supporting Columbus view, about the original population of the Caribbean:

> put no value on gold and other precious things. They lack all manner of commerce, neither buying or selling, and rely exclusively on their natural environment for maintenance. They are extremely generous with their possessions...

I need to say, in parenthesis, that up to now that view of the original inhabitants is not taught in schools to this day! It is the European view, the colonising view of warlike Caribs and docile Arawaks, all slaughtered by Europeans, which is taught. Not men and women in harmony with their natural environment, manufacturing 'balls of cotton thread' which even now we do not make! Hostile forms of ownership dictate that the cotton is to be grown, exported as lint, to be returned to us, as thread, as cloth, as clothes, even though we produce 'the best sea-island cotton in the world.' Or, in the case of pineapples 'the sweetest pineapples in the world', yet hostile forms of ownership and control determine that we should use tinned pineapple juice and pineapple slices from Hawaii. Prime Minister Lester Bird and others such as he, are not disturbed at all by this state of affairs. They rest like babies asleep in the arms of hostile ownership, producing alienated labour and estranged persons in consequence. They claim only to use 'guile' to get 'a little more' for alienated labour, the job here and there, which they disburse, while getting by "guile" – better known as corruption – a great deal more for themselves. That type recurs and recurs in all territories, in all languages of the Caribbean archipelago.

Columbus, as I said, was the first to define the type, their purposes and intentions, conscious or unconscious, and their view of the people of the region. In this regard Columbus wrote of the Caribbean population this:

> They would make excellent servants. With fifty men we could subjugate them all and make them do whatever we want.

All that has changed between Columbus and Prime Minister Lester Bird is that with monopoly control of the electronic media, with the police and army, and exerting control if not over the judiciary then the judicial process, they can and do subjugate them all and make them do whatever they want in the service of hostile ownership in pursuit of the sole principle of material self-interest. This is so, be it for Vesco, de Savary of St James' Hotel, Gerald Bull of space Research, Rob Barratt of Royal Antigua, Wexelman of Heritage Quay and King's Casino or Lester Bird of Antigua Isle. The list could go on and on and on and on.

Then Lamming, who never reinvents the wheel, preferring always to go to the best source, and as he quotes John Esquemeling, coming some two hundred years after Columbus, who wrote that 'from the very beginning of their conquests the English, French, Dutch, Portuguese, Swedes, Danes...all other nations that navigate the ocean, have frequented the West Indies and filled them with robberies and assaults.'

There are those professionals and intellectuals who aid and abet those incessant robberies and assaults on the Caribbean and its people. While there are those who have resisted, following the Caribs, Arawaks and African slaves, these robberies and assaults.

Also aiding and abetting the process of robberies and assaults on the Caribbean and its people is the academic whom Lamming describes as 'often a specialist of great competence and very limited interests' and who is not an intellectual in the sense as Lamming says of 'primarily concerned with ideas – the origin and history of ideas and the ways in which ideas have influenced and directed social practice.' Divided to the bone, this Caribbean academic, Caribbean in origin, but educated in the Euro-American western way, pretends that he lives in the best of all possible worlds, is indifferent to anything outside his area knowledge, and lives only to get his 'dues of barley and of wheat' or schemes to get more than his due.

But there is a fourth category of intellectual who Lamming is pleased to bring to our attention. I guarantee it will surprise you and should bring you to a new awareness of the Caribbean and what it means in this critical elaboration of consciousness. Writes Lamming:

> There is a fourth sense in which the word intellectual may be applied to all forms of labour which could not possibly be done without some exercise of the mind. In this sense the fisherman and the farmer may be regarded as cultural and intellectual workers in their own right. Solid practice has provided them with a considerable body of knowledge. If we do not regard them as cultural and intellectual workers, it is largely, I think because of the social stratification which is created by the division of labour, and the legacy of an education system which was designed to reinforce such a division in our modes of perceiving social reality.

Lamming who, as I said before, never reinvents the wheel gives this most apt quotation from an authority on the subject. Here is Professor Woodville Marshall as quoted by Lamming:

> Peasant activity modified the character of the original plantation economy and society. The peasants were the innovators in the economic life in the community. Besides producing a greater quality and variety of subsistence food and livestock they introduced new crops and/or reintroduced old ones. The peasants initiated the conversation of those Plantation territories into modern societies. In a variety of ways they attempted to build local self-generating communities. They founded villages and markets, they built churches and schools, they clamoured for extension of educational

facilities, for improvements in communication and markets; they started the local co-operative movement. Peasant development was emancipation in action.

Every schoolgirl and boy should be required to learn by heart that passage. It is vital to their inventory of becoming, and the understanding and incorporation of it into the Caribbean personality is so, so vital, to our liberation from hostile ownership and control, and to our emancipation from alienated labour.

But as Lamming says the educated lawyer, like Prime Minister Lester Bird, doctor or academic does not see that an alternative consciousness and authentic way of being was being forged by the peasants and women. As Lamming says the other type 'the specialist technocrat does not really see these peasants and women' or vendors and traders. 'His technical agenda' writes Lamming 'does not register them as a critical political force because he is the product of a new intellectual formation: the technocrat who believes that the efficient management of a modern society is essentially a technical operation. If you can identify the appropriate technologies, and recruit a certain calibre of personnel with the right kind of managerial expertise. It really does not matter what electoral games are played or who wins since the correct decisions will ultimately be implemented by those whose technical expertise is indispensable to this process. Politics and ideology are viewed as an antiquated pastime.' Lamming quite aptly calls this malady 'technophilia,' and as he says, 'I do not yet know its cure'. The malady persists. So does the hostile ownership and control. So do the politicos who ceaselessly aid and abet this process as political mercenaries, accumulating private wealth through State power. PM Lester Bird is only one of the best (or is it worst?) known examples.

Those who read this book by Lamming will want to say of him, as the great poet, the Dean of Haitian letters Felix Morrisseau-Leroy said of Dessalines

Only I know what you are for us
Lamming, our bull
Lamming, our blood
Lamming, our two eyes
Lamming, you are guiding light.

Coming, Coming Home, is a vital to the eventual Caribbean homecoming.

SECTION 5

Extract of Novel in Progress: Columbus: A View From the Other Side

Columbus – Another View

Extract from a novel in progress
By George Lamming

The main story is set within what is described in my novels as the *Ceremony of the Souls.* This is a moment in Haitian mythology when the *Dead* return to discuss and dispute with the *Living* all those issues which were left unresolved when death separated them. The issues in the drama presented here derive from the fact of European conquest over what has been described as the Indies, and the legacy of this enterprise for all who were involved. The main story is narrated from the point of view of the violated hosts: Arawaks (Tainos) and the Caribs (Kilinagos).

Dominica will serve as the location or tonelle where the confrontation is mediated. In Haitian mythology, the tonelle is the sacred meeting ground to which the *Dead* and the *Living* are summoned by the houngan (priest of the occasion) or the mambo (priestess). It is the duty of the *Dead* to offer a full and honest report of their past relations with the *Living*, just as it is the responsibility of the *Living* to confront the meaning of the past if they are to discover any course of action which may help them towards reforming their present condition.

The extracts presented here are divided into two sections. In the first, Columbus is arrested and about to be taken to Spain for trial. In the second, instead of a Spanish trial, Columbus is confronted by the Mambo in the *Ceremony of Souls.*

Part 1

Town square. Columbus stripped naked to waist, hands and legs in chains. White hair falling loose down the sides of face, beard long, unkempt. Guard drags him across the street. Crowd shouting insults. He appears incredibly calm, except for occasional twitch of the mouth or rapid flicking of the eyelids. Voices giving evidence of the Admiral's crimes.

FIRST VOICE

> To Castile for trial,
> Dirty foreigner.

SECOND VOICE

> Try him here. Let us be
> his real judges.

THIRD VOICE

> Execution. I say execution
> without trial.

FIRST VOICE

> I was put in prison for
> crimes he invented. He
> stopped my rations of food
> for a month. Just water
> and biscuits with worms
> and lice over everything you eat.

SECOND VOICE

> He tried to degrade every
> noble Spaniard who stood
> up to the tyrant. Drove us
> like common native slaves to
> dig in the river and the rocks
> for gold he was going to steal.

THIRD VOICE

> And he stole the Queen's
> pearls. Put everything in
> hiding that was the property
> of the sovereigns. Yet the
> queen trusted him.

FIRST VOICE

> He deceived the queen
> more than once. Not only
>
> with the pearls, but playing
> he was the saint come out to
> convert heathens to the Faith.
> And sodomising the natives.
> That's what he was. A sodomite.

SECOND VOICE

> Not one native ever became
> a convert. Except the slaves
> he sent back to Seville. He was
> always looking for a bargain.

> *An Indian woman makes a passage*
> *Through the gathering, encouraged*
> *by one of the Spaniards.*

INDIAN WOMAN

> He murdered my husband with
> his own hands. Because my husband
> wouldn't start a war among
> his own people. He was ordering
> us to make war on our own families.
> We could be Christians if you take
> him away.

The woman turns and is led away
by the Spaniard who came with her.

FIRST VOICE

And you did worse things
than murder. Ask the women in Cibao
what happen there. Crimes no Christian dare mention.

COLUMBUS

(The voice is heard as in
interior monologue, melancholy
and a little perplexed.)

If it's new for me to complain
about the world,
it's custom of maltreating
me is very old. A thousand battles
I have fought with it, and I have
come to be such that there is none
so vile as not dare insult me.

THE SOUND OF A HORN AND BELL
EXPRESSING JOY AT HIS DISGRACE
THE GATHERING BECOMES MORE AGITATED
BY HIS APPARENT CALM.

FIRST VOICE

The thief was not satisfied
to make himself rich. But all
his family. The brothers who
come out here with him. Commanders
each one.

SECOND VOICE

And his sons at the
Court. Acting as his spies
right under the sovereign's nose.

FIRST VOICE

> I say execution without trial.

COLUMBUS

> (interior monologue)

> And these are men whose only
> aim in coming to the Indies was
> to amass as much wealth as they can
> by any means and return home
> speedily. I recognize them, and
> I swear there are among them
> men who are not worthy of baptism
> in the eyes of God or man.

THIRD VOICE

> Governor, Vice Roy, Admiral
> of the Ocean Sea! And a
> foreigner who never tells
> anyone who was his real father.
> Killed his wife, for all we
> know.

FIRST WIFE

> Always secrets. How could a bloody
> weaver's son, if that is true, get
> to marry a lady who claims noble
> rank. Even in Portugal where he
> seduce her.

SECOND VOICE

> He was always full of
> secrets and tricks. He stole from
> other men's papers, everything
> he claimed he knew. Everything
> stolen from honest to God sailors.

FIRST VOICE

> And to bargain with the Sovereigns
> for ownership of the lands
> he might discover! Never saying what he
> was really up to, what it is he had in mind.

SECOND VOICE

> No passage back to Castile
> until he says where he is
> hiding the queen's gold.

THIRD VOICE

> Yes, where. We know about
> the pearls. But you have gold
> nuggets in hiding. Where?

VOICES

> Where? Where? Where?

COLUMBUS

> (interior monologue)
> (the voice seems weary)

> I would very gladly rid myself of
> this whole business of it were honourable
> towards my queen to do so.

> *THE SOUND OF THE HORN AND BELL ARE HEARD*
> *INTERRUPTING COLUMBUS. FEELING OF GREAT*
> *JUBILATION AMONG CROWD.*

COLUMBUS

> (interior monologue)
> (tone of exhaustion remains)

> I did not come on this voyage to
> navigate for gain, honour or wealth,

that is certain. For then the hope of all
such things was dead. I came to your
Highnesses with honest purpose and sincere
zeal, and I do not lie. I humbly beg
that if it please God to remove me hence,
you will aid me go to Rome and other
pilgrimages. May the holy Trinity guard
and increase your lives and high estate.

*COLUMBUS IS DRAGGED ACROSS STREET TOWARDS
PRISON.*
*THERE IS CLAPPING AND SOUND OF BELL. A PICNIC
ATMOSPHERE.*

*COLUMBUS IN DUNGEON. HE STUMBLES ABOUT FROM
TIME TO TIME,*
*ON OCCASIONS APPEARS DELIRIOUS. BUT THE VOICE
IS NOW HEARD AGAINST THE BACKGROUND OF BELL
AND HORN.*
*HE IMAGINES HE IS ADDRESSING THE CROWD OUTSIDE
THE PRISON AND THE SOVEREIGNS AT THE SAME TIME.*
*VOICE EXPRESSES CONFIDENCE AND CONVICTION IN
HIS INTEGRITY.*

COLUMBUS
Seven years I was at your royal court
where all to whom this undertaking was
mentioned, unanimously declared it to be a
delusion... All wished to cover the ignorance
in which they were sunk, hiding their little
knowledge by speaking of difficulties and expense...

*HE RETURNS TO SITTING POSITION, STRUGGLING TO
REACH HIS*
*SHOULDER WITH HIS BROW. HE RESUMES HIS
STANDING POSITION*
SHUFFLING ABOUT.

COLUMBUS

> Difficulties, expense. Of all this
> they had no conception. Now everybody,
> down to the very tailors, seek permission
> to make discoveries. They go forth to
> plunder, and it is granted them to do
> so. It is they who prejudice my
> honour and do very great damage to the
> enterprise.

COLUMBUS

> (interior monologue)
> (his expression is bitter, head bent in despair)
>
> I have been very much aggrieved that
> they have sent to enquire into my
> conduct a man who knew that, if the
> reports he sent back were damaging,
> he would remain in charge of the
> Government here. I have not spoken
> to him to this day, nor has he allowed
> anyone to speak to me, and I swear
> that I cannot think why I am a prisoner.

> *COLUMBUS STOOPS FEEBLY TO HIS KNEES*

COLUMBUS

> I came here with such earnest love to serve
> these princes, and I have served with
> a service that has never been heard or
> seen. I entered upon a new voyage
> to a new heaven and a new earth which up
> to then had lain hidden...
> Of the new heaven and the new earth,
> which our Lord made as St. John writes
> in the Apocalypse, after he had spoken
> of it by the mouth of Isaiah. He made me

the messenger, and He showed me where
to go.
I went to take possession in her royal name.

*AN ABSOLUTE STILLNESS DESCENDS
OVER THE DUNGEON AND THE SOUNDS
OUTSIDE AS HE SPEAKS THE
LAST SENTENCE.*

COLUMBUS
Weep for me, whoever has charity,
truth and justice!

Part 2

INSIDE THE TONELLE

MAMBO
We have come to bear witness to this ceremony of souls which
is an original gift from Africa transformed after her turbulent
meeting with Europe in the disfigured homelands of the
Arawak and Carib Indians from Haiti to Antigua, Dominica,
St. Lucia, St. Vincent, Grenada, St. Kitts, and Nevis.

The MAMBO or priestess is between 30 and 40, a striking
black woman dressed in
white, with a headwrap. Her arms and neck are decorated with
emblematic jewelry. The tonelle is decorated with ververs or
symbols of various deities, small drums suspended from a peg,
pictures of a ship, plates of stones which serve as protective
charms, chains and iron bars, a bell, a rainbow, the Virgin
Mary, candles placed at four corners of the tonelle. There is a
table and chair. A pole (the centre pole) rises from the centre
of the floor to the roof and indicates the stairway down which
the deities descend to enter the tonelle.
The Mambo casts a last fleeting look around and picks up the
asson, a large calabash filled with seeds and a sacred rattle, tilts

her head back, chin pointing to the circle where the pole meets the roof. She shakes the asson. Immediately it is supported by the drums. It is a powerful sound that is felt throughout the countryside.

COUNTRYSIDE DAY

A dog barks, cocks begin to crow; there is the agitated sound of small animals, agouti.

INSIDE THE TONELLE

The Mambo suddenly stops. The silence that descends upon everything has the quality of a church. Her hands are raised in an arch round the pole and pointing towards the roof of the tonelle.

MAMBO
    In the name of God, of the Spirits
    I am asking the Saints, the Dead,
    You who are my only defense against
    all enemies, do not stop helping me
    during my life, and especially now
    in my conduct of this reunion between
    the living and those who reside below
    the waters...

MAMBO
    (addressing Columbus)

    The living accuse you of crimes inflicted on these islands.

COLUMBUS
    No man is ever separated from the reputation of his country.

MAMBO
    They say you were born in Italy. Some say otherwise.

COLUMBUS

I was born. That I know. But always I had this vision of being somewhere else before that birth... travelling forever before I discovered Genoa.

MAMBO

...Where your father was a weaver. But the record does not say
For certain.

COLUMBUS

I say my birth gave me no anchor. There was no anchor.

MAMBO

...There was a family...mother, father, brothers...Family is what you call an anchor. You have no memory of childhood as an anchor?

COLUMBUS

I had no anchor. I travel through childhood like an ocean, without latitudes, no hourglass or compass...Travelling. I travel forever before that first landing in Genoa. I was a stranger even there, even then.

MAMBO

That's why your life was made a secret...Your wife...a secret. Your mistresses...secrets...Your arguments before the queen about the voyage...hiding a secret...The logs you wrote on that same voyage always conceal a secret...The maps...the means you travel by. The letters you sent back to your sovereigns... buried their meaning in secrets. Why? Why?

COLUMBUS

(in sort of trance, crosses himself)
Since and before I was born, He had me in his most watchful care... He caused my name to sound marvelously in the land. The Indies, so rich a part of the world, He gave me for mine own. Of the barriers of the Ocean Sea which were closed to

such mighty chains, He gave me the keys...Among Christians I had an honourable name.

MAMBO

Honourable?

COLUMBUS

You know the men who conspire to damage my name.

MAMBO

Truth is the only conspiracy now working against you. It is not a secret that your journals show admiration for the people you met when you first arrive in these islands...

COLUMBUS

They brought me many gifts

MAMBO

Parrots and balls of cotton...

COLUMBUS

The birds and the flowers were uncommonly beautiful...I almost wanted to stay there for the remainder of my days.

MAMBO

They put no value on gold...neither buying nor selling.

COLUMBUS

They were generous with their possessions.

MAMBO

...With 50 men you could subjugate them all, and make them do what you want

COLUMBUS

In exchange for the Faith

MAMBO
>In exchange for Death, Cristobal Colon. You led the slave raid in Cibao…captured almost 2000 Indians, male and female… selected 500 for export to Spain…distributed the rest among your men on condition they were going to settle on the island. …Of the exported slaves half died before they reached Spain… Two hundred were too sick to walk when they arrived.

COLUMBUS
>Servitude was their refuge from the barbarism of their neighbours who lived on human flesh.

MAMBO
>…Cannibalism was the slander you invent to hide what is not a secret. Before your fourth and last voyage, more than half of original population has been murdered by work in the mines, and the musket…Before long, all were exterminated. No secret that.

COLUMBUS
>…There were Indians of civil manners and there were savages. My intervention postponed many a disaster. Indians came to me by the thousands begging to be taken to Spain and safety from the savages who had already destroyed many of their numbers. That is the truth.

MAMBO
>That is why we are here. To weigh the truth…

COLUMBUS
>Their King, Guacanagari, placed his own coronet on my head…He was a royal guest on my own ship…He wanted to accompany me back to Castille with his wives and family. We were friends. He would have given his life for me.

MAMBO
>(Loudly)
>He did!

COLUMBUS

> (Wounded by memory)
> The savages! It could only be the savages who envied his manners. (After a pause) You know of the massacre at Navidad?...We left 38 of our men on the first voyage...The Indians surprised them one night and slaughtered every one... Their private organs were chopped up and scattered about.

MAMBO

> The private organs were the Spaniards' undoing. Even the savage knows when his wives are insulted.

COLUMBUS

> The Christians were without protection...

MAMBO

> The Spaniards were beyond anyone's control. It is an accusation many make against you...

COLUMBUS

> ...How innocent the men who make it!
> As a governor sent to Sicily or to a city or two under settled government where the laws can be fully maintained, as such a governor they judge me.

MAMBO

> How did you want to be judged?

COLUMBUS

> I should be judged as a captain who went . . .to conquer a people warlike and numerous...who lived in highland and mountains, having no settled dwellings. A wild people...I conquered for our sovereigns the King and Queen of Spain, another world, whereby Spain, where was called poor, is now most rich.

MAMBO

> ...There is some justice in that claim.

COLUMBUS

Justice. Justice....My errors have not been committed with intention to do ill...I believe their highnesses gave me credit when I say so. The Queen stood for justice.

MAMBO

You rode beside her in pomp after your first voyage.

COLUMBUS

She stood for justice.

MAMBO

But she did not rule against the order for your arrest to be sent home for trial. Did she think you had failed to control the settlements? You were the Governor.

COLUMBUS

...I cannot think why I am a prisoner. I came with such earnest love to serve these princes, and I have served with a service that has never before been heard of or seen. I entered upon a new voyage to a new heaven and a new earth which our Lord made, as St John writes in the Apocalypse...He made me the messenger and He showed me where to go. I went to take possession of all this in her royal name...

MAMBO

You think the sovereigns betrayed your trust?

COLUMBUS

I had no anchor. Among a rabble who decided beforehand that I was not fit, I had no anchor. Always I felt my confidence slip.

MAMBO

The accusations of cruelty are true?

COLUMBUS

Accusations of cruelty?

MAMBO

> The punishment you ordered for insubordination.

COLUMBUS

> ...They condemned me to a style of rule that was not in my nature. And I had no anchor.

MAMBO

> Then the accusations are true?

COLUMBUS

> No truer than the circumstances which forced me to assume real command. Yet I was careful to ensure that such men as masons and those of other trades who came out without pay should have their wages paid to their wives back home. I was merciful to those in need.

MAMBO

> But they accuse you of a greed for gold.

COLUMBUS

> ...Gold brings souls to paradise.

MAMBO

> Their accusation is true.
> You went to the end of the world looking for gold.

COLUMBUS

> To Solomon on one journey they brought six hundred and sixty quintals of gold. David in his will left three thousand quintals of gold on the Indies to Solomon to aid him in building of the temple, and according to Josephus, it was from these lands.

MAMBO

> ...Gold. Gold. In every letter to the sovereigns you excite their imaginations about the quantity of gold you have found. Even when there was none. Gold. Gold.

COLUMBUS

> I had no other anchor...Poor...in Seville no roof over my head save in an inn or tavern where often I lack the wherewithal to pay the score.

MAMBO

> You were making this complaint long after your material comfort was secure.

COLUMBUS

> I wanted no more than the honors and privileges due to me by the articles of agreement the sovereigns endorsed.

MAMBO

> That would have made you richer than the King.

COLUMBUS

> I had no other anchor.

MAMBO

> ...To go beyond the reach of other men. Power was the vocation you were looking for.

COLUMBUS

> To stand out. To go beyond, always beyond. There I would discover my anchor.

MAMBO

> That's why you came to these islands And the Indian savages were proof
> You could go beyond
> We were your anchor.

INT. TONELLE NIGHT

The Mambo is at the table. Her mood is compassionate. Columbus has his back to her.

MAMBO

Are men to be judged according to the customs and opinions of the age in which they lived? Can any wrong be justified by the conviction which they held to be honourable?

SECTION 6

Annotated Biographies

Selected Annotated Biographies and Important Events

Louis James

Louis James is a scholar of Victorian and Caribbean literature. James taught at universities in Africa and Asia, and at the University of the West Indies. He is today Emeritus Professor and honorary member of the Centre of Colonial and Postcolonial Studies at University of Kent, an associate editor for the Victorian Periodicals Review, and an editorial advisor for the *Journal of West Indian Literature*, the biannual publication of the departments of Literatures in English of the University of the West Indies.

A literary critic, his interests have noticeably shifted between Victorian literature and West Indian literature. In the 1960s, he published the literary history of Victorian England, *Fiction for the Working Man* (1963) and *Print and the People* (1976) and his book on Caribbean literature *The Islands in Between* (1968). The volume, which contains examinations of works by Roger Mais, V.S. Reid, George Lamming, Derek Walcott, Andrew Salkey, John Hearne, V.S. Naipaul, and Wilson Harris is often considered to be the first published collection of West Indian criticism. In 1972 he wrote an essay on Lamming's *In the Castle of My Skin* entitled 'The Sad Initiation of Lamming's "G" and Other Caribbean Green Tales'. James is also credited as the first scholar to write a full-length study of Jean Rhys, which appeared in 1979. His most recent work on West Indian literature is *Caribbean Literature in English* (1998).

H.G. de Lisser

Author and journalist, Herbert George de Lisser was born in Falmouth, Jamaica on December 9, 1878 to parents of Afro-Jewish descent. His father, also named H.G. de Lisser was the editor of a small newspaper in Trelawny and later became an editor of the *Gleaner* when the family moved to Kingston. After the death of his father, de Lisser abandoned his formal education to find employment to support the family although he was only 14 years old. After working in several menial positions, he was eventually hired as an assistant in the library of the Institute of Jamaica, which proved to be a formative experience; there, he became proficient in French and Spanish languages and Caribbean history and politics.

De Lisser worked as a proofreader for the *Gleaner* before being offered a writing position for the *Jamaica Times*. In 1903, he became an associate editor at the *Gleaner* and editor-in-chief only a year later, becoming at the age of 26, the youngest ever editor-in-chief of the periodical where he would remain until 1942.

De Lisser frequently published his own literary writings in the *Gleaner*, including a serialised version of his first novel *Jane, a Story of Jamaica*. His well-known novels include *Jane's Career* (1914), which has received much critical attention, its sequel *Myrtle and Money* (1942), *Susan Proudleigh* (1915), *Under the Sun* (1936), *The Rivals* (1921), *Sins of the Children* (1928), and *The Crocodiles* (1933). *The White Witch of Rose Hall*, published in 1929 is perhaps his most famous novel.

Scholars of de Lisser's work have noted a strong racial bias present within his journalism and novels. As a writer of literature, de Lisser seemed interested in the colour line and depicting miscegenation. As a journalist he wrote against the efforts to attain self-government. He was the general secretary of the Jamaica Imperial Association and founded *Planter's Punch* as its unofficial organ in 1920, the same year he received the C.M.G. of the British Empire for Journalistic and Literary Achievement.

He died May 19, 1944, the year Jamaica received the right to self-government

Montego Bay 1947 Conference on Federation

The Montego Bay 1947 Conference was the occasion during which the West Indies Federation was first seriously promoted. Towards the end of the Second World War, the United Kingdom supported the development of a self-governed federal union of its territories in the West Indies to reduce the cost of administration. The colonies had considered federation as a step towards full-independence. On March 14, 1945 Colonial Secretary Oliver Stanley communicated that he would assemble a conference on federation if the legislatures approved such an endeavour. The new colonial secretary Arthur Creech-Jones convened the Conference on Closer Association of the British West Indies, which took place September 11–19, 1947.

At the conference the Standing Closer Association Committee was established and charged with the task of developing proposals on a federal structure. Another matter of the conference that proved to be a source of conflict was the discussions on the nature of a federal constitution and the timetable for the adoption of such a document. Federalists advocated entering federation with the preparation of a constitution; conversely, gradualists preferred the eventual unification of services, a customs union, enactment of uniform legislation, and a uniform currency. Jamaica had not been present for the preceding meetings of British Guiana and West Indian Labour Conferences in 1938 and 1944 during which a resolution for federation and self-government was unanimously passed. On the first day of the Montego Bay Conference, D.J. Judah conveyed that Jamaica wanted to postpone a decision on federation. Albert Gomes of Trinidad, a federalist, conveyed that the British West Indies would federate without Jamaica if necessary. Chief Minister Alexander Bustamante asserted that Jamaica risked being burdened by the smaller and economically weaker islands and could achieve independence without a federation. A compromise was reached with the passing of a resolution expressing the desirability of federation and to continue drafting a federal constitution and with the unification of services. British Guiana and British Honduras did not accept the resolution. The Montego Bay Report was published in 1959.

Samuel Selvon

Trinidadian novelist, poet, and journalist Samuel Dickinson Selvon was born May 20, 1923. Selvon attended Naparima College in his hometown of San Fernando, then enlisted with the British Royal Naval Reserve in 1940 as a wireless operator. While serving in the navy he read widely and the rich depictions of England in the works of Richard Jefferys inspired Selvon to become a writer and record in prose images of life in his country.

From 1946 to 1950 he edited the literary section of the *Guardian Weekly*, the magazine published by the *Trinidad Guardian*, a post that permitted him to publish his own poems, though under pseudonyms. Some of these short pieces were later anthologised in *Forever Morning: Selected Prose 1946-1986*. He also published in *Bim* magazine and sold his material to the BBC. At a time when West Indian literature was viewed as a nascent literary field, Selvon was very supportive of poets and short story writers. He became acquainted with a number of Caribbean writers who would achieve great prominence.

Selvon migrated to London in 1950, where he could not secure a permanent job as a journalist. He did find work as a civil servant at the Indian Embassy. Two years after his arrival in London, Selvon published his first novel, *A Brighter Sun*, which extensively portrayed peasant life in Trinidad, as he had resolved to do after the Secomd World War. This work is notable for its use of dialect, keenly demonstrating the differences in the creolised languages of the Afro – and Indo-Trinidadians, generational differences in assimilation amongst Indo-Trinidadians, and American imperialism with the construction of the Churchill-Roosevelt Highway. With the success of *A Brighter Sun*, he became a professional writer. In 1954, he followed with *An Island is a World*, and in the 1956 *The Lonely Londoners*, a critical look at West Indian immigrants after the Second World War and the British Nationality Act of 1948. *Ways of Sunlight*, a collection of short stories that included his well-known 'Brackly and the Bed' was published in 1957.

In 1978 Selvon left London for Calgary, Alberta where he was writer-in-residence at the University of Calgary. Though he did not return to his native land to live until the end of his life, he visited often and continued to write about the land in his works. He was a prolific writer producing ten novels including (1973), *Turn Again Tiger* (1978), the follow up to *A Brighter Sun*, *Moses Ascending* (1975) and *Moses Migrating*, both conceived as sequels to *The Lonely Londoners*.

Selvon returned to Trinidad in December of 1993 and died there on April 16, 1994.

Vic Reid

The writer Victor Stafford Reid was born on May 1, 1911 in Kingston, Jamaica. While his formal schooling ended with his graduation from Kingston Technical High in 1929, it was Reid's home edification in Jamaican folk culture that would influence his writing most. He travelled to England, Africa, and the United States, but only called Jamaica home. He served as chairman of the Jamaica National Trust Commission and as a trustee of the Historic Foundation Research

Centre in Kingston. In 1960 Reid received a Guggenheim fellowship which allowed him to live and work in New York, frequenting Harlem to be with his good friend Langston Hughes.

As a novelist Reid wrote to educate younger Jamaicans in their history and culture. His first novel, *New Day*, published in 1949, depicts the Morant Bay Rebellion of 1865. Reid recounts this important time in Jamaican history in Jamaican dialect, capturing the speech of the people. This was the first time the voice of narration was written in dialect, a fact that causes Louis James in *The Islands in Between* to argue that it is the first distinctively Jamaican novel. Reid was committed to giving Jamaican people a history written from their perspective and one for which they could feel immense pride. Reid wrote four historical novels for children: *Sixty-Five* (1960), also about the Morant Bay Uprising; *The Young Warriors* (1971), which portrayed the Maroons; *Peter of Mount Ephraim* (1971), on the slave rebellion of 1831; and *The Jamaicans* (1978), about the guerilla leader Juan de Bolas who fought Spain in the seventeenth-century. Consistent in his works is a sense of urgency to reconceive the conventional narrative of a historical event to counter the imperial bias present. His other novels are *The Leopard* (1958), which was written to provide a more accurate history of the Mau Mau uprisings in Kenya; *Nanny Town*, a portrait of the now legendary maroon queen, Nanny; and a biography of Prime Minister Norman Manley entitled *The Horse of Morning* (1985).

Reid was awarded a Silver Musgrave Medal in 1955, a Gold Musgrave Medal in 1978, the Order of Jamaica Award in 1980, and the Norman Manley Award for Excellence in Literature in 1981, amongst several other awards. Reid died August 25, 1987.

John Hearne

Born in 1926 to Jamaican parents in Montreal, Canada, John Hearne moved to his parents' native country at the age of two before leaving Jamaica at the age of 17 to serve as an air gunner with the Canadian Royal Air Force during the Second Word War. After the war he studied history at Edinburgh University where he also worked on the university newspaper. The years after the completion of Hearne's studies at Edinburgh are characterised by frequent travel between Jamaica and England to teach. In 1950 Hearne returned to Jamaica to teach at his alma mater Jamaica College before leaving two years later for England, where he worked as a supply teacher for the London City Council. He travelled again to Jamaica and taught at Calabar High School between 1955 and 1957 before briefly returning to England. After 1961 he returned to Jamaica and was very active in community and government. He held a position in the Public Relations Office, tutored in the Extra-Mural Department of the University of the West Indies until 1967. From 1967 to 1974 he was secretary of the Creative Arts Centre which is the performing theatre of the University of the West Indies at Mona. He was also executive chairman in the Agency for Public Information, special assistant to Prime Minister Michael Manley, and Chairman of the Council of the Institute of Jamaica.

Drawing on autobiographical elements, particularly those relating to his experiences of belonging to an economically privileged family, Hearne explores the complexities of racial identification and its relationship to class in his novels. The protagonists of his novels are often middle-class West Indians participating in or being affected by larger societal shifts. The protagonist of Hearne's first novel, *Voices Under the Window* (1955), is a young lawyer who unknowingly performs racial passing. Hearne won the Llewellyn Rhys Prize for this novel. Hearne's second novel, *Stranger at the Gate* (1956) depicts a lawyer who dies for the Communist movement. Cayuna, a fictional island, remains the setting for Hearne's other novels, which move away from an overt look at politics to arguing the importance of interpersonal relationships. His other works are: *The Faces of Love* (1957), which was printed in the United States as *The Eye of the Storm*; *The Autumn Equinox* (1959); *The Land of Living* (1961); and *The Sure Salvation* (1981).

George Headley

The first black captain of the West Indies cricket team, George Alphonso Headley was born in 1909 in Colon, Panama to a Jamaican mother and Barbadian father. He moved to Jamaica at the age of ten. As a teenager, Headley earned a reputation as a very gifted cricket player and was invited to join the St Catherine Cricket Club. In 1927 Headley was chosen to play against the visiting English team captained by Lionel Tennyson and scored 211 out of 348, making him a renowned batsman. He was selected to play for the West Indies in the 1929–1930 inaugural Test tour and when he was set to bat at number three, he broke the barriers of race and class that govern the game. Headley, a working class black man was batting in the spot usually reserved for members of the plantocracy and those of similar social standing. This sent waves through the colonies of the British empire. Headley performed impressively, scoring 703 in eight test innings and became known as the best West Indian batsman and a rival to the Australian legend Bradman. In fact, only Bradman holds a better record of scoring centuries than Headley. The competition between Headley and Bradman stirred pride in West Indians, who took to inverting the comparison and jokingly called Bradman the 'white Headley.' Headley was named the Wisden cricketer of the year in 1934. In 1948 Headley became the first black man to captain the West Indies cricket team. He died in 1983. Headley is featured in a number of books on cricket in the West Indies, including C.L.R. James's memoir *Beyond a Boundary* (1963) and Michael Manley's *A History of West Indies Cricket* (1995).

Eric Williams

Trinidad and Tobago's first Prime Minister, Eric Eustace Williams was born in Port of Spain, Trinidad on September 25, 1911. As a student at Tranquility Boys primary school, Williams was one of eight students to win the government-financed 'exhibitions' earning him a scholarship to attend college. He chose to matriculate to Queen's Royal College in Port of Spain, a formative environment that would impress upon him an interest in foreign languages that would later aid his research around the Caribbean. In 1931 Williams won the prestigious Island Scholarship to pursue an Honours Degree in History at Oxford University, defying his father's wishes for him to study law or medicine. In 1938 William earned a doctorate in History from Oxford. His dissertation, *Economic Aspects of Abolition of West Indian Slave Trade and Slavery* challenged the notion that abolition of slavery in the British West Indies was motivated by humanitarianism and instead asserted that it was largely an economic decision.

After graduation Williams accepted the post of Assistant Professor of Political and Social Science at Howard University in Washington, D.C. He taught a course in world civilisation and created the three-volume textbook *Documents Illustrating the Development of Civilisation.* The newly formed Anglo-Caribbean Commission offered Williams a part-time research appointment, which he would hold until accepting a full-time position in Trinidad as Deputy Chairman of the Caribbean

Research Council of the Commission in 1948. A Julius Rosenwald research fellowship allowed Williams to travel around the Caribbean in 1940 and resulted in his works, *The Negro in the Caribbean* (1942); *Capitalism and Slavery* (1944), an extension of his doctoral dissertation; and *Education in the West Indies*, which was published in 1950 after being rejected by publishers for five years as a response to his argument that students of the West Indies should have opportunities to pursue advanced education within the Caribbean instead of having to leave for the metropole.

In 1954, after his return to Trinidad Williams started a series of public lectures in the Trinidad Library in Port of Spain intended to educate the people in their history and economic present. Tensions between Williams and his supervisor due to their intellectual and political differences led to a decision not to renew his contract with the Caribbean Commission in 1955. Afterwards, he embarked on a lecture tour around Trinidad between July 1955 and January 1956, during which he gave his first major political speech 'My Relations with the Caribbean Commission, 1943-1955.' On January 5, 1956, Williams and his supporters launched the People's National Movement which under William held a strong anti-colonial stance and supported the West Indies Federation. The PNM won the nation's elections eight months after its founding making Williams the Chief Minister from 1956 to 1959 then Premier from 1959 to 1962. On leading the country to its independence from England, Williams became the first prime minster in 1962. He died in office on March 29, 1981.

The Anglo-American Caribbean Commission

The Anglo-American Caribbean Commission (AACC) was an agency created by the governments of Great Britain and United States to conduct research and supervise economic and social programmes in the region. The Commission consisted of six members with three members from each country; one member from each country served as co-chair. In the United States the Commission was affiliated with the Department of State and the Department of the Interior. It reported directly to the President. In the United Kingdom it was associated with the Colonial Office in London, and in the West Indies it was part of the Development and Welfare Organisation.

The announcement of the AACC came on March 9, 1942, two years after the nations came to the agreement that the United States would provide Britain with 50 old warships in exchange for 99-year leases on military bases in the British West Indies. This coincided with the occurrence of enemy submarine warfare in the Caribbean. Consequently, the Commission was concerned with war-related initiatives upon its founding. One of the major projects of the AACC was the Emergency Land-Water Highway, which operated from October 1942 to September 1943. This programme was the institution of a shipping route designed to alleviate famine in the area caused by the interference of enemy submarines. The commission also developed the West Indies Schooner Pool to facilitate intercolonial trade, recruited labour from the Bahamas and Jamaica for work in the United States, and established a venereal disease programme to protect members of the United States military stationed in the Caribbean.

The AACC established the Caribbean Research Council in August 1943. The purpose of the Council was to supervise scientific, technological, social, and economic research in the region and serve as advisory body to the Commission. It did not convene until 1947 in Port of Spain, Trinidad. During the first meeting the Council resolved to include Haiti, the Dominican Republic, and Cuba in its next project concerning agriculture and livestock. The membership of the Council included representatives from the United States, Great Britain, and the Netherlands.

The West Indian Conference was also created as an advisory body to the Committee. It held its first meeting in Barbados in 1944. The West Indian Conference differed from the AACC and Caribbean Research Council Consultations in its membership; present at its meetings were delegates from the territories and France, Canada, and the Netherlands as observers.

In October 1946 a four-party agreement was signed in Washington D.C. to formally admit France and the Netherlands to the Commission, which was renamed the Caribbean Commission. The amended commission was granted more influence for it could now approach territories directly instead of making recommendations to the United States and British governments. The Caribbean Commission also set up a central secretariat and a secretary-general as head of the secretariat. In 1946, these headquarters were established in Trinidad with Lawrence W. Cramer, the former governor of the U.S. Virgin Islands serving as secretary-general.

The Caribbean Commission was succeeded by the Caribbean Organisation in 1961 and headquarters moved from Trinidad to Puerto Rico. The Caribbean Organisation was dissolved in 1965.

Aimé Césaire

Aimé Césaire was born on June 26, 1913 in Basse Point, Martinique. After learning to read and write in the home of his grandmother, Césaire later attended Lycée Schoelcher in Fort-de-France where he earned a scholarship to attend the elite secondary school Lycée Louis-le-grand in Paris. There his examination of African American literature as his dissertation 'The Theme of the South in African American Literature' earned him a *diplome d'etudes*. During his stay in Paris he met Leopold Sedar Senghor, the future first president of Senegal, and reconnected with Leon-Gontran Damas, a French Guianese poet and politician, and together they founded the literary review *L'etudiant noir* and the *négritude* movement.

After this eight-year stay in Paris, Césaire returned to Martinique as a literature teacher at Lycée Schoelcher in 1939 and shortly after published *Notebook of a Return to my Native Land*, which remains one of his most famous works. In 1941, Césaire and his wife Suzanne Roussi started the cultural journal *Tropiques*, in which he published his poetry. Césaire's political life began in 1945 when he was elected mayor of Fort-de-France and deputy in the Constituent Assembly on the French Communist Party ticket. Still, he continued publishing collections of poetry with anti-imperialist themes and a notable surrealist aesthetic, including *The Miraculous Weapons* (1946), *Beheaded Sun* (1948), and *Lost Body* (or disembodied body) (1950).

In the early 1950s, Césaire became disillusioned with the French government's promises of economic improvement in Martinque, which with the championing of Césaire, had now become an overseas department of France instead of a colony. His famed essay, Discourse on Colonialism was published in 1950 then again in the journal *Prescense Africaine Paris* in 1956. Around this time, the Communist Party in France lost influence and Césaire sensed increasing discrimination within the party leading him to break with it in 1956 and found the Parti Progressive Martiniquais in 1958. Césaire published *And the Dogs*

Were Silent in 1956, a play based on an earlier poem and while his collection of poetry, *Ferrements* followed in 1960 he would find theatre a suitable medium to get his political messages to the public. These plays explored the condition of black peoples throughout the world: *The Tragedy of King Christophe* (1963) depicted Haiti's first and last emperor, Henri Christophe commenting on neocolonialism in Africa; *A Season in the Congo* (1966) was about Zaire's first prime minister, Patrice Lumumba; and *A Tempest* (1969) a reworking of Shakespeare's *The Tempest* from the colonised Caliban's perspective. Towards the end of his life, Césaire remained active in politics. He served as the President of the Regional Council of Martinique from 1983 to 1988. Césaire died in Fort-de-France on April 17, 2008.

Nicolás Guillén

Born in the town of Camagüey in 1904, Afro-Cuban poet Nicolás Guillén would become one of the most influential literary figures in the Caribbean. After his father was assassinated in 1917 for being involved in the Cuban revolutionary movement, Guillén became a typographer for the movement. He later received a degree at the Instituto and commenced studying for a law degree at the University of Havana, but left to pursue a career as a journalist and activist in his native province publishing *Al margen de los libros de estudio (Apart from the text books)* as an apology for leaving law school.

In the late 1920s, Guillén became acquainted with Langton Hughes who would prove influential to his career by suggesting Guillén focus on Cuban music in his work as Hughes had done with jazz. Hughes would later translate Guillén's poems into English. By 1930, Guillén was a distinguished journalist and the publication of *Son Motifs* made him a celebrated poet. The eight poems comprising *Son Motifs* are written in Afro-Cuban vernacular and explore black themes while onomatopoeically recreating the rhythms of Son, a popular Cuban style of music that features Spanish guitar and African percussion. Guillén followed with *Songoro consongo* in 1931 and *West Indies, Ltd.* in 1934. The political messages of revolution and pride in the African blood in Cuban veins also received much attention. Guillén's verses were so stirring that the Grenet brothers, Lecuona, Amadeo Roldán, Alejandro Garcia Carturla, Silvestre Reveultas and composers set his poems to music.

In 1937 Guillén travelled to Spain to report on the Spanish Civil War and recorded the experience in a long poem *Spain: A Poem in Four Anguishes and One Hope*. Also in 1937, Guillén formally joined the Cuban Communist Party and pursued public office as the mayor of Camagüey in 1940 and as a senatorial candidate for the Communist Party in 1948, but was defeated in both attempts. In 1953 upon return from Chile, Guillén was denied reentry to Cuba at the command of dictator Fulgencio Batista and consequently spent years living in exile in Paris and Argentina. In 1954 he was awarded the Stalin Peace Prize, which was renamed the Lenin Peace Prize. When Guillén returned to Cuba after the Revolution in 1959 Fidel Castro asked him to organise the National Union Writers and Artists of Cuba (UNEAC), of which he became president in 1961. Guillén died on July 17, 1989.

Andrew Salkey

Andrew Salkey was born to Jamaican parents in Colón, Panama on January 30, 1928, where his father worked in the Canal Zone. Migrating to Jamaica at the age of two, Salkey was raised by his grandmother then by his mother upon her return. There he became familiar with the folklore of the country and developed a special interest in Anancy tales, which would be reflected in his writings as he would publish a number of books featuring the trickster figure including his popular collection of original short stories *Anancy's Score* (1973) and *Anancy Traveller* (1992). Salkey attended St George's College and Munro College in Jamaica, before pursuing a bachelor's degree in English literature at the University of London. After graduating in 1952, Salkey stayed in London and taught English language and literature and worked for the BBC as an interviewer and scriptwriter where he became associated with the programme *Caribbean Voices*, which helped launch the careers of many of the major writers from the Caribbean.

Characteristic of Salkey novels are the use of dialect and autobiographical elements, including the absent father and coming of age. He wrote five novels: *A Quality of Violence* (1959), *Escape to an Autumn Pavement* (1960), *The Late Emancipation of Jerry Stover* (1968), *The Adventures of Catallus Kelly* (1969), and *Come Home, Malcome Heartland* (1976). Between 1964 and 1980 he wrote eight novels for children: *Hurricane, Earthquake, Drought, Riot, Jonah Simpson, Joey Tyson, The River that Disappeared*, and *Danny Jones*.

Though committed to sharing Jamaican culture in his work, Salkey was also interested in the Spanish Caribbean and edited *Writing in Cuba Since the Revolution* (1977) and wrote a collection of poems, *In the Hills Where the Dream Lives: Poems for Chile* (1979) for which he won the Casas de las Americas poetry prize. He wrote travel books for the region, *Havana Journal* and *Georgetown Journal: A Caribbean Writer's Journal from London via Port of Spain to Georgetown, Guyana.*

Salkey was influential in forming a Caribbean literary canon as he edited several literary anthologies: *West Indian Stories* (1960), *Stories from the Caribbean* (1965), *Caribbean Prose* (1967), *Island Voices: Stories from the West Indies* (1970), *Breaklight: An Anthology of Caribbean Poetry* (1971) and *Caribbean Essays: An Anthology* (1973). He was also active in the founding of the Caribbean Artists Movement and supported Bogle-L'Ouverture, the first major British publishing house for Black authors. Salkey also served on the editorial board of the magazines *Caliban, New Letter,* and co-founded the magazine *Savacou.*

In 1976 he left England to teach literature and creative writing at Hampshire College in Amherst, Massachusetts. Salkey died in April 1995 in Amherst, MA.

Edgar Mittelholzer

Born in 1909 in New Amsterdam, British Guyana, Edgar Mittelholzer was one of the first West Indian professional writers. According to Mittelholzer's autobiography *A Swarthy Boy* (1963), his father William Austin Mittelholzer was a 'confirmed negrophobe' who expressed displeasure at his son's 'swarthy' appearance. Mittelholzer's early attempts at becoming a writer were less than successful. In 1929, he wrote his first novel, *The Terrible Four,* for which he could not find a publisher. His second novel *Creole Chips* was self-published in 1937. The rejections continued but Mittelholzer persevered until his novel *Corentyne Thunder* was published in 1941 in London. In December of that year Mittelholzer left Guyana for Trinidad as a recruit with the Trinidad Royal Volunteer Naval Reserve. Although his military career was short-lived for he received a medical discharge in August 1942, he settled in Trinidad to write.

With the aim of becoming an author, Mittelholzer left Trinidad for England in 1947. He took a job at the Books Department of the British Council where he met the husband of Virginia Woolf, Leonard

Woolf who in 1950 published the manuscript Mittelholzer finished in Trinidad, *A Morning at the Office*. By 1952 Mittelholzer had two more published works, his third novel *Shadows Move Among Them* (1951), and the first volume of his *Kaywana Trilogy*, *The Children of Kaywana* (1952). In the same year Mittelholzer became the first West Indian to be awarded a Guggenheim Fellowship for Creative Writing.

The award took Mittelholzer, now living off his earnings as a writer, first to Canada then to Barbados where he wrote *The Life and Death of Sylvia* (1953); the second volume of his trilogy *The Harrowing of Hubertus* (1954); and the ghost story *My Bones and My Flute* (1955). Mittelholzer returned to England in 1956 and continued regularly publishing novels; however the criticism became increasingly negative and it was becoming harder for him to find publishers for his work. Ultimately, this led him to commit suicide in Surrey, England on May 5, 1965.

Mittelholzer published more than 20 books throughout his career, including *The Weather in Middenshot* (1952), *A Tale of Three Places* (1957), *Kaywana Blood*, (1958), and *The Aloneness of Mrs Chatham* (1965). His novels are known for their attention to setting and detailed descriptions of weather.

V.S. Naipaul

Indo-Trinidadian writer Vidiadhar Surajprasad Naipaul was born on August 17, 1932 in Chaguanas, Trinidad. Naipaul's father was the aspiring writer Seepersad Naipaul. His mother was from the influential Capildeo family. Naipaul was educated at Queen's Royal College in Port of Spain and studied English at Oxford University in England after winning in 1950, a prestigious scholarship sponsored by the Trinidadian government. Naipaul has lived in England ever since.

After Oxford Naipaul worked for the BBC as a broadcaster on *Caribbean Voices* from 1954 to 1956. He wrote reviews and articles as a freelance journalist for publications such as the *New Statesmen* and *Times Literary Supplement*. Naipaul began working on the fiction that would make him one of the most eminent writers from the Caribbean. In the late 1950s he published his first three novels, *The Mystic Masseur* (1957), *The Suffrage of Elvira* (1958), and *Miguel Street* (1959). Published in 1961, *A House for Mr Biswas* was Naipaul's first major work and may be his most famous. The protagonist is based on Naipaul's father and illustrates the individual's search for identity within the confines of an established Indo-Trinidadian community.

Naipaul's writing is centred on the problems of colonialism and the complications of decolonisation, and moreover the relationship of the individual to the post-colonial homeland and to the imperial nation. His novels have received much scholarly attention focusing on his seemingly unflattering depictions of the third world individual and denunciations of multiculturalism. As a critic and literary figure Naipaul complicates the image of the post-colonial West Indian writer for he appears to communicate an irredeemable inferiority of the region. Furthermore, Naipaul refutes the title of West Indian writer. His other major works include *The Mimic Men* (1967); *A Bend in the River* (1967), which is set in Africa; *Guerrillas* (1975); his memoir *An Enigma of Arrival* (1987); and *A Way in the World* (1994), a fictional history of colonialism. Naipaul has also written a number of non-fiction books based on his travels around the Caribbean, India, and Africa: *An Area of Darkness* (1964), *India: A Wounded Civilisation* (1977), *India: A Million Mutinies Now* (1990), *The Middle Passage: Impressions of Five Societies – British, French and Dutch in the West Indies and South America* (1962). Naipaul is also the subject of a number of full-length studies and biographies.

Naipaul has won a number of notable literary honours, including the Llewellyn Rhys Memorial Prize in 1958, the Somerset Maugham Award in 1961, David Cohen British Literature Prize in 1993, and after many nominations Naipaul won the Nobel Prize for Literature in 2001. He became a Knight of the British Empire in 1990.

Kamau Brathwaite

As a writer of literature and a scholar, Kamau Brathwaite is one of the most prominent voices on the subject of Caribbean history, culture, and literature. He was born Lawson Edward Brathwaite in Bridgetown, Barbados on May 11, 1930. Brathwaite attended Harrison College and was awarded a scholarship to study history at Pembroke College, Cambridge. He graduated in 1953 then earned a certificate in education.

Between 1955 and 1962 Brathwaite worked with the Ministry of Education in Ghana. There Brathwaite flourished as a writer; he wrote poetry that was published in the Caribbean literary magazines *Bim*, and

Kyk-Over-Al, and also in Cambridge University journals. While in Ghana he wrote plays for children's theatre that were later published as *Four Plays for Primary Schools* (1964) and *Odale's Choice* (1964). In 1962 he was employed by the University of the West Indies as an extra-mural tutor in St Lucia. In 1963 Brathwaite accepted the post of lecturer in history at the University of the West Indies in Mona, Jamaica.

In 1965 Brathwaite returned to England and enrolled in University of Sussex as a doctoral student in Creole society. He received his D.Phil in 1968. During his studies he co-founded the Caribbean Artists Movement and edited its literary magazine *Savacou*. He continued teaching at UWI, Mona and was appointed professor of social and cultural history in 1983. He has most recently taught as a professor of comparative literature at New York University.

As a poet and an academic Brathwaite interrogates similar issues in these different mediums. His scholarly texts include "Jazz and the West Indian Novel," which was published in *Bim* in 1967; *Folk Culture of the Slaves in Jamaica* (1970); *The Development of Creole Society in Jamaica 1770-1820* (1971); and a number of articles. Brathwaite published his first book of poetry, *Rights of Passage* in 1967 as the first volume of a trilogy. Its sequel was *Masks and Islands* in 1968, and the trilogy was completed in 1973 published as *The Arrivants: A New World Trilogy*. His other major collections of poetry include *Other Exiles* (1975); *Black and Blues* (1976) for which he won a prize in the Cuban Casa de las Americas poetry competition; *Mother Poem* (1977); *Sun Poem* (1982); *Middle Passages* (1994); *Black and Blues* (1995); *Ancestors* (2001), and *Born to Slow Horses*, for which he won the Griffin Poetry Prize in 2006. He won the Neustadt International Prize for Literature in 1994, and has received the Guggenheim Fellowship, and the Fulbright Fellowship amongst other honours.

M.G. Smith

Anthropologist Michael Garfield Smith was born in Kingston, Jamaica on August 18, 1921. From September 1941 to May 1942 he studied English literature at McGill University in Quebec, Canada after winning an Island Scholarship. During the Second World War, Smith enlisted in the 17th Duke of York's Royal Canadian Hussers and was stationed in Normandy, France, Holland, and Germany. After the War he enrolled at University College London intending to study law. In 1946 Smith switched to social anthropology. He conducted field research in Zaria, Nigeria between May 1949 and December 1950 that lead to his 1960 book *Government in Zazzau: 1800-1950*. It received acclaim for its novel combination of historical, sociological, and anthropological perspectives.

After graduating Smith accepted a research fellowship at the Institute of Social and Economic Research of the University of the West Indies in Jamaica. Smith's research would become the definitive studies of the ethnography of Caribbean in the 1950s and 1960s. Smith theorised pluralism, a way to analyse the cultural diversity in the Caribbean. He published *The Plural Society of the British West Indies* in 1965, *Pluralism in Africa* in 1969, *Race and Stratification in the Caribbean* in 1974, and *Pluralism, Politics and the Ideology in the Creole Caribbean* in 1991. Smith published 21 books in all.

In 1961 he taught at the University of California in Los Angeles, then in 1969 he returned to University College London as chair of Social Anthropology. During the six years he held the position, Smith made the department the most prestigious social anthropology department in the United Kingdom. The late Jamaican Prime Minister Michael Manley offered him the post of cabinet-level social policy advisor to the Jamaican government. He was awarded the Order of Merit in 1972.

Smith's final teaching post before retiring was as the Franklin M. Crosby Professor of the Human Environment at Yale University. He was awarded the Wellcome Medal for Anthropological Research, the Curl Bequest Essay Prize, and the Amaury Talbot Book Prize. Smith died in 1993.

Smith was also a poet. His nationalist poem 'I saw my land in the morning' is regularly anthologised. A compilation of Smith's poems were published in 2003 as *In the Kingdom of Light: Collected Poems of M.G. Smith*.

Lloyd Braithwaite

Sociologist Lloyd Ewen Braithwaite was born in Belmont, Trinidad on July 16, 1919. Braithwaite qualified as a solicitor in 1944 but did not further pursue a legal profession, choosing instead to work for the Social Welfare Department of the Civil Service. He entered London

School of Economics in 1946 to earn an undergraduate degree in sociology. While at London School of Economics, Braithwaite was housed in the colonial students residence, Nutford House, an experience that may have inspired his work *Colonial West Indian Students,* which was published posthumously in 2001. In this book Braithwaite examines the discrimination faced by West Indian students in Britain and the factors that influence their upward mobility upon return to their native countries. Braithwaite is considered to be one of the founders of Caribbean sociology. 1953 he published the seminal document 'Social Stratification in Trinidad' and would publish nearly 30 articles and books on aspects of life in the West Indies. His range was wide-reaching as he wrote about fertility differentials amongst various populations, cultural integration, education within the West Indies and abroad, the West Indies Federation, and West Indian industrialisation, to name a few of his subjects.

After receiving his degree, Braithwaite accepted a position at the Institute of Social and Economic Research at the University of the West Indies. In 1965, he became a professor of sociology. In 1969, he became Pro-Vice Chancellor of the University of the West Indies in St Augustine, Trinidad, which he held until 1984. Braithwaite died on January 10, 1995.

Presence Africaine

Presence Africanie was in the 1950s the primer journal of African and African Diaspora thought, literature and culture. Founded in 1947, the initial committee of patrons comprised of individuals like: Andre Gide, Jean-Paul Sartre, Albert Camus, Leopold Senghor, Richard Wright and Aimé Césaire. The idea for the journal came from Alioune Diop a Senegalese philosopher, with the stated objective to 'rehabilitate the collective memory of the peoples of Africa…To bring new life to the Africans from inside their culture.' The first issue of the journal published articles by Senghor and Wright as well as by Sartre and Camus. It also reproduced some essays of Edward Blyden. In the second issue we find articles by the Haitian writer, Jacques Roumain and an essay by Wright amongst others. The journal quickly became a 'larger publication enterprise, an intellectual group and a cultural movement.' In the words of Leopold Senghor, the journal was of 'great importance to those who struggle for the ideas of *'Negritude.'* It was seen by many as the 'primary instrument of the Negritude movement.' In general the journal became a major voice in the decolonisation of Africa and the Caribbean.

As an intellectual group *Presence Africanie* organised a series of conferences which are of seminal importance to radical anti-colonialism and black radicalism. The first of these conferences was the First Congress of Black Writers and Artists held at the Sorbonne in 1956. The theme of the congress was 'Modern Western Culture and Our Destiny.' In attendance were delegates from, the USA, Africa, the Caribbean, the Pacific and India. One participant recalls the conference this way:

'And we were all there…I particularly remember Langston Hughes …and there was Richard Wright…and there was Frantz Fanon… Alioune Diop and Aime Cesaire worked hard to organise it.'[1] George Lamming, Jean Price Mars and Cheikh Anta Diop attended this conference as well. Other congresses organised by the journal were the Second Congress of Black Writers and Artists which was held in Rome in 1959, the creation of World Festival of Black Arts, organised in 1966 and held in Senegal and Nigeria in the 1977.

Today the journal continues to be published in Paris.

Sylvia Wynter

Theorist, cultural critic, playwright and novelist, Sylvia Wynter is one of the Caribbean's premier intellectuals and thinkers. In her early intellectual practice, Wynter draws extensively and deeply from radical anti-colonial thought and today she still considers herself profoundly shaped by the anti-colonial struggles of the 20th century. She was born in Cuba of Jamaican parentage and grew up in Jamaica, where she attended St Andrew High School. In London she attended the University of London and in Spain the University of Madrid. In the late 1950s she wrote for the BBC programme *Caribbean Voices*. One of her most important plays at the time was co-authored with Jan Carew, *The University of Hunger* a clear reference to the poem and work of Martin Carter. In the late '50s she wrote the novel, *The Hills of Hebron* which was first published in 1962. Wynter returned to the Caribbean in 1961 first to Guyana and then to Jamaica. In Jamaica she taught Spanish Literature at the University of the West Indies, co-founded and wrote extensively for the *Jamaica Journal*, contributed regular columns and articles for the *Daily Gleaner*; sat on the committee to determine the criteria for national heroes and wrote the framing document in 1971, *Jamaica National Heroes*. She also wrote the following plays, *Ballad for a Rebellion: Epic Story of Morant Bay Rebellion; Brother Man, Rockstone Anancy: A Magical Morality* (1970 pantomime co-authored with Alex Gradussov) and *Maskrade*.

In this period of her intellectual life Wynter's essays and articles focused on issues of decolonising Caribbean history while developing a theoretical practice of subaltern studies in culture and literature. In a period of Caribbean intellectual history in which various theories of Caribbean society emerged, she advocated the theoretical conception of *indigenisation*. For Wynter this was a concept which allowed for the understanding of Caribbean history, culture and literature from the perspective that black cultural resistance to colonialism was an indigenous one. She writes:

'The history of the Caribbean islands is, in large part, the history of the *indigenisation* of the black man. And this history is a cultural history not in 'writing', but of those *"homumculi"* who humanize the landscape by peopling it with gods and spirits, with demons and duppies, with all the rich panoply of man's imagination.'

In the 1970s, Wynter left Jamaica for the US. There she was associated with the Institute of the Black World, taught at various American universities including Stanford where she remained for many years. In the US, Wynter's intellectual trajectory and work can be divided into two periods. In the first she was deeply influenced by the black liberation movement of the period and her unpublished manuscript, *The Native Intellectual* is a remarkable synthesis of grappling with the wider canvas of the Americas not just the Caribbean. This preoccupation and influence still remains with her. In her second period she begins to work on opening up the entire episteme of Western thought. Working through Fanon's theory of sociogeny Wynter has argued for a mode of being in which we replace our present conception and practices of *Man* with the *Human*. She notes that as humans 'we only exist in the "cosmogonic" or "webs of significance" chartering terms by means we have always already autopoetically enacted...as specific modes of *kind*.' From this perspective Wynter argues for a new conception of the human which will create new grounds for us as human beings overturning what she calls the 'ethno-class terms of Man overrepresented as being the human itself.' Wynter presently lives in California where she is writing about these issues. A collection of her Caribbean essays *We Must Learn to Sit Down Together and Talk About A Little Culture: Decolonising Essays. 1967-1984* and the novel, *The Hills of Hebron* have just been republished.

Martin Carter (1927–1997)

Martin Carter was a major poet of the English speaking Caribbean in the 20th century. Guyanese by birth his first published volume of poetry in 1954, *Poems of Resistance* was described as, 'one eloquent refusal to be dehumanized by imperialist bayonets and colonial arms.' Carter was a major poetic voice in the anti-colonial moment of 20th century Caribbean history observing and creating an inventory of the passages between colonialism and political independence. In the 1950s, he was closely associated with the Peoples Progressive Party then led by the Marxist politician Cheddi Jagan. His first poems appeared in the party journal, *Thunder.* Critics view him as belonging to the Caribbean poetic tradition that includes, Derek Walcott, Kamau Brathwaite, Claude McKay, George Campbell, Aimé Césaire and of course Nicolás Guillén amongst many others. In 1956, he was interned by the British colonial government. His poems were smuggled out of prison and read at political rallies and trade union meetings. Regarded as a 'political poet' Carter's poetry became so popular in Guyana and because they were often read in public their verses became etched in the minds of many Guyanese. In the 1950s one of his most important poems, 'University of Hunger' has the following lines:

> is the university of hunger the wide waste
> is the pilgrimage of man the long march
> The print of hunger wanders in the land
> The green tree bends above the long forgotten
> The plains of life rise up and fall in spasms
> The huts of men are fused in misery…

Between 1967-1970, he was the Minister of Culture resigning from the Burnham government claiming that 'the mouth is muzzled by the food it eats to live.' Although never formally involved in Guyana's political process again, he was sympathetic to radical politics of Walter Rodney. On Rodney's political murder he wrote:

> Assassins of conversation
> They bury the voice
> they assassinate, in the beloved
> grave of the voice, never to be silent.

Carter's poetic voice was a complex one securely anchored in a Caribbean sensibility, in Lamming's words he was an 'authentic' voice. But perhaps one of the best descriptions of him is that by Eusi Kwayana, who wrote, 'His poetry was not a political instrument, but his politics was an expression of his poetry.' Some of Carter's major poems can be read in the following books: *Selected Poems*, Martin Carter and *Poems by Martin Carter* (eds.) Stewart Brown & Ian MacDonald.

Roberto Fernandez Retamar

One of Cuba's most distinguished intellectuals, Retamar is a poet, literary critic and essayist. Since 1955 he has been a professor at the University of Havana and has been the president of Casa de las Americas, one of the most important Cuban cultural institutions. Considered along with the Nicaraguan intellectual Ernesto Cardenal and the Chilean poet Nicanor Pawa to be one of the founders of the "conversational poetry" movement, his best known work in English is *"Caliban" and Other Essays* (1989).

Note

1. Cited in V. Y. Mudimbe (ed.), *The Surreptitious Speech* (Chicago: University of Chicago Press, 1992) p. 35.

Contributors

Andaiye is one the Caribbean's leading radical political figures, social and political thinkers and public intellectual. A founding member of the Working People's Alliance in Guyana she was a co-founder of Red Thread and a member of Women International Network Wages for Caring Work.

Clevis Headley is Associate Professor of Philosophy and current chair of the Philosophy Department at Florida Atlantic University. He was a founding member and Vice-President of the Caribbean Philosophical Association.

Tim Hector was a radical political leader in Antiguan politics and founder of the Antigua Caribbean Liberation Movement. The publisher of the newspaper, *Outlet,* Hector for many years wrote until his death one of the most important newspaper columns in the Caribbean, *Fan the Flame.*

Glyne Griffith is Associate Professor in the Department of English and the Department of Latin American Studies, Caribbean Studies and US Latino Studies at the University of Albany, State University of New York.

Supriya Nair is Associate Professor of English at Tulane University where her research interests are Caribbean and African Literature, cultural studies and feminist theory. She has written extensively on George Lamming.

Sandra Pouchet Paquet, Professor of English at the University of Miami and a leading literary scholar on Caribbean literature. She is also the editor of *Anthurium* a journal on Caribbean literature.

Ngũgĩ wa Thiong'o is one of Africa's leading writers and novelist, he is currently Distinguished Professor of English and Comparative Literature at the University of California, Irvine. He has recently published his memoirs, *Dreams in a Time of War-A Childhood Memoir.*

Index

www.ingramcontent.com/pod-product-compliance
Lightning Source LLC
Chambersburg PA
CBHW030910050726
47498CB00003BA/669

9789766375157